BROADWAY MUSICALS

The Biggest Hit and the Biggest Flop of the Season

1959 to 2009

49TH ST. N.Y.C.

T MISBEHAVIN

SAT SEP 10 1988

26

3:0

D 1

MAJESTIC THEATRE
245 W. 44TH ST. N.Y.C.
THE PHANTOM
OF THE OPERA
2:00P SAT DEC 10 198

$15.00

VIRGINIA THEATR
245 WEST 52ND STR
CARRIE

8:00P TUE MAY 03

04644857BE0074 130

NO REFUNDS NO EXCHANGES

RMEZ40

2

F 1

$20.0

F

M   109

IMPERI

249 WEST

The Shubert Organization

DREAMGIRLS

8:

THU DEC 06 1984 C   8

DEC'8R

27

th STREET THEATRE
CHESTRA $15.00
TICKET COMPANY

CRAZY FOR

141996838049

AIMPBE042809E

P2543993609

PE0421E OMP

EVENT CODE

$

PRICE & ALL TAXES INCL

ORCH
SECTION/BOX

CO   2x

G 102
ROW   SEAT

PAL400C

24MAR94

212-239-620

.com p

ANNIE 2

JAN 20 1990

LHSM

G 102

COM

ORCH
SECTION/BOX

ORCH CENTER
SEAT

All Taxes Incl if Applic

NO REFUNDS/NO EXCHANGE

BEAUTY AND THE BEAST

THE PALACE THEATRE
1564 BROADWAY, NYC
THU APR 21 1994

IMPERIAL THEATRE
249 WEST 45TH STREET, NYC
BILLY ELLIOT
THE MUSICAL
7:00 PM TUE
APR 28, 200

42609

0RCHO

SEC

B

×INCLUDES $0.00 FACI
MAIMP2108-0426-M23

2 MAIMP2108-0426-M23

JAMES
246 WEST 447
"GOOD N
EVENINGS AT

3B
105

ORCHESTRA

FEB'RY FRI

14

1975

PRICE

Maximum r
Mezz., Balc
resale restri
to support
License gra
refunding p

ROUNDABOUT THEATRE COMPANY PRESENTS 113

ROUNDABOUT THEATRECOMPA

CABARET
AT STUDIO 54
Mon, January 14, 2002   8:00 PM
Doors Open 1 Hour

COM
$0.

FRNT

Row or
Table:

in Seat:

NOV 02 1990   10/1

ORCHI

K 10

K

$40.0

ORCH

CO   1x

G 111
ROW   SEAT

MAR601C

10JAN9E

CQ0127E ORCH

EVENT CODE

$ 0.00

PRICE & ALL TAXES INCL

G 111
ROW   SEAT
SECTION/BOX

ORCH CENTER

COMP

All Taxes Incl if Applicable

ADM.$

NO REFUNDS/NO EXCHANGES
THE CAPEMAN
* * *
MARQUIS THEATRE
211 W. 45TH, NYC
TUE JAN 27 1998 7:00PM

U01/04

30 P. M.
UARY

7

1975

MINSKOFF THEATRE
ORCHESTRA $12.00

BROADWAY MUSICALS

The Biggest Hit and the Biggest Flop of the Season

1959 to 2009

PETER FILICHIA

APPLAUSE
THEATRE & CINEMA BOOKS

An Imprint of Hal Leonard Corporation

Published in 2010 by Applause Theatre & Cinema Books
An Imprint of Hal Leonard Corporation
7777 West Bluemound Road
Milwaukee, WI 53213

Trade Book Division Editorial Offices
33 Plymouth Street, Montclair, NJ 07042

Printed in the United States of America

Book design by Leslie Goldman

Library of Congress Cataloging-in-Publication Data

Filichia, Peter.
Broadway musicals : the biggest hit and the biggest flop of the season,
1959 to 2009 / Peter Filichia.
p. cm.
Includes bibliographical references.
ISBN 978-1-4234-9562-8
1. Musicals—New York (State)—New York—History and criticism. I. Title.

ML1711.8.N3F55 2010
792.609747'1—dc22
2010026856

www.applausepub.com

Contents

2 1969–1979

3 1979–1989 118

4 1989–1999

5 1999–2010

Preface

"In fifty years or so
It's gonna change, you know…"

T hose lines that Roxie Hart and Velma Kelly sang near the end of *Chicago* turned out to be true where the Broadway musical was concerned. The last half-century has brought many profound changes.

The look and sound of the shows. The advent of amplification and synthesizers. More daring subject matter. The importance of an established brand name. Many fewer performers on stage and in the pit. Many more producers on a single show. Corporate sponsorship. Different marketing techniques. Routine standing ovations. An ever-burgeoning tourist market. Old theaters gone, new theaters built. Nudity.

And, of course, bigger budgets and more expensive tickets.

If the fans of the Broadway musical who died in 1959 were Billy Bigelowed into returning today, they'd be mighty surprised at what was now playing in the theaters between Forty-first and Sixty-fifth Streets. Once they got inside the theater, they might even be shocked.

Still, what hasn't changed is that every year there's one musical that the public will pay most any price to see. That, of course, is the biggest hit of the season.

And every year there's *at least* one musical that the public can't be bothered to see, even at steep discounts or free of charge. That, of course, is the biggest flop of the season.

We're only dealing with musicals, Broadway's prime commodity. So non-musical hits from the last fifty years, be they as long-running as *Deathtrap*, *Barefoot in the Park*, or *Sleuth*, are nowhere to be found. That's also true of their short-lived brothers *A Race of Hairy Men*, *Song of the Grasshopper*, and, of course, *Moose Murders*.

Only musicals that appeared Broadway—or planned to go there—have been considered. No matter how great a hit an off-Broadway show was (*The Fantasticks*) or how short-lived (*Postcards on Parade* closed in previews), it won't be part of our survey.

"The season" has been defined in the oldest, most classic way, the one used by the authors of *Theatre World* and *The Best Plays* annuals: June 1 through May 31 of each year.

The traditional "season" doesn't always match up with the Tony Awards season, which for many years used April 15 as its cutoff date. That's why *How to Succeed in Business Without Really Trying* and *A Funny Thing Happened on the Way to the Forum*, both members of the 1961–1962 season, each won a Best Musical Tony—because *How to Succeed* opened in October and *Funny Thing* debuted the following May, a full twenty-three days after the Tony cutoff. But for our purposes, they both belong to the 1961–1962 semester, which is why you'll read about one and not the other.

Many criteria were employed in determining each season's biggest hit and biggest flop. Like it or not, money made or lost was a prime consideration. After all, that's the time-honored show business definition of a hit and a flop.

But also taken into consideration were the length of a musical's original Broadway run, the response from the critics, and the voting from the various awards committees.

Judged to be as important as all the other criteria, though, were a show's expectations.

You'll find that much of the time, the biggest flop of the season was the musical that originally seemed the most promising. With the track record that the writers, directors, and stars had, theatergoers, investors, and even the press were licking their lips in anticipation.

Then they read the script . . . or heard the score . . . or saw the show.

And then their feelings completely changed.

A preponderance of our biggest flops were musicals that closed out of town. A show that dared not brave Broadway can almost always be considered a bigger disaster than one that came to New York, even if only for a performance or two.

Expectations could be a factor in the biggest hit of the season, too. If a show with *low* expectations became a smash, it made the hit seem all that much bigger. Prospects originally seemed woefully dim for *Man of La Mancha* and *1776*, but they turned out to have extraordinary receptions, runs, profits, honors, and history.

Determining which musical was the biggest hit of the season was far easier than zeroing in on which was the biggest flop. For one thing, there are always far fewer hits than flops, so the playing field isn't as wide. For another, most seasons had one show that was clearly head and shoulders above the pack in critical reception, grosses, awards, and runs.

Most readers may find themselves nodding with the choice I made for most of the biggest hits of the seasons. Sure, a show's winning the Best Musical Tony was helpful, but while thirty of the fifty hits did just that, twenty of them didn't.

But some may take issue—or even angry umbrage—with my choice for the biggest flop of the season. Even when one factors in exorbitant financial losses, oh-so-short runs, humiliating response from the critics, snubs from the awards committees, and low expectations to boot, often a clear "winner" among the losers cannot be gauged with 100 percent accuracy. We'll have to occasionally agree to disagree.

Thanks to my agent, Linda Konner, who's also the love of my life.

Thanks, too, to Val Addams, Ken Bloom, Michael Buckley, Wayne Bryan, Jay Clark, Bill Cox, Brian Drutman, Joshua Ellis, Larry Fineberg, Alan Gomberg, Marc Grossberg, John Harrison, Kenneth Kantor, Skip Koenig, Peter J. Loewy, Joe Marchese, Kevin McAnarney, Marc Miller, Dick Minogue, Matthew Murray, Richard C. Norton, Rick Pender, Paul Roberts, Howard Rogut, David Schmittou, Bob Sixsmith, Ron Spivak, Ryan Stotts, Robert Viagas, and the late, great David Wolf. They're among the biggest hits I've ever encountered.

PETER FILICHIA
October 30, 2009

BROADWAY MUSICALS

The Biggest Hit and the Biggest Flop of the Season

1959 to 2009

1

1959–1969

1959–1960

THE BIGGEST HIT
The Sound of Music

Let's start at the very beginning.

Actually, let's start thirteen years earlier than *The Sound of Music*.

In 1946, Mary Martin was appearing in a London musical flop called *Pacific 1860*. One of her lines was "The very first thing the Austrians do in the morning is sing." Little did Martin know that about a dozen years down the road, she'd have one of her most illustrious roles as a singing Austrian in *The Sound of Music*.

This is one of those times when the most anticipated musical of the season actually turned out to be the biggest hit of the season. Over the years, *The Sound of Music* has been accused of being sticky-sweet and no more than an old-fashioned operetta. When it opened, the town's two biggest critics—Brooks Atkinson of the *New York Times* and Walter Kerr of the *Herald-Tribune*—respectively said, "disappointing" and "too sweet." And once the movie went from hit to phenomenon, out came all those "Sound of Mucus" jokes.

But the original *Story of the Trapp Family Singers* by Maria Augusta Trapp (Note: No "von") shows that bookwriters Howard Lindsay and Russel Crouse, lyricist Oscar Hammerstein, and composer Richard Rodgers more often than not made the property less sweet.

One must concede that the former Maria Augusta Kutschera was much more experienced than the musical's Maria. Her own story tells us that she was actually a college graduate going for a master's. When she arrived at the Trapps' door, the Captain said—giving her "a warm and hearty handshake" as the housekeeper poured a glass of wine—"Welcome, welcome, and may you never have a successor." Lesser composers and lyricists would have made this moment a glass-clinking song.

Maria Augusta said that one Trapp child was sick and bedridden. Her name? Maria. Rodgers and Hammerstein would have been well within their rights to write a sickbed song called "Maria's My Name, Too." Luckily, they didn't.

As for the Captain, he was actually the type to "shower the children with presents and surprises." That could have made for a treacly scene, too. However, the Captain did use a whistle to call the seven kids, whose names the collaborators changed to protect the audience. Johanna, Martina, and (needless to say) Maria are names that sing, but Agathe, Hedwig, Rupert, and Werner aren't.

Before Maria Augusta arrived, the real Trapp kids were well beyond do-re-mi basics. One was already taking piano lessons. But one night Maria Augusta did sit down and encouraged them to sing "Silent Night," which they'd learned from their father—who came in and joined them. "Then," wrote Maria Augusta, "we sang all twenty-two verses."

And you thought "Do-Re-Mi" went on too long.

Actually, it doesn't. Among Broadway's more brilliant songs, is there any one more taken for granted? What could have been a better teaching tool than a description of each note in the scale paired with a visual image?

Soon after "Silent Night" came Christmas, to which Maria Augusta dedicated an entire chapter. Aren't the collaborators to be commended for avoiding a sentimental scene set on that holiday?

And how about the real-life episode in which Maria decided to leave, but was forced to stay when the housekeeper broke her leg? (Shades of *42nd Street*!) For guidance in fulfilling her new duties, she read *The Golden Book for Housewives*. The collaborators could have had Mary Martin scurrying around the kitchen, making many mistakes and much hilarity. But that would have been cheap, easy humor.

The Captain was indeed engaged when Maria Augusta arrived, but to a woman named Yvonne, not Elsa. In the book, she's even colder than she is in the musical, telling a Trapp daughter upon seeing the children in their new playclothes, "A decent lady doesn't wear pants." Lindsay and Crouse retained her plan to ship the kids off to boarding school—and her later assertion to Maria that "The captain is in love with you."

As in the musical, Maria Augusta retreated to the convent, where she first consulted not a nun but a priest—then the Mistress of Novices, and then the Mother Abbess. The last-named told Maria Augusta, "I assembled the community . . . we prayed to the Holy Ghost and we held council, and it became clear to us that it is the Will of God that you marry the captain." (My, that was easy!) There is also the implication that the nuns had assumed that once Maria went to the Trapps, she wouldn't be returning—and that they were frankly pretty happy to be rid of her.

What Maria Augusta then tells us would have made for a sweeter and sillier musical scene. For when she returned, the Captain sent the kids to ask if she "liked" him. Once they reported that she indeed did, he came in while she was on a ladder cleaning a chandelier, and asked her to marry him—almost causing her to fall off the ladder. She told the Captain the nuns' directive, and he replied—and this is exactly the way Maria Augusta wrote it—"Th-they s-s-said I have to m-m-m-marry you." Bless the collaborators for excising this moment!

After Maria Augusta and the Captain marry, the book is boring for quite some time, for it has no conflict. Maria Augusta wrote in a travelogue style about life in Austria, and dedicated eight pages to telling how the family once celebrated Lent.

Not until page 112—when Rupert is already in med school—are Hitler and the Nazis even mentioned, and then only in passing. The big problem, introduced on 113, was that the Trapps' bank went bust, so they became insolvent, forcing everyone to pitch in and work. While that's a considerable conflict, it's not nearly as dramatic as the Nazi threat. By putting the family in graver danger, the musical's four collaborators gave the Trapps a chance to stand up and fight for something nobler than money. Again, for all the talk about the show's sentimentality, Rodgers and Hammerstein didn't succumb to a cheer-up song in which the family whistled while they worked to keep poverty at bay.

Truth to tell, though, the Trapps did not escape by climbing every mountain and fording every stream. Maria Augusta made clear that to reach America, they merely took a train and an ocean liner. Note, too, that the book offered no Liesl-and-Rolf romance. Rodgers and Hammerstein undoubtedly inserted it because they'd often had success with secondary lovers (Will and Ado Annie in *Oklahoma!*, Carrie and Enoch in *Carousel*, Cable and Liat in *South Pacific*, and Lun Tha and Tuptim in *The King and I*).

As merely the biggest hit of the season, the musical probably wouldn't have come in for all the years of criticism it garnered as the monster Hollywood hit of 1965 and beyond. *Mad* magazine had its own "Do-Re-Mi" parody: "Dough means cash for all of us of us / Ray for musicals like this! / Me, a star, so big that by / Far, we couldn't really miss! / So insipid is the plot / La dee dah, although we know / Te - dious it is a lot /It will bring us back much dough-oh-oh-oh."

And as the show's first Maria unknowingly presaged her own fate with that comment on singing Austrians, the film's Maria, Julie Andrews, could little know what was in store when she and Carol Burnett did a parody of the show in their 1962 Carnegie Hall TV special. Here, Andrews headed the Swiss Family Pratt. Mike Nichols, still sixteen months away from his first directing success, cowrote devilish turns on "My Favorite Things" (including "pigs' feet and cheese") and "Do-Re-Mi," which as "Ding-Dong Yum-Yum-Yum" included many infantile sounds.

Fifty years after the musical's birth, the references, parodies, and revisionings continue. In 2007, the Salzburg Marionettes did a puppet version of *The Sound of Music* that actually brought on a marionette deer during "Do-Re-Mi." It was presumably there to illustrate the first line of the famous refrain, rather than to suggest that a deer ran rampant through the Trapp home. In the second act, the deer returned, once more prancing across the puppet stage—until the audience heard a gunshot that blew off the deer's head, exploding it into a dozen or so pieces. Then an actual human being—clad in a Nazi uniform—was seen, from the waist down, walking across and overwhelming the puppet stage, holding a rifle. Director Richard Hamburger was going to make certain that no one called his *Sound of Music* sticky-sweet.

And in 2008, a rock musical called *Next to Normal* evoked the show when a distraught bipolar mother, looking through her medications sang to Rodgers' melody, "These are a few of my favorite pills." Never mind "Dolly'll never go away again;" *The Sound of Music* really never will.

The Sound of Music. November 16, 1959–June 15, 1963. 1,443 performances.

The Biggest Flop
The Pink Jungle

Don't think pink.

Playwright Leslie Stevens had written two Broadway comedies that had lasted a total of twenty-seven performances before he succeeded with *The Marriage-Go-Round* in 1958. The boulevard comedy is now forgotten, but when Stevens' new musical *The Pink Jungle* went into rehearsal, it was approaching its first anniversary on Broadway

In fact, *The Marriage-Go-Round* would still be running when *The Pink Jungle* closed on the road.

Joseph Anthony, who'd staged Stevens' hit—and, more significantly, *The Most Happy Fella*—would direct. The score was by Vernon Duke, who'd penned the melodies to "Autumn in New York," "April in Paris," "I Like the Likes of You," and "I Can't Get Started." Recently, he'd started writing his own lyrics, and would do so for *The Pink Jungle*.

Admittedly, aside from *Cabin in the Sky*, a modest hit in 1940, Duke had written six failures. But theater pundits felt it was only a matter of time before he got the right property and right star to showcase his songs.

He'd have the star in Ginger Rogers. After being noticed in Broadway's *Girl Crazy* in 1930, Rogers had immediately gone Hollywood. Decades later, when her film opportunities had officially evaporated, she'd retreated to Broadway in a comedy called *Love and Let Love*. It ran but fifty-one performances in '51, but the feeling was that if Rogers were to appear in a musical, theatergoers would still flock to see Fred Astaire's most famous partner once again singing and dancing.

In *The Pink Jungle*, Rogers would play Tess Jackson, a female executive at Eleanor West, Limited, a successful cosmetics house. Ms. West, Tess told us, "gives a good massage. Full of hate." Now that West has died, Tess is a strong contender to become the company's next president.

Death, though, doesn't keep West from appearing on the scene. Playing her as a ghost—officially called "The Shade of Eleanor West"—was Agnes Moorehead. (In a few years, she'd become known throughout the nation for playing the not dissimilar role of a witch in TV's *Bewitched*). Eleanor may be seen and heard "only while assisting a love match."

Tess has three other female rivals for the post. Her main one is Chris (Maggie Hayes), who's engaged to Brian (Leif Erickson), one of West's sons, to whom Eleanor would like to give "my short course on jiu-jitsu." But all four contenders show their mettle in "A Hundred Women in One," by dispensing beauty secrets in song. "If you're cursed with black mustaches / We'll convert them into lashes." The executives also tell their customers that they can charge their treatments on Diners Club—which must have torn down the house in those days when all one could charge on a Diners Club card was dinner.

Tess dons many disguises so that West's sons and her rivals don't recognize her. One ruse has her playing a hostess in a restaurant, which goes well until Pierre (René Paul), whom she's been dating, walks in. That allows Tess to come down to the footlights and sing "It's Tough to Be a Girl," which offers such lyrics as "Should you meet a charmer who makes you melt / Get yourself a chastity belt." (The script establishes that Tess hasn't yet slept with Pierre, Eisenhower-era innocence being what it was.)

What Tess doesn't know is that Chris is in the restaurant, too, tape-recording her conversation. So when Pierre winds up stealing the ad campaign that West Limited had already in place—"The girl who looks like a tramp but you sense is really a homebody"—Tess is fired for presumably leaking the information.

Tess decides the only way she'll get herself back in the company is by "La Digging Pour la Gold" and marrying one of the sons. She picks David (Ray Hamilton) and, after a night at the Persian Room, says, "I could have danced all night." (Beware a musical that uses a quotation from a better musical to make a point.)

The next day in Central Park, David sings, "I'm free as the air, free to love you, free to savor your kiss." (Perhaps Duke shouldn't have written his own lyrics.) When Tess sees how sincere he is, she decides she can't go through with her plan. Unaware of this, Chris works to subvert the romance, as does Brian—though when he meets Tess in Central Park, he's charmed by her and the surroundings: "There are heights to scale / Lovely boats to sail / Bears and monkeys to tease in the zoo." (No question, Duke shouldn't have written his own lyrics.)

Harvey (Gavin Gordon), Eleanor's widower, comes to the park, too, and somehow gets a banana cream pie right in the face—and soon the first act ends. And, as anyone can tell you, the first act of a musical tends to be better than the second.

In the office scenes, there were projections of beauty products and not-so-healthy-looking skin. One stage direction said, "An anatomical cross section of dermis flips in looking like a lasagna." That doesn't sing, does it?

The creators were true to their title, and did think pink: another stage direction said that when Tess meets David for the date, she "carries a pink picnic basket over one arm and holds the string on a cluster of translucent pink balloons." But the musical never made its planned Broadway opening on January 14, 1960 at the Fifty-fourth Street Theatre, Broadway's favorite house of flops. Instead, *Pink* had closed in the red.

> *The Pink Jungle.* October 14, 1959, in San Francisco–December 12, 1959, in Boston. No New York performances.

1960–1961

THE BIGGEST HIT
Camelot

But it almost was the biggest flop of the season.

Of course, expectations were high. Bookwriter-lyricist Alan Jay Lerner and composer Frederick Loewe's *My Fair Lady* had conquered Broadway in 1956, and their *Gigi* had overwhelmed Hollywood in 1958. No motion picture had ever won every Oscar for which it was nominated, but *Gigi* went nine for nine in '59.

What next? Lerner's associate Stone Widney gave him T. H. White's *The Once and Future King*. The tale of Arthur, Guenevere, Lancelot, and the magician Merlyn seemed to have the requisites for a great musical: big characters and big events. (Hard to believe, though, that Lerner's original title was *Jenny Kissed Me*; that sounds more apt for a boulevard comedy à la *Boy Meets Girl* or *Dear Ruth*).

When collaborators have a hit, they're often inclined to assemble the same staff for their next show. *Camelot* had *My Fair Lady*'s director (Moss Hart), choreographer (Hanya Holm), set designer (Oliver Smith), and even Robert Coote, who'd played Pickering, as the bumbling King Pellinore.

Most importantly, Julie Andrews, *Fair Lady*'s fair lady, would be Guenevere. Rex Harrison, though, was not asked to portray Arthur. He was British enough, but was already fifty-two years old; better let thirty-four-year-old Welshman Richard Burton play it.

Also not asked to participate was *Fair Lady* producer Herman Levin. This time, Lerner, Loewe, and Hart would do the producing themselves—and split the 50 percent of the profits that producers get once a show pays off.

Even in those pre-Internet days of 1960, word traveled fast from the Toronto and Boston tryouts that *Camelot* was in trouble. The character of Pellinore had a tendency to nod off every now and then, but he wasn't the only one to fall asleep during *Camelot*'s four hours. Then came Lerner's bleeding ulcer and Hart's heart attack. Everyone might have thought about praying to Guenevere's St. Genevieve—save the spurned Levin, who may well have enjoyed those reports. Maybe there wouldn't be any profits for the greedy creators to split.

Camelot limped into town and opened at the Majestic on December 3, 1960 to a majority of not-so-hot reviews. Sure, there was a $1 million advance, but even in that era when the best seat sold for less than $10, such an advance would be eaten up fast.

Had *Camelot* opened before *Fair Lady*, it might have been well appreciated on its own considerable terms. Arthur is a king who never loses the common touch, a genuinely nice guy who admits, "I'm not accomplished at thinking"—which is more than many rulers would deign to admit. Still, he's thought enough to put in motion the plans for a civilized kingdom. An audience—and Guenevere, his arranged-marriage bride—can easily sympathize with him.

Most musicals take the whole night to get to a wedding; these two are heading off to theirs at the end of act 1, scene 1. What could possibly happen next?

Lancelot. Sure, Guenevere sees him as "overbearing and pretentious"—and hates that he takes himself so seriously—but she'll take him more seriously once he brings the knight he's just killed back from the dead. Lancelot bows to her, but just as Anna in *The King and I* bows lower to her monarch, so too does Guenevere now bow lower still to Lancelot. Can an affair be far behind?

Should we be surprised that Guenevere cheats? Even before she meets Lancelot, she very openly sings about "The Lusty Month of May." The song may seem a happy-go-lucky romp, but the lady does refer to "those dreary vows that ev'ryone takes, ev'ryone breaks." Guenevere has already done the former; she'll do the latter in due time—and Arthur knows it.

Lerner and Loewe missed a grand opportunity here. At the end of act 1, when Arthur considers Lancelot and Guenevere's future, he delivers a long speech. But this is a musical, so why didn't the songwriters musicalize the moment? Imagine *Carousel* if Billy Bigelow had come forward and spoken a soliloquy instead of singing a musical one. A musical bolt of lightning for Arthur might have made a huge impression on critics. Instead, Arthur's big song was "How to Handle a Woman," in which he sensitively concluded that "The way to handle a woman is to love her, merely love her, love her, love her." (That from Lerner, who would marry no fewer than eight times.)

In act 2, Guenevere grows. In her first-act immaturity, she wanted to be "competed for" and "cause a little war." Now both her wishes come to pass, and she regrets them. Guenevere tries to do the right thing, and every reason she gives Lancelot explaining why they shouldn't consummate their relationship is a good one.

Camelot may well be the first genuinely serious look at adultery in musical, theater, where a grown illegitimate child such as Arthur's Mordred was an anomaly. Hence, when the magical first act gave way to a suddenly dramatic second act, some theatergoers may have been unnerved. For all the talk of civilization, Guenevere is to be burned at the stake.

Another problem: How many theatergoers walked into the Majestic assuming they were about to see a true slice of English history, and not just the magical Arthurian Legend? Were they confused when Arthur started singing that an actual law prevented July and August from being too hot? That winter officially had to end on March 2? Indeed, Arthur literally means everything he says in the title song, but audiences could be excused if the messages didn't sink in. Most historians agree there never was a King Arthur, and the idea of a magical kingdom in which a knight can bring a dead man back to life is, to say the least, wishful thinking. While *Camelot* is a great name for a musical, *The Arthurian Legend,* however stodgy, might have better informed the public that make-believe was a big part of the show.

People liked the Columbia original cast album, though. It was #1 on the charts for six weeks, in those days when adults bought albums for themselves and singles for their children. The disc stayed on the Top 100 for three years, and produced a hit song in "If Ever I Would Leave You," Lancelot's sincere declaration of love to Guenevere.

Savvy Columbia record producer (and president) Goddard Lieberson had learned long before *Camelot* that the second side of a cast album should start with the show's hit song, even if that meant reshuffling the order of the songs as they appeared in the show. In *Camelot*'s case, that meant "If Ever I Would Leave You"—sung beautifully by that new white-hot heartthrob Robert Goulet.

Yes, Robert Goulet. Though Lerner's first choice was Christopher Plummer (who auditioned with "Till There Was You"), Goulet got the part. *Annie* lyricist and director Martin Charnin says, "People don't realize how great Goulet was before he made himself into a joke." That's why, fifteen years after *Camelot*, *A Chorus Line* hopeful Bebe, remembering her youth, cried out "Robert Goulet! Robert Goulet! My God, Robert Goulet!" Just as Lancelot breathed life into that dead knight, Goulet breathed life into the show.

And for the first—and certainly not the last—time in this book, we come to *The Ed Sullivan Show*, that Sunday night stalwart that was broadcast from eight to nine at a theater on Broadway and Fifty-fourth Street. Sullivan often allowed a song and a scene or two from a current Broadway show, but when *My Fair Lady* was approaching its fifth anniversary on March 15, 1961, the host thought he should devote the entire broadcast to it. Lerner shrewdly said that he'd only allow half the show to be devoted to his past hit; *Camelot* would have to be featured, too.

While the nation may have been familiar with Burton from such films as *The Robe* and *Alexander the Great*, and with Andrews from Rodgers and Hammerstein's *Cinderella*, their chemistry together in charming songs (as well as Goulet doing his hit) made for a long line at the Majestic Theater's box office the next morn. What audiences saw on TV made them dismiss what the critics had written.

When the Tony nominations came out a month later, *Camelot* was denied a Best Musical nod, but the creators had to be comforted by rising grosses. (Besides, in those days, the Tonys weren't on national TV, so their impact on business was negligible.)

Yet when theatergoers who loved *Camelot* on record came to see the musical on stage, they must have been flummoxed to find two songs missing: Guenevere's "Then You May Take Me to the Fair" and the Knights' "Fie on Goodness." Lerner had excised them, thinking the show too long. By now, he was in charge of the show; Hart was in the last nine months of his life.

Even Merlyn, who could see into the future, apparently never told *Camelot*'s creators that it would play 873 performances—a long run in those days.

Though it closed on January 6, 1963, the show was back in the public consciousness by the end of the year, when a different T. H. White—historian Theodore H. White—asked the just-widowed Jacqueline Kennedy what music her husband had liked—and she mentioned *Camelot*.

Ever since Mrs. Kennedy's offhand remark, *Camelot* has stayed in the public consciousness as the unofficial name of the John F. Kennedy administration. How lovely that a time cherished by so much of the nation should be named for a Broadway musical. But can you picture the Kennedy years referred to as the "*Jenny Kissed Me* Era" (though many a Jenny probably *did* kiss JFK)?

Camelot. December 3, 1960–January 6, 1963. 873 performances.

THE BIGGEST FLOP
Wildcat

Casting against typecasting.

February 19, 1961. Once again, *The Ed Sullivan Show*. On stage is a ramshackle Stutz Bearcat, looking utterly defeated. There's Paula Stewart, playing a young woman named Janie. She hopes that the mechanic who's tinkering around under the car will be able to fix it. But the mechanic can't and eventually emerges from down under—as the *Sullivan* studio audience goes wild.

Because that "mechanic" is Lucille Ball.

Actually, Ball is playing Wildcat Jackson, who's deep in the south of Texas. Her latest scheme is to lie her way into getting men to work for her so they can strike oil. But her motivation is a good one: her sister, Janie Jackson is lame, and she wants to make a better life for her.

Though you'd never guess it from that description, bookwriter N. Richard Nash said he wrote *Wildcat* specifically for Ball. Ball's famous alter ego, one Lucy Ricardo, never had to deal with an infirm sister. The audience didn't want to hear about any latter-day Laura Wingfield. What it wanted from *Wildcat* was unmitigated fun.

At least that night on the *The Ed Sullivan Show*, they were going to get it. After Ball inadvertently hit her head on the running board—and ad-libbed a "Boinggg!"—she gave the introductory dialogue to the show's big hit, "Hey, Look Me Over." Alas, she said the word "damn" as Nash's book called for—only then remembering that she was back on TV, and that she'd better correct herself and add a quick "darn" to wipe it away.

Ball fearfully raised her eyebrows, afraid that she'd just gotten herself into trouble. But most everyone pretended not to have heard the "profanity." Nothing was going to keep them from enjoying the song they'd already been hearing on the various TV variety shows (which, in those days, routinely celebrated new Broadway songs). Now, though, they'd hear the hit from *Wildcat*'s one and only star, one of the first superstars made from TV.

There were others that season. Jackie Gleason had already come to Broadway with *Take Me Along*, and Phil Silvers opened *Do Re Mi* shortly after *Wildcat*. But in the fifty years this book covers, Broadway never anticipated or greeted a bigger or more beloved star than Lucille Ball. An astonishingly high percentage of American homes had seen Ball play Lucy McGillicuddy Ricardo more than two hundred times. Over the past nine years, no one had been more welcomed into the nation's living rooms than she. Now, only a matter of months after the last of the Ricardos' adventures had aired on April 1, 1960—thirty-three days before she and costar-husband Desi Arnaz were actually divorced—viewers were once again seeing Lucy on the tube.

But would they dare to buy tickets? For the past two weeks, *Wildcat* had been dark. Only fifty-three days into the run, the exhausted Ball had received "doctor's orders" to stop performing. Now, a day before performances were to resume at the Alvin, Ball would appear on Sullivan's show in hopes of jump-starting some momentum.

At forty-nine, Ball was certainly no kid, but she should have been able to do eight performances a week. What probably fatigued her was the stress of carrying a show for which she was not right. As Norma Desmond had informed filmgoers a decade earlier, "Great stars have great pride." Ball wanted a new hit to show her ex-husband and former costar—whom *she* had made a star—that she could reinvent herself. Broadway was still the nation's most prestigious entertainment venue, and she'd conquer it.

While she sang "Hey, Look Me Over," Ball looked completely at home and satisfied, as if her Broadway gamble had paid off. And indeed it was her own gamble; she'd put up the entire $300,000 to get the show on. While bookwriter Nash and director-choreographer Michael Kidd would be the nominal producers, Ball was really in charge.

Her bigger gamble was entrusting the score to lyricist Carolyn Leigh and composer Cy Coleman. Their Broadway résumé as a team had included only one song: "You Fascinate Me So" for *John Murray Anderson's Almanac* in 1953. On her own, Leigh had had a bit more Broadway experience, for she wrote the lyrics to Mary Martin's *Peter Pan*—until she was replaced. Yet her pop song work with Coleman had resulted in "The Best Is Yet to Come," "Firefly," and "Witchcraft"—all solid hits. Ball must have hoped that they'd provide *Wildcat* with this level of quality.

They virtually did. Much of Coleman's *Wildcat* music is extraordinarily catchy. It was an impressive debut for a composer who would captivate five thousand Broadway audiences in the next-half century.

With *Wildcat*, Leigh had a chance to exercise an earthy sensibility that she'd had to leave out of the teddibly British *Peter Pan*. In "Hey, Look Me Over" alone, the heroine sings the salty "Don't pass the plate, folks, don't pass the cup. I figure whenever you're down and out, the only way is up" as well as "Don't thumb your nose, bub. I'm a little bit short of the elbow room." Leigh wrote plenty of other spirited expressions in the show: "Look out for the claws . . . You bet your booties . . . It ain't Little Eva or Mother Machree . . . I'll be swacked and pickled in moonshine. I'll be piked and peddled for coal oil . . . Cookin' grub and pinnin' up didees . . . Why would you throw a girl a belt then behave as if she actually smelt?" Here was a distinctive voice.

After Ball and Stewart finished "Hey, Look Me Over," Sullivan embraced Lucy, then said, "You know, ladies and gentlemen, down through the years—because she's given the country, the whole world, as a matter of fact, so darn much enjoyment—Lucille Ball, I'd say that you are probably the best beloved star in show business." Lucy responded with a slight nod and a wonderfully heartfelt, "Thank you, Ed."

Such sincerity wasn't necessarily what she'd been giving theatergoers at the Alvin. Since the tryout at Philadelphia's Erlanger Theater, Ball had failed to abide by one of show business's great maxims: "Let them come to you." When she saw that her Wildcat Jackson was failing to please, Ball reverted to playing Lucy Ricardo, adding her trademark "Waaaah!" cry after one song. She even bent the dialogue to include a reference to the Ricardos' neighbor Fred Mertz. But a quintessential professional such as Lucy must have realized that in pandering to the audience's needs, she was going backward, not forward.

Nevertheless, her solid *Sullivan* performance ensured that next day, as with *Camelot*, there was a rush at the box office that brought *Wildcat* to capacity. But what's harder than returning to a job you hate after your vacation ends? Ball missed more performances in late March. Granted, when she came back in April, she was doing standing-room-only business (which was $65,717 a week in those days).

But on April 22, Lucy collapsed on stage. She returned for most—but not all—of the month, making Wednesday evening, May 24, her final performance. She'd apparently decided that she'd suffered enough in making trying to make *Wildcat* something it just wouldn't be: a hit.

Ball could certainly afford to lose the $300,000, but she didn't close *Wildcat* because she was spending good money after bad; she just didn't want to expend good energy after bad money. Someone named Betty Jane Watson took over, which is why *Wildcat* closed in just a little more than a week. From then on, Ball spent an inordinate part of her career playing someone named Lucy—be it Carmichael, Carter, or Barker. They were all variations on Mrs. Ricardo and, for the most part, made her audiences mighty happy.

Wildcat. December 16, 1960–June 3, 1961. 172 performances.

1961–1962

The Biggest Hit
How to Succeed in Business Without Really Trying

The Tony is one thing, but . . .

October 14, 1961. It's been forty-six months since any musical has opened to unanimous raves—with seven out of seven newspaper critics agreeing. Forty-seven musical productions have opened in that time, but none has been able to match the feat last accomplished by *The Music Man* on December 20, 1957.

After opening tonight, *How to Succeed in Business Without Really Trying* will easily break the streak. It will be the last time any musical accomplishes this, for two years to the day later, New York is left with six daily newspapers when the *Mirror* folds.

But did it deserve a Pulitzer Prize?

Granted, the musical was a hilarious send-up of the business world, thanks to Abe Burrows. Not only did he direct, but he also resuscitated Jack Weinstock and Willie Gilbert's original attempt at adapting of Shepherd Mead's spoof of how-to manuals.

Mead's book, also called *How to Succeed in Business Without Really Trying*, is the one that J. Pierrepont Finch (Robert Morse) is reading in between washing windows at the World Wide Wicket Company, Inc. "If you have education and intelligence and ability, so much the better," the book tells him. "But remember, thousands have reached the top without any of these qualities."

Finch plans to get inside the building and get ahead. When he enters, he crashes into company president J. B. Biggley (Rudy Vallee), who irascibly chews him out. Finch isn't flustered; he goes to personnel and blithely says that he "just bumped into" Biggley, who sent him here. He isn't lying—but he sure isn't telling a clear truth, either.

Though Finch is merely assigned to the mail room, secretary Rosemary

Pilkington (Bonnie Scott) still lusts for him—to no avail. When she asks her friend Smitty, "What's the opposite of a sex maniac?" Smitty (Claudette Sutherland) replies, "A businessman."

Finch charms Miss Jones (Ruth Kobart), Biggley's secretary, while getting in a bad word about Bud Frump (Charles Nelson Reilly), Biggley's nephew. Frump fears Finch, and hatches a plan to get him in trouble. Bud knows that "secretary" Hedy La Rue (Virginia Martin) is his uncle's girlfriend, so he sends her to his rival. As Hedy tells Finch, "A secretary was ordered to be assigned to you. I'm your assignation."

Our "hero" resists the bait, and even gets promoted when his own boss falls for La Rue. There seems to be no stopping Finch, who does take time to semi-fall in love with Rosemary. Says Hedy, "Guess I'll wait for that pigeon until after he's married."

Once Finch is head of advertising, Frump plans to destroy him by giving him an idea to start a TV quiz show that his uncle has already vetoed. But when Biggley sees the show as a chance to feature Hedy, he approves. Alas, Hedy has been given important information about the quiz show in advance, and blabs it on live television. (The parallel with the 1950 TV quiz show scandals was definitely implied and intentional.)

Everyone blames Finch, who seems utterly ruined until CEO Wally Womper (Sammy Smith) learns that Finch was once a window washer—just as he was once. Finch emerges triumphant.

Certainly it was a great deal of fun, and Frank Loesser's score was equal to the task, with sharp lyrics. (In "A Secretary Is Not a Toy," he wrote, "Her pad is to write in / And not spend the night in.") However, the score and the cast album never reached the popularity of smash Broadway hits of yore—a harbinger that few saw at the time. In the years to come, cast album sales would fall dramatically as Baby Boomers' taste for rock dominated the market.

Nevertheless, the show became so successful that Milton Bradley, creator of such board games as Go to the Head of the Class and Candyland, created a *How to Succeed in Business Without Really Trying* board game. The lid stated, "This is not a serious game." That was fitting for a musical that wasn't serious, either.

So how could such a broad spoof get the Pulitzer? Sure, give it the Tony and the New York Critics Circle Award, but *How to Succeed* wouldn't seem to honor Joseph Pulitzer's ideal of rewarding "the original American play performed in New York which shall best represent the educational value and power of the stage in raising the standard of good morals, good taste, and good manners."

After all, Finch is single-minded about getting ahead, and so ambitious that he usurps other people's ideas, stretches the truth, plays his colleagues against one another, and doesn't mind double-crossing anyone. All this occurs in an arena where male executives routinely ogle and try to seduce their secretaries. Granted, the business world hadn't yet had its consciousness raised, but one couldn't easily find "good morals, good taste, and good manners" in this musical.

But a juggernaut is a juggernaut. The following season, the Pulitzer Board of Directors rejected the drama jury's vote to award a Pulitzer to Edward Albee for his *Who's Afraid of Virginia Woolf*—because it found the script wasn't "uplifting" and contained too much sexual permissiveness and coarse language. *How to Succeed* could have been said to have many of the same flaws. Perhaps in a small way, *Virginia Woolf* died for its sins.

How to Succeed in Business without Really Trying. October 14, 1961–March 6, 1965. 1,417 performances.

THE BIGGEST FLOP
A Family Affair

"We'll never hear from those guys again."

The *Billy Barnes Revue* closed in a week, and *Kwamina* in a month. *Kicks & Co.* and *We Take the Town* didn't even make it to New York.

But what makes *A Family Affair* the biggest flop of the season is that its quick failure and no-name creators made all Broadway confidently say, "We'll never hear from those guys again."

Good guess. The two bookwriter-lyricists had had a play flop earlier in the season. The composer had only provided dance music for two shows. The producer had no Broadway producing credits, just as the director had no Broadway staging credits. And when a show lists "choreography by" one person and "musical numbers staged by" another, something's wrong in the dance department. No wonder *A Family Affair* could only get a booking at the woebegone Billy Rose Theater, all alone on Forty-first Street.

When nobodies like this flop, they fade away now and forever. Except that composer John Kander went on to write *Cabaret*, *Chicago*, and plenty of other hits. The book was cowritten by the brothers Goldman; James would later write *The Lion in Winter* and the libretto to *Follies*, while William would write *The Season* (the great book about the Broadway semester of 1967–1968) and the screenplay to *Butch Cassidy and the Sundance Kid*. The director was Harold Prince, who would stage *Company*, *Follies*, *Sweeney Todd*, and plenty more. Even Linda Lavin, who had a few small parts, would wind up a Tony winner.

One never knows, does one?

The show, based on no source material, could have been titled *Uncle to the Bride*. While many musicals take all show long to get a man to propose to a woman, *A Family Affair* started with that proposal—and then proceeded through all the headaches of planning a wedding, where every friend and relative has an opinion.

Alfie Nathan (Shelley Berman) has been caring for niece Sally (Rita Gardner) ever since her parents died. Now that she's getting married to Gerry (Larry Kert), chaos erupts between Alfie and Tillie (Eileen Heckart), the groom's mother. Because Tillie eloped and missed out on a big wedding, now she's going to stage an extravaganza. Never mind that Sally, Gerry, Alfie, and Tillie's husband, Morris (Morris Carnovsky) don't want that. Never mind, too, that this will be a financial stretch for these middle-class Jews (Alfie's a real estate broker, Morris a furrier) who—surprise!—don't live in New York, but in suburban Silver Hills, Illinois.

And so it goes with the wedding consultant, reception site, gown, bridesmaid's dresses, going-away outfit, shower, cake, bachelor party, and rehearsal. What William Goldman said of *How Now, Dow Jones* in *The Season*—"With a plot like this, are you surprised to learn that there was trouble out of town?"—applies to his own show. In later years, though, Goldman would fully admit, "*A Family Affair* just wasn't good enough to be a hit."

Says agent Richard Seff, who represented Kander at the time, "Jerome Robbins was interested in directing, which made Leland Hayward interested in producing—but when Robbins decided that he wouldn't, Hayward said he wouldn't, either. But I so believed in this show that I got my cousin Andrew—who spells his last name Siff—to produce it."

Non-singers in musicals had started appearing more frequently after *My Fair Lady* got away with it in 1956, but the practice reached its apotheosis with *A Family Affair*; the three top-billed performers had virtually no Broadway singing experience. Though Shelley Berman had made five albums, they were spoken-word comedy LPs. Berman was a stand-up comic—no, make that sit-down comic, for he was often found on a stool with a mock telephone to his ear, pretending to have a hard time with bureaucratic operators and receptionists who never quite answered his questions or gave him the party for whom he was looking.

Nevertheless, Berman had sung on Broadway sixteen times in *The Girls Against the Boys* in 1959—just as many times as Heckart had sung on stage. Though she was known for such dramatic properties as *The Bad Seed*, *A View from the Bridge*, and *The Dark at the Top of the Stairs*, the husky-voiced actress had also done a stint at City Center singing "Zip!" in *Pal Joey*.

Carnovsky was in his fortieth Broadway show in forty years, but his only musical was Kurt Weill's *Johnny Johnson*. Given that Carnovsky played "Chief of the High Allied Command" in that one, he wasn't required to do much singing.

Just the thought of these stars' voices may have caused recording companies to turn down the chance to record *A Family Affair*. This was still the golden age of original cast albums, when record companies often provided some or all of a show's capitalization in exchange for the coveted right to record the show. Yet in this same season when Columbia backed eight shows, Capitol five, and RCA Victor three, all these labels turned down *A Family Affair*.

"I made it my mission to get it recorded," said Seff. "I finally convinced United Artists to do it." It was that company's first-ever original cast album.

Harold Prince admitted in his autobiography, *Contradictions*, that he was originally offered the chance to direct the show, though he'd never staged a show on Broadway. "All" he'd done was coproduce five musicals, four of which had made money. But after Prince had resisted temptation and turned down *A Family Affair*, the job went to Word Baker, who two seasons earlier had directed the still-running *The Fantasticks*. There his ingenue had been Rita Gardner (married at the time to playwright Herb Gardner), whom he now made his ingenue Sally.

"But I had to audition, believe me," recalls Gardner.

Once the show was found wanting in Philadelphia, Prince was asked to come to see it. He saw enough there to make him commit to his first directorial assignment.

Says Gardner, "I still remember how I cried when I heard that Word was fired. But Hal was so kind to me. He said, 'I understand how you feel, but let's try to put this together and make it work.'" (Gardner also says that Berman was less nice to her, but chooses not to elaborate.)

The actor playing opposite Gardner was less worried that he'd be fired by Prince, for Kert had played Tony in Prince's coproduction of *West Side Story*. Eight years later, he'd also star in Prince's *Company* as Bobby, the man who couldn't make a commitment to any woman. But in this musical, Kert's character sure could commit. Indeed, the first words in the show were his "Will you marry me?"

Not only was Baker fired, but so was choreographer John Butler, whose big credit was providing the "dream" choreography for Menotti's opera *The Consul* a dozen years before. He was replaced by Bob Herget, though two of Butler's numbers, "The Right Girl" (which the cast would later perform on *The Ed Sullivan Show*) and "Revenge"—both centering on Berman—were retained; Butler got specific credit for each in the program.

"Revenge" allowed Alfie to fantasize about what he'd like to do to Tillie—and, even more importantly, it allowed Berman to pause the song each night, get on the phone, and do one of his trademark telephone operator routines. Oddly, though, the routine had him talking to an answering machine—in an age when such machines didn't yet exist. Could it be that the Goldmans and Kander invented that device?

The set resembled a wedding cake, which sounds cute and novel, but Prince felt the show needed a more realistic approach, and did what he could to change David Hays' design. And though Heckart wanted the show closed in Philly and Berman got testy about changes, Prince did get the piece to Broadway, and always took pride in how much he'd improved it. Even Heckart came around; she eventually requested that her funeral open with "My Son, the Lawyer" played from the show's original cast album.

That album was a lackluster single-sleeve job with a modest summary of the plot on the back. But it was wrapped in a pink paper ribbon that proclaimed, "First original cast album recorded on 35mm film."

The album would have done better to have given a cast list. One jaunty, Dixieland-inspired song, "Harmony," was said to be sung by "Osterwald, Conforti, Lavin, and DeLon." At least Bibi Osterwald and Jack DeLon's names were billed on the front cover, but who were the others? Gino Conforti, who'd become the original Fiddler on the Roof, and Linda Lavin, who played multiple roles, including "Quiet Girl."

"This show was important to my career," says Lavin. "Once Hal took over, he gave me more to do. And when he was casting '[It's a Bird . . . It's a Plane . . . It's] Superman' four years later, he chose me for a featured role"—prompting then–*Times* critic Stanley Kauffmann to say that Lavin should be in every musical. "I always thought he was the brightest critic of them all," Lavin says with a smile.

The best that Howard Taubman, the *Times* critic who reviewed *A Family Affair*, could say was "some numbers are lively." Walter Kerr in the *Herald-Tribune* wrote that the show had "genuine charm," and that it was "innocent, easygoing, and pleasant," but those aren't words that make people rush to the box office.

A Family Affair was one of the comparatively few musicals that didn't specifically identify the authors of the book, music, and lyrics, but simply said the show was "by James Goldman, John Kander, and William Goldman." It's now easy to infer that Kander wrote the music and the Goldmans did the book and lyrics, but a look at the script that Music Theatre International leases for stock and amateur productions states that while the Goldmans did the book, James Goldman and John Kander wrote the lyrics.

Not that the show gets done much. "Gay" used as a term for "happy" was dated even by 1962. What's even more dated is the belief expressed in the song "Every Girl Wants to Get Married."

Said Seff, "It wound up losing all $350,000, but it wasn't all for naught. For I also represented Fred Ebb, who at the time was writing with Paul Klein, a composer who wanted to leave show business. So I took Fred to see *A Family Affair*, and afterwards, he said to me, 'Yeah. I could write with that composer.'"

Indeed he could—and he did for the next forty years. In 1977, Ebb even took "Mamie in the Afternoon," one of the songs that *A Family Affair* had dropped out of town, rewrote it as "Arthur in the Afternoon," and put it in his and Kander's *The Act*.

By then, both he and Kander had each won a Tony, while Prince had won four for Direction of a Musical. Both Goldmans had won Oscars, too.

We *did* hear from those guys again.

A Family Affair. January 27, 1962–March 24, 1962. 65 performances.

1962–1963

THE BIGGEST HIT
Oliver!

Our very first British megahit.

And for the first time in this book—but certainly not the last—we come in contact with producer David Merrick.

Do young 'uns know how famous Merrick once was? In the movie of *Valley of the Dolls*, Merrick is mentioned as the producer of *Take Me, Darling*, the musical in which Neely O'Hara stars. In an episode of *The Mary Tyler Moore Show*, in which Murray has written a play, the Broadway producer who's said to reject it is David Merrick.

Merrick was notorious. Tom Jones, whose *110 in the Shade* (1963) and *I Do! I Do!* (1966) were produced by Merrick, remembers the vivid red of the producer's office walls, a color that, around Broadway, came to be known as "David Merrick red." Says Jones, "You had to stand there while he sat. David didn't provide furniture, all to keep his visitors ill at ease." Some years later, Jones admits, when he was writing an original musical, *Celebration*, he patterned the character of Mr. Rich, the vain, self-centered, nouveau-riche bully, on Merrick.

Howard Kissel, in *The Abominable Showman*, his biography of Merrick, states that when Merrick went to Vietnam with *Hello, Dolly!*, he sought out generals in order to learn their ambush tactics so that he could put them theatrically into play.

Whether widely loved or widely feared, not many producers are famous enough to get record albums named after them. But in 1964, RCA Victor released *David Merrick Presents Hits from His Broadway Hits*, with a "David Merrick red" cover. John Gary and Ann-Margret sang songs from *Hello, Dolly!*, *110 in the Shade*, *Stop the World—I Want to Get Off*, *Subways Are for Sleeping*, *Carnival*, *Do Re Mi*, *Irma la Douce*, *Take Me Along*, *Gypsy*, *Destry Rides Again*, *Fanny*, and the biggest hit of this season, *Oliver!*

Merrick would often brag on late-night talk shows that he carried his passport with him at all times, so that if he suddenly heard about a hit in London (such as *Look Back in Anger*) or Paris (*La Plume de Ma Tante*), he could grab the next plane and buy it. So not long after *Oliver!*—a musical version of Charles Dickens' *Oliver Twist*—opened in London on June 30, 1960 to West End raves, Merrick was flying to England.

Oliver! was one of the comparatively few musicals whose book, music, and lyrics were the work of one person. Lionel Bart had had a good deal of pop music success before he wrote the lyrics for one West End hit (*Lock Up Your Daughters*) and the entire score for another (*Fings Ain't Wot They Used T'Be*). But *Oliver!*

was judged to be more than just a hit. It was given the ultimate compliment: it was as good as an Americna musical.

Bart couldn't notate his music, but could only conceive it in his head. Still, "As Long as He Needs Me" became a hit and signature song for Georgia Brown, who portrayed Nancy, the doomed lover of Bill Sikes (Danny Sewell). Bart had a way with words, too. Years before Ben and Jerry came up with a certain ice cream flavor, Bart had Mr. Bumble (Willoughby Goddard) refer to himself as a "chubby hubby."

Merrick quickly snatched up *Oliver!* for America, putting the show on a cross-country tryout that would begin on the West Coast and culminate in New York on December 27, 1962. He talked RCA Victor into the rare concession of releasing the cast album long before the New York opening. One problem with that was that the record couldn't be called an original Broadway cast album when the show finally debuted at the Imperial, for by then Michael Goodman, who'd been playing the Artful Dodger, had been replaced by one David Jones.

Just before opening, though, Merrick decided to postpone the first night for a week. His hope was that the citywide newspaper strike, which had begun on December 8, might be solved in a few days. With no free publicity or reviews from newspapers, Merrick "helped" by going on the radio and reading his own (rave) review of the show. Then he applied for membership in the New York Critics Circle.

When the newspapers came back after 114 days out, Merrick took out heavy newspaper ads. But the following year, when sales were starting to lag, Merrick decided to have two numbers from *Oliver!* broadcast on prime-time TV.

No larger television viewing audience ever saw a sequence from a Broadway musical than the 73 million that saw *Oliver!* on *The Ed Sullivan Show* on February 9, 1964. Georgia Brown did "As Long as He Needs Me" and joined Bruce Prochnik, playing Oliver, in "I'd Do Anything."

To be fair, most of those 73 million had tuned in to see a new hot pop group called the Beatles make their American television debut. But *Oliver!* benefited. Kissel states in *The Abominable Showman* that in the summer of 1964, scalpers were selling tickets to *Oliver!* for a higher price ($27.50) than they were getting from Merrick's new white-hot hit, *Hello, Dolly!* That, he wrote, "may have been increased by the number of families in New York for the World's Fair." A case could be made that these families may have seen *Oliver!* on *Ed Sullivan.*

What David Jones noticed when he performed on *Ed Sullivan* that night was that the audience response was far greater for the Beatles than for *Oliver!* He then decided to abandon Broadway and pursue a pop career. Within two years, as a member of the Monkees, he was singing on the number one album in the country.

As for David Merrick, *Oliver!* was the fifteenth of thirty-four musicals that he produced. Considering his prolificacy, one might be surprised to find that only two of those shows were Tony winners: *Hello, Dolly!* (1964), and *42ⁿᵈ Street* (1981). *Oliver!* lost to *A Funny Thing Happened on the Way to the Forum,* which had opened too late for the previous year's Tony race. Bet when Merrick saw *Oliver!* in London that summer night in 1960, he thought had he had his first Best Musical Tony in the bag.

Oliver! January 6, 1963–November 14, 1964. 774 performances.

THE BIGGEST FLOP
Hot Spot

There's little peace in the Peace Corps musical.

One could argue that the biggest flop of the season was *Mr. President*. It had a book by Howard Lindsay and Russel Crouse, who wrote *Life with Father*, still today the longest-running non-musical in Broadway history. It would be staged by Joshua Logan, the only director to have helmed two musicals (*Annie Get Your Gun* and *South Pacific*) and one play (*Mister Roberts*) that each ran over 1,100 performances. Most significantly, its score was by Irving Berlin (no credit list necessary).

But, while *Mr. President* was an intense disappointment, it did run for more than seven months, and made back some of its money because of its mammoth advance sale. (In those days, that meant more than $1 million—which was equivalent to more than 150 sold-out performances. Today, a show with a $1 million advance can't sell out a week.)

Mr. President's big mistake was detailing the life of a president in office only for act 1. In the second act, Stephen Decatur Henderson (Robert Ryan) lost his bid for re-election. "You Need a Hobby," sang his wife, Nell (Nanette Fabray). Why take such a big character and reduce him for the last half of the show?

One could also argue that the biggest flop of the season was *Sophie*, which lasted only eight performances. But only one famous name was attached to this one: Steve Allen, an early "Tonight Show" host and the leading man of *The Benny Goodman Story*. Though he wasn't as heralded as songwriter, Allan provided the score for this musical version of the life of rotund and rowdy vaudevillian Sophie Tucker (Libi Staiger).

The reviews weren't good, and the novice producers closed as soon as they could. Still, Allen believed in his songwriting ability, and on Wednesday, May 15, 1963—exactly a month after *Sophie* opened—he took out a full-page ad in *Variety*. "What the Critics Say about the Score of *Sophie*," it proudly proclaimed, followed by quotes from some critics, including a blue-chipper from the esteemed Walter Kerr of the *Herald Tribune*: "Richard Rodgers is famous for his 'wrong note.' Mr. Allen may become famous for always arriving at the right note."

Did Kerr really admire Allen's music that much? No. What he actually wrote was "Richard Rodgers is famous for his 'wrong note.' Mr. Allen may become famous for always arriving at the right note, and you have no idea how monotonous that can be." Allen just cut off the quotation where he saw fit.

But the biggest flop of the season has to be *Hot Spot*, mostly because it starred the beloved Judy Holliday. How many other performers could say they'd won an Oscar (for *Born Yesterday*, beating out Bette Davis and Gloria Swanson) and a Tony (for *Bells Are Ringing*, besting no less than Julie Andrews in *My Fair Lady*)?

The lead producer was Robert Fryer, who'd produced such hits as *Wonderful Town*, *The Desk Set*, and *Redhead*. To direct, Fryer hired Morton "Tec" DaCosta, who'd given him a hit in *Auntie Mame* and, admittedly, a big 1959 flop, *Saratoga*.

Hot Spot was a musical about the then-very-topical Peace Corps that had been started by President John F. Kennedy. Enlistee Sally Hopwinder (Holliday) tried to do some good in the mythical land of D'hum. The book was by Jack Weinstock and Willie Gilbert, the librettists *of record* of *How to Succeed in Business Without Really Trying* but Abe Burrows considerably rewrote their work. *Hot Spot*'s music was by Mary Rodgers, whose father had just won a Tony for writing music and lyrics (Richard Rodgers; *No Strings*) and whose son would someday do the same (Adam Guettel; *The Light in the Piazza*). Mary was no slouch, for she'd written the delightful music for *Once upon a Mattress*.

The most obscure name was Martin Charnin, the lyricist, who would have a huge success by conceiving, directing, and lyricizing *Annie* fourteen long years later. Charnin now remembers how matters quickly became shaky for *Hot Spot*, partly because Holliday was romantically involved with esteemed jazz saxophonist Gerry Mulligan.

"I'll never forget being at a rehearsal where Tec was directing, and Gerry was in the house," he says. "Tec told Judy to move in a certain way, and she looked right through him and looked to see what Gerry was thinking. Gerry shook his head no, and Judy said, no, she wouldn't do as he asked. It wasn't too much longer that Gerry was our new director and Tec was literally taken out on a stretcher."

Sheila Smith, who had a featured role, insists,

It had *nine* directors. I checked my 1963 journal, and saw that we started rehearsals on January 2 and previewed in Washington on February 4 before opening the next night. DaCosta departed on February 17, and they let his associate Myles Eason take over till they could find someone else. He was still there when we closed in Washington on February 23, though Bob Fosse came in just "to help" on February 19. That's the best he could do, because his baby with Gwen Verdon was soon due. [Nicole Fosse would be born on March 3.]

Robert Fryer took over the direction on February 25, though he'd never directed before. Cy Feuer, who was famous as a producer—but at least one who had directed—came on February 27, the day we opened in Philadelphia. But before we closed there on March 16, Marty Charnin assumed the duties on March 3, Arthur Laurents on March 9, Richard Quine from March 16 to 26.

Quine did have some experience directing Broadway properties: *The Solid Gold Cadillac*; *Bell, Book, and Candle*; and *The World of Suzie Wong*—but only in their later screen transformations. His Broadway experience was solely as an actor, in a small role in the short-running *Very Warm for May* in 1939, and in the straight play *My Sister Eileen*, originating the role of Frank Lippencott, the drugstore employee who took a shine to the younger Miss Sherwood. To be fair, Quine did direct the 1955 film musical of *My Sister Eileen* (which, as every true musical enthusiast can tell you, was not the same property as *Wonderful Town*). Those credits, though, apparently gave him enough clout to come in and direct *Hot Spot*—at least for a while.

"But," says Smith, "Myles Eason came back on March 23—maybe because he was the only one to have the original working script. Add to that Bob Linden, the associate producer who acted like a director on March 12 in the way he gave notes, and Herb Ross on March 27."

Weinstock and Gilbert's book had its share of helpers, too. Says Smith, "Herb Gardner, Comden and Green, Jerome Chodorov, and Marshall Barer all came in. Milton Rosenstock replaced Franz Allers as conductor. And Sondheim wrote one new song for Judy." (That was "Don't Laugh," which has received some recordings over the years.)

"We started previews March 19," says Smith. "We played thirty-five of them, which was really unheard of in those days, especially when you'd already been out of town."

Finally Fryer opened the show. Said the critics, "It isn't any good" (Kerr, *Herald-Tribune*), "smother(s) the prodigious and ebullient Miss Holliday" (McClain, *Journal-American*), and "new depths of grim" (Nadel, *World-Telegram and Sun*).

And in the end, out of those nine directors, no one took credit for either for direction or choreography, though Herbert Ross was the one who eventually did or supervised both.

Ross just didn't want his name on another flop. He'd choreographed seven in a row (*A Tree Grows in Brooklyn*, *Three Wishes for Jamie*, *House of Flowers*, *The Body Beautiful*, *The Gay Life*, *I Can Get It for You Wholesale*, and *Tovarich*), and didn't need to add one more to his resume.

Little did Ross know that four more flops were coming: *Anyone Can Whistle*, *Kelly*, *Do I Hear a Waltz?*, and *On a Clear Day You Can See Forever*. That's when he started making plans to go to Hollywood, where his real success began, as the director of *The Turning Point*, *Soapdish*, and five Neil Simon films, including *The Sunshine Boys*.

But he never did a movie of *Hot Spot*.

Hot Spot. April 19, 1963–May 25, 1963. 43 performances.

1963–1964

THE BIGGEST HIT
Hello, Dolly!

Wow, wow, wow, fellas . . .

It's a rare musical theater enthusiast who doesn't know that David Merrick gave Jerry (*Milk and Honey*) Herman a mere weekend to write songs for his planned musical version of Thornton Wilder's *The Matchmaker*.

Herman went home and absorbed the story of Dolly Gallagher Levi, the Yonkers widow who entices the wealthy Horace Vandergelder to New York City, ostensibly so he can meet much younger widow Irene Molloy. (Of course, Dolly plans to get Vandergelder for herself.) While Vandergelder's away, his employees—Cornelius and Barnaby—will play. Cornelius comes to New York and winds up winning Irene for himself, while Vandergelder hooks up with you-know-who.

So went the play; so Herman went to work. He returned first thing Monday morning and offered four songs that so impressed Merrick that the producer said, "Kid, the show is yours."

According to original Cornelius Charles Nelson Reilly, though, at least one melody came from Herman's trunk. Because Reilly had appeared in one of Herman's first efforts—the off-Broadway revue *Parade* in 1960—he already knew much of the songwriter's oeuvre. Said Reilly, "The melody to 'Put On Your Sunday Clothes' originally had lyrics that went, 'The spirit of the chase is what it's all about.'"

But is there any smash hit with more secrets than *Hello, Dolly!*? What about the story behind "Before the Parade Passes By"? Charles Strouse and Lee Adams first wrote the song for *Dolly* director-choreographer Gower Champion, who'd staged their *Bye Bye Birdie* in 1960.

Said Pat Tolson, *Dolly*'s original stage manager,

Yes, that's true. I still remember [dance arranger] Peter Howard playing it for Gower and me. Gower didn't like the song, and said that even though he'd been specific to Strouse and Adams as to what he needed, they'd let him down. But he did like the title, and asked Jerry Herman to write a song with that same title.

Herman said, "My proudest moment on the show was coming up with 'Before the Parade Passes By' while under the gun." Tolson reported, "When he did, Strouse and Adams said they'd sue, which made Michael Stewart—who worked with them on *Bye Bye Birdie*—furious."

Strouse says,

Without exaggerating, I've never seen a more horrific atmosphere than *Dolly* in Detroit. The first night, after Jerry went into shock that we were there, we were walking along the corridor of the hotel, a door opened, a hand came out, and it literally pulled Lee into the room. It was Mike [Stewart], who said, "Don't listen to anything Gower says! And report everything to me!" It was like a Peter Sellers spy film. Nobody was talking. It was just awful.

"Before the Parade Passes By"—a number for Dolly (Carol Channing)—replaced "Penny in My Pocket," a song for Vandergelder (David Burns) in which he told of his accumulated wealth and catalogued his many possessions, plenty of which were brought out on stage. "What was sadly lost," said original cast member Randy Phillips, "was that Dolly also came out with a big bolt of red fabric—which would turn into the dress that she'd wear to the Harmonia Gardens."

All this happened after the show had been called "a blue baby" by Detroit's leading drama critic. Champion, galvanized by the poor notices, would not let the company rest, not even on November 22, 1963, after John F. Kennedy had been assassinated. Though that that night's performance would obviously be canceled, Champion used the time to rehearse the company and make changes. "He put a box of Kleenex near the footlights," Channing recalls. "If anyone wanted to cry, he could get a tissue, wipe the tears—and then return to work."

Reilly called the experience "a living hell—though I wouldn't have wanted to be in any heaven instead." Given Reilly's previous association with Herman, one might assume that the composer-lyricist had urged Champion to hire the actor—despite Reilly's fey persona—in what becomes a romantic role. But Herman explains,

No. I saw a real leading man in that part, with a voice that sounded more like John Raitt's. Gower explained that if all the characters were a little off-center, the show would have a cartoon flavor, and that's what he was looking for. That's why Freddy Wittop's costumes were so brightly colored, too, and why we had two girls as the front and back of horses in horse costumes, so the show would be a cartoon. It was wonderful to be told that at the time, for it made me write in a style I wouldn't have otherwise used.

Before the show moved to Washington, there was talk of restoring a song previously cut from the Harmonia Gardens sequence, in which an entertainer sang, "The Man in the Moon (Is a Lady)" to replace the still-not-working "Come and Be My Butterfly." That didn't happen, so two years later, Herman used "The Man in the Moon" in *Mame*. (Turnabout is fair play; a song then written for Mame herself—"Love Is Only Love"—wound up in the film of *Hello, Dolly!*)

But *Dolly*'s title number worked wonderfully right from the beginning. As for those Harmonia Gardens waiters who celebrate Mrs. Levi, Herman named them Harry, Louis, and Manny, respectively (and respectfully) for his father and two uncles.

Regarding the song that preceded it in the show, Strouse reports, "Bob Merrill wrote 'Elegance'," confirming what musical theater enthusiasts suspected for years. After all, the lyric "All the guests of Mr. Hackl are / Feeling great and look spectac-alar" seems to have been written by the same man who wrote, "Kid, my heart ain't made of marble / but your rhythm's really har'ble" for that same season's *Funny Girl*.

Says Strouse, "Bob once told me he made over a million dollars from that one song." Strouse, however, doesn't offer to disclose what he and Adams have earned by providing at least the title to "Before the Parade Passes By."

But it all worked out by opening night. Channing recalled that Champion, right after seeing Dolly's unanimous raves, said to her, "Isn't this better than sex?" Channing said she replied (and imagine this in her trademark basso profundo voice), "Well, I wouldn't know."

It's a rare show that opens to raves and then is still fine-tuned. Credit to Champion for believing he could do still better. He replaced "Come and Be My Butterfly" with a polka contest. Herman, though, thought it "bland," and preferred his song: "I have always missed it."

The show is still a little lumpy, but it rings. Would the uneducated Vandergelder really say the grammatically precise "To whom can you turn when the plumbing is leaking?" In "So Long, Dearie," Dolly sings to Horace, "I'm going to learn to dance and drink and smoke a cigarette"—but earlier in the show, we saw her *teaching* people to dance. Maybe that's why, when Pearl Bailey took over the role in 1967, she changed the lyric to "I'm gonna learn to hootchy-kootch."

The cast album—helped by Louis Armstrong's number one rendition of the title song—sold eighty thousand copies its first week. It would be the traditional Broadway musical's true last hurrah on disc. For by 1964, the oldest of the baby boomers were now getting jobs and making money while still living at home. In their youth, they'd had to save their pennies to buy 45 singles at eighty-nine cents each; now they could easily afford $3.98 for mono albums and $4.98 for stereo ones. The only real show song they'd be buying would be "Till There Was You," thanks to its being on side two of *Meet the Beatles*.

Dolly sold out until summer 1965, when Ginger Rogers succeeded Channing. After Martha Raye and then Betty Grable took over, the show was running out of box-office gas. But when Pearl Bailey and Cab Calloway headed an all-African-American company, rave reviews resulted, and business was back to capacity.

Merrick seemed to be the smartest man on Broadway for thinking of such a plan, but even he was taken by surprise. He'd mounted this black company simply as a new tour, but after the tumultuous reaction in its initial stop in Washington, he decided to fire Grable and company and bring the black cast to New York. *Dolly* would eventually break *My Fair Lady*'s long-run record, but it wouldn't have been able to do it without Bailey and Calloway's terrific shot in the arm.

As a result, *Dolly* was the first-ever musical to still be running on Broadway after its movie version came and went. The 1969 film, starring Walter Matthau (okay, Barbra Streisand, too), has endured much criticism, but screenwriter Ernest Lehman did make one improvement: Irene Molloy (Marianne McAndrew) figures out that Cornelius (Michael Crawford) is not a wealthy man. In Stewart's version, she does not—and one would have to be very stupid not to see through his nervousness at going to a much too expensive restaurant.

Following Bailey came Phyllis Diller (yes—and the eccentric comedian played it straight) until Ethel Merman took over. She was in place for the closing. Theater historian Skip Koenig reports that Merman's curtain speech after minutes of tumultuous cheers included "Well, I don't know about you, but I'm going out for some Neapolitan ice cream!"

But *Dolly* wasn't remotely through. On Broadway alone, there have been three revivals (one with Bailey, two with Channing). Sure, the show became a cliché; that's what happens to superhits. James (*A Chorus Line*) Kirkwood liked to tell of seeing a sign in Los Angeles that said, "Jesus, save us from Hell" but was amended by a graffiti artist to say, "Jesus, save us from *Hello, Dolly* revivals." (Pretty erudite graffiti artists out in L.A., wouldn't you say?)

Eventually a plaque was installed outside the theater: "David Merrick's production *Hello, Dolly!* celebrated its 2,718th performance on September 9, 1970 at the St. James Theatre and became the longest running Broadway musical in history." The plaque was there for a few months until someone ripped it from the wall.

But *Dolly* itself endures. *Wall-E*, the 2008 Pixar-Disney-Buy-n-Large film, started with the words "Out there, there's a world outside of Yonkers," in Michael Crawford's distinctive voice. *Wall-E* director Andrew Stanton knew the song because he'd played Barnaby in his high school's production. So Stanton has had

Wall-E—an acronym for Waste Allocation Load Lifter Earth-Class—take time out from his busy schedule of trash-compacting to watch a VHS tape of a movie made 849 years earlier. Yes, even in 2815, someone is watching *Hello, Dolly!*

Hello, Dolly! January 16, 1964—December 27, 1970: 2,844 performances.

THE BIGGEST FLOP
Anyone Can Whistle

Sondheim strikes out—in more ways than one.

In late 1963, as he readied his newest musical, Stephen Sondheim had only known Broadway success. *West Side Story* (1957), *Gypsy* (1959), and *A Funny Thing Happened on the Way to the Forum* (1962) were not only hits, but classics that would be performed on the world's stages for decades to come.

Of course, Sondheim "only" wrote the lyrics for the first two, and his score to the third wasn't that well received. Still, for someone thirty-two going on thirty-three, he had quite a track record.

Now he'd return to working with Arthur Laurents, his *West Side* and *Gypsy* librettist, on that most difficult of musical theater animals: the original musical. This time, they wouldn't have master director-choreographer Jerome Robbins; Laurents would direct. He'd staged only one Broadway musical, the fascinating failure *I Can Get It for You Wholesale*, in 1962. There—and here—his choreographer was Herbert Ross, who, as we've seen, had only known failure.

The first page of Laurents' script says the show must be played on a "pop-art cockeyed" set, so that sets the atypical tone. An unnamed town is desperate to fake a miracle in order to entice some tourists into traveling there and spending their dollars. What else can its citizens do, given that they'd "manufactured a product that never wore out"? (There's a subject for a musical that's never been tackled: planned obsolescence.)

Whistle was always said to be ahead of its time. First, America's cities hadn't yet reached the crisis mode; today, the show could be easily set in at least a dozen depressed American cities. The show also cited "people who made other people nervous by leading individual lives," four years before hippies and *Hair* said much the same thing. Religion wasn't put up on a pedestal, either, as Fay (Lee Remick), the maybe-crazy, maybe-not heroine, spoke of preferring "the miracles of man, such as the wheel, the alphabet, and the pyramids."

Fay was quite the crusader for individual rights, too, as was her likewise maybe-crazy, maybe-not confederate J. Bowden Hapgood (Harry Guardino). He proved that people will put their faith in charisma instead of using their heads, selling them on his logic: "The opposite of left is right. The opposite of right is wrong. So anyone who's left is wrong."

That's terrific Sondheim wordplay, but he had more to say here, too, especially in "Everybody Says Don't," where he urged audiences to "make a noise"—again, a few years before the youth of American actually did. Had hippies heard this song, they might not have taken to Sondheim's Broadway sound, but they would have embraced what he was saying.

But in early 1964, that wasn't at all what Broadway wanted to hear. The wound of the Kennedy assassination needed to be healed. Who knew that in fewer than ten years there would be a political irony: In the show, mayoress Cora Hoover Hooper (Angela Lansbury) employed a corrupt official named Magruder (James Frawley). In 1973, one Jeb Magruder would be known to all Americans as one of the less-honest executives in Nixon's Watergate-tainted administration.

Harvey Evans played John—married to his boss, June, who won't give him a raise because "He's not worth it." He recalls the uncertainty, even hostility, that dogged the show in Philadephia—as when Nancy Walker came at the request of management to see the show, possibly to replace the now-nervous Angela Lansbury—or when, after one performance, during the curtain calls, "A man in the front row gave us a thumbs-down gesture; Harry Guardino returned it by giving him the finger."

New York critics collectively wound up doing both. During this same season, when *Barefoot in the Park* opened to unanimous raves from the six daily critics—and *Abraham Cochrane* (and plenty of others) debuted to unanimous pans—*Anyone Can Whistle* opened to three raves and three pans. No critic was indifferent.

Why has no other musical that has run nine performances or fewer stayed in a musical theater enthusiast's mind as strongly? The original cast album made it happen.

Those who bought the original LP were surprised when they took the disc out of the sleeve and saw only four bands on the first side; even some ten-inch original cast LPs from the forties had more songs to a side. But Sondheim was starting to experiment with long song forms, so "Simple," almost thirteen minutes long, took up quite a bit of Side One.

But Sondheim's music wasn't as complicated as it would be in years to come. Keys and time signatures rarely changed, and, despite the iconoclastic nature of the show, an inordinate number of songs say "Moderato" on the sheet music.

Don Walker's orchestration suited the score, and included a galvanic rideout for "The Miracle Song"—which had a lyric that went, "Glory hallelu, you fin'lly came through!" Sondheim would again and again come through for the American musical—as did Columbia Records president Goddard Lieberson.

He wasn't required to record the score, but did—even though the show's closing would obviously curtail sales. Before this, the only musical that failed to reach double figures and still got an original cast album had been *Man in the Moon* (1963), a Bock-Harnick tuner for children that was released on a children's label. But Lieberson would give *Anyone Can Whistle* the grade-A treatment that he'd thus far afforded to only ten other musicals in his tenure: the ornate, double-fold jacket with the extra page inside.

More miraculously, *Anyone Can Whistle* would be released on four-track tape, *eight*-track tape, cassette, and CD. Without this documentation of the score, *Whistle* would not have been heard, reheard, talked about, argued about, and—in the end—mostly appreciated.

The 1995 Carnegie Hall concert with Bernadette Peters as Fay, Madeline Kahn as Cora, and Scott Bakula as Hapgood might not have happened, or the 2010 Encores! Concert, either. Some months later, producers who were searching for a performer to play Mame were reassured by this album that Angela Lansbury could sing theater music.

Whistle proved that even a show that ran a mere week could have an afterlife. Since then, more than two dozen musicals that have numbered nine performances or fewer have recorded cast albums. None have done as well, to be sure, but everyone dreams of having his show enjoy as strong an afterlife and a redeemed reputation. Because of that original cast album, *Anyone Can Whistle*, to paraphrase the biggest hit of this same season, will never go away again.

Anyone Can Whistle. April 4, 1964–April 11, 1964. 9 performances

1964–1965

THE BIGGEST HIT
Fiddler on the Roof

A palpable hit song.

What was the biggest hit song from a 1960s Broadway musical? These would seem to be the contenders:

"A Lot of Livin' to Do" (*Bye Bye Birdie*)
"Aquarius" (*Hair*)
"As Long as He Needs Me" (*Oliver!*)
"Big Spender" (*Sweet Charity*)
"Cabaret" (*Cabaret*)
"Gonna Build a Mountain" (*Stop the World—I Want to Get Off*)

"Good Morning, Starshine" (*Hair*)
"Hair" (*Hair*)
"Hello, Dolly!" (*Hello, Dolly!*)
"Hey, Look Me Over" (*Wildcat*)
"If Ever I Would Leave You" (*Camelot*)
"If He Walked into My Life" (*Mame*)
"If I Ruled the World" (*Pickwick*)
"I Gotta Be Me" (*Golden Rainbow*)
"I'll Never Fall in Love Again" (*Promises, Promises*)
"The Impossible Dream" (*Man of La Mancha*)
"The Joker" (*The Roar of the Greasepaint—the Smell of the Crowd*)
"Let the Sunshine In" (*Hair*)
"Make Someone Happy" (*Do Re Mi*)
"On a Clear Day You Can See Forever" (*On a Clear Day You Can See Forever*)
"Once in a Lifetime" (*Stop the World—I Want to Get Off*)
"Once upon a Time" (*All-American*)
"People" (*Funny Girl*)
"Promises, Promises" (*Promises, Promises*)
"Put on a Happy Face" (*Bye Bye Birdie*)
"(S)he Touched Me" (*Drat! The Cat!*)
"What Kind of Fool Am I?" (*Stop the World—I Want to Get Off*)
"Who Can I Turn To?" (*The Roar of the Greasepaint—the Smell of the Crowd*)

Of those twenty-eight, "Hello, Dolly!" seems the likely winner, through its 1964 chart-topping Louis Armstrong recording that hit #1 the week of May 9, 1964. (And in the era when the Beatles were white-hot.)

But actually, "Hello, Dolly!"—from the second-longest-running musical of the decade—must settle for being the second-biggest hit song from a 1960s Broadway musical. The biggest hit song from a 1960s Broadway musical comes from the longest-running show of the sixties.

The musical is *Fiddler on the Roof*, and the song is "Sunrise, Sunset," with music by Jerry Bock and lyrics by Sheldon Harnick. It showed us the inner thoughts of Tevye (Zero Mostel) and Golde (Maria Karnilova) as they saw their daughter Tzeitel (Joanna Merlin) marry the Tailor Motel Kamzoil (Austin Pendleton). "Is this the little girl I carried? Is this the little boy at play?" Tevye sang, before Golde mused, "I don't remember growing older; when did they?" What parent couldn't relate to that universal truth?

"Sunrise, Sunset" became a standard despite not getting a representative recording from a famous artist. The other songs listed above became associated with the likes of Tony Bennett, the Fifth Dimension, Robert Goulet, Anthony

Newley, and Barbra Streisand. No one of such stature had a breakthrough hit with "Sunrise, Sunset." Even when alto jazz saxophonist Cannonball Adderly released an album of *Fiddler*'s songs, he included the dropped "Dear Sweet Sewing Machine" and "Chavaleh"—the latter was even released as a single—but not "Sunrise, Sunset."

Yet "Sunrise, Sunset" is a true "standard"—the term used for a song that remains in the public consciousness for decades after its first release. Some would say that the twenty-eight above-named songs are standards, too. Yes and no, for many of them aren't heard very much these days.

But for the last four decades, the band at any wedding, bar- or bat-mitzvah has been virtually guaranteed to play "Sunrise, Sunset."

"Sunrise, Sunset" may turn out to outlast *Fiddler on the Roof*, the show that finally broke *Life with Father*'s record 3,224-performance Broadway run. But the success didn't come easily. Bock and Harnick made no fewer than three attempts to write a song called "Why Gentile, Why Jew?" before discarding it. The show's original opening number was "We Never Missed a Sabbath Yet." In it, the younger daughters ask to go out and play, only to have Golde tell them there's still too much work to do. Hodel, meanwhile, is reading instead of working, causing her mother to mutter, "With a million things I really need / God gives me daughters who can read!"

In the middle of it, though, were a few bars of music for what would eventually become the opening number, "Tradition." Originally it had lyrics that went, "There's noodles to be made, and chickens to be plucked, and liver to be chopped, and challah to be baked." Great opening numbers aren't created overnight, though "Tradition" was in place in July, 1964 when the company headed for its out-of-town tryout in Detroit.

People are always asking, "What comes first—the music or the lyrics?" There are demos in which Bock is playing the piano, and humming or "da-da-da"-ing, and they prove he wrote at least some of *Fiddler*'s melodies before Harnick provided lyrics. What became "The Tailor Motel Kamzoil," "Sabbath Prayer," and—yes—the blockbuster hit "Sunrise, Sunset"—were all melodies in Bock's head before they were words on Harnick's pad.

In a year in which nine of the sixteen musicals on Broadway had title songs, *Fiddler* almost made it ten. Harnick did write lyrics for the Fiddler's theme, heard just before "Tradition." It begins, "Away above my head / I see the strangest sight / A fiddler on the roof / Who's up there day and night." It concludes with "A fiddler on the roof / A most unlikely sight / It might not mean a thing / But then again, it might."

For the second year in a row, our biggest hit of the season was a big flop in Detroit. Director-choreographer Jerome Robbins had a second-act ballet, "Chaveleh," that lasted more than ten minutes; it eventually was cut down to a glorified move across the stage, as Tevye rued that he must spurn his daughter Chava (Tanya Everett) because she has married a Christian. (Bookwriter Joseph

Stein's early précis said that "Tzeitel tells Tevye that Chava is here; he accepts her." That certainly didn't come to pass in the finished product.)

Dropped in Detroit was the delectable, humorous, and moving "When Messiah Comes." It came near show's end, when Mendel (Leonard Frey), the rabbi's son, said to his father, "We've been waiting for the Messiah all our lives. Wouldn't this be a good time for him to come?" Tevye then stepped forward and sang, "When messiah comes / He will say to us / 'I apologize that I took so long / But I had a little trouble finding you / Over here a few, and over there a few.'" It was a funny song, at least at the start, but became progressively more serious. Audiences that began laughing at the start of it were asked to change their reactions in the middle. Eliminating the song made it easier for them.

After its semi-acclaimed film version opened in November 1971, *Fiddler on the Roof* played eight more months on Broadway. Throughout its 1964–1972 run, *Fiddler* kept its $9.90 top. Never mind that *On a Clear Day You Can See Forever* went to $11.90, or that *"It's a Bird . . . It's a Plane . . . It's Superman"* soared to $12, or that *Zorba* danced up to $15; *Fiddler* held firm, as all holdover shows did in those days. Not until the late seventies did yesteryear's hits begin raising their prices when the new hits came along and upped the ante. *A Chorus Line* charged $15 when it opened, but was asking $60 when it closed fifteen years later.

In the sixties, though, such a practice was unthinkable. Perhaps that's why producer Harold Prince came to the erroneous conclusion in 1974, "I don't think a show will run longer than *Fiddler*'s 3,242 performances on Broadway."

Fiddler on the Roof. September 22, 1964–July 2, 1972. 3,242 performances.

THE BIGGEST FLOP
Pleasures and Palaces

Did we see the same show?

How tempting to name *Kelly* the biggest flop of the season, for it ran only one night (February 6, 1965) and lost an unprecedented $650,000. (Today, when show loses $650,000, its producers brag about the hit they had.)

Kelly may well have inspired the longest article ever written about a Broadway musical in a mainstream magazine: Louis H. Latham's "Has Anybody Here Seen *Kelly*?" ran twelve pages (when pages were a large 10½ by 13½ inches) and sported eleven pictures. It appeared in the April 24, 1965 edition of the *Saturday Evening Post*—which is ironic, in that *Kelly* opened on a Saturday Evening with a closing notice already Posted.

But *Kelly* wasn't a high-profile show. Its four producers had never mounted a Broadway musical. Yes, its music was by Mark "Moose" Charlap, composer of the beloved *Peter Pan*—but then Jule Styne was called in to buttress his work.

The bookwriter-lyricist was Eddie Lawrence, whose only professional credits were as a performer.

And here's Herbert Ross again, this time, though, as both director and choreographer. He'd done that double duty only once before on Broadway, in a revival of *Finian's Rainbow* that had lasted a week.

And speaking of *Finian's*, its original leading lady, Ella Logan, would star in *Kelly*. It was to be her first Broadway appearance since *Finian's* had closed seventeen years earlier. But, while Logan played the Philadelphia and Boston tryouts, she never made it to New York. *Kelly* nearly didn't, either.

Its closing freed Leon Janney, who played a restaurateur in the show, to join *Pleasures and Palaces* as a Russian politico. Now he'd be working with real pros. The score for this one was by Frank Loesser, whose *Where's Charley* (1948), *Guys and Dolls* (1950), and *The Most Happy Fella* (1956) had all been hits, not to mention his most recent show, *How to Succeed in Business Without Really Trying* (1961), which ran longer than any of the others. Bob Fosse would choreograph and direct. He'd won three Tonys for the former, and might well have won one for *Redhead* (1959) had there been a Best Director of a Musical prize in those days. (Amazingly, there wasn't until 1960.)

Pleasures and Palaces was based on Sam Spewack's *Once There Was a Russian*, a play he had written without his usual collaborator-wife Bella. That may have been a mistake; together they'd written the hit comedies *Boy Meets Girl* (1935) and *My Three Angels* (1953)—not to mention the book for two musical hits, *Leave It to Me* (1938) and *Kiss Me, Kate* (1948). Perhaps for this musical version, Sam should have asked for his wife's help, but instead he had Loesser join him as bookwriter.

The original play concerned the passionate relationship between Russia's Catherine the Great (Francoise Rosay) and Prince Grigory Potemkin (Walter Matthau)—and what happens when American naval hero John Paul Jones (Albert Salmi) comes to visit. Catherine wants to impress him as much as Anna and the King yearned to wow their foreign dignitaries. Little do Catherine and Potemkin know that Jones is down and out, for the U.S. government has lost faith in him following the sinking of his ship. But Catherine believes that Jones will help in the war against the Turks. Potemkin is angry that his queen is making decisions without him—a reminder that she, not he, has the ultimate power. Catherine would be even angrier with him, though, if she knew that he's taken up with Sura (Julie Newmar), countess and sex fiend.

Once There Was a Russian opened on February 18, 1961—and closed the same night. Obviously, this musical version—first called *Holy Russia!* and then *Ex-Lover*—was intended to run longer. United Artists Records thought it would, and put up much of the $450,000 budget. (Hmmm, why didn't the more prestigious Columbia, RCA Victor, or even Capitol offer to invest in a Loesser show? That alone was not a good sign.)

Fosse cast John McMartin and Phyllis Newman as Jones and Sura. McMartin had been in four straight Broadway flops, but his Theatre World Award–winning stint as Billy Jester in *Little Mary Sunshine* was still fondly remembered. Newman had appeared on Broadway in *Subways Are for Sleeping*, cowritten by her husband Adolph Green—but she makes clear that nepotism did not get her cast. "Husband or no husband, I had to audition five times," she says. "It was the first time an actress got a part by *not* sleeping with the author."

Newman proved, too, that she deserved the job, winning the Best Featured Musical Actress Tony over fellow-competitors Barbra Streisand and Barbara Harris.

After *Subways* closed in 1962, Newman became a well-known TV presence. As the Detroit playbill stated, to do this musical, she "withdrew from two weekly television shows in which she was starring . . . *To Tell the Truth* and *That Was the Week That Was*." Newman also was the first woman ever to substitute for Johnny Carson on the *Tonight Show*.

Fosse took a brave chance with his leads by casting two English stars. Alfred Marks, who'd play Potemkin, was a British comedian well-known enough in England to have an eponymous TV series, *Alfred Marks' Time*. Hy Hazell, who would portray Catherine, was making her second attempt to get to Broadway in a musical. Her first, *Lock Up Your Daughters*, an import in which she had starred in London, had closed in Boston in 1960.

Pleasures and Palaces seemed to be headed for the same fate. Fosse fired Marks and replaced him with Jack Cassidy. (The unimportance of the Tonys in those days before they were nationally broadcast is proved by Cassidy's not even mentioning in his *Pleasures* playbill bio that he'd won for *She Loves Me*.)

The show, as seen in Detroit, begins with the Russian militia offering Potemkin a musical "Salute," though he doesn't pay much attention to it: "I Hear Bells," he sings of the bells tolling over St. Petersburg, musing on the power and glory they represent. That business done, Potemkin goes to Catherine's boudoir, where she senses he hasn't been faithful to her. "My Lover Is a Scoundrel," she sings, proving that women were attracted to bad boys long before recent times. But once Catherine meets Jones, she's ready to betray Potemkin. Jones, the ever-so-Puritanical American, isn't. "To Marry," he admitted in song, is the American thing to do.

Meanwhile, Potemkin and Sura get out of town on horseback to have some time to themselves (and to glorify one another in song as sexual "Thunder and Lightning"). When Potemkin returns, he goes to Catherine, who despite her suspicions can't help telling him, "I Desire You." Potemkin judges it politic to match her word for word in the next chorus.

Catherine comes to the conclusion that she is "Truly Loved." But Sura, feeling less secure, gives Catherine her recent sexual résumé in song ("Sins of Sura"). Luckily (or all too conveniently), Sura is standing over a trap door just as she is about to confess her latest lover—who pulls the lever that makes her disappear.

With that as a first-act curtain, the show soon would soon disappear, too.

Though the reviews in Detroit were terrible, Fosse believed he could save the musical. He convinced Loesser and producer Allen B. Whitehead (who represented Loesser's company, Frank Productions) to book another out-of-town engagement and delay the Broadway premiere at the Lunt-Fontanne. The Shubert Theater in Boston was the choice.

Then, suddenly, Loesser changed his mind and closed the show. Its shuttering meant that a one-performance comedy achieved the seemingly impossible: it outran its musical version. And poor Leon Janney experienced two closings in sixty-three days in shows that averaged a half a Broadway performance each.

The Monday night after the closing, Newman appeared on *The Tonight Show* as Carson's guest, where she told of the struggles with the show and let the nation hear the title song, "Pleasures and Palaces." Hazell went home to London, where she was more appreciated; by year's end, she was starring in *Charley Girl*. It would be a six-year smash—though quality-wise, not much better than *Pleasures and Palaces*.

And why the failure? Fosse maintained that he and his collaborators had been working on three different shows. He wanted a farce, Spewack preferred high comedy, and Loesser was writing in a comic opera vein. Moral of the story: Having great talents is not enough, if those talents don't see eye to eye on what the material should be.

Pleasures and Palaces. March 11–April 10, 1965, in Detroit. No New York performances.

1965–1966

The Biggest Hit
Man of La Mancha

Talk about an impossible dream's coming true.

The composer, Mitch Leigh, has written little more than jingles. The lyricist, Joe Darion, has had one Broadway catastrophe, while the bookwriter, Dale Wasserman, has had one straight-play flop.

Director Albert Marre, after staging the successful *Kismet* in 1953, has had twelve flops in a row, including the recent *Never Live over a Pretzel Factory*. Now, for this musical, he insists that his wife, Joan Diener, get the lead—even though she hasn't worked on Broadway since he hired her for *Kismet*.

Hal James, one of the two producers, has never produced, while the other, Albert Selden, has had four previous Broadway productions that averaged thirty-nine performances. Only Kapp Records, a minor label, is willing to invest and make a cast album, after heavyweights Columbia, RCA Victor, and Capitol all passed.

In an era when shows still try out in Philly, Boston, or Baltimo', their show is going *where*? East Haddam, Connecticut? Where's that?

And it's a musical of *Don Quixote*, yet? A story about having "The Impossible Dream"?

Man of La Mancha certainly achieved one. "We'll make golden history," Quixote sang, and this musical indeed did. It won the Best Musical Tony, ran almost six years, became one of the most recognizable titles in Broadway history, and has had four Broadway revivals. A 1989 episode of the TV series *Quantum Leap* even had a *La Mancha*–themed episode. After auditionee Michelle Pawk sang a song from the score, John Cullum, playing a director, exclaimed, "Not since Joan Diener have I heard it done so well!"

Who'd have thought it? John Bowab, associate producer on both *Sweet Charity* and *Mame* that same season, says, "Back then, everyone was saying to us, 'Oh, you've got the Tony wrapped up—but which of your two shows will win it?' And *Man of La Mancha* came out of nowhere and eclipsed both."

It didn't start out promisingly. In his book *The Impossible Musical*, Wasserman says that he thought his TV teleplay *I, Don Quixote* might make a good musical. He entrusted noted poet W. H. Auden to do the lyrics, but soon saw there was a profound difference between poems and lyrics.

So Joe Darion came on in 1964 and wrote a song for the scullery maid/prostitute Aldonza, called "What Kind of Animal Am I?" Just two years earlier, though, Anthony Newley and Leslie Bricusse had created a gold-record standard called "What Kind of Fool Am I?" Shouldn't have Darion have worried that he'd come up with too similar a title?

As for the show's most illustrious hit song, Wasserman claims, "I the bookwriter wrote, 'To dream the impossible dream, to fight the unbeatable foe' . . . The lyricist then wrote, 'To dream the impossible dream, to fight the unbeatable foe'—whereupon through the alchemy of contractual usage, the words became his forever." (Actually, that's a very common experience for bookwriters.)

After the tryout at Connecticut's Goodpeed Opera House, *La Mancha* found that necessity would mother their invention. Because no Broadway theater owner wanted the show, the producers were forced downtown to the then-dark ANTA Washington Square Theater on the campus of NYU. It had been a temporary prefabricated house that Lincoln Center Repertory Theatre used until its own uptown theater was ready in 1965.

But no Broadway musical had ever been set on a thrust stage with semicircular seating around it. Designer Howard By took full advantage of this to make *La Mancha* look novel and exciting. It thrived there for more than two years, until the theater had to make way for a new NYU building. (The prefabricated theater was purchased by Trinity Square Repertory Company in Providence, Rhode Island, which shipped it to a nearby warehouse and planned to raise the money to reconstruct it. That never happened.)

La Mancha moved to the Martin Beck, a regular proscenium house. By then, it had become a classic that no longer needed to rely on the different look that had helped catapult it to success. The show that had opened two years to the day after the first Kennedy assassination had a message that became a favorite one of the latter part of the sixties: Are the insane really more sane than the sane?

And speaking of insanity, Gerianne Raphael, who played Fermina in the original cast, says, "Originally there was a scene where Richard Kiley drank urine from a chalice. But he told the director that he absolutely refused to do that."

Wasserman stated in his book that people sent him "a flood of mail" that said, "The play changed my life." He believed it "reawakened the ideals of adolescence, ideals that had died in the attrition of living." And yet Wasserman told "what happened to the team that had created this 'classic' . . . with success they became alienated. Then antagonists. And finally, enemies."

La Mancha is supposed to be a beautiful celebration of the human spirit, but the creators apparently didn't buy their own message.

Man of La Mancha. November 22, 1965–June 26, 1971. 2,328 performances.

The Biggest Flop
Little World, Hello!

So near, yet so far.

In 1968, when *The Producers* debuted, film audiences would hear Max Bialystock say of *Springtime for Hitler*, "This play is guaranteed to close on page four."

Little World, Hello! virtually did. This Broadway-bound musical stopped production four days before it was to start rehearsals.

Its subject was Jimmy Savo (1890–1960), a vaudevillian who played the original Dromio of Syracuse in *The Boys from Syracuse*. He also appeared in *What's Up?* (1945), Lerner and Loewe's first musical, in a role called the Rawa of Tanglinia.

But soon after, Savo lost a leg to cancer and moved to Poggio, Italy, with his wife Nina, who had inherited a castle. He detailed their adventures in assimilation in his 1947 book *Little World, Hello!*

After he died, Mrs. Savo decided to have him memorialized in a Broadway musicalization of his book. Though she had never written a musical, she had penned a novel called *The Green Bird*, which had inspired a musical called *Royal Flush*, a big flop of the 1964–1965 season. Despite having Eddie Foy, Jr. and Kaye Ballard in the cast, it opened in New Haven and died in Philadelphia.

Mrs. Savo wrote her libretto to *Little World, Hello!*, which interested a just-starting-out producer, Jack Beekman. He did say that she needed a collaborator, so she reluctantly agreed. Novelist Lee Cooley was Beekman's choice. While he was at it, Cooley decided to direct the show, too. Choreographing would be Matt Mattox, who'd done the dances for *Jennie*, Mary Martin's 1963 disappointment.

Both music and lyrics would be provided by Dick Manning, who'd never written a Broadway musical but had collaborated on a slew of pre-rock-era pop hits: Perry Como's "Hot Diggity Dog" and "Papa Loves Mambo," as well as "Allegheny Moon" and "Gilley, Gilley, Ossenfeffer, Katzenellen Bogen by the Sea." (Don't laugh; that 1954 opus made it to #18 on the America charts and #7 in England's Top Ten.)

Little World, Hello! would star Pinky Lee. If you can't remember him, can you remember Pee Wee Herman, who may well have taken his look and style from him?

Lee (1907–1993), born Pincus Leff, became famous during the early days of children's TV, what with his checkered coat, shirt, and hat, as well as a slight speech impediment. In 1954, *The Pinky Lee Show* was the six-times-a-week lead-in for the iconic *Howdy Doody*. Pinky's young audience was quite unnerved during one 1955 episode when Lee dropped to the floor, appearing to have a heart attack. No, it was just his sinuses that had acted up, but plenty of parents and network affiliates thought if Pinky wasn't in the pink, he shouldn't be on live TV. Hosting a short-lived series that featured Claymation stalwart Gumby didn't provide much income, so Lee, like so many unemployed performers, now looked to Broadway.

He'd been there only once before, nearly a quarter-century earlier, in a 1942 revue called *Wine, Women and Song*—in which, coincidentally, Jimmy Savo also appeared.

Beekman had no problem raising the money, thanks to John C. Cohan (never to be confused with George M.), who owned a few radio and television stations in Southern California. He agreed to provide the entire $440,000 for over-the-title billing right after Beekman's. As was the standard with such agreements, they'd split the profits fifty-fifty.

Not that there would be any.

Little World, Hello's curtain was to rise on Central Park, where characters known as Moochers would sing, "Hey, Gimme, Jimmy," establishing that Savo was the type of guy who just couldn't say no to any request for money, no matter who made it of him. Luckily, Savo got home to his Central Park West digs before the Moochers completely cleaned him out.

But the next day he returned to the park to play with the children, whom he loved to make laugh—and whom he loved to tell his philosophy of life in the title song. "Little World, Hello, hello, hello, little world / Say hello, and shake my hand, my friend / Though it might be raining cats and dogs—nearly stepped into a poodle—say, it's a beautiful day / Let's pretend it's raining rainbows."

Jimmy's so busy with them that he doesn't even see that he's loved by the uninspiredly named Jane Foster. But he eventually notices, without much provocation or reason, and they wed. Then comes that trip to Italy where they claim that castle. First, though, Jimmy must get over his queasy stomach, brought to life in the song "O Salty Sea."

The Savos finally arrive and take a donkey named Stupidina (the subject of a song by the same name) to the castle, where a whole new group of Moochers are very glad to meet what they assume to be very wealthy Americans.

Jimmy soon becomes immersed in the life of the locals. After the flute-playing shepherd Tonio sings "Loneliness," and Jimmy tries to cheer him in "A Very Fortunate Man," Savo entertains Poggio's child population with "Nino and Dino and Gino."

And then there's Veneranda, a lovely lass who feels she has "Got to Get Away from Here," because the native men try to bed her and the native women envy her (and call her "The Little Witch" in song). Veneranda's best feature is said to be her very attractive toe, and there's a song devoted to that, too.

Jane eventually takes Veneranda to the Big City, where the girl soon realizes that while there's no place like Rome, there's also no place like home. When she returns, the townspeople demand that she "Choose! Choose! Choose!" a husband. She does: Tonio.

With that ostensibly happy ending, Jimmy sings "If I Could Buy a Dream," in which he wishes that the world could be "a million laughs" where "no one would cry." Then he and Jane leave on Stupidina.

With a cast of sixty, *Little World, Hello!* was to start rehearsals on January 10, 1966, with a Philadelphia opening on February 28, a Boston debut on March 15, and a Broadway opening on April 16 "at a theater to be named later," which is always an ominous sign.

But Mrs. Savo took umbrage at the way Cooley was characterizing her late husband, and when Beekman told her that her contract did not allow her a voice in the matter, she demanded that the dispute be settled by arbitration. (Cooley had been through worse; he'd been a radio announcer in Italy until Benito Mussolini didn't like the way he was delivering the news. His deportation soon followed.)

The arbitrators were playwright Elmer (*Street Scene*) Rice, producer Elaine (*Anastasia*) Perry, and a theatrical lawyer. All three sided with Beekman. Mrs. Savo then started talking about appeals to the Supreme Court.

By now, Cohan was having second, third, and fourth thoughts about *Little World, Hello!* He refused to put up any more money than he had advanced, and that was the end of it.

More information on Pinky Lee can be easily found on Google, though you'll find many more references to a female porn star who's usurped his name.

Little World, Hello! Closed four days before the first rehearsal.

1966–1967

The Biggest Hit
Cabaret

Perfectly Marvelous

Who expected anything from *Cabaret?* A season earlier, composer John Kander and lyricist Fred Ebb had debuted with *Flora, the Red Menace*, a two-month flop. Its low point was a song in which a character who stuttered put marbles in his mouth à la Demosthenes, and sang, "Urgh, uh, ooh, ga, brggh"—as a love song, yet.

When we last left *Cabaret*'s producer-director Harold Prince, he'd just finished directing *A Family Affair* to no avail. He'd had three directorial flops since. But as a producer, he was riding high with the still-SRO *Fiddler on the Roof*, which was on its way to becoming the longest-running-ever Broadway production. The word was out: Prince could produce a hit, but not direct one. Sure, he'd beautifully staged *She Loves Me* (1963), but the public hadn't responded.

And here was *She Loves Me*'s bookwriter, Joe Masteroff, trying again on *Cabaret*. He'd adapted Christopher Isherwood's *Berlin Stories* and John Van Druten's play *I Am a Camera*, which could at best have been called a moderate success on the basis of its seven-month run in 1951–1952.

A musical that centered on the Nazi movement? Sure, *The Sound of Music* dealt with Nazis, too—but that show suggested they'd eventually be defeated. *Welcome to Berlin*, as *Cabaret* was first called, was conceived to show the rise of Nazism, reiterating that the movement was destined for some great success long before it declined and fell.

Perhaps such a show could thrive with solid names in the cast, but Prince hired nobodies for the three biggest roles. Jill Haworth, who'd previously only played small parts in movies, would be Sally Bowles, the not-so-talented and apolitical chanteuse who believes that allure will make her rich. (Interesting that her signature song, "Don't Tell Mama," was a Charleston—a style of music that was dated by the time *Cabaret* begins in 1929. Sally's already behind the times.)

Bert Convy, who'd previously done even smaller roles in musicals, would portray Cliff Bradshaw, an American novelist who comes to Berlin for local color—and must decide whether he'll smuggle information for the Nazis in order to make a quick buck. And who was this Joel Grey who'd play the emcee in the cabaret where Sally worked?

Sure, Jack Gilford, who'd done well in Prince's *A Funny Thing Happened on the Way to the Forum*, was signed, but in a secondary role: he'd play Schultz, an elderly fruit seller who courted Fraulein Schneider, his landlady (and Sally and Cliff's) by bringing her a pineapple. When word got out that that scene would be conveyed in song, Broadway naysayers smelled another marbles-in-his-mouth atrocity.

The cast's only blue-chip name was Lotte Lenya, Kurt Weill's widow, as Fraulein Schenider. Lenya may have been best known from Bobby Darin's inserting her name in his million-selling rendition of her late husband's song "Mack the Knife." But the soon-to-be-sixty-eight-year-old actress hadn't been on stage in years, and had never been one whom Broadway audiences flocked to see.

What's more, *Cabaret* had the nerve to charge a $12 top—the highest on Broadway. This in a season when you could spend less money to see Barbara Harris in *The Apple Tree*, the new musical by the *Fiddler on the Roof* authors, directed by Mike Nichols, who'd had three consecutive hits. And then there were those two musicals produced by David Merrick: Mary Martin and Robert Preston in *I Do! I Do!*, a Gower Champion show; and, the most anticipated of all, the musical version of *Breakfast at Tiffany's* with Mary Tyler Moore and Richard Chamberlain. There can only be so many hits a season; how could *Cabaret* possibly survive with those three behemoths as competition?

As it turned out, *Cabaret* would rack up more performances (1,165)—and more Tony Awards (eight)—than those other three musicals *combined*. After *New York Times* critic Walter Kerr proclaimed it "a stunning musical, brilliantly conceived . . . you'd be wise to go to it"—and most other aisle-sitters made similar observations—*Cabaret* moved from the Broadhurst to the Imperial to take advantage of the latter's additional 250 seats.

Cabaret also got an unexpected boost by being the first show to win a Best Musical Tony on national TV. This was the first year that the Tonys were broadcast nationally, resulting in many ringing telephones the next day.

But *Cabaret* didn't start out sure-handedly. When it began its pre-Broadway tryout in Boston on October 8, 1966, it was nearly three hours long. It got off to a great start with "Wilkommen," where emcee Joel Grey let the audience know that he was someone to watch. Haworth, though, didn't do well by her songs (including the tuneful title one), and that would start a decades-long debate about Sally Bowles: Isn't she *supposed* to be a bad singer? But if she is, how can she entertain us?

Nobody much liked Convy, either—or was it the role? *Cabaret*'s eventual history would see Broadway and Hollywood bestow nominations or awards on performers playing Sally, the Emcee, Schultz, Schneider, and even Kost, a prostitute who had maybe seven minutes of stage time; no one who's played Cliff ever has received as much as a nomination.

Most daunting of all was a sequence that took place in the middle of act 1, when Sally and Cliff went for a stroll in a park. They walked in front of a white scrim, where a man in a wheelchair begged Sally for a few marks. Behind the back-lit scrim, a prostitute came on to Cliff ("I do anything for money—anything at all"), just before a short man on a soapbox began shouting angrily in German. One didn't need the scrim removed to know it was Hitler. As Sally and Cliff walked off in terror, the man in the wheelchair turned out to be Grey, jumping up and letting us know he was hardly infirm, but pretended in order to get a few marks.

The scene was powerful, yes, but perhaps too powerful. Prince reluctantly dropped it after a few Boston performances. Aside from the substitution of "Perfectly Marvelous" for "Roommates" (when Sally moves in with Cliff), no other songs were added or subtracted; the book was just shortened, and what had been a three-act musical became a two-acter.

What was always in place was a fascinating concept: often, a song done on stage in the cabaret would comment on what the characters were experiencing. So when Schneider, a Gentile, was beginning to fear what a marriage to a Jew would hold for her, the Emcee danced with a gorilla, and proclaimed that she didn't "look Jewish at all" to demonstrate the Nazis' beliefs were becoming increasingly popular. *Cabaret* became the missing link between early-sixties musical comedy and early-seventies concept musicals, and influenced musicals for many seasons to come.

But that line comparing a gorilla to a Jew infuriated many Boston theatergoers. After scores of complaints, Ebb changed the line to "She isn't a meeskite at all"— referring to a song that Schultz sang at a party. ("Meeskite" is a Yiddish term for "ugly person.")

Director Bob Fosse reinstated the original line for his 1972 film, but he had to; "Meeskite" had been dropped from the film along with the romance of Schultz and Schneider; they were replaced by a younger couple enduring their own amorous difficulties.

Not as many, though, as Sally and Brian (the renamed Cliff, repatriated as an Englishman). When Brian saw that Sally was becoming obsessed with a new friend, he told her, "Screw Maximilian!" After she enjoyed taunting him with "I do," wasn't she surprised when he replied, "So do I"?

Fosse's movie won eight Oscars, including one for him as director, and almost upset *The Godfather* as Best Picture. It was Fosse's first jewel of a 1972 directing triple crown that would include an Emmy for *Liza with a "Z"* and a Tony for *Pippin*.

Cabaret returned to Broadway in 1987 with Joel Grey, who inserted "I Don't Care Much," a Kander-Ebb song that Barbra Streisand fans remembered from a 1963 recording. Indeed, it was in *Cabaret*'s original script, though it was cut even before Boston. This revival limped through the season, and lost money.

But *Cabaret*'s biggest stage success was to come. In 1998, hotshot director Sam Mendes staged a much more sexually frank version that, at 2,377 performances, doubled the original's run.

It was a bitter pill for Grey to swallow. For more than thirty years, he'd never been able to surpass the role that landed him a Tony and an Oscar, but at least he'd had the pleasure of hearing people say, "Yeah, but no one can play the Emcee like Grey." No, not until the unknown Alan Cumming. While Grey's Emcee seemed to be hiding behind his face full of white makeup, Cumming offered his own face and no apologies for being sexy and sleazy. Mendes had the Emcee pay the price, though, in a masterstroke at show's end: the Emcee opened his trench coat to reveal a concentration camp uniform branded with a yellow star and pink triangle.

Cabaret, which had been wildly successful when first released to stock and amateur markets, now got a second life there, too. As Bert Silverberg, a theater professor at the Community College of Rhode Island, astutely remarked, "Everybody used to play the Emcee exactly the way Joel Grey did. Now they wouldn't think of playing that way, but only Alan Cumming's way."

Cabaret. November 20, 1966–September 6, 1969. 1,165 performances.

THE BIGGEST FLOP
Breakfast at Tiffany's

The first musical to close in previews.

Even before it announced its leading lady, *Holly Golightly* just had to be THE musical of the season.

David Merrick had the idea: a musical version of *Breakfast at Tiffany's*. Only a few years earlier, Truman Capote's novella had been made into a marvelous film. Audrey Hepburn played the farm girl who came to New York and reinvented herself as a sophisticate—but wasn't above sleeping with a man if, earlier in the evening, he'd given her "$50 for the powder room."

Abe Burrows, whose last musical was *How to Succeed*, was then riding a straight play smash with *Cactus Flower*. He'd provide the book and direction. Bob Merrill would do the score, as he'd done three times before; even his least successful effort, *Take Me Along*, ran more than a year. That was buttressed by *New Girl in Town* in 1957 and *Carnival* in 1961, both of which made money and yielded a Tony or two.

Merrill's biggest success, though, was his most recent show, *Funny Girl* (1964)—though here he'd "only" written lyrics (including "People") to Jule Styne's music. Barbra Streisand was originally believed responsible for the show's success, but when *Holly Golightly* went into rehearsal, *Funny Girl* had been running for nearly a year without her— and still had almost a year left in its run.

So far, so great. And then Merrick nabbed one of the sixties' most beloved TV stars to portray Holly: Mary Tyler Moore, formerly Laura Petrie on *The Dick Van*

Dyke Show. On a few musically themed episodes, Moore had displayed solid song and dance abilities. Now, not long after winning her second Emmy for the series, she'd make her Broadway debut.

To play Jefferson Claypool, a struggling writer and the new man in Holly's life, Merrick hired another name from the pop culture market: Richard Chamberlain, who'd made teen girls (and their mothers) swoon as television's Dr. Kildare. *Photoplay* had named him TV's Most Popular Male Star for three straight years.

Because Merrick's *Dolly!* had been a best-selling LP of 1964, its issuer, RCA Victor, made an arrangement with Merrick. It would invest significantly in each of his musicals for the privilege of recording their cast albums.

Merrill did have a difficult obstacle: the well-regarded 1961 film featured an Oscar-winning song, "Moon River," by Henry Mancini and Johnny Mercer. What would Merrill write and put in its place? On the other hand, when Merrill did *Carnival*—a musical version of the 1954 film *Lili* that also sported a popular song in "Hi, Lili, Hi, Lo"—he came up with an acceptable substitute, "Love Makes the World Go 'Round." So perhaps there was no reason to worry.

Oh, yes, there was—plenty, in fact, that would (to paraphrase a Merrill lyric) rain on everyone's parade. What ticket-buyers failed to realize from that full-page ad they saw in the Times was that Burrows was not the show's first director; Joshua Logan was, and had left soon after he saw what the authors had written. Burrows was the third writer hired; Nunnally Johnson and Sidney Michaels had each taken a crack at the show, and had admitted defeat.

Says Richard Chamberlain, "The gypsies and (choreographer) Michael Kidd were saying from the beginning that it wasn't good. I couldn't tell—though I should have known when we didn't have a second act when we started rehearsing. Abe was directing the first act during the day and writing the second act at night. I was having such a great time, though, even with the bad reviews, because the audiences in Philadelphia, where we first stopped, and then in Boston, were so nice to us."

The best musicals are built on big characters and big events; Holly, though flamboyant, kept too many cards too close to her vest to be a triumphant heroine. Perhaps Merrill should have given her more introspective songs to let us know who she really was. As for Jefferson, he had to spend much of the evening looking astonished at this free spirit, reacting to what she did. That's not much for an actor to play.

As a result, the reviews in Philadelphia were bad, and the ones that came weeks later in Boston were worse. Kevin Kelly of the Boston Globe was so outraged that even two months later, when a musical called *Sherry!* opened, he called it "so awful that it makes *Holly Golightly* look like a nostalgic work of art, and no, I'm not kidding."

There was a scene in which Holly ruminated to Jefferson about her beloved brother Freddy, and how much fun she had teasing him when they were young.

She'd taunt him with a chant: "Freddy is a dumb [sic] and a big dumb bunny / Freddy's half-cockeyed; Freddy runs funny / Freddy's got cooties in his head / Freddy, Freddy, Freddy pees in bed."

But what Boston also saw at the end of the first act was Holly receiving a telegram, opening it, reading it, writhing in agony, and singing the chant once again. Only this time, "Freddy's got cooties in his head" was rhymed with "Freddy, Freddy, Freddy's dead"—as the curtain fell.

In a party scene, Moore had to navigate around a singing and dancing chorus while carrying an enormous bowl of glop—"clam dip, that damn dip," she called it. There was a scene where Jeff returned to a bar he hadn't been to in a long time. The bartender took one look and said, "Jefferson! Jefferson Claypool!" Not the most scintillating dialogue.

But Merrick displayed his showmanship and made an unorthodox move to shake things up. He hired as his new bookwriter someone who'd never worked on a Broadway musical, though he'd certainly had written a big hit four years earlier with *Who's Afraid of Virginia Woolf?*

Yes, Edward Albee, who immediately stressed that Holly's best friend Mag (Sally Kellerman) was a lesbian. He also decided to make Holly a figment of Jeff's imagination, a character he was writing. Both he and Merrick thought the show's title should return to its original name; hence, *Breakfast at Tiffany's* was (re)born.

"Why Merrick had Albee come in, I'll never know," says Chamberlain. "As you'd suspect, he really made it into a darker show, one that nobody knew what to make of, because all those dark Sondheim shows were still in the distant future." In fact, the yellow window cards and three-sheets that had once sported the tagline "a new musical comedy" soon had little yellow stickers added to obliterate the word "comedy."

Burrows was encouraged to stay as director, but was insulted when removed as bookwriter; for decades, he'd been considered Broadway's best play doctor, so he believed he could nurse this show to health. Denied that chance, he resigned, and the assignment went to Joseph Anthony, veteran director of twenty-one Broadway productions (including *The Most Happy Fella* and *Mary, Mary*, the longest-running play of the sixties—but *The Pink Jungle*, too).

Ten songs were dropped in Boston (including one called "Scum-Dee-Dum"), and eight added, including "Home for Wayward Girls," which does sound as if it would be right at home in an Edward Albee musical. *Breakfast at Tiffany's* came to the Majestic Theater on December 12, 1966 with more than 125,000 tickets sold for the next four months. Thus, no matter what the critics said, the show could run at least until spring even if another person never approached its box-office window.

"As nice as audiences had been out of town," says Chamberlain, "they were so terrible in New York. They hated us, I mean, *hated* us. They actually shouted at us from the audience. I can still see Mary going offstage and bursting into tears as soon as she reached the wings."

But Merrick then made the greatest grandstanding moves of his entire fifty-four-year career. After the fourth preview, he told the press, "Rather than subject the drama critics and the theater-going public—who invested one million dollars in advance sales—to an excruciatingly boring evening, I have decided to close the show." For a season or so afterwards, Merrick, in every *Playbill* biography, eschewed mentioning the two dozen hits he'd already had, but chose to use, "Mr. Merrick is best-known as the distinguished producer of *Breakfast at Tiffany's*."

Says Chamberlain,

I was heartbroken. Angela Lansbury, Ruth Gordon, and Gower Champion told me that it was good for me to be in such a spectacular flop, because up till then, I'd had this big success with *Dr. Kildare*, so everyone in the country knew who I was, and I had a nice recording career with MGM Records, too. They all said to me, "Show business is hard, and it's important for you to get used to it."

Merrill salvaged two of the songs: "Stay with Me" went into his 1978 musical *The Prince of Grand Street* (which we'll soon meet), and "Lament for Ten Men"—a purposely obfuscating title for a song that really should have been called "Dirty Old Men," but that would have given away the joke—later surfaced in the London version of Merrill and Styne's musical version of *Some Like It Hot*.

Had Merrick not closed the show, RCA Victor undoubtedly would have recorded a cast album, and hearing iconic star Moore singing it would have been a treat, especially in the (eventual) title song, a lovely waltz. A bootleg LP made from a tape of an actual performance did surface some years later. More astonishing, in 2000, record producer Robert Sher brought Faith Prince and John Schneider into a studio to play Holly and Jeff, and got Kellerman to reprise her role. The result was a lavish two-CD set that included songs from Philadelphia, Boston, and Broadway—indeed, most everything that Merrill wrote for the musical.

And did Merrill ever come up with the right song as a substitute for "Moon River?" No, he solved the problem by not writing an analogous song for that spot in the show.

As for Moore, the *Breakfast at Tiffany's* script called for someone to tell her early in the show, "You'll be a thoroughly modern lady," and in fact her next job would be in the film *Thoroughly Modern Millie*. There she had a line, "The world of the stage just doesn't seem to suit me." How did Moore feel saying this less than a year after she didn't make it to opening night with *Breakfast at Tiffany's*?

Breakfast at Tiffany's. December 12–December 14. 4 previews, no official performances.

1967–1968

The Biggest Hit
Hair

An innovation in costuming.

June 3, 1968. *Hair* at the Biltmore Theatre, New York City. It's the end of the first act, where a number of young men and women will strip and appear nude on stage. It's not a long scene, and the lighting isn't bright, but one can definitely make out unprecedented full-frontal nudity.

As soon as the house lights come up, a policeman officiously walks down the center aisle. He starts telling the capacity crowd that everyone is being taken into custody for attending such a lewd event.

Throughout his stern speech, many in the audience are giving glassy smiles to the people around them. *Is this for real?* Some are waiting—or at least hoping—that the cop will soon give an "only kidding" wave.

The now-notorious musical, which started previews without incident on April 11, has continued unbothered since its April 29 opening. But perhaps today the police decided, "Okay, enough is enough; we're gonna raid that house of filth on Forty-seventh Street." After all, this is the same theater where Mae West's *Pleasure Man* was shut down for indecency. That was nearly forty years ago, but who says that the law has eased up this much?

So much of the audience is taken in—not taken to jail, but "taken in," in that they believe what they are hearing. Finally, after too many minutes of waiting, the "policeman" does indeed give an "only kidding!" wave and a big smile. Now, with all pretense of authority gone, he sheepishly walks up the aisle.

The sound of nervous laughter and boos is loud. Until *Hair,* nudity has never appeared so frankly on Broadway; flesh-colored stockings, strategically placed pasties, and other illusions have sufficed. No wonder many in the audience thought they were about to experience their first fingerprinting, and were already wondering whom to contact when offered their one phone call.

That policeman wasn't part of the 1977 or 2009 Broadway revivals, of course; by then, audience members wouldn't have believed he was on the level or felt in the least threatened by him. Since *Hair,* scores of Broadway shows—and easily more off-Broadway—have sported nudity, and the law has never once made an incident of it.

Natalie Mosco, one of the original cast members who was part of that infamous scene, recalls, "They told us that if we would go naked, they'd give us an extra dollar fifty a performance. A dollar fifty! I told them that if I took that little money for getting naked, I'd feel like a whore—but I would do it for free. That way, I'd feel okay about it."

The back cover of the original Broadway cast album proudly proclaimed, "All the songs in this album have been recorded complete and unexpurgated as they are performed on the Broadway stage." After *Hair*, lyrics that previously would have been censored would now be recorded as is, in a nod to "the mind's true liberation." And finally, *Hair* deserves credit for its fearless integration. "Black Boys" and "White Boys" were respectively celebrated by white girls and black girls, in frank fashion.

The men behind this were co-bookwriter-lyricists Gerome Ragni and James Rado. Both had been actors, and would act in *Hair*; Ragni was the worldly-wise Berger, while Rado was the more innocent Claude.

These roles were far from their usual fare. Rado had played meek George Nowack in a 1964 Boston production of *She Loves Me*. (A then-unknown Jane Alexander was one of the shoppers.) Some months later, Ragni played in the ensemble of the Richard Burton *Hamlet*—which may have spurred his including "What a Piece of Work Is Man" in *Hair*. In 1965, Ragni had been cast in the Ronald Ribman play *Harry, Noon and Night*, but left before opening. The lyric "I'm hairy, noon and night" was his way of making it up to Ribman.

The composer was Galt MacDermot, a newcomer to Broadway, but no kid. Though *Hair* agreed with the current line "Don't trust anyone over thirty," MacDermot was now almost forty—and yet his music sounded young. It couldn't be described as acid rock, but, compared to the show that had opened just before *Hair*—*The Education of H*Y*M*A*N K*A*P*L*A*N*—there was some battery fluid present.

Recalls MacDermot, "I used to stop by music publisher Nat Shapiro's office and talk jazz, which I love. In 1960 I even got a Grammy when Cannonball Adderley did my song 'African Waltz.' But then Nat said he had a feeling that I'd be good for this show that these two guys were doing. I wrote the score in two weeks."

That's impressive, especially his settings of "My Conviction," "Frank Mills," and "Let the Sunshine In"—none of which had a rhyme scheme; yet MacDermot's music makes them all sound natural. On the other hand, while "What a Piece of Work Is Man" is also rhymeless, MacDermot strangely put the musical stresses in the wrong places—just as he would often do three years later in *Two Gentlemen of Verona*, his other setting of Shakespeare to music.

Though this was hardly show music as Broadway knew it, *Hair* would represent the last time that so many of a musical's songs would be pop hits. "Easy to Be Hard," by Three Dog Night, was on the charts for twelve weeks, peaking at #4. "Good Morning, Starshine," by Oliver, rested comfortably for eleven weeks, reaching #3. That, though, was bested by the Cowsills' recording of the title song, on the list for thirteen weeks, and making it to #2. But the champ was a mini-medley by the Fifth Dimension that paired "Aquarius" and "Let the Sunshine In." It stayed on the charts for sixteen weeks, six at #1.

The original cast album itself was on the Top 100 for 151 weeks—almost three years—with a 13-week stint as the top album in the land. And while some Broadway hits had occasionally released foreign-language recordings in America (*My Fair Lady* in Spanish, *Irma la Douce* in French), *Hair* opened the floodgates. Big-city stores offered recordings in Danish, Dutch, Finnish, French, German, Hebrew, Norwegian, Portuguese, Spanish, and Swedish.

And yet, *Hair* was conventional in many ways. The hippies of "Aquarius," the show's opening number, performed the same function as the 'merry villagers' of many an operetta. And Ragni, stepping forward to say, "My name is Berger," evoked the clumsy-exposition days when another hairy actor (albeit with muttonchops, not tresses) would have been deputized to state, "I am the town's burgomeister." When Claude sang, "I Got Life," he was offering much the same worldview as "I Got the Sun in the Mornin' (and the Moon at Night)." The show even included a type of dream ballet—albeit a drug-induced one—in which Claude imagined his life as a soldier in Vietnam. Finally, *Hair* even had a traditional curtain call in which the cast sang the title song—just as the casts of *Dolly* and *Mame* did.

Successful as it was, *Hair* was victimized by its own producer. Michael Butler erred in scheduling his opening fourteen days after the Tony cutoff. Had Butler been more efficient, *Hair* would have won the 1967–1968 Best Musical award, easily besting lame-duck winner *Hallelujah, Baby!* The following year, when *Hair* was finally eligible, it was the oldest of the four nominated shows, and couldn't compare or compete with the newly minted *1776*. (It probably finished third, behind *Promises, Promises*). *Hair* had to wait until 2009 to win its Tony, as Best Musical Revival.

Hair. April 28, 1968–July 1, 1972. 1,750 performances.

THE BIGGEST FLOP
Mata Hari

Die! Die! My Darling!

This season, there were a large number of candidates for this honor.

Should the biggest flop be *Here's Where I Belong*? It was a one-performance disaster whose two wordsmiths would go on to win six Tonys, a Pulitzer, and an Oscar between them. The book for this musical version of John Steinbeck's *East of Eden* was written by Terrence McNally (though he did take his name off it before opening night). The lyrics were by Alfred Uhry, who later did better with *Parade*, *The Last Night of Ballyhoo*, and *Driving Miss Daisy*. (Only Robert Waldman, the show's composer, has found success elusive.)

In the final years of the twentieth century, much was made of *Phantom*'s falling chandelier, *Miss Saigon*'s rising helicopter, and *Sunset Boulevard*'s floating mansion. But such eye-popping devices didn't originate with the British musicals. *Here's Where I Belong* planned to have the curtain rise on a street-sweeping machine motoring onto the stage, as a chorus sang that "There'll Be Sweeping Changes Around Here." But the producer decided the effect would be too expensive for his budget. He was Mitch Miller—yes, the same Mitch Miller who used to go on TV and have audiences sing along with him.

Another biggest flop contender is the thirty-one-performance *Darling of the Day*—despite music from the composer of *Gypsy* and *Funny Girl* (Jule Styne) and the lyricist of *Finian's Rainbow* and *The Wizard of Oz* (E. Y. Harburg).

The story was based on Arnold Bennett's 1895 novel *Buried Alive*. British painter Priam Farll (Vincent Price) isn't favored by Queen Victoria, so he and his butler Henry Leek (Charles Welch) leave England. When Edward VII assumes the throne, he summons Farll home to offer him a knighthood. But Leek suddenly dies, and when a clerk mistakenly puts Farll's name on the death certificate as the deceased—and Leek as the survivor—Priam sees this as a lovely opportunity to begin a new life. He even falls in love with a local who has the felicitous (if silly) name of Alice Challice (Patricia Routledge). Now—how can he make a living? And shouldn't he tell his wife the truth about himself?

Unlike *Here's Where I Belong*, which got no cast album, *Darling*'s score was released on vinyl, cassette, *and* eight-track tape—astonishing for a month-long flop. While it only got one Tony nomination—for Routledge as Best Actress in a Musical—and was long gone by awards time, Routledge still won—though she did tie with *Hallelujah Baby!*'s Leslie Uggams (whose show ran more than nine times as long).

Fascinating, isn't it, that each winner was in a Jule Styne show? And speaking of Styne—through the seventies and eighties, when he was asked to perform at parties, he was most likely to play "Let's See What Happens" from this score. He often said it was, of all the songs he wrote, his favorite.

Some may cavil that Styne couldn't be right for a British score, because he was so quintessentially American. They'll point out that *Peter Pan* was his only Broadway show with a British locale, and that his eight contributions to that score were either about Neverland or all took place there. But they forget that Styne was British by birth, having been born in London in 1905.

But at least those two musicals made it into town. One musical didn't.

November 20, 1967. The National Theatre, Washington. Opening night of *Mata Hari*, which is about to spawn one of musical theater's most infamous stories. After a tied-to-a-post Mata Hari (Marisa Mell) is shot by a firing squad,

Mell slumps forward. But one of her eyelashes becomes loose, and is hanging. The dead Mata lifts her hand to pull it off. It's the biggest laugh the audience gives the show that night.

Mata Hari closed in Washington in eighteen days. But, like Mell, it wasn't officially dead.

September 12, 1968. The Hotel Gotham. Backers audition for a new off-Broadway musical called *Ballad for a Firing Squad*. It's actually *Mata Hari* all over again, but bookwriter Jerome Coopersmith, composer Edward Thomas, and lyricist Martin Charnin feel that this new version needs a new name.

Charnin starts the evening by saying, "Welcome to an evening without David Merrick," citing the producer who mounted the previous version. There's rancor here, because Merrick hired Vincente Minnelli to direct, and wouldn't fire him when Charnin, Thomas, and Coopersmith found him wanting.

They raise some money that night, thanks in no small part to Charnin's mesmerizing rendition of "Maman" with Thomas playing guitar behind him. The song shows a soldier writing to his mother, informing her of what's going on at the front—and not employing euphemisms. As he sang, Charnin reinforced the valuable theatrical lesson that if an actor wants the crowd to weep for his character, he must elicit their sympathy by remaining strong. Charnin did exactly that while singing, "I'm afraid, Maman, we are done / They have gas, Maman; we have none."

This off-Broadway version would be staged by Charnin—"and if we fail this time," he told potential backers, "it will be our failure."

Indeed, the show did fail, this time after five performances. But again it was more the fault of the producer, who was alleged to be somewhere between incompetent and financially unscrupulous.

Mediocre reviews, of course, didn't help. "But another problem," said assistant director Larry Fineberg, "is that the show depends on turn-of-the-century European opulence, with plenty of salons. Instead, it looked as if it cost a nickel at the Theatre de Lys (now the Lucille Lortel Theatre)."

But a third of a century later, *Mata Hari* received a cast album, thanks to a revival at the York Theatre Company. It allowed listeners to see that this two-time disaster had great worth.

In the stirring "Is This Fact?" Captain LaFarge faces the truth that the cabaret entertainer known as Mata Hari is a spy. LaFarge and his wife go to see her act, in which she sings the delightful (and all-too-true) "Everyone Has Something to Hide." Afterward, LaFarge hides his attraction to Mata Hari and his boredom in his marriage, singing to his wife "How Young You Were Tonight." Madame LaFarge will soon be hiding the truth from her friends when she pleasantly sings to them that "I Don't See Him Very Much Anymore." She knows that business isn't the only thing keeping her husband away from home, and that war isn't occupying all his thoughts. She's in denial when she sings, "I try to understand /

When he takes away his hand."

"You have no idea what I've been through," Mata Hari sings to LaFarge in an intoxicating and jaunty song—all meant to throw him off the track. It's quite different from the song she sings at the end of the show, "What Might Have Been," which has a haunting semi-Weill feel to it. Along the way comes the stirring antiwar song, "Hello, Yank!" and, of course, "Maman."

So Mell's gesture was actually metaphorically prophetic. *Mata Hari* didn't quite die in Washington.

Mata Hari. November 18–December 9, 1967, in Washington, D.C.
No New York performances.

1968–1969

The Biggest Hit
1776

But we know how it's going to turn out!

"It's a masterpiece, I say / They will cheer ev'ry word, ev'ry letter," sings John Adams in *1776*, about Thomas Jefferson's Declaration of Independence. The same could—and should—be said of Peter Stone's book, based on Sherman Edwards' conception, for the 1969 Tony-winning musical.

Stone's work is the best libretto that the musical theater has ever seen. Devotees of *Gypsy* will cite that as Broadway's quintessential book, but, as great as it is, much of the plot and a number of characters and situations came directly from Gypsy Rose Lee's memoir. Indeed, Lee even divided her book into "acts," and ended "act 1" with June's leaving and Rose's determination to continue.

Stone and Edwards had the more difficult task of poring over congressional transcripts, letters, journals, and biographies, and then making a musical out of them. They had to decide which of the fifty-six delegates to keep, eventually whittling the number to twenty—sometimes combining many characters into one. How's that for *e pluribus unum*?

Edwards, a high-school history teacher and successful pop songwriter ("See You in September"), originally wrote the score and the script that told of the struggle in getting the Declaration of Independence written, approved, and signed. Producer Stuart Ostrow told Edwards that he needed a bookwriter, and Stone took the job. He respected Edwards' important plot as well as the essential tone: that these hitherto dry-as-dust historical characters would be passionately and three-dimensionally human.

The writers made John Adams (William Daniels) maddening, Richard Henry

Lee (Ronald Holgate) egomaniacal, Samuel Chase (Philip Polito) gluttonous, and Rhode Island delegate Stephen Hopkins (Roy Poole) an older man who kept confusing one Carolina with another. Thomas Jefferson (Ken Howard), meanwhile, craved sex with wife Martha (Betty Buckley), while Benjamin Franklin (Howard DaSilva) craved it from any fair lady.

It takes a witty man to write a witty man, and Stone was up to the task of recreating Franklin, the Dean of Aphorisms. But he didn't make the mistake that *Baker Street*'s (1965) authors had made with Sherlock Holmes four seasons earlier, by giving their detective the inevitable "Elementary!" line before act 1, scene 1 was over. Stone instead had Franklin in his first scene say a line that sounds like vintage Ben, but would have been unfamiliar to the audience: "Treason is a charge invented by winners as an excuse for hanging the losers." Adams then gave voice to the audience's reservation about seeing the play in the first place—"I have more to do than stand here listening to you quote yourself"—but that gave Franklin the chance to disarm us with "No, that was a new one!"

Not until three minutes are left in the show does Stone finally give Franklin a line with which audiences are familiar: "If we don't hang together, we shall most assuredly hang separately." By that point, *1776* has the audience enthralled, and the crowd finds itself delightedly saying, "Oh! Is that where that comes from?" Had Stone seeded the quote in the first ten minutes, the audience would have rolled its eyes heavenward and heaved sighs of disgust.

In the opening song, where the Continental Congress is battling Adams' attempt to secede from England, Benjamin Franklin isn't present. If he were, that familiar visage would surely pull focus from John Adams, the mover and shaker behind independence, whom we must get to know. Saving the recognizable Franklin for the top of the next scene also gets a nice laugh from the audience as soon as the lights come up.

In Adams, Stone created a galvanic character who doesn't mind that Franklin, Jefferson, and Lee tell him to his face that he's "obnoxious and disliked," because, he retorts, "I'm not promoting John Adams; I'm promoting American independence." But his main adversary, John Dickinson (Paul Hecht) of Pennsylvania, who is resolutely against independence, sees them as one and the same.

So when Adams is trying to stall a vote that would sink American independence, he suggests a written declaration. He's asked, "What sort of declaration?" as our eyes half-close in anticipation of his inevitable response: "A Declaration of Independence!" No. Stone instead has Adams say, "Oh . . . you know . . ." fudging because he doesn't himself know. It's one of the few times the resolute Adams is stumped.

How thrillingly Stone wrote him, especially later, when his own allies stress that there's no time, the vote on independence is tomorrow, they're still many colonies short of unanimity, so it's hopeless. But a great man knows there's enough time if he uses it correctly.

To make Dickinson even easier to hate, Stone gives him the show's worst joke. When the congressional secretary, trying to track down a missing delegate, asks, "Where's New Jersey?" it's villain Dickinson who offers the groan-inducing quip "Between New York and Delaware."

But Stone didn't make Dickinson a fool, knowing the musical would be stronger if the man gave good reasons for not wanting to break from England. We see Dickinson's point when he roars, "Would you have us forsake Hastings and Magna Carta, Strongbow and Lionhearted, Drake and Marlborough, Tudors, Stuarts, and Plantagenets?" When he lists the seemingly insurmountable odds—"No army, no navy, no ammunition, no treasury, no friends"—we find ourselves nodding our heads, even though we want Adams and independence to prevail. Stone makes it a fair fight between worthy opponents, and that's a great ingredient in his achievement.

The authors created two vital components in *1776*'s success: the day-by-day wall calendar that shows us how many more days there are until July 4, and the tally board that tells exactly how many colonies are now voting for independence and how many aren't. We see on June 28 that only six out of the must-be-unanimous thirteen have voted "Yea." We know everything's going to be wrapped up in six days—but how? As Otis Guernsey wrote when naming *1776* to his *Best Plays of 1968–1969,* "When you entered the theater, you knew how it was going to turn out. After a half-hour, however, you weren't so sure." Indeed, while sitting in the theater, an audience begins to think, "There *is* no United States of America! They're breaking the news to us as gently as they can—by telling us through a marvelous musical!"

The calendar and tally board are the reasons that the 1972 movie version, despite featuring virtually all of the original cast, doesn't work as well. Because the cinematographer only occasionally takes us to those scorekeeping devices, we don't know or remember how near or far the Declaration is from being ratified. A theatergoer must be able to check the score whenever he needs to, not when Hollywood thinks it's time.

The tote board was purposely constructed so that the yeas were on the left (just as "yea" advocates were on the left), and that "nays" were, as one song goes, "to the right, ever to the right, never to the left." But lyricist Ed Weissman points out that "That's an anachronism. 'Right' and 'left' originated just before the French Revolution. When the Estates-General met in 1789, it soon fell apart and became the national assembly; as the revolution began, the left and right seating reflected the split between the revolutionaries and the Ancien Régime."

DaSilva quit a number of times before the show opened because a song he liked was taken from him. (Originally, Adams and Franklin shared a bed in a New Brunswick inn, where a prostitute came to visit them in the middle of the night.) But DaSilva eventually returned, and played the opening week despite enduring severe heart problems. He did have to be hospitalized soon after, and missed the recording session.

One can see why; the show endured much tryout stress. "Momma, Look Sharp" moved from a New Brunswick battlefield setting to the congressional chamber. "He Plays the Violin" was written late, but not as late as "The Egg." When Edwards sat to write a new song in New Haven, he was inspired by the show's logo, where a little eagle with an American flag in its beak came out of an egg. Though one might assume that artist Fay Gage, having read the script, had been spurred by "The Egg" to create her whimsical logo, she actually came up with it on her own, and wound up inadvertently spurring the song.

There's the temptation to say that *1776* didn't need a score; it would have made a great play. Exhibit A is the thirty-six-minute scene in which not a note of music is sung—from "The Lees of Old Virginia" to "But, Mr. Adams"—which will now and forever be the longest non-musical stretch in the history of musicals. Edwards had written a few tunes for the spot, but none worked.

And Edwards, it must be admitted, wrote a very odd score. The music is angular, occasionally dissonant, with atypical rhythms and structures; it has not a single A-A-B-A song. The lyrics, too, are problematic, with many imperfect rhymes (views/mute; sage/leg). There are even more false accents (compro-MISE; independen-CY; parti-CIP-le), and the humor behind one song totally depends on them: Lee enjoys adverbs, because each ends with his name: Immediate-LEE. Short-LEE. But Stone's great book conquered all these deficiencies.

1776 director Peter Hunt had worked with Ken Howard in a 1968 production of *How to Succeed,* and thought he'd be an ideal Jefferson. But Howard was already in *Promises, Promises,* which had opened to rave reviews and was destined to run for years. Still, in that hit, Howard only sauntered on in act 2, punched Chuck (Jerry Orbach) in the nose, took his sister Fran (Jill O'Hara) offstage, and left. So Howard gambled and took the bigger role, and never regretted the choice. He claims that he came up with one of the show's best sight gags: Jefferson, in trying to write the Declaration, scratches a word on a piece of paper, and then crumples it. He does the same thing again. The third time, though, he crumples it before he even has a chance to write a word, as if the thought he had was so inept he must rid himself of it.

But how accurate is *1776?* Historical writer William Martin, author of *Citizen Washington,* says that George Washington's dispatch ("What brave men I shall lose before this business ends") read in the show was not written until late August 1776, at the Battle of Long Island.

Martin also says that Richard Henry Lee was not a happy-go-lucky egomaniac but an austere, tight-lipped, no-nonsense Southern puritan—"and," he says, "the most powerful orator in Congress next to Adams."

That Adams and Franklin conspired to get Martha Jefferson to Philadelphia is also spurious. "Martha was very ill, too sick and depressed to even write a letter," Martin says. "She couldn't have traveled there, and certainly wouldn't have had the energy to sing about [Jefferson's] playing the violin."

Martin takes issue with Rutledge's claim that "The Deep South speaks with one voice." "There was a minimum of thirteen voices," he insists, because within those thirteen, there were state congresses, too. A third of the people were on the right, a third on the left, and the other third in the middle, trying to decide, trying to hold center, or waiting to see what would happen. That was the main problem facing Washington, who learned that Congress gave him more trouble than the British ever did.

He doesn't buy Ben Franklin's statement in the show that he couldn't come up with a declaration because "the things I write are only light extemporanea." Instead, says Martin, Franklin demurred because he was "a learned guy, but wasn't completely beloved, so he knew that if he wrote it, the declaration would be tarred with his brush. He brought baggage to the table that Jefferson didn't."

Sherman and Livingston, who in the show bow out of the writing, also could have done it, says Martin. "Though would they have come up with something as perfectly worded? When John tells Jefferson, 'You write ten times better than any man in Congress,' he was right.

"But," says Martin, "It's impossible to tell a story the way the historians want you to tell it. Those writers knew their job—to be as true as possible to the letter of the times, but always true to the spirit of the times. They knew that they were writing an entertainment. If they wanted to give us history, they'd have sent us to a great historian."

1776 made history in another way. In the early years of the Tony Awards, billing determined the category in which a performer could be nominated. So because William Daniels was billed below the title and not above, he was considered a Best Featured Musical Actor. But John Adams is clearly the show's lead, mover and shaper. He's involved with nine of the show's twelve songs, and featured prominently in six. So when he got his Best Featured Musical Actor nomination, he refused it, saying he belonged in the Best Musical Actor category.

This made Ron Holgate very happy, for he was (correctly) nominated in the Best Featured Musical Actor category, and won because Daniels abdicated. Also benefiting from the Tonys' mistake was Jerry Orbach, who won the Best Musical Actor Tony for his role in *Promises, Promises*. Had Daniels been placed in that category, he would have won.

Daniels' falling on his sword did result in a change of Tony rules. From then on, common sense rather than billing put people in the correct categories—pretty much.

1776 was not a hit in London. With lines such as like "The king is a tyrant" and "We say to hell with Great Britain!" Ostrow didn't expect it to be, so he allowed Alexander H. Cohen, a frequent producer of musical flops, to produce it there. It lasted forty-nine performances.

Still, *1776* emerges as the most gripping and palatable history lesson ever taught. Interesting that it's a show about a cause that seemed hopeless a scant six days before it succeeded. For the musical itself almost closed in New Haven after a disastrous premiere—but, a mere month later, opened in New York to unanimous raves. In a way, history repeated itself.

1776. March 16, 1969–February 13, 1972. 1,217 performances.

THE BIGGEST FLOP
Love Match

Can you picture Queen Victoria singin' and dancin'?

In 1977, a showcase of songs by lyricist Richard Maltby, Jr. and composer David Shire took place at Barbarann, a Forty-sixth Street restaurant. *Starting Here, Starting Now* included "I Think I May Want to Remember Today," in which a woman told of her love for a certain young man whom she'd known since childhood. "Oh, Albert," she sang. "My, how you've grown!"

The name "Albert" wasn't arbitrarily chosen. Originally, he was Prince Albert (1819–1861) and the singer was Queen Victoria (1819–1901)—both the subjects of Maltby and Shire's 1968 musical *Love Match*.

The leading lady would be Patricia Routledge, who we saw win a Best Musical Actress Tony for *Darling of the Day* despite its thirty-two-performance run. Now Broadway was looking forward to seeing her as Victoria.

She'd be reunited with her *Darling* director Noel Willman, best known for staging *The Lion in Winter* and *A Man for All Seasons.* (He won a Tony for the latter.) Of the two producers, Elliot Martin had sponsored the 1,007-performance smash *Never Too Late* before turning to such prestige projects as a *Dinner at Eight* revival and O'Neill's *More Stately Mansions.* Because Martin was also the director of the Center Theatre Group in Los Angeles, he booked the show there.

The other producer was Ivor David Balding, who'd recently had a big off-Broadway hit with Bruce Jay Friedman's *Scuba Duba.* Now he made arrangements for the show to premiere at a new theater in—yes—Phoenix.

Balding had originally signed a little-known composer named Milton Kaye (husband of Shannon Bolin, Meg Boyd in *Damn Yankees*) for the $475,000 project. Soon, though, Maltby and Shire had the job. They'd started collaborating when they were students at Yale. Their 1958 *Cyrano* starred Yalies John Cunningham (Cyrano), Dick Cavett (Ragueneau), Austin Pendleton (Ragueneau's Assistant), Carrie Nye (Lise), and Bill Hinnant (Porter). Playing both Bellerose and "Townsperson" was Bart Giamatti. He wasn't only Paul Giamatti's father, but also the commissioner of baseball for 154 days in 1988–89 before he died of a heart attack.

Though Maltby and Shire were clearly talented, they hadn't had much luck. *The Sap of Life* (1961) had closed quickly off-Broadway, and *How Do You Do, I Love You*—about computer dating—died in a 1967 summer stock tryout. Perhaps their fortunes would change with *Love Match*, with newcomer Laurence Guittard as Albert; he'd been spelling Jose Ferrer, David Atkinson, and Hal Holbrook as Don Quixote at *Man of La Mancha*'s matinees.

Newcomer Christian Hamilton's book had Victoria looking back on her life, starting with her eighteenth birthday, when she was "a fearful, foolish girl." Lord Melbourne (Michael Allinson) will help her to change, so she'll be ready when she becomes Queen. "You'll Have It Beautiful," he sings to her— meaning not just her regal career, but also her romantic life.

Enter Albert (Laurence Guittard), Prince of Saxe-Coburg-Gotha, Germany, her cousin who's being groomed as her husband. But Victoria suddenly and unexpectedly becomes queen—and immediately takes to it. "Play It Again," she insists of the fanfare the held trumpets are giving. That part of her life is set; but what of Albert?

He expects that she'll soon invite him to London, and during "The Packing Song" he prepares all his luggage—only to unpack and pack again, for she doesn't summon him for a full year. By then he's furious, and makes clear, "You're not going to trifle with me."

Before he arrives, though, Victoria realizes she's more drawn to Melbourne. That's "As Plain as Daylight," she sings, though he resolutely refuses even to entertain the thought; he is, after all, forty years older.

So when she sees Albert, she displaces her hostility on him—until she realizes how attractive he is. That's when she decides, "I Think I May Want to Remember Today."

Albert is a no-nonsense type who puts his cards on the table. "I like landscapes with hills and brooks / I don't like the way England looks," he sings, before reaching the song's title, "You Should Know These Things of Me." When the time comes for them to dance, Albert is astonished when they start to polka. "Victoria! You're leading!" he says, to which she answers, "Albert! Of course!"

Victoria leads in another way: She proposes to him. Now they waltz in "A Beautiful Surprise," and Victoria finally allows him to lead as the act 1 curtain falls.

Act 2 starts with Victoria offering "to conjugate our conjugal life: President, indicative. Future, perfect." It's "A Wonderful Life," she sings. Victoria feels that way until she learns she's with child.

"Never Again," she decides—especially because propriety demands that she not been seen by the public in her condition. But a year later, she must admit, "I the Queen Regnant / am pregnant again"—probably the only time a lyricist could aptly use those two words in rhyme.

And so it goes—until she's seen with nine children. Now when she sings the song, it's "Never again / Children like mine will come never again."

History demands that the show end sadly, for Albert dies at forty-two, and Victoria never fully overcomes her grief. Now when she sings, "Play It Again," she is longing to see him "just one more time."

Could 1968 audiences be made to care about Victoria and Albert? While the public had made a hit of *Victoria Regina* in 1935, many theatergoers back then still had a memory of the Queen on the throne. By the late sixties, far fewer had any interest in the overweight and unattractive monarch.

As for Maltby and Shire, by the time they got to Phoenix, they'd dropped four songs and added six. In Los Angeles, Maltby now admits to having been so desperate that he wrote that Victoria got over Albert by singing "Today Is the First Day of the Rest of Your Life"—a then-trendy sixties expression. Anything to make the tender if stodgy story more au courant. But it didn't work.

Shire would reach his greatest success in 1980, when he received an Oscar for composing the theme to *Norma Rae*—with a different lyricist, one Norman Gimbel. As we'll see, Maltby will have two "biggest hits" later in this book—both without Shire. Though the two were still collaborating fifty years after *Cyrano*, their greatest successes have come without the other. But together, they do make beautiful music and lyrics.

"What I'll always remember," says Maltby, "is that when we asked Christian to rewrite the book, he said no. When we asked why, he said, "Because I have a rich wife.""

Love Match. Opened November 3, 1968, in Phoenix, and closed January 4, 1969, in Los Angeles. No Broadway performances.

2

245 W. 44TH ST. N.Y.C.
THE PHANTOM
OF THE OPERA
2:00P SAT DEC 10 198
The Shubert Organization
SAT SEP 10 1988
LOCATION
249 WEST
249 WEST 4
BILLY
7:00 PM
APR 28,
*INCLUDES $0.00 FACI
2 MAIMP2108-0426-M23
NO REFUNDS/N
BEAUTY AND
THE PALACE
1564 BROADWA
THU APR 21,199
24MAR94
ROUNDABOUT THEATRE COMPANY PR
CABARET
AT STUDIO 54
Mon, January 14, 2002 8:0
Doors Open 1 Hour B
COMP
All Taxes Incl. If Applicable
246 WEST 44
"GOOD N
EVENINGS AT
FEB'RY
14
1975
PRICE
ORCHESTRA
3B 105
CQ0127E ORCH G 111
EVENT CODE SECTION/BOX ROW SEAT
$ 0.00 ORCH CENTER
PRICE & ALL TAXES INCL
NO REFUNDS/NO EXCHANGES
THE CAPEMAN
MARQUIS THEATRE
211 W. 45TH. NYC
TUE JAN 27,1998 7:00PM
10JAN98
MAR601C
NOV 02 1990
MINSKOFF TH
ORCHESTRA

1969–1979

1969–1970

THE BIGGEST HIT
Applause

Taking on a movie masterpiece.

In the landmark 1968 gay play *The Boys in the Band*, Michael says that one of his hyper-effeminate friend Emory's favorite things is "*All About Eve*—the screenplay of which he will recite verbatim." Playwright Mart Crowley could have chosen a number of other films that are popular with gays, but this had to be the one.

As Comden and Green wrote in *Applause*'s cast album's liner notes, *All About Eve* is "a very special film with an army of millions of fiercely loyal aficionados who love and cherish every frame, word and gesture with the defensive clucking passion of an outraged mother hen."

(They *did* mean gays, don't you think?)

But given that *All About Eve* won the 1950 Best Film Oscar suggests that even heterosexuals must have admired this intoxicating story about glamorous star Margo Channing and Bill Sampson, her frequent director and current love. That he's some years younger than she threatens Margo, especially when über-fan Eve Harrington comes on the scene. Though Eve meets Margo in October, after watching her umpteenth performance of Channing's star vehicle *Aged in Wood* by noted playwright Lloyd Richards, by June she's already starring in Richards' new play. (My, shows got on fast in those days, didn't they?) And while Margo loses a good role to Eve, she doesn't lose Bill to her, too.

In 1968, producers Joseph Kipness and Lawrence Kasha hired three-time Tony nominee Sidney Michaels to write the book. They later supplanted him with Comden and Green. This legendary pair had also been librettists for most of the shows for which they'd provided lyrics, but lyricist Lee Adams, along with partner Charles Strouse, had already been signed for the score. Comden and Green might have balked—we do lyrics, too, or we walk—but they signed to do only the book. Soon after came a big break: Lauren Bacall agreed to play Margo Channing.

The show was titled *Welcome to the Theater*, then *Make Believe*, then *Applause, Applause*, before that was cleaved in two. As soon as the musical played its Baltimore tryout, some of those mother hens railed that the stage replacement for acerbic critic Addison DeWitt—Stan Harding, played by Ray Becker—sure wasn't the wit DeWitt was; that Birdie, Margo's Girl Monday-through-Friday, had morphed into male hairdresser Duane (Lee Roy Reams); that Mitteleuropean producer Max Fabian had become standard-issue producer Howard Benedict (Robert Mandan); and that Phoebe, the stagestruck young lass who, in a manner of speaking, played Eve Harrington to the real Eve Harrington, had been completely omitted.

The musical's creators didn't cavalierly discard these characters. Kipness and Kasha couldn't get the rights to the film, only to "The Wisdom of Eve," the story by Mary Orr (about a Margola Cranston) that had inspired it. Because *All About Eve*'s writer-director, Joseph L. Mankiewicz, had created DeWitt, Birdie, Fabian, and Phoebe, Comden and Green couldn't use them. (Considering how many characters Mankiewicz created, how surprising to find that Miss Caswell—a DeWitt date and "the Marilyn Monroe role"—was in Orr's original story.)

In 1968, while Strouse was writing the musical version of Mankiewicz's most famous film, he was also writing the background score for Mankiewicz's current film, *There Was a Crooked Man*. Recalled Strouse, "Joe's biggest piece of advice was to make a song from the movie's most famous line, 'Fasten your seat belts; it's going to be a bumpy night.'" Strouse and Adams decided to do that for the moment when an out-of-control Margo, utterly irate with Eve, utters this immortal warning to her party guests.

While the film opened with Margo sitting and watching Eve win "The Sarah Siddons Award," Comden and Green did better by having Margo herself present the Best Actress in a Play prize at the Tonys.

The action flashed back to Eve and Margo meeting after the opening of the latter's musical. Friends come backstage with a host of conflicting opinions: in a song called "The Well-Wishers," the actors in the Baltimore production sang, variously, "It's a bomb," "It's a hit," "If you want entertainment, this is it,"— everything from "It won't run" to "It's the best thing that Margo's ever done"—all leading to the final line, "I love your coat."

The lyrics were purposely clichéd, but did they need to be heard at all? The song was replaced with "Backstage Babble," in which nonsense syllables alternated with words: "Openings are really ba ba a dah / So exciting, ba ba da, ba da"—meaning that the chatter that goes on at openings isn't interesting, and who's listening, anyway?

In Baltimore, Bill (Len Cariou) then sang to Margo "It Was Always You," a perky song, but director-choreographer Ron Field preferred a ballad. Strouse said he hadn't written a good ballad since "Once upon a Time," from his 1962 flop *All-American*. Field insisted, and said he didn't care if Strouse wrote "Once upon a Time" backwards. As a listen to replacement "Think How It's Gonna Be" proves, Strouse consciously did just that.

Comden and Green had Eve state that she comes from Madison, Wisconsin and that she worked with "our local dramatic society. We did Pinter and Albee." Considering what community theaters usually do, everyone should suspect Eve right then and there. But everyone buys the story that her husband Eddie died in Vietnam—still a hot-button word in 1970 when the war was still raging.

In the film, after Ms. Harrington told her sad backstory, Margo's maid Birdie famously quipped, "Everything but the bloodhounds snappin' at her rear end!" That reference to nineteenth-century melodrama was much too dated, so

Comden and Green came up with a beauty of an update for Duane: "Wow! It's like being in group therapy!" Because Duane was written as an out-and-proud gay whose sexuality was treated matter-of-factly Reams could play him as a human being and not a limp-wristed cliché.

Lest we think Comden and Green too ahead of the curve, their stage directions say that Margo, Eve, and Duane go to a "place that is filled with people. All of them are dancing, and it becomes apparent all of them are male." How demure! Today, a playwright would simply say "a gay bar." Going there, though, was a smart move for *Applause*. Imagine the commotion if a star of Margo's magnitude arrived there on the night she opened her new hit.

Margo invites Eve back to her apartment, where Strouse and Adams made great theatrical hay by having Margo see herself in an old movie on TV, and mock herself in "Who's That Girl?" replete with boogie-woogie music to set the forties mood. But at the end of the scene comes an important detail missing in *All About Eve*. Margo exits for bed, and Eve, left alone, reprises a few lines of her earlier song, "The Best Night of My Life." She isn't singing to impress anybody; these are just her internal thoughts, but her expressing them allows the audience to assume she's on the level, and that Margo's later suspicions mean she is simply, in Bill's words, "paranoid."

Soon, though, comes the famous scene where Eve is on stage, holding Margo's dress in front of her, taking some deep bows to an imaginary audience—until Margo catches her. In the film, Eve is mortified; in *Applause*, the script directs her to be "composed."

Producer Howard Benedict originally had three songs, none of which would be retained by the Broadway opening at the Palace. At least in Baltimore, he got to sing a charmer to Eve, which started, "We trade our lives for just some good reviews / For 'Smashing'—*New York Times* / 'Terrific!'—*Daily News*." Actually, if Strouse and Adams had followed the movie more closely, Bill might have sung this song. After all, in the film, he did have a harangue about "The theater! The theater!" Perhaps the songwriters felt that a song listing all the facets of show biz would be too on-the-nose.

Howard's other two dropped songs didn't even make it to Baltimore. "God Bless" was his duet with Margo, in which they argued about her taking time off to visit Bill in Rome. "The Loneliest Man in Town" was his come-on to Eve. Recalls Strouse, "We'd originally written that for Jack Cassidy to sing to Lois Lane in '[*It's a Bird . . . It's a Plane . . . It's*] *Superman*.'"

At least Mandan retained his role. Diane McAfee, portraying Eve, was fired in Baltimore, with Penny Fuller taking over. Despite the heartbreak, McAfee can't have regretted getting cast, because she met Brandon Maggart (portraying playwright Buzz Richards) in the production. They eventually had two daughters who went into the business, too: Maude Maggart and—yes—Fiona Apple. (Notice, too, that in the film, Richards' first name was Lloyd. That had to be changed, for by 1970, a real Lloyd Richards was well known as the director of five shows on Broadway, including the original *A Raisin in the Sun*.)

In the film, Eve gets a speech about the value of applause, but rather than risk another on-the-noser, the musical took us to Joe Allen's where a gypsy (Bonnie Franklin) begins to talk about the rigors of show business, while chorus members Renee Baughman, Sammy Williams, and Nicholas Dante stand behind her. Those three would make Franklin's points more boldly in five years when they originated roles in *A Chorus Line*.

"Applause" was one of the great production numbers of the seventies. The original cast album doesn't do it justice, for it eliminates the section where Joe Allen's waiters put some tables together, make an impromptu stage, and do snippets from *Rose Marie*; *Hello, Dolly!*; *Fiddler on the Roof*; *Cabaret*; *The Boy Friend*; and *West Side Story*, but changing the lyrics to accommodate the word "applause." They also aped the nude revue *Oh! Calcutta!* by stripping to their boxers, which had been greatly ventilated to show their bare bottoms. (Theatergoers who saw *Applause* and went to Joe Allen's afterwards expecting to see this kind of spontaneous performance must have been disappointed when it didn't materialize.)

For Bill's welcome-home party, Comden and Green again did *All About Eve* one better by having Eve wear one of Margo's hand-me-down dresses; that way, when Bill comes in and sees her from behind, he mistakes her for Margo and caresses her. They also invented a game requiring each party guest to wear on his back a sign with the name of a famous person on it. The wearer would not know his own identity, but would have to guess by comments people made about that person.

Would such sophisticated New Yorkers really play such a game? Whether they would or not, the game did allow for another improvement over the screenplay. To help Eve to guess that her "identity" is Freud, Bill lies down on the couch to be "analyzed"—just as Margo comes in and finds them in a compromising position. Fasten your seat belts.

Many have wondered why Margo lets Eve become her understudy after she stops trusting her. The film never addressed the issue, but *Applause* did—albeit unconvincingly. Howard tells her, "You don't have understudy approval in your contract." Hmmm, big star that Margo is, why doesn't she? Comden and Green probably agonized over this line, but may have felt that it at least acknowledged the point many have raised: Margo was starting to sour on Eve, so she would have put her foot down and demanded a different understudy.

Margo's subsequent tirade against Eve included a line that certainly wasn't in the 1950 film: "Let her run naked off-Broadway." Her rage also resulted in an aria called "Welcome to the Theater." Sang Margo, "Welcome to the world of fears and jeers and tears"—but an early demo proves that what Adams original wrote was, "Welcome to the world of fears and *queers* and tears." One wonders if the lyric was changed some time after June 28, 1969, when the Stonewall riots occurred.

In the film, there's the scene at the Richards' country house where Karen Richards drains the gas tank so that Margo can't catch the train back to the city for her performance. But would Radcliffe-educated Karen be likely to know how to empty a tank by using a hose to siphon it? She'd undoubtedly never attempted such a stunt, so she probably wouldn't have been successful at it. Besides, where did Karen put that full tank's worth of gas—in the wine bottles that she, Margo and Lloyd had drained at dinner? Chances are that there'd be some residue on the ground by the car, not to mention the distinctive odor of gasoline. Considering that Margo is a major smoker, *All About Eve* might have ended right there with a scene worthy of an action movie.

In *Applause*, the plot is still there. The audience doesn't see the scene in the car between Margo and Karen (Ann Williams); instead, Margo returns to the country house, where she warns, "At eight-thirty, I start doing the play, no matter what." It's a reminder of another era when shows began a half hour later than they do now.

Margo then has a nice moment not in the film. She calls Eve, who is doing the role in her place, and warns her about a difficult second-act costume change. Lest Margo be too nice, though, once she's off the phone, she says that she hopes Eve "stinks."

Karen rues draining the tank in the felicitous song "Good Friends." Comden and Green had her faint at song's end, which ended the scene. It made for a nice blackout, but also must have turned Margo's suspicions on Karen as the culprit. But give Comden and Green credit for eventually addressing the issue that the film didn't. There, Margo never figures out what Karen did; in *Applause*, Karen eventually confesses her sin to Margo, who says she figured it out many moons ago, anyway.

In that country house scene, Margo mentions that she has to do a coffee commercial the next day; that resulted in another Comden and Green improvement. While in the movie, Margo simply goes to lunch the next day; in *Applause*, she has to show up for work and tape the commercial—a difficult thing for a devastated and grieving person, and certainly harder than merely sitting and having lunch. Another improvement: though both the film and the musical had Bill show up, in *Applause*, he doesn't merely comfort Margo, but helps direct her in the commercial—an oblique way of saying, "I'm here for you, I'll make this better, and we're gonna be all right."

While one misses Addison DeWitt, *Applause* makes producer Howard Benedict the one who will "own" Eve and steer her future. That makes more sense, for a producer would have more power to make her dreams come true than a critic would.

Eventually Margo decides not to worry about Eve's ascension, because "Love Comes First," as her eleven o'clock number stated. *Applause* press agent Susan L. Schulman credited Louis Botto of *Look* magazine for suggesting that Strouse and Adams come up with something greater. And so they did, a song called—

yes—"Something Greater." (Strouse later recycled some of the melody of "Love Comes First" into "You, You, You" in *Annie 2*, and then "Above the Law" in *Annie Warbucks*.)

Love Comes First. Something Greater. *Applause* is another property that believes that true love is much more important than professional success. Perhaps it is. But in *All About Eve*, that isn't quite what Margo says. She says that she'll no longer play roles too young for her, and not that she's abandoning her career to joyously clean out the drain in the sink. Still, musicals often preach romance above all (though Stephen Sondheim's *Company*, opening less than a month after *Applause*, would change that).

Like *Anyone Can Whistle*, *Applause* opened to three raves and three pans— but it enjoyed a very different fate. Only twenty days after it opened, Bacall won Best Musical Actress, Ron Field both Best Director and Best Choreographer, and *Applause* Best Musical. In a year when there was no separate awards for book or score, Comden, Green, Strouse, and Adams all got trophies along with producers Kasha and Kipness. The only miscue on Tony night was during the title song, when a chorus member on roller skates fell on his *gluteus maximus*. And yes, each waiter did strip to his boxers and show his *gluteus maximus*, too.

Applause ran more than two years in an era when a hit was expected to last about that long. When Bacall left, the producers had an inspired notion: Anne Baxter, the movie's *Eve*, became *Applause*'s Margo. Arlene Dahl, who followed her, finished out the run.

For a Tony-winning commercial musical, *Applause* doesn't show up much. In 1996, there was a revival with Stefanie Powers as Margo that started a planned twenty-six-stop tour at the Paper Mill Playhouse in Millburn, New Jersey—only to close after its next engagement. During the late seventies, Charles Strouse was often referred to in print as Charles (*Bye Bye Birdie*, *Applause*, *Annie*) Strouse. By the end of the eighties, he was Charles (*Bye Bye Birdie*, *Annie*) Strouse.

Still, though more than eighty musicals have had longer original runs on Broadway, *Applause* was the biggest hit of its (weak) season. Luckily for it that *Company* opened days too late to compete that Tony season, for the Stephen Sondheim-George Furth masterpiece might well have won the Best Musical prize.

Schulman recalls that Bacall did not live up to her reputation as difficult and profane. "It was such a good time in her life," Schulman says. "She was in love with her leading man, the show was a hit, and while she'd never won any kind of award, here she was, beating out Katharine Hepburn (nominated for *Coco*) for the Tony. Even today, when I see her, I don't expect her to remember me, so I say, 'Hi, it's Susan Schulman'—and she always says right away, 'I know who the fuck you are.'"

Applause. March 30, 1970–July 27, 1972. 896 performances.

The Biggest Flop
Gantry

Let the audiences—and the critics—come to you.

One could make a case that *Jimmy* was the biggest flop of the season. The show had a song called "One in a Million"—and one was probably the number of dollars the show made back from the $1 million investment during its eighty-four poorly attended performances.

The "Jimmy" in question was James J. Walker (1881–1946), New York's mayor from 1926 to 1932. Walker had already rated a song in a Pulitzer Prize–winning musical ten years earlier. In *Fiorello!* he was lauded because he "kept the subway to a five-cent fare." But Walker was far more famous for his drinking, gambling, carousing, taking bribes, and not paying attention to corruption among his aides. Honest men such as Fiorello LaGuardia deserved musical comedies; scalawags such as Walker didn't. A fictional con man such as Harold Hill is one thing, but a real-life rogue of whom many theatergoers had bad memories is a different story.

At least bookwriter Melville Shavelson (who'd written *Beau James*, a film about Walker) didn't try to hide Walker's warts. Neither did Bill and Patti Jacob; their first song, "The Little Woman," shows Walker being told by his cronies that he can cheat and connive as long as he projects the image of a good husband. Once he agrees, the cronies gleefully sing, "The city's now for sale." And audiences were supposed to laugh in delight?

The Jacobs wrote "Will You Think of Me Tomorrow as You Think of Me Today?" which was to mirror "Will You Love in December as You Do in May?" a genuine twenties hit that Walker cowrote. In those days, that's what you did; witness *Funny Girl*'s Jule Styne and Bob Merrill writing "My Man" as "The Music That Makes Me Dance." Today, songwriters wouldn't write a new pastiche, but would just use the original song.

Despite *Jimmy*'s $1 million loss, let's call *Gantry* (as in Elmer) the biggest flop of the season—not just because it ran one night, but also because its plan to get feedback from out-of-town critics was the biggest flop idea of the season, too.

Going out of town was becoming more and more expensive, so producers Joseph Cates and Jerry Schlossberg had a brainstorm: instead of going to neighboring states and getting critics' opinions, why not preview in New York and bring the critics to see the show? Afterwards, the appraisers could write a review for their hometown papers if they chose. But if they preferred, they could just relate to the creative staff what they liked, what they didn't, and what they'd suggest should be done next.

Five were invited from Boston, including the esteemed Elliot Norton, "the dean of American drama critics," from the *Record-American*. Four were from

Washington, headed by Richard Coe from the *Post*. That left three from Philadelphia, including Charles Petzoid of the *Daily News*, who wrote that the plan "could kill this city as a tryout town. It would leave only proven hits."

The New York Times, the *New York Daily News*, and the Associated Press weren't happy with the scheme, either. They felt that if the out-of-towners reviewed a show in New York during the thirty-one scheduled previews, they should, too.

So Cates and Schlossberg scuttled the plan. Their telegrams to the dozen critics read,

> We did not realize at the time that principles of media competition were involved. Our thought was that your constructive criticism would serve to help us improve and polish the show for its opening night, but various managements of the local press took exception because competing papers would now have priority. We now understand their objections.

Gantry had Robert Shaw billed above the title as the charismatic and flawed Elmer Gantry. Rita Moreno, playing Sharon Falconer, the holy woman for whom he lusts, was billed below, but the typeface of her name was exactly the same size as Shaw's and the show's title.

The music was by Stanley Lebowsky, the musical and vocal director for *A Family Affair* and *Breakfast at Tiffany's*. Choreographer Onna White had done the dances for eleven previous musicals to reach Broadway, but this would be her first (and last) directorial assignment.

The book was by Peter Bellwood, who'd never written a musical before, and would never have another one on Broadway. Lyricist Fred Tobias could brag that he'd been represented as a Broadway lyricist, but considering that the musical was the three-performance *Pousse-Café* in 1966, he would have been better off not bragging.

Gantry opened and closed on Valentine's Day, 1970, after getting no valentines from the critics. And Petzoid's fear that inviting out-of-town critics to New York previews would leave Philadelphia with no tryouts and only road shows? That happened anyway.

Gantry. February 14, 1970. 1 performance.

1970–1971

The Biggest Hit
No, No, Nanette

Broadway discovers its past as it never has before.

In a twenty-year-span, producer Harry Rigby has managed to get only four shows to Broadway, all of which flopped. Now, in 1969, he wants to revive a forty-five-year-old show called *No, No, Nanette*. Everyone tells him that Broadway wants new musicals, not revivals.

Then Ribgy meets Cyma Rubin, who got her fortune the way most women did then—by marrying a second time. Her husband is Sam of Revlon cosmetics fame. Rigby tells Rubin that a *Nanette* revival could be the hit of the seventies—under four conditions.

First, the leading lady must be played by Ruby ("You're going out there a youngster, but you've got to come back a star") Keeler. Second, Patsy Kelly, the sassy comedienne who began her film career in 1929, must play her maid. Third, directing will be thirties film legend Busby Berkeley. Fourth, the musical director will be Buster Davis, who's helmed orchestras of four shows, all flops, but is now writing his memoir, which he calls *Ask Her If She's Got a Brother*. (It will never be published.)

Mrs. Rubin agrees, and her husband puts up virtually the entire $500,000 budget for a musical that sounds very old. Jimmy Smith (Hiram Sherman) is a Bible salesman who's now at the dangerous age. He flirts not only with Winnie from Washington (Pat Lysinger), but also with Betty from Boston (Loni Zoe Ackerman) and Flora from Frisco (K.C. Townsend). Jimmy's wife, Sue (Keeler), suspects nothing, but her best friend, Lucille (Helen Gallagher), decides to tell her what's going on. Lucille soon has problems of her own, because she'll suspect her husband Billy (Bobby Van) of infidelity, too.

And who's Nanette (Carole Demas), and how does she fit into all this? She's Sue's "protégée" who's smitten with young Tom. Enamored though she is, Nanette feels she should experience life a little more before she settles down. But Tom sure doesn't want Nanette to commit a no-no.

The original's pre-Broadway tryout in 1925 was surely the strangest ever. *Nanette* opened in Chicago, ostensibly for a few weeks, but it became a sensation and lasted forty-nine weeks there. Then came four (!) national companies before the show even opened on Broadway for 321 performances. Clearly, though, it wasn't all smooth sailing, for during rehearsals and the tryout, producer-director H. H. Frazee replaced the performers who portrayed Jimmy, Lucille, and Nanette.

And that was nothing compared to the bloodletting that Cyma Rubin would cause. Starting with the first rehearsal and right down to the show's final tryout stop in Baltimore, no fewer than thirty-five were fired—including Harry Rigby. Sherman gave way to Jack Gilford, and Demas to Susan Watson. Berkeley would direct in name only, and his successor, Bert Shevelove, would considerably rewrite the book, and add a few songs that weren't part of the original.

The critics and public didn't care. The former raved, and the latter flocked to the Forty-sixth Street Theater. Hmmm, producers thought, is nostalgia what the public wants?

Few had thought so. Take the twenty years before this *Nanette* opened: Broadway played host to only eight commercial musical revivals: *Music in the Air* (1951); *Of Thee I Sing, Shuffle Along,* and *Pal Joey* (1952); *Porgy and Bess* (1953); *Finian's Rainbow* (1960); *Annie Get Your Gun* (1966); and *The Boy Friend* (1970). Most were faithful recreations of the originals, and most flopped.

Because *No, No, Nanette* didn't, money men started looking to the past instead of the present for their future productions. In the next twenty years, Broadway saw sixty-nine musical revivals—fourteen of which were presented with one or more additional songs and/or substantial changes to the book. Those producing often said, "We're bringing the show into the" followed by the number of the current decade. So many changes were often made that a new word was spawned: "revisal."

In the last two decades, the pattern hasn't ceased. For better or worse, *No, No, Nanette*'s two lasting contributions to Broadway were the revival and the revisal. These became so plentiful that in 1977, the Tonys initiated a category for both play and musical revivals, and, in 1994, gave Best Revival of a Musical a category all its own.

Finally, there's no truth whatsoever to the oft-told story that Frazee—also then the owner of the Boston Red Sox—sold Babe Ruth to the New York Yankees in order to finance *Nanette*. What Frazee really did was unload Ruth in 1920 in order to buy three theaters in New York and two in Chicago.

No, No, Nanette. January 19, 1971–February 3, 1973. 861 performances.

THE BIGGEST FLOP
Lolita, My Love

A musical of WHAT?!?!

Some would say the biggest flop of the season was *Follies*, given that it lost $665,000. Many more who consider *Follies* a complete masterpiece would say, "Bite your tongue."

They've got a point, and not just because the show ran 522 performances.

How could the biggest flop of the season have the greatest production number of the post-war era? "Who's That Woman?" written by Stephen Sondheim and choreographed by Michael Bennett, acknowledged that at any reunion of showgirls (which, on one level, *Follies* was), one of them is going to suggest that they all do their favorite number from way back when. But to have these old showgirls mirrored by the ghosts of their beautiful-girl former selves was brilliant. So was Sondheim's making the lyric to include a mirror, too.

Sondheim's wordplay was at its peak here. For "Can That Boy Fox Trot?" Carlotta Campion (Yvonne DeCarlo) rationalized her dimwitted lover's deficiencies by arguing, "But who needs Albert Schweitzer / when the lights're / low?" Even better: In "Uptown-Downtown," Phyllis (Alexis Smith) expressed her two contradictory selves, singing, "She sits / At the Ritz / With her splits / Of Mumms / But then she pines / For some steins / With her village chums / But with a Schlitz / In her mitts/ Down at Fitz- / roy's bar / She thinks of the Ritz, oh / It's so / Schit-zo." In a mere forty-one words making up only two sentences, there are twelve (count 'em, twelve) rhymes.

And yet, Sondheim dropped both those songs in hopes of writing something better. Fans are still arguing over whether "The Story of Lucy and Jessie" is better than "Uptown-Downtown," but virtually everyone agrees that "Fox Trot?" isn't as potent as "I'm Still Here."

This massive, epic musical can even boast of fascinating stage directions: when aged showgirl Sally first approaches her old boss, impresario Dimitri Weisman, according to bookwriter James Goldman, "He hasn't a clue who she is . . . Either he used to lay her or he thinks he did."

Playing Sally was Dorothy Collins, Sondheim's first choice. He'd admired her performance in a stock production of *Do I Hear a Waltz?* Considering how many times Sondheim had gone on record as regretting his decision to write lyrics for that musical, how nice to hear that at least one good thing came out of his working on it.

Waltz's choreographer, Wakefield Poole, left theater to become a gay porno movie pioneer. But he did make one great contribution to American musical theater. When he heard that Hal Prince had accepted a *Follies* logo before he saw what David Byrd had designed, he insisted that Prince look at what Byrd had done. Prince did—and of course chose the now-legendary logo.

More than a reunion, *Follies* was metaphorically about the death of show business. How fascinating that such a message was delivered during the same year that *The Ed Sullivan Show* went off the air after a twenty-four-season run. Then, six months after *Follies* closed, *Life* magazine ended its thirty-six-year run as a weekly magazine. Broadway was wounded, because each had heralded many musicals and put them front and center before the nation. That would happen no longer.

Follies, a veritable phantasmagoria, became more and more legendary as time went on. In 2007, when Encores! decided to revive it, many people decried the decision, saying the company had done it just because it knew it would make a lot of money. The biggest flop of the season was now considered to be a cash cow.

Such a reclamation hasn't happened for the two other contenders for the crown of the biggest flop of 1970–71. One was *Prettybelle*, Jule Styne and Bob Merrill's first collaboration since *Funny Girl*. The plot: Southern housewife Prettybelle Sweet (Angela Lansbury) discovers that her late husband, the town sheriff (Mark Dawson), was terrible and torturous to minorities in ways she couldn't have begun to fathom. The revelation sends her off the deep end, and she begins bringing home the young men her husband harmed, and then, in a strange way of compensating for their indignities, sleeping with them.

Audiences in Boston were utterly repulsed at the idea of Lansbury acting so carnally. But the show might have worked if Prettybelle had decided to compensate for her husband's behavior by taking young men into her home to school them—while the townspeople was convinced that she was bedding them. There was nothing wrong with Styne's music, peppered with a country twang, which was very adventurous for this brassy sixty-five-year-old—or with Lansbury's galvanizing performance.

So *Prettybelle* closed in Boston—but *Lolita, My Love* closed in Philadelphia and then—after its authors hastily decided to give it one more try—opened and closed in Boston, too. A musical that twice closes out of town has to be the biggest flop of the season.

The ad campaign for Stanley Kubrick's 1962 film of Vladimir Nabokov's most famous novel asked, "How did they ever make a movie of *Lolita*?" Nine years later, Broadway would ask a better question: "How did they ever make a musical of *Lolita*?"

"They" were bookwriter-lyricist Alan Jay Lerner and composer John Barry. Columbia Records, which had backed Lerner's two most popular and famous musicals, *My Fair Lady* and *Camelot*, decided to plunge in again. This time, the company wouldn't sell a single album, because it wouldn't make the recording.

Here's what wound up in Boston: The overture alone sounds ominous before we met Clare Quilty (Leonard Frey), who's taking a break from writing *The Cross of Rabbi Fineberg*, the love story of a rabbi and a priest. Quilty is hosting a hedonistic party, which allows him to sing, "Going Going Gone," about the ephemeral nature of the human body.

A frantic Humbert Humbert (John Neville) arrives and accuses Quilty of stealing away his Lolita, whom he hasn't seen for "two years, ten months, and four days," the all-too-easy way for a writer to establish a character's obsession. When Humbert pulls out a gun, Quilty tries to downplay the situation by saying, "Careful; you might shoot your toe off and then you'd only have five"—a much-too-clever reference to the six-toed sloth.

Humbert shoots Quilty dead, and addresses the audience: "How many of you have ever committed murder?" He then tells us what brought him to it: his passion for the aforementioned Lolita. "Although the mature woman stimulates my glands," he said, "it's the passing tot of twelve or thirteen who turns me into a hell furnace of desire." That wasn't easy for an audience to hear, so Lerner wisely added, "Following my nervous breakdown," in the hope of eliciting some sympathy for the character.

Humbert takes us back in time to his arrival in Ramsdale, Vermont, to teach adult ed—an important detail, for it shows that he's not actively looking to prey on young girls; if he were, he'd have got a job in a middle school. Looking for a room to rent takes him to the home of Charlotte Haze (Dorothy Loudon), who's having a tough time with her teenage daughter, Lolita (Denise Nickerson). That the kid never listens prompts Charlotte to sing "The Same Old Song." Loudon was riveting in delivering the pulsating Barry melody, even with the constant interruption of Lolita's "Oh, mother!" screech.

Charlotte is taken with Humbert. "I was expecting a European, but you're just English," she says confidently. Prying to find out his marital status, she is delighted that he was "Divorced in Paris! How romantic!"

Humbert, disgusted, tries to extricate himself from renting the room—until Lolita enters. One look is all it takes to change his mind. By today's standards, Charlotte seems naïve in that she doesn't immediately suspect that Lolita is the reason he's staying.

Lolita and Humbert chat, and when she mentions that she'd like a swimming pool, there's a double dose of double entendres—"You must be very hot," he tells her, and she answers, "You don't look so cool yourself." And while many a musical has had a man sing a love song the moment he first sets eyes on his beloved, Lerner and Barry felt they'd better draw the line there and not cross it. Instead, Humbert enthusiastically tells Lolita, "I'd be delighted to help you with your homework." After she says, "Terrific!" he immediately asks her, "*When?*"

Not today, because it's "Saturday," as Lolita sings to a nice bubble-gum melody. Though Lolita was established as fourteen—Nickerson's actual age—the actress had a voice that made her sound much more like ten-year-old Annie Warbucks. Sue Lyon in the film was more mature, and while audiences seeing her with James Mason may have felt uncomfortable, audiences at *Lolita, My Love* were more unnerved by a seemingly much younger girl with an older man.

Humbert says, "My knuckles brush against her blue jeans. I almost lose consciousness," and relishes "that glimpse of flesh between her thigh and ankles." By the time he encourages Lolita to go swimming, the audience is pretty repulsed. The writers tried to ameliorate the situation by writing "In the Broken Promise Land of Fifteen." In what could be musically described as a benign tango, Humbert remembers his first girlfriend, who drowned while they were swimming. That, too, helped explain his obsession with young girls, but still, audiences were more inclined to yell out, "Come on, Humbert! Move on!"

Later, when Lolita visits his room, Charlotte comes in, chides her daughter for bothering him, and tells Humbert, "I am sorry for this intrusion." He responds with an ultra-dry "Which?" And she still doesn't catch on. We do, because we know that in his diary he's described Charlotte as "a walrus in heat." You'd think she might catch on when Humbert gives a lecture (attended by Quilty) on the subject of "Nymphets." But she doesn't—maybe because she's too blinded by love.

Charlotte takes Humbert for a (hopefully) romantic dinner at "Sur les Quias de Ramsdale, Vermont," singing, "Who could ever dream you could reach Paris on the Interstate Highway 93?" The song becomes cancan-like in exuberance, the two dance, and the number turns into a showstopper—the only one of the evening. The problem was that Loudon made the audience fall in love with her, and had them rooting that she'd get her man—that he'd straighten out and be a good stepfather to Lolita.

It doesn't happen. After Charlotte goes for broke by writing Hubert a letter sighing, "There's no one at the organ in the chapel of my heart," he decides to marry her just to stay close to Lolita. In his head, the marriage ceremony takes an unusual turn: "Do you, Lolita's mother, take this man to be Lolita's stepfather?" The chorus sings, "Ave Lolita," adding a bit of blasphemy to the proceedings.

When Charlotte learns that Humbert has sent Lolita candy at camp, she chides him, not for making a romantic gesture, but because she disapproves of candy. ("Fructose!" Loudon snarled, making the word sound very funny.) "She's mad," Humbert responds drolly. "I'm sick—but she's mad."

He fantasizes about killing Charlotte in "Farewell, Little Dream, Goodbye." (One lyric: "Let her pass on / With the gas on.") He knows that he could never go through with it—but then Charlotte goes snooping, finds his diary, reads how he really feels about her and Lolita—and runs helter-skelter into the street where she's killed by a car. Humbert's melody stays the same, but the song becomes more up-tempo and carefree as the lyric changes to "Hello, Little Dream, Hello." And the audience was supposed to sympathize or even enjoy this as the curtain came down on act 1.

In act 2, Humbert takes Lolita on a rainbow tour of America. Eventually he has to tell her, "Your mother is dead." That was mercifully not set to music, but audiences still had to watch the kid cry. Worse, Humbert complained to us, "Why do women always have to cry?" Everything isn't about you, Humbert.

"Promise me you'll never leave me," a desperate Lolita says, prompting him to sing, "I'll buy you bubble gum, sandals, and jeans; perfume, potato chips, and movie magazines." He saw it as enough. Audiences didn't.

At a motel, he gets a call from a man whose voice we recognize as Clare Quilty's. "Who's that finger-lickin' chicken in your room?" he asks. Turns out that Quilty has designs on Lolita, too, because she's "youth at her youthiest."

So, as hard a time as audiences had in dealing with Humbert's lust, now they were given a triangle with two perverted men savoring a pre-pubescent. Does this sound box-office to you?

But Quilty just wants a quick and cheap thrill, making the besotted Humbert the more pathetic of the two. "I know she's being unfaithful to me," he moans. To Lolita, it's "The Same Old Song," as she reprises her mother's complaint. "You can't torment me like this," he pleads. "I love you too much." That cuts no ice with Lolita, who wants to have fun with her peers. "They're racing their cars / and playing guitars / but I'm so adored / I've got to be bored." (Barry's melody was much too perky here.)

"How Far Is It to the Next Town?" covered nearly ten minutes of music, in which Humbert and Lolita crossed many state lines. It was a good song, too, but that couldn't change the fact that both the plot and the production were doomed to a most unhappy end. Lolita escapes on the journey, marries, and drives Humbert to Quilty's door and murder.

What's more, Ming Cho Lee's set was done on the cheap; instead of genuine interiors, mere house frames were offered, with a square or two of wallpaper positioned here or there so audiences could imagine what the rooms looked like. They would have preferred to see them whole.

Walter Kerr called *Kelly*, the second biggest flop of the 1964–1965 season, "A bad idea gone wrong." *Lolita, My Love* was actually a bad idea gone right—in that a theatergoer couldn't have expected a better musical of Nabokov's novel or Kubrick's movie.

But would anyone have asked for a musical of *Lolita* in the first place?

Lolita, My Love. February 16, 1971, in Philadelphia–March 27, 1971, in Boston. No New York performances.

1971–1972

THE BIGGEST HIT
Grease

Quality uncontrol.

Anna conquered the King, Dolly bested Vandergelder, Adelaide got Nathan to marry her, Maria changed Captain von Trapp. Musicals usually have women emerge victorious over men.

Until *Grease*—one of the comparatively few musicals where the female eventually goes along with what the male wants. Sweet Catholic ingenue Sandy Dumbrowski (Carole Demas) doesn't get her teen boyfriend Danny Zuko (Barry

Bostwick) to dress preppy and acquire culture. Instead, Sandy, according to the stage directions, emerges at the end with "a wild new hair style, black motorcycle leather jacket, skin-tight slacks, gold hoop earrings," and looks "more alive than she ever has . . . smoking a cigarette" which she "French inhales."

More surprising is that Sandy caves in soon after wild girl Rizzo (Adrienne Barbeau) admits to her that she may be pregnant. Many theatergoers might have assumed that Rizzo's apparent fate would be a cautionary tale for Sandy. The innocent lass's constant resistance of peer pressure would seem to have been a wise choice, after all. If she continues to maintain her conservative behavior, she'll never find herself in Rizzo's difficult position.

But the 1950s that *Grease* wanted on stage represented the first time (and not the last) that peer pressure trumped time-honored family values. The respect of your friends and acquaintances had become more important than that of your family, school, and church. Society had changed; *Grease* knew it, and told the truth.

How could any author deny that being a teenager in the fifties meant anything but following the crowd? The baby boomers and even the "silent generation" that came before had seen many a Sandy capitulate in real life; why shouldn't they see one do the same on stage?

Now that message has been spread by many a high school drama club— and middle school drama clubs, too. Almost every night of the year, some teachers and parents wish that Sandy would come to a different conclusion. She never will.

So this musical that opened downtown on Valentine's Day, 1972 wasn't quite a valentine to the fifties. When *Fiddler* was winding down to its July 1, 1972 closing, few would have believed that this little musical that had limped uptown from the Eden (now a movie multiplex) and hoped for the best at the Broadhurst would in 1979 strip it of its crown as the longest-running show in Broadway history.

That such an uncelebrated show would do it surprised Broadway. *Grease* was nominated for seven Tony Awards, and won none. Indeed, it was the first musical in the Tony-era to set the long-run record without benefit of a single Tony. *My Fair Lady*, *Hello, Dolly!*, and *Fiddler on the Roof* had all won Best Musical Tonys before it, and every long-runner that surpassed it—*A Chorus Line*, *Cats*, and *The Phantom of the Opera*—did too.

But the wildly successful film version did win two People's Choice Awards in 1979, for Favorite Musical Motion Picture and Favorite Overall Motion Picture. *Grease* gave the people what they wanted—even though there were still plenty of people who wished that people didn't want it.

Grease. February 14, 1972–April 13, 1980. 3,388 performances.

THE BIGGEST FLOP
On the Town

Too soon, too soon . . .

As we saw, producers assumed that *No, No, Nanette*'s success meant that theatergoers were getting nostalgic and wanted revivals. *On the Town* would be the next of the 112 musical revivals that would open during the remainder of the millennium.

It's the story of Chip, Ozzie, and Gaby, three sailors on a day's leave in New York. They decide to spend it looking for Miss Turnstiles, with whom Gaby has fallen in love just from seeing her poster on the subway. En route, Chip winds up with a randy cabbie named Hildy, and Ozzie meets up with dizzy anthrolopogist Claire de Lune.

Boston saw Jess Richards as Chip, Bill Gerber as Ozzie, and Kurt Peterson as Gaby. New York only saw Richards, as Remak Ramsay and Ron Husmann respectively took over the other roles. Both of them, though, were approaching the age when a person can be elected president of the United States (thirty-five), and they looked too old to be a contemporary of the much younger Richards.

It was a rich female cast. Phyllis Newman (Claire) had already won a Tony, and four other women eventually would: Donna McKechnie (Ivy), Bernadette Peters (Hildy), Marilyn Cooper (Hildy's roommate Lucy Schmeeler, a person who'd developed a cold), and Carole Bishop (later known as Kelly Bishop).

Nanette hadn't been seen in more than forty-five years, and the 1971 critics either hadn't seen it or didn't remember it that well. *On the Town* had debuted less than twenty-seven years earlier, and many critics had seen not only the original choreography by Jerome Robbins, but also his oft-revived ballet, *Fancy Free*, on which *On the Town* was based.

So the revival that opened on Halloween got a trick rather than a treat on November 1. Though it's "All Saints' Day" on the Roman Catholic calendar, the critics were no saints. "Robbins, it seems, has had the last laugh as well as the first," wrote Clive Barnes in the *Times*. "Field ran the inevitable risk of comparison and its inevitable result of coming off second-best," stated Martin Gottfried in the *Post*.

Broadway would have to wait more than twenty years before another revival outran *Nanette*'s 861 performances (*Guys and Dolls*' 1,143), but only ten weeks before one would outrun *On the Town*'s 73 (*A Funny Thing Happened*'s 156). And yet, revivals kept coming—because young, untested producers had an easier time raising money for a familiar title than for a new musical. The public would look at an ad and say with delight, "Ah! They're bringing back *Peter Pan*!"— not caring who "they" might be.

On the Town. October 31, 1971–January 1, 1972. 73 performances.

1972–1973

THE BIGGEST HIT
Pippin

Do you think advertising on TV might work?

When *Kismet* opened on December 3, 1953, New York's newspapers were on strike, and would be for the next few weeks. Of course, *Kismet*'s producer Charles Lederer was glad that no one could read Brooks Atkinson's assessment in the *Times* ("Assembled from a storehouse of spare part ... stupefying ... some of the most fearful poetry of our time") or Walter Kerr's in the *Herald-Tribune* ("Arabian nights nonsense ... would sell its soul for a joke, and the jokes should be better at that price.")

But Lederer would have liked theatergoers to know that John Chapman in the *News* called it "a gorgeous show" and that Richard Watts in the *Post* decided that Alfred Drake was "at his best in *Kismet*, which is saying a lot." (Yes; his previous musicals included *Babes in Arms, Oklahoma!*, and *Kiss Me, Kate*.)

Lederer had also been told by his pals Alfred Lunt, Lynn Fontanne, Helen Hayes, and a few others that he had a good musical on his hands. But how could he let the public know? Well, what about that newfangled invention called TV? What if he got Lunt, Fontanne, Hayes, et al. to go on live TV and say how wonderful *Kismet* was?

They did, and by the time the newspapers came back, Lederer didn't have to worry about whether anyone had seen the *Times* or the *Trib*. *Kismet* was already a hit with the public. Lederer then returned to advertising in the papers and magazines, the way everyone had done for the last century or two.

But why didn't Lederer continue with the medium that had saved him? Why didn't other Broadway producers say, "Hey, if TV worked for Charlie, it might work for me, too?"

Someone did, but not until nineteen years later: Stuart Ostrow, producer of *Pippin*.

Roger O. Hirson's book and Stephen Schwartz's score were ostensibly about the son of Charlemagne, but at heart the story of a young man who's trying to find himself and isn't having an easy time of it. Long before Princeton sought his purpose on *Avenue Q*, Pippin (John Rubenstein) went looking for his. Pippin went to war with men and to bed with women. He touched a breast, looked at the audience, and said, "I found it!" Theatergoers laughed, because older-and-wiser they knew that, no, he hadn't found what life is really all about.

But then they were awestruck at one of director-choreographer Bob Fosse's most brilliant moves: one actor held Pippin's arms, another held his legs, and they lifted him in the air. A young woman rolled underneath the spot over which he was suspended; the actors quickly thrust Pippin onto her, then immediately raised him high; the young woman rolled away, and another took her place. The same action occurred over and over again, always with a different young woman. Pippin's "making love" to these women had all the emotion of a pants-pressing machine doing its daily duty. What a unique way of showing mindless sex.

Discouraged Pippin then turned to revolutionary means to right his father's wrongs. But he was uneasy when his head wore the crown. Nothing stuck or satisfied—until he met Catherine (Jill Clayburgh), a single mother. He fell as much in love with her as he did with her son Theo (Shane Nickerson). Pippin realized that becoming a spouse and a parent may not mean a terribly exciting life, but it is a worthy and rewarding one.

So what to use on the commercial? Rubenstein singing "Corner of the Sky"? The song came to be heard at least once at every audition for every musical in the next couple of decades, but it wasn't chosen for the ad.

What about Irene Ryan doing her number, "No Time at All"? A decade earlier, Ryan had played Granny Clampett, a key character in the nation's number one TV show, *The Beverly Hillbillies*. Letting potential theatergoers know that they could see her live and on stage might be wise.

Of course, Ryan was in just one scene, playing Pippin's grandmother. Yet "No Time at All," a paean to living life to the fullest, wound up as the musical's biggest showstopper. An enormous piece of "parchment" sheet music flew in from the wings with Gregorian chant notations and lyrics so the audience could sing along. Given the tuneful nature of the song, the crowd didn't find retaining it at all difficult, even after one hearing.

Near song's end, Ryan sang, "Now I could waylay / Some aging roué / And persuade him to play in some cranny / But it's hard to believe I'm being led astray / By a man who calls me Granny." One might infer that the tale wagged the dog— that Schwartz added these lines once Ryan had been cast. After all, "cranny" and "granny" had two syllables, while in each of the previous sections, the corresponding lines had ended with one-syllable words.

But Schwartz swears,

> I wrote that before Irene joined the show. I think, though, that that's what made [director] Bob Fosse think of getting her for the role. The lyric did go through a change much earlier—where I rhymed "play on some sandbar" with "grandma." But I knew it was a really bad rhyme that I had to fix, though I liked the concept of the joke. I thought, let me do "cranny" and "granny." In fact, I almost changed it when she was cast, because I thought it was tacky. But no one else seemed to be bothered by it, so I let it go.

Finally, though, Ostrow and his advertising agencies, Ingram and Jeff Ash and Blaine-Thompson, decided to feature the work of the man who'd received the production's best reviews: Fosse. This can't have sat too well with Schwartz, for during rehearsals, Fosse had taken total control of his musical and barred Schwartz from the theater. Yet Fosse was said to have saved the show, so seeing eventual Tony winner Ben Vereen (who essentially played *Pippin*'s emcee) and two dancers offering a minute of show did cause people to rush the Imperial to see the other two hours.

The show became the biggest hit of the season—but not solely because of the commercial; there had to be quality here, or it wouldn't have happened. After all, every season since, plenty of shows have taped and aired TV commercials to no avail.

Pippin also scored because Schwartz's music was wonderfully tuneful as well as diverse. (Who expects a finale to begin in waltz tempo?) As for the book, only *Follies'* libretto has been more unjustly maligned.

But the show may be most remembered for making the television commercial an integral part of Broadway advertising. Ostrow says,

> Looking back on it now, I have mixed feelings about it. Yes, it revolutionized the way shows are marketed, but it also added a significant amount to the budget, for now you just have to have a television commercial. If you don't, you're just not an important show. The public can ignore you and not feel as if it's missing anything. And that's not right.

Pippin. October 23, 1972–June 12, 1977. 1,944 performances.

THE BIGGEST FLOP
Via Galactica

Maybe the checks didn't bounce, but the actors did.

Actually, a case can be made that the biggest flop of the season was Galt MacDermot. The composer who started out with *Hair* and later had the Tony-winning *Two Gentlemen of Verona* suddenly had two enormous flops in a nine-week span in 1972.

The first, *Dude*, reunited him with *Hair* co-librettist/lyricist Gerome Ragni, who demanded that management tear out seats from the Broadway Theatre to create "an environment" that brought tons of dirt onto the stage. The producers, though, were contractually obligated to return the house to its previous condition once the show closed. The irony was that fifteen months after *Dude* succumbed, the next tenant, an atypical production of *Candide*, tore out the seats once again to create another environmental staging (without the dirt, though).

Dude is a picaresque in which the main character is simply known as He. It was He who got slapped by the critics, who crushed the rest of the show, too. In this contest where representatives of both God and the Devil fight to get He to side with them, God is simply known as "33." Was Ragni trying to imply that God is only one-twentieth as effective as the Devil, whose number is thought to be 666?

Husband and wife Adela and Peter Holzer produced. The former later went to jail for financial improprieties. MacDermot says, "My mother, who was a very good judge of character, always said, 'I don't trust that woman.'"

Only thirty-eight days after *Dude* closed (after sixteen performances), MacDermot had an even bigger failure with *Via Galactica*. It started with a Storyteller (Irene Cara) who introduced us to the year 2972. One assumes that if Via Galactica had lasted into 1973, the year would have been changed to 2973. But the show didn't.

In 2972, Earth's citizens refer to their home planet more grandly than their 1972 audience did, namely as "the Earthly Paradise." That's because everyone born in this era is given at birth a headpiece that he must wear at all times, one that makes him happy, no matter what else happens to him.

Raul Julia left his leading role in MacDermot's *Two Gents* to play Gabriel Finn, who's driving along in his spaceship, minding his own business, when he's space-jacked. The perpetrators are Hels Mikelli (Damon Evans), a revolutionary, and his pregnant girlfriend, April Whitney. (She was played by a performer known simply as Edloe, though people who remembered her performance as Ermengarde in the more conventional Broadway production of *Hello, Dolly!* might also have remembered her full name, Edloe R. Brown, from *Dolly*'s playbill.)

Hels brings Gabriel to his home, an asteroid named Ithaca—a song calls it "The Other Side of the Sky"—where April is happy to be again, free from the conformity that the so-called Earthly Paradise demands. "Take Off Your Hat," everyone sings to Gabriel, regarding that oppressive headpiece, and he does— though he is wary of Ithaca's king, Dr. Isaacs (Keene Curtis). Something must be terribly wrong with Isaac's body, given that he is always encased in a box with only his head poking out. Or does he have a body at all?

In the film version of the 1956 comedy *The Solid Gold Cadillac*, actress Laura Partridge complains that she doesn't like to do Shakespeare because "They don't let you sit down unless you're a king." It was true of the king in *Via Galactica*, too. Dr. Isaacs was obviously a physician who couldn't cure himself.

Rather than sit, in a box or not, the king's subjects flew in weightless gravity around the stage. That is, they bounced on trampolines, an idea that came from director Peter Hall (yes, *that* Peter Hall, the head of Britain's Royal National Theatre). Hall, who started his Broadway directorial career in 1958 with a Tony nomination for *The Rope Dancers* and ended it forty-one years later with a revival of one of his greatest hits, *Amadeus*, also had spaceships fly over the audience in the perfect house for the show—the ever-so-sterile Uris Theater (now the Gershwin). *Via Galactica* was the venue's very first attraction.

A man who never comes out of his box runs the risk of being cuckolded by his wife, and, indeed, Gabriel is soon consorting with Mrs. Omaha Isaacs (Virginia Vestoff). Their eventual children decide that they'd rather be on earth. The messages—"Youth always rebels" and "Be it ever so conformist, there's no place like Earth"—were familiar, even if the setting wasn't.

Perhaps influenced by the pop opera success of *Jesus Christ Superstar*—both on record in 1969 and on Broadway in 1971—the show offered no dialogue. The credit read "Musical Book by Christopher Gore and Judith Ross." The latter was the author of the 1966, four-performance boulevard comedy *Happily Never After*. How did she get a job writing a sci-fi musical? Her husband, George W. George, was one of the show's producers. Ms. Ross had so little to put in her *Playbill* bio that she padded it with "All of Miss Ross's scenes have been set to music by Galt MacDermot, a departure from the Broadway musical tradition."

Dude at least got a semi-original cast album, recorded on MacDermot's own record label, Kilmarnock. The album proved that much of the music is terrific. The overture starts off in a genuinely majestic fashion, and the songs that follow are both tuneful and fun (though Ragni wasn't above writing a non-autobiographical song about penis size: "I'm Small").

For *Via Galactica*, though, MacDermot didn't go to the expense of hiring an entire cast to record the score, but just had one of the pit musicians, guitarist Billy Butler, record an instrumental album. Guess he would have preferred real lyrics over a "musical book by Christopher Gore and Judith Ross."

Via Galactica. November 28, 1972–December 2, 1972. 7 performances.

1973–1974

THE BIGGEST HIT
The Magic Show

When you've got magic, who needs an out-of-town tryout?

The story was simple. Meek young magician Doug (as in Henning) and his meeker assistant, Cal (Dale Soules), are looking for a showbiz break. Everybody's got to start somewhere, so they try the Hi Hat, a seedy club in Passaic, New Jersey.

Cal wishes that Doug would give her a break, too, for she's in love with him. When Doug is advised to get a beautiful assistant, Cal tarts herself up, and is devastated when Doug solves the problem by conjuring up the exotic Charmin (Anita Morris, wife of the show's director Grover Dale).

The book by Bob Randall included such well-worn sentiments as "Believe in yourself" as well as a career-vs.-love subplot and a rival magician, Feldman (David Ogden Stiers), who through his sheer incompetence served only to bolster Doug's image. Of course all ended happily, with both Doug and Cal achieveing both romantic and professional success.

Henning had a pencil-thin body and slightly thicker mustache. What he didn't have was any kind of singing voice. Composer-lyricist Stephen Schwartz purposely wrote around him, creating ten songs in which Henning didn't open his mouth. So everyone else in the company sang the opening number, "Up to His Old Tricks," which introduced the audience to "Doug, the magic man."

Meek Cal sang "Lion Tamer," in which she longed to be more than she was, and "West End Avenue," which became a cabaret staple for the rest of the decade. In "Style," the tuxedoed Feldman told the blue-jeaned Henning that he had to sharpen his look.

Henning did deliver dialogue, though rather less subtly than we're used to seeing in the lowest levels of community theater. His overdone and *actory* reactions to every stage moment, however, didn't stop the Tony committee from giving him a nomination as Best Featured (that's debatable) Actor (that's more debatable) in a Musical.

Why? His magic, of course. Henning could put a man on a motorcycle in a large box, and seconds later make both appear somewhere else on stage. He got Cal to float on jets of water jutting out of the floor and kept her in suspended non-animation—then trumped himself by putting Cal in a body bag, lockeing her in a trunk, and, only a few seconds later, trading places with her—somehow changing his clothes in the process. And, oh yes, he made an elephant disappear from the stage, too.

And that's why *The Magic Show* ran almost five years. When it closed, only seven musicals had had longer Broadway runs: *Fiddler, Dolly, My Fair Lady, La Mancha, Oklahoma!,* Schwartz's own *Pippin,* and *South Pacific.* Had *The Magic Show* played a little more than three more weeks, it would have bested the last two, too.

By now, the baby boomers who had dropped in to see *Hair* were paying a bit more attention to Broadway. Some of them had even given birth to young children who might enjoy a magic show. If there were good songs attached (there were), who cared if the story was formulaic (it was)?

The Magic Show is the first of the hits in this book to have succeeded without the benefit of a pre-Broadway tryout in some far-off city. Two weeks of preview preceded the opening. Other producers sure took note of that.

What's more, of the 137 musicals that opened on Broadway during the 1970s, *The Magic Show* was one of the mere even dozen that were filmed. While half the Tony-winning musicals of the seventies weren't made into movies, *The Magic Show*, which couldn't even get a Best Musical nomination, was.

At least in a manner of speaking. A performance at the Queen Elizabeth Theatre in Toronto was filmed in 1981. It shows all too well Henning's embarrassing acting limitations, but it also beautifully displays his skill—if, of course, you can believe what's stated at the very start of the film: "All the magical effects and illusions in this motion picture were filmed in front of a live theatre audience. No trick photography or special editing has been used to modify, in any way, the illusions performed in this film."

Those who saw *The Magic Show* on stage would assure you that the claim was utterly true.

The Magic Show. May 24, 1974–December 31, 1978. 1,920 performances

The Biggest Flop
Rachael Lily Rosenbloom (and Don't You Ever Forget It)

Yesterday's disaster might be today's hit.

While Grover Dale and Anita Morris were involved with the biggest hit of the season, midway through the same semester they were involved in the biggest flop of the season: *Rachael Lily Rosenbloom (and Don't You* Ever *Forget It)*.

Paul Jabara, who cowrote the book, music, and lyrics, was twenty-five years old. Nevertheless, he was a Broadway performing veteran, having appeared in *Hair* in 1968. He'd had West End experience, too, playing King Herod in the London *Jesus Christ Superstar.* There he became friendly with Superstar's producer, Robert Stigwood, convinced him to mount the world's first disco musical.

Rachael Lily's curtain rose on the Forty-sixth Annual Academy Awards, which would actually be held on April 2, 1974, a date that *Rachael Lily* never lived to see.

The eponymous Ms. Rosenbloom (Ellen Greene) is dressed to kill, though before we can discover for which award she's been nominated, we flash back to a scene that the program describes as taking place at "Brooklyn garbage cans." Rachel, not yet boasting a second "a" in her name, writes a fan letter ("Dear Miss Streisand") to her favorite star from her own hometown. Rachel informs the star that she'll pay tribute to her by taking the "a" that Streisand dropped from "Barbara" and adding it to hers.

(Streisand doesn't answer.)

Rachael's life isn't at A-level, though, not with her job at the Fulton Fish Market. She dreams of having her own radio show, and soon takes off for Hollywood, the site of so many fantasies—and of real-life experiences that would have been better left to fantasy. Nearly naked chorus boys paid tribute to Rachael, who becomes a gossip columnist (as noted in the song "Rona, Mona and Me," the first two names referencing the real-life Rona Barrett and Mona Ferrett, the animated character who spoofed her.)

There was plenty of lamé, and plenty that was lame. Says Greene, "They gave me forty pages of changes overnight, every night. I was young and didn't know enough to be scared."

Director Ron Link, on the other hand, did. He was replaced by Tom Eyen, best known as the author of *The Dirtiest Show in Town.*

Hits don't have playbills that say both "Choreography by Tony Stevens" and "Choreography supervised by Grover Dale." (The latter supplanted the former, and was responsible for the first-act closer in which the "Dykettes" kill a woman they never liked—the aforementioned Anita Morris).

With such song titles as "Seduction Samba," "Rachael Gives the Dish," "Cobra Woman," and the oxymoronic (and moronic) "Silver Diamond Rhinestone Glasses," *Rachael* was the first out-and-out gay Broadway campfest. In 1973, though, that style of entertainment was too avant-garde for the still-conventional theatergoer. Of course, that the show was hard to follow and often made little sense didn't help. Says Kelly (then Carole) Bishop:

> What I remember most were all the drugs that were circulating. I was standing in a beautiful evening gown from Neiman-Marcus waiting for the curtain to go up, and the stage manager ran out and threw a popper out my nose. I mean, I'm a party girl, but I was thinking, "What is this? I don't believe it." I never saw so many drugs around—not to mention apricot brandy, which seemed to be at every lunch hour.
>
> I knew before we started that this would be my last chorus job, and if I hadn't known it, I would have known it soon after we started rehearsals. That it was such a terrible show made it worse. But we did have huge audiences, because people wanted to come and laugh at us, and just couldn't stay away.

Nevertheless, Stigwood and his coproducer, music legend Ahmet Ertegun, knew that critics could keep people away easily enough. They closed the show during previews at a $500,000 loss.

Recalls Greene, "I concentrated so much on what I was doing, I didn't even know *Rachael* was closing. Everyone else did. Everyone in the audience did, too. I was told during the middle of our last performance."

Better fates were in store for many. In addition to Dale and Morris finding themselves in a smash by season's end, Greene would have a triumph in both the stage and film versions of *Little Shop of Horrors*. Tom Eyen would write the book and lyrics to *Dreamgirls*.

And while Rachael fictitiously attended the Forty-sixth Annual Academy Awards, Jabara was himself at the Fifty-first, where he received a Best Song Oscar for "Last Dance." Later that year, he and "Last Dance" would win for Best Rhythm and Blues Song at the Twenty-first Annual Grammys, too. The final irony: he would work with his idol Streisand as a coproducer of her *Broadway Album*.

But long before any of that happened, Stevens and his assistant Michon Peacock, who also danced in the show, called director-choreographer Michael Bennett. They wanted to meet and talk about the frustrating lives that dancers lead. The following month, Bennett invited them and other dancers, including some *Rachael* cast members, to chat. Among them were Bishop, Wayne Cilento, and Thomas Walsh—who would wind up in a Bennett show that would be the biggest hit of the 1975–1976 season.

The irony is that *Rachael* may have been ahead of its time. Today, the So-Bad-It's-Good Musical is a genuine genre, thanks to the success of *The Rocky Horror Picture Show* and *Little Shop of Horrors*. Broadway campfests have included *Monty Python's Spamalot*, *Xanadu*, and *Young Frankenstein*, though off-Broadway has played host to many more, from *Evil Dead: The Musical* to *Zombie Prom*, not to be confused with *Zombies from the Beyond*.

Don't be surprised if *Rachael* someday gets another chance.

Rachael Lily Rosenbloom (and Don't You Ever Forget It). November 26, 1973–December 1, 1973. Seven previews.

1974–1975

The Biggest Hit
The Wiz

Add black to the colors of the rainbow.

October 20, 1974. The Mechanic Theater, Baltimore. Director Gilbert Moses III comes out to make a pre-curtain speech, which is never a good sign. He apologizes for the not-yet-ready show, noting that one actor has taken ill, another has been replaced, and there was no time for a technical rehearsal.

The show has a novice bookwriter in William F. Brown, and an equally inexperienced songwriter in Charlie Smalls. Producer Ken Harper was recently a program affairs director at a radio station. Hence, the crowd is not optimistic. Moses senses that, and crows, "But some day, you'll brag that you were here this night."

Many of those people probably did just that, and are still bragging today that they were at the world premiere of *The Wiz*—an urban black twist on *The Wizard of Oz*.

But the show that night in Baltimore turned out to be far worse than Moses had predicted. There was a surfeit of corny jokes. When Dorothy (Stephanie Mills) arrived in Oz, she was told that she was talking to the Munchkins. "But they're doughnuts," she said. When the Wicked Witch of the West, here named Evillene (Mabel King), said, "A plague on both your houses!" an underling cried, "Not my summer place, too!"

A song called "Which Where, Which What, Which Why?" for the Good Witch (here named Addaperle; Clarice Taylor) was awful. As the Scarecrow, TV personality Stu Gilliam merely went through the motions. Butterfly McQueen—Prissy of *Gone with the Wind* fame—played the Queen of the Field Mice, and seemed somewhere between intoxicated and hung over.

Of course what everyone wanted to know was what Smalls would do with the scene where Judy Garland sang "Over the Rainbow." How could he hope to come up with what is often cited as the best song to ever grace a musical motion picture?

Smalls solved the problem by writing no song at all for that moment. One could argue that none is necessary, for many connected with *The Wizard of Oz* in 1939 thought the number extraneous. There was quite a debate back then on whether or not it should stay in the picture.

The Wiz did lose a lot by not bringing in its Wicked Witch until the top of act 2. Unlike the film, where the foursome is very much aware of the power and wrath of their enemy, Dorothy, the Scarecrow, the Tin Man (Tiger Haynes), and the Cowardly Lion (Ted Ross) have no idea what they're up against, and that gives them less to fear—and less for the actors to play.

Despite Moses' optimism, he was soon fired. Geoffrey Holder, the show's costume designer, took over the direction. He eliminated McQueen's role, but allowed her to stay on and understudy Addaperle. He did, however, retain the five field mice—including Phylicia Ayres-Allen, who later changed her last name when she married footballer Ahmad Rashad.

Gilliam, certain that he was in a titanic failure, asked to be released, and Holder agreed, promoting seventeen-year-old understudy Hinton Battle to Scarecrow status. (Little did anyone know that between 1981 and 1991, Battle would win three Tonys as Best Featured Actor in a Musical.) Last but hardly least, Megs, playing the demanding role of Toto, was replaced by Nancy.

After an engagement in Detroit, *The Wiz* came to New York, got decent enough reviews, and, in a weak season, went on to win a Tony and run more than four years.

Some of the success was the result of a term that would show up more and more as the decades continued: "brand-name recognition" of a beloved film. There was a new generation that was coming to the theater, people who didn't want to be challenged by the way musicals—especially Stephen Sondheim's—were going.

Ironically enough, Sondheim would be a great champion of *The Wiz* in multiple published interviews. Who knows how many super-sophisticated musical theater enthusiasts attended *The Wiz* solely on his say-so?

The Wiz also made substantial inroads in getting the black audience to the musical theater. That had been happening slowly, but surely, by way of previous seasons' *Purlie*; *Don't Bother Me, I Can't Cope*; *Don't Play Us Cheap*; and *Ain't Supposed to Die a Natural Death*. But none did it as well as the household-name sensation of *The Wiz*.

The Wiz. January 5, 1975–January 28, 1979. 1,672 performances.

THE BIGGEST FLOP
Good News

W. C. Fields was right about working with animals.

How tempting to choose the show that would run 2,920 performances in London but could only muster 45 here. But the modest musical known as *The Rocky Horror Show* (with no one famous connected with it) wasn't expected to take Broadway by storm, anyway. The property's fame would come instead from midnight showings of the film version.

So instead let's go to December 15, 1973, at the Colonial Theatre, Boston. *Good News*, a revisal of the 1927 smash hit about college life, *was* expected to succeed all over again. First off, there's that terrific DeSylva-Brown-Henderson score, with such hit songs as "Good News," "Lucky in Love," "Just Imagine," "The Best Things in Life Are Free," and "The Varsity Drag." Plus, Harry Rigby—the producer who'd initiated the wildly successful *No, No, Nanette* revisal and produced the moderately successful *Irene* revisal—made sure that score was buttressed with more of the trio's hits, including "Button Up Your Overcoat," "Life Is Just a Bowl of Cherries," "You're the Cream in My Coffee," and "Keep Your Sunny Side Up." All great songs.

Truth to tell, stars Alice Faye and John Payne, exhumed from the entertainment industry's mothballs, were uncomfortable in their roles as, respectively, an astronomy professor and a football coach. Stubby Kaye fared better as the coach's assistant.

But, oh, that young cast cutting up behind them! There was a winning Wayne Bryan as Bobby, the young man on whom Babe (a sensational Barbara Lail) had set her sights—though he was afraid of her old boyfriend, a linebacker (a delightfully dumb Joseph Burke) who was named Beef for a reason. Charming Scott Stevensen played Tom, the football hero who was happy that he was going to land rich girl Pat (a delicious Jana Robbins) if Tait College won the big football game (which of course it did). And considering that this Boston preview was set to kick off a year-long road tour before the production settled into the St. James, there was ample time for Faye and Payne to get comfortable.

Good News played its year-long run on the road, came in to town, and bombed at the St. James. How did it happen?

Bryan feels that the show reached its apex when it played San Francisco in May 1974, partly because San Franciscans welcomed Faye and Payne, who had starred in the 1943 film *Hello, Frisco, Hello*. But it's a long, long time from May to December, and by the time *Good News* got to the St. James, it was limping. Director Abe Burrows and choreographer Donald Saddler were gone; replacing them to do both jobs was Michael Kidd, who, ironically enough, had been choreographer to director Burrows on the original *Guys and Dolls*.

But Rigby was still confident, because he had a good idea: a running joke for Kaye that had him perpetually searching for the Tait team mascot. He would come in first with a duck, then later a skunk, and later still a llama, all of which would be rejected. But, at the very end of the show, the entire cast would run in, screaming with fear, "Mad elephant! Mad elephant!" not understanding that it had just met the team's new mascot. Then Kaye would triumphantly bring in the pachyderm and assuage everyone's fears before ending the show with a reprise of the show's title tune.

Bryan remembers Rigby saying with excitement, "Broadway hasn't seen a live elephant since 1935, when *Jumbo* opened! The audience is going to go crayyyyyy-zeee!" (By the way, Bryan does a wonderful imitation of Rigby's squeaky voice. As with Carol Channing—whom, incidentally, Rigby sounded quite a bit like—anyone quoting Harry Rigby tries to reproduce the *sound* of the words as well as the sense.)

Of course, getting all these aforementioned animals wasn't easy, but luckily a woman who kept such creatures was found in the wilds of New Jersey. "All I remember," Bryan says, "is that her name was Bunny and she was six months pregnant at the time."

As the animals' first performance approached, Bunny brought them all to the theater, except the elephant, who, she explained, had suddenly fallen ill. Still, the dialogue had been written and rehearsed, so it was put in, even though there wasn't yet an elephant on the premises to make the audience go "crayyyyyy-zeee!" The performers were going crayyyyyy-zeee, though, because, as Bryan recalls, "backstage was starting to smell like a carnival, and the llama just wouldn't stop spitting at us."

Some days later, the elusive elephant was deemed fit for both travel and performance. But Kaye had had no time to work with him. The decision was reluctantly made to have Bunny bring on the elephant. But in what would she be costumed? Bunny blithely offered the outfit she used to wear when she worked for Ringling Brothers. With time a-wastin' and no money for a new costume in the now well-over-budget production, everyone reluctantly agreed that that Bunny's duds would have to do.

There was a setback, though, when the elephant arrived and Bunny had to admit that on the trip in, the poor thing had suffered from diarrhea. Hence, Bunny had to spend much of the performance not preparing for her big entrance or getting into her costume, but cleaning off the other animals who'd been dirtied during their ride into town.

Finally, though, the big moment came when the chorus rushed in from the wings, screaming for their lives, "Mad elephant! Mad elephant!" And then, Bryan remembers, from offstage, everyone heard a painfully slow *thunk . . . thunk . . . thunk . . . thunk . . . thunk.*

Finally, out came Bunny in her Ringling suit, which wasn't zipped all the way up her back because she was so heavy with child. Still, she pulled on the rope, and finally (*thunk . . . thunk . . . thunk . . . thunk . . . thunk . . .*) the elephant lumbered on—in chains, which didn't make it seem like such a "mad" elephant. Indeed, its appearance was more sad than spontaneous.

Thunk . . . thunk . . . thunk . . . thunk . . . thunk.

Finally, Bunny and the beast reached center stage. Bunny reached into a handbag that looked awfully 1974 for a show set in the thirties, found a peanut, and fed the treat to the elephant, who dutifully ate it. Once that was done, *thunk . . . thunk . . . thunk . . . thunk . . . thunk,* until it was offstage.

"And," said Bryan, "the audience didn't go 'crayyyyyy-zeee,' but just sat there in stunned silence—the type of silence that's far more silent than silence."

After one more performance, Bunny and her charges were fired. Without them, *Good News* finally opened at the St. James and met its biggest-flop-of-the-season fate.

Good News. December 23, 1974–January 4, 1975. 16 performances.

1975–1976

THE BIGGEST HIT
A Chorus Line

A hit from a mere workshop.

When those who cherish *A Chorus Line* reminisce about the show, they often first think not of a musical sequence, but of a non-musical moment.

It involved Paul (Sammy Williams), the only one of the seventeen on the line who did not have a song or even a substantial segment of one to call his own. Paul did, though, have his own monologue while no one else was on stage.

He told the heart-wrenching story of growing up gay, feeling alienated, and being dismissed even by school officials who'd have found life easier if he'd dropped out. Soon Paul was working as a female impersonator at a seedy drag club. One night, his parents discovered him just before he went on stage. To his surprise, his father expressed a sentiment of love he'd never before delivered.

That monologue is one reason why many young teenage boys today don't look in the mirror and say, as Paul did, "You're fourteen and you're a faggot." Closeted gays who attended from 1975 to 1990 came away with more courage after seeing that they weren't alone in the world. Today, A Chorus Line reminds us that times have changed, and that's cause for celebration.

But there was another moment in A Chorus Line—a much subtler one—that also helped pave the way for gay acceptance. It occurred during the monologue delivered by Gregory Gardner (née Sidney Kenneth Beckenstein, and played by Michel Stuart). He told of adolescent angst and erections while making out with a girl—a scenario the straight men in the audience seemed to relate to and enjoy.

By the time Gardner told the audience he was gay, it was too late for the homophobes to turn against him. They'd already come to like him, and now they couldn't go back on that just because of his sexuality, could they?

A Chorus Line represented Michael Bennett's third professional engagement at the Shubert Theater. He'd been Dancer in the flops Here's Love (1963) and Bajour (1964). But in 1975, his billing was markedly different: he'd "conceived, choreographed, and directed" one of Broadway's greatest artistic and commercial successes. He certainly had Joseph Papp to thank, for the famed producer gave him workshop space and plenty of encouragement.

Because Chorus Line composer Marvin Hamlisch had been the dance arranger on Henry, Sweet Henry (1967), which Bennett had choreographed, many assume that the two met there. Actually, they'd met a year earlier, after Hamlisch saw A Joyful Noise and was impressed with Bennett's choreography. (So was the Tony nominating committee; it gave Bennett a nomination, a pretty nice compliment for a show that ran twelve performances.) Hamlisch says, "After seeing Michael's work on that show, I put his name in my address book, not under 'M' or 'B,' but 'G' for 'genius.'"

And yet, Bennett fired Hamlisch from Chorus Line when the composer questioned his judgment one time too many. "And wouldn't you know," said Hamlisch, "[his lyricist] Ed Kleban stepped right up and said he'd be happy to write the music for the show, too."

Musicals about show business have traditionally had a tough time. So why did A Chorus Line become a record setter? Because it wasn't about becoming a star, but just getting a job— which everyone can relate to. This very day, hundreds of thousands of people will go on job interviews that have nothing to do with dancing, but throughout the process, they'll be thinking, "God, I hope I get it," "God, I really blew it," or "God, I think I got it."

Four "boys" and four "girls" were what director Zach (Robert LuPone) had to choose for his chorus. During previews at the Newman Theatre downtown, Bennett famously had Zach reject Cassie (Donna McKechnie), his old girlfriend. He later relented, and had Zach hire her.

Says McKechnie,

Cassie's getting the job made an enormous difference to me. Her rejection was so close to the bone to all the rejections I'd ever experienced. I felt utterly defeated, as if I'd immediately have to go to therapy. I tried to think that Cassie would be heroic and brave and just go audition for another show, but it was much easier getting chosen. It also made me happier for Cassie and Zach. They may not have the relationship they had before, but now that he's chosen her and they'll be doing the show together, they might have a friendship, or at least a good working relationship.

Soon after opening on Broadway, McKechnie was on the cover of *Newsweek*. "I got all this attention, and some cast members expressed some bitterness and jealousy over it," she says. "What a shame, I thought. Here's the most important show in my whole career and I can't say it was a great experience. But when I returned to the show eleven years later, it *was* great. The cast was entirely new, and they loved doing it with me."

Cassie's getting chosen meant someone else wouldn't be chosen. Says Carole (Kelly) Bishop, the original Sheila,

At the workshops, Michael would sometimes play Zach. When he did, he'd choose different people for the chorus each time. That way, he'd keep us on edge, and we wouldn't get complacent that we knew in advance that we'd be chosen and somehow telegraph that to the audience. And do you know that that stinker never chose me any time he played Zach? Not once! That was his way to zing me. But he did give me one great moment.

Bishop means at the very end of the show, after Zach makes his eight choices, and the other nine auditioners leave. Sheila walks off, only to stop and turn, ready to tell him a thing or two—before she thinks twice, turns again, and walks off silently.

Says Bishop,

Cassie originally had that moment, when Zach didn't give her the part. Back then, I'd cross to get my bag stage left, and head up to the diagonal in the upper right, as she was standing there staring at Zach. I'd then walk up and put my arm around her, and take her with me. But then one day Michael came in and said, "Okay, as of tonight, Donna's gonna get the job, so Kelly, after you cross and get your bag, go up where Donna was, stop, turn around, and then leave."

Musical theater mavens might assume that Bennett would have called her Carole, not Kelly, for she was born Carole Bishop; not until *Chorus Line* was up and running on Broadway did she change her name to Kelly.

"Michael just liked calling me Kelly, and did it early on," she says.

And since he was God, everyone in the production started calling me Kelly, too. The thing was, that year at the Tonys, when they announced that the winner was Kelly Bishop, a lot of people who know me were really upset, because they thought the presenter had got my name wrong.

A Chorus Line was influential, too, for Bennett had developed his show, not through out-of-town tryouts or previews, but through two workshops, where authors could experiment without the pressure of critics or audiences. As we'll see in the seasons to come, the workshop system would have its assets and liabilities.

But there were no liabilities here. On September 29, 1983, *A Chorus Line* broke the long-run record set by *Grease*, playing performance 3,389. Many Broadway fans breathed a sigh of relief. For almost four years, they'd been embarrassed that a spoof had held the title; before that, only quality works had.

And yet, both *Grease* and *A Chorus Line* did have one odd thing in common: Both mentioned Troy Donahue (1936–2001), a teen heartthrob of the late fifties and early sixties. When one adds in Broadway revivals, *Grease* wound up mentioning his name ("As for you, Troy Donahue") 5,447 times, while *A Chorus Line* ("If Troy Donahue can be a movie star, then I can be a movie star") cited him 6,896 times. Those 12,343 mentions have kept alive the name of this minor actor who would otherwise now be forgotten.

In *Chorus Line*'s 2006 Broadway revival, the passing of time gave some of bookwriters James Kirkwood and Nikolas Dante's lines newly weighted meanings. "There's no work anymore," and "They're not doing big musicals like they used to" were true in 1975—but truer still in 2006. At least this revival had exactly the same number of people in the cast—twenty-six—as it originally had.

When director Zach announced that the unnamed musical for which these people have been auditioning would have "a two-month out-of-town tryout," that practice was all but gone in 1975, let alone in 2006. Paul says he and his family went to "Forty-second Street, and we'd come out of one movie and go to another and another movie." They could still do that today—though now they wouldn't even have to leave the building, what with the multiplexes there. There's a description of a television set as "one of those great big things." Today, when a TV is "big," we're talking about the sheer size of the screen, while in those days, we'd have been referring to the gargantuan cabinet that contained all that complicated machinery.

If the show had been written in the twenty-first century, a few seconds could be shaved off its running time, for the assistant director wouldn't need to run off stage to find a phone and call that doctor when Paul injures himself; everyone would immediately pull a cell phone from his dance bag.

Some of the lines show how some things still haven't changed for the better. There's poignancy in Mike's statement, "We're no better off than athletes," for today, actors are of course far worse off than athletes. When *A Chorus Line* originally opened, the average baseball player's salary was $44,700. It's now $2.82 million. In fact, the financial dam broke open for baseball players in 1975, when the show debuted; that's when courts handed down the ruling that players need not be bound by trades, and could be free agents.

Safe to say and sad to say, the average Broadway dancer's salary has not remotely kept pace.

A Chorus Line. July 25, 1975–April 28, 1990. 6,138 performances.

THE BIGGEST FLOP
1600 Pennsylvania Avenue

Not quite the expected bicentennial celebration.

With America's bicentennial coming up, it just had to be celebrated through a quintessentially American art form: the musical. Alan Jay Lerner had an idea for one, and sought as his collaborator America's greatest living composer: Leonard Bernstein.

Bernstein had been away from Broadway for almost two decades, since 1957, when *Candide* was closing and *West Side Story* was opening. After that, he made some attempts to musicalize *The Skin of Our Teeth* and Brecht's *The Exception and the Rule*, but nothing came of them.

Lerner got Bernstein to agree, *and* got Coca-Cola, virtually America's official drink, to put up the money for what would become *1600 Pennsylvania Avenue*— a look at the first one hundred years of the White House (1800–1900).

That Lerner and Bernstein had very different work habits didn't help," says Erik Haagensen, who was hired by the Bernstein estate in 1995 to reconstruct the show for a concert reading. "I've been told that they didn't even write the show while in the same room. Lerner would be on Long Island and Bernstein would be in Fairfield, Connecticut. Helicopters would fly over Long Island Sound and take the material back and forth to each of them."

Not unlike the then-popular PBS series *Upstairs, Downstairs* (1971–75)—

which told of an upper-crust family as well as its servants—*1600* would tell of the presidents (Ken Howard) and their first ladies (Patricia Routledge) from 1800 to 1900, as well as their black servants Lud (Gilbert Price) and Seena (Emily Yancy),who'd eventually marry. Though the most famous White House residents would come and go, the symbolic Lud and Seena would always be the same servants (and much the same age) throughout the century. However, we'd first meet Lud as a child (Guy Costley), when Mrs. Adams sang to him, "Take Care of This House." Lud promised her that he always would.

There was another dimension to the show as well: Howard, Routledge, Price, and Yancy were first and foremost established to be playing *performers* who were hired to enact the story of the White House. This gave the show an extra dimension—one that many felt made matters more confusing.

Says Haagensen

> The show was to open with a song called "Me." The white actor playing the presidents and the black actor playing Lud argued that the show was "all about me." In another song called "What Happened?" the chorus eventually responded with, "We're here to polish a play / Not to fix the whole U.S.A."
>
> But Lud and Seena were intended to be the leads. The question is, will Lud and Seena decide to stay in the White House, or will they go? Will they continue to pursue the promise of America, or will they say that that promise has been betrayed and abandoned?

So *1600* would comment on race relations in America—which might make it less of a bicentennial celebration, mightn't it?

And if indeed Lud and Seena were the leads, the title should have reflected that; *1600 Pennsylvania Avenue* indicates that we're going to learn about the presidents and (perhaps) their wives.

Still, hopes were high for *1600*. How fitting that it would play the three cities that had served as the nation's capital: first Philadelphia, then Washington, and finally, New York. But just as New York enjoyed the shortest period as the nation's capital, *1600* experienced fewer performances on Broadway than it did in the two other cities.

Of all the dropped songs Haagensen found, two in the second act fascinated him the most. "First came 'American Dreaming,' which was the nervous breakdown of the actor who's been portraying Lud," he says. "Portraying him has upset him more and more, because he feels he's playing an Uncle Tom. So he refuses to go on with the show. But both actors become disgusted with the content of the play. At the end, they each sing, 'Spotlight! Spotlight! Take it away from me!'"

That song at least made it to Washington. But Haagensen found a crucial piece of music that never even made it into rehearsal: the "switch scene," which was almost a quarter of an hour long.

Says Haagensen,

> The actor playing Lud looked at his understudy and said, "I want to play your role." So the understudy took over as Lud, thus freeing the actor who had been playing him to leave the White House as a free black. After he then went off to establish himself successfully in business, he returned and lorded it over the people still working in the White House. He was very cynical, for while he'd taken advantage of the American system, he hated America. That's quite a change from the person who'd had "Take Care of This House" sung to him as a child, and had always clung to that.
>
> But eventually he stopped this scene and said, "I can't do this." The actress playing Seena then responded with a song called "Can You Love?"—saying that one must love, no matter what he's faced with, and that's the best way to deal with it. That was to be the climax of the show, and it was musically adventurous.

But audiences might have been flummoxed by the sheer scope of the music— or that the issues facing a black man in America might have been too cutting for predominantly white Broadway audiences.

What was added during the Philadelphia run was a stirring new opening number called "Rehearse!" "It's a catchy tune, but it's wrong emotionally for what the show was supposed to be," says Haagensen. "It suggests the show will be cheerful, when it really was a meditation on important issues about America."

"Rehearse" also shows that Lerner was acknowledging that *1600* had its own problems. For the cast sang straight out to us, "Rehearse and don't stop / And if we do and if we don't drop / it's gonna be great!"

It wasn't. Bernstein was especially humiliated by the quick failure. While Capitol Records had been signed to record the cast album, he wouldn't allow it. But in 2000, ten years after Bernstein's death, his estate approved an abridged version of the score. Called *White House Cantata* and released on the classical label Deutsche Grammophon, it was a too-operatic rendition with most of the political material conspicuously missing.

But of course it included "Duet for One," which many of *1600*'s attendees still speak of more than a third of a century later. It took place at the 1877 inauguration, where two First Ladies—the outgoing Julia Grant and the incoming Lucy Hayes—showed that they didn't much like each other. As Routledge went from Mrs. Grant to Mrs. Hayes and back again, she flipped a funny little headpiece to differentiate the two. Routledge delivered this tour de force with great force—not to mention charm, vivacity, and wit.

Broadway has never seen her again. And to think that her first Broadway musical, *Darling of the Day* (1968), was written by the composer of *Gypsy* and the lyricist of *Finian's Rainbow*, and that this, her next one, was written by the composer of *West Side Story* and the lyricist of *My Fair Lady*—and still she only managed runs that averaged 20.5 performances.

Says David Patrick Stearns, music critic for the *Philadelphia Inquirer*, "One time I was talking to Bernstein, and he told me that he had finally figured out a solution to the show and written it on the back of an envelope. He went on to other things—and then, when he wanted to revisit *1600*, he couldn't find the envelope or remember what the solution was."

1600 Pennsylvania Avenue. May 4–8, 1976. 7 performances.

1976–1977

The Biggest Hit
Annie

Caring deeply for a comic strip character.

Some would argue that the biggest hit of the season was the revival of *Oh! Calcutta!* After all, 5,959 performances, even at the 572-seat Edison Theatre, was impressive. But it was a spoken-word revue with an occasional song, so we can't call it a genuine musical.

Running less than half as long—but a true Broadway musical that was a hot ticket (which *Oh! Calcutta!* never was)—was *Annie*.

It was the brainchild of Martin Charnin, who, as an actor, originated the role of Jet "Big Deal" in *West Side Story*. Is there a possibility that hearing two words in "Gee, Officer Krupke" night after night planted a seed in Charnin's head that would grow to fruition almost two decades later?

The words? "Leaping lizards"—the expression that comic strip heroine Little Orphan Annie made famous.

Nevertheless, after Charnin brought on Thomas Meehan to write the book, they both decided that they would veer from Harold Gray's 1924–1968 comic strip—and not just because Gray hated Franklin D. Roosevelt. Little Orphan Annie's Daddy Warbucks had had a serious (and right-wing political) slant and didn't offer much emotion. So Charnin and Meehan would supply that.

Annie did what an audience didn't expect it to do: Care—and care deeply. Who couldn't get emotionally involved with a little girl who desperately wanted to find her parents?

To escape the fury of Miss Hannigan (Dorothy Loudon), Annie (Andrea

McArdle) takes her chance when Grace Farrell (Sandy Faison), secretary to millionaire Oliver Warbucks (Reid Shelton), shows up at an orphanage. Grace has come to take home a young boy whom Warbucks will entertain during the Christmas holidays, but Annie convinces her that a girl will do. Annie is right; soon Warbucks comes to love her and wants to adopt her. What's surprising is that Annie refuses his offer; she's still resolute on finding her real parents.

That leads to one of the show's most poignant moments, one that is sadly missing from the cast album. After Daddy Warbucks promises Annie that "You Won't Be an Orphan for Long," the stirring march stops abruptly as Warbucks then softly sings his interior thoughts: "What a thing to occur / finding them / losing her." That he's willing to give her up so that she could be happy makes us love him, too.

Of course, it all ended happily, with good songs, strong emotion, and one good in-joke. Annie's second act opens with a radio show on which "the lovely Boylan Sisters" appear; in the thirties, NBC sponsored the Moylan Sisters— Marianne Moylan, all of seven, and Peggy Joan Moylan, merely five.

Charnin claims that the first lyric he wrote was "The sun'll come out tomorrow." But when Charles Strouse is involved, there's a good chance the music came first, for of all the Broadway songsmiths, Strouse is probably the one who recycles his songs most frequently. The melody he eventually used was based on a theme he'd written for a TV special. In addition, "Something Was Missing," the waltz in which Daddy Warbucks expresses his love for his stepdaughter-to-be, was originally the razzmatazz, up-tempo "You Rat, You," from the 1969 film *The Night They Raided Minsky's*.

As for character names, we may infer that at least two came before the music—Drake, the butler, and Mrs. Pugh, the maid—for Charnin wrote, "When you wake / ring for Drake / Drake will bring your tray" as well as "When you're through / Mrs. Pugh / comes to take it away."

Charnin directed, too. Many assumed that once Mike Nichols saw the tryout at Goodspeed and became lead producer, he took over. "No," says Stuart Ostrow. "I'm the one who talked (coproducer) Roger Stevens out of replacing Charnin with Nichols."

Though Loudon deservedly won the Tony for playing the dipsomaniac (and just plain maniacal) orphanage leader Miss Hannigan, thirteen-year-old McArdle dazzled in the title role. There have been thousands of Annies since, but McArdle had to be the first kid to get it right—after being promoted from her role as an orphan named Pepper when the original Annie, Kristin Vigard, didn't work out. McArdle showed Annie's spunk without being obnoxious, and displayed the character's vulnerability without being cloying.

Much as Peter Stone saved a Ben Franklin witticism for late in the show, Meehan didn't use "leaping lizards" until deep in the second act, by which point audiences had forgotten about it. If he'd put it in one of Annie's first speeches—as less gifted writers would have done in order to quickly establish her character—crowds would have groaned.

Annie won the Tony, Drama Desk, and New York Drama Critics Circle Awards for Best Musical, but it was not awarded that prize by the Outer Critics Circle (whose members write in New Jersey, Connecticut, and points beyond). In fact, the Outer Critics Circle declined to choose a Best Musical winner that year, but *Annie* did win that organization's award as "Most Refreshing Musical." That must have been a first, and may well be a last.

With such a reception, the vertical sign that sat atop the Alvin's marquee was changed from A-L-V-I-N to A-N-N-I-E. Throughout the six-year run, no one seemed to notice and/or mind that the action takes place in only two weeks' time. That's a very short span for a man to decide that he loves a little girl he's just barely met.

And who would have guessed that fifteen years after the closing, "It's the Hard Knock Life" would become a popular rap song? Singer Jay-Z was watching the movie version of *Annie* and was "mesmerized" (his word) by the orphans' gritty ability to withstand the rigors of their life. He could relate to that, and Messrs. Strouse and Charnin became the richer for it. (But can you imagine a rap singer sitting down to watch *Annie* in the first place?)

In 2006, Showtime aired *Life After Annie*, a documentary in which ex–cast members reminisced about playing Annie or other orphans on Broadway or on national tours. During the final credits, audiences were taken to an *Annie* reunion, where each of these now-grown women threw themselves on the floor and once again sang "It's the Hard Knock Life." Then they got up, joined arms, and performed "You're Never Fully Dressed Without a Smile."

In other words, these women were doing their own version of "Who's That Woman?" from *Follies*.

Annie. April 21, 1977–January 2, 1983. 2,377 performances.

The Biggest Flop
Hellzapoppin'

Just call it "Hell."

Back in the thirties, *Tobacco Road* was the longest-running show in Broadway history, followed by *Abie's Irish Rose*. In third place was a comic musical revue called *Hellzapoppin'*, which ran from 1938 to 1941, amassing 1,404 performances.

Now there'd be a *Hellzapoppin'* revisal that would run 1,404 performances fewer.

There were no stars in the original production, but the 1977 version would be headed by Jerry Lewis, making his official Broadway debut. The show would begin with Lewis in tights and leotard, auditioning for *Hellzapoppin'* itself in an obvious *Chorus Line* parody. Unlike the obedient dancers auditioning for Zach, Lewis gave his trademark immaturity to the director-choreographer. The other dancers eventually carried him off, returning without him to do the opening number. The lyrics started, "It's a helluva night, Hellzapoppin'! Nothing's gonna go right."

In the long run—make that *short* run—they were correct.

There were attempts to profit from Lewis' persona as a klutz, so he fell into the orchestra pit. An actor playing the Stage Manager was there to give him an introduction, after which Lewis took a bow—to the displeasure of the Stage Manager. "In the legitimate theater, you don't bow until the final curtain, which this may be."

Not far from the truth.

Lewis then started his monologue with "For the next two and a half hours," which prompted "Voice in Balcony" to yell out, "How long?" When Lewis reiterated the time, the Voice said "Oh, my God!" after which the audience heard a gunshot. After another man in the audience tried to sell two tickets to *The Wiz*—and an usher (Jill Choder) tried to straighten out a seating problem—we heard that Voice in Balcony once again. Lewis was astonished the man was still alive. Said the usher, "He's the producer."

There must have been times when *Hellzapoppin'*'s producer, Alexander H. Cohen, did feel as if he should shoot himself. He'd first tried to get this show on ten years earlier, when Soupy Sales headed a version that played Montreal's Expo '67—and died there. Cohen was an associate producer on the (melo)dramatic hit *Angel Street* in 1941, but had always wanted a great big Broadway musical smash of his own. He tried with *Of V We Sing, Bright Lights of 1944, Make a Wish, Courtin' Time, Rugantino, Baker Street, A Time for Singing, Dear World,* and *Prettybelle.* Those nine musicals amassed only 731 Broadway performances.

This time Cohen had hired librettist Abe Burrows, of *Guys and Dolls* and *How to Succeed* fame. For songwriters, he hired the less illustrious Hank Beebe and Bill Heyer, whose modest off-Broadway hit, *Tuscaloosa's Calling Me . . . but I'm Not Going,* was still running.

But Cohen was all about Big. "I always wanted to become the master of the grand gesture," he liked to say. Indeed, he got NBC to put up $350,000 (of the $1.3 million) so that scenes from *Hellzapoppin'* could be broadcast on its *Big Event* on February 13, 1977, the show's opening night at the Minskoff. Not only that, Cohen would see to it that the open space underneath the office building that went from Forty-fourth to Forty-fifth Street would be renamed "The Jerry Lewis Arcade."

The show's big running gag was that Lewis would start a sentence and often be interrupted. Some original *Hellzapoppin'* interruptions were included, such as the delivery boy who carried a plant down the aisle and searched the audience for Mrs. Jones, to whom he was to deliver it. In the second act, the delivery boy returned, still looking for her—but by now, the plant had grown into a small tree.

There were novelty acts interspersed, including Bob Williams and Louie, the latter being a dog who just stood uninterested while his "master" enthusiastically encouraged him to do some tricks. Lynn Redgrave was on hand to add a little class. But of course the emphasis was on Lewis, who also played a balloonist who's about to cross the Atlantic, until an interviewer tells him everyone who's tried before has perished; the supposed fun was seeing how scared Lewis got.

Lewis also played an anchorman who couldn't say the word "environmentalist," a cuckolded husband, and a sailor who wandered into a "Make a Record" booth at an amusement park. Upon hearing a voice say "twenty-five cents please," the sailor parted with the quarter, but that wasn't the last of the voice. It became a tyrannical director who made overbearing demands and literally turned the modest recording into a big production number. It was an excuse to bring the first act to a big finish.

The second act began with Lewis playing a techie for a rock band, setting up their equipment so they can sing "Doin' the Frisbee." That allowed the rhyming line "People said, 'Who can that whiz be?'" Certainly not Lewis, who was pelted by Frisbees spinning near his head no matter which way he moved.

Lewis then judged a Miss Hellzapoppin' contest, with one entrant from each state. But even Cohen wasn't a big enough spender to offer fifty contestants, so the competition was limited to representatives from the thirteen original colonies. In a nod to consciousness-raising, all the contestants walked off when Lewis asked their measurements. By default, Mrs. Pringle, the aged pageant organizer, won the contest.

Then came a big dance number for Lewis. The lyrics started, "Some people can't dance without their taps on / Others can't dance without funny caps on."

(Really?)

"Still others can't move till the spotlight snaps on / I think they're all insane."

"Insane?" The word seems a little strong for the situation until we realize it's there to provide a rhyme for the song's title, "All I Need Is My Cane."

It would all culminate with a sketch that had Lewis reprise one of his most famous roles, the "Nutty Professor." Here, the professor wanted to send a man to the sun, though he wouldn't volunteer himself. ("I peel.") It led to a song, "Let's Put a Man on the Sun" whose opening line was followed by "The whole business sounds like fun."

Strangely enough, in the eleven o'clock number Lewis gave the spotlight to Choder. "A Miracle Happened," she sang, about getting her chance. The show came to a close with her joining Lewis center stage in a big dance number.

But one other ingredient from the original *Hellzapoppin'* was still supposed to happen. As theatergoers left, they'd see in the lobby an enormous overgrown tree on which the delivery boy would be sitting, still looking for Mrs. Jones. Cohen didn't bring the tree to any of the three out-of-town engagements, but was saving it for the Jerry Lewis Arcade.

It never made it there, and neither did the show. After *Hellzapoppin'*, Cohen had ten musicals to his credit—but the same 731 Broadway performances.

Hellzapoppin'. November 22, 1976, in Baltimore–January 22, 1977, in Boston. No New York performances.

1977–1978

THE BIGGEST HIT
Ain't Misbehavin'

No book, no dialogue, no stopping it.

The biggest hit of the 1977–1978 Broadway season owed a great deal to the biggest off-Broadway hit of 1967–1968.

Back then, *Jacques Brel Is Alive and Well and Living in Paris* put four singers on an off-Broadway stage to sing a few dozen of an obscure Frenchman's obscure songs—and put drinks in front of its patrons. It lasted 1,847 performances, an off-Broadway total then surpassed only by *The Fantasticks* (of course) and *The Threepenny Opera*.

Yes, Broadway pundits said, but that was off-Broadway, where audiences don't expect much, and where little shows can be produced. Don't try putting one song after another with no plot on Broadway.

Some did, anyway. *Noel Coward's Sweet Potato* opened in 1969, and ran two months. The early seventies saw evenings devoted to Dietz and Schwartz (*That's Entertainment!*), Ogden Nash (*Nash at Nine*), Sammy Cahn (*Words & Music*), Harry Chapin (*The Night That Made America Famous*), and the eponymous *Rodgers and Hart*. None ran longer than four months, and *That's Entertainment!* played two days.

In 1977, though, two such shows did well. *Side by Side by Sondheim* had narration, which made for a fuller evening. It would last a year, but *Beatlemania* would more than double that with its John, Paul, George, and Ringo clones. Yes, Broadway said, but that was bringing in a non-theater crowd. You couldn't expect conventional theatergoers to accept such a small enterprise.

But after an anthology of Thomas "Fats" Waller's songs called *Ain't*

Misbehavin' opened at the Manhattan Theatre Club on East Seventy-third Street on February 8, 1978—and scored mightily—producers suddenly stopped worrying that such a show might be too small for Broadway—where, within three months, the "musical" was ensconced. When the Tony nominations were announced, *Ain't Misbehavin'* garnered five—coincidentally the exact same number of cast members it had.

Of the five, the production won three, for featured actress Nell Carter, director Richard Maltby, Jr.—and Best Musical. Never had such a small show won the Big Prize.

Once producers noticed that winning the Tony on the cheap was possible, they sought the same kind of gusher. Suddenly there was value in a show where the audience came in knowing the songs, and already liked many of them.

So after *Ain't Misbehavin'*, the deluge. Dozens of similar anthologies opened celebrating the dead (Johnny Mercer; *Dream*), the alive (Burt Bacharach; *The Look of Love*), and the somehow-still-alive (*Eubie*, as in Blake, then ninety-five years *very* old). Some songwriters were associated with Broadway (Jerry Herman; *Jerry's Girls)*, while some were not (Mitchell Parish; *Stardust)*. Some took notice of the illustrious (Rodgers and Hammerstein's *A Grand Night for Singing; The Gershwins' Fascinating Rhythm)*, while others recalled the forgotten (Johnny Burke; *Swinging on a Star*) or the previously unsung (Louis Jordan, *Five Guys Named Moe*).

But more than twenty years would pass before another such musical revue— *Smokey Joe's Café*—would surpass *Ain't Misbehavin'*'s run. And while that would be the biggest hit of the 1994–1995 season, it wouldn't win the Best Musical Tony. Only *Ain't Misbehavin'* can lay claim to the small bookless revue that got the big run *and* the big prize.

But right now there are producers out there aiming to match that achievement with another small-cast revue.

Ain't Misbehavin'. May 9, 1978–Feb 21, 1982. 1,604 performances.

The Biggest Flop
The Prince of Grand Street

A Jewish show in New York! (Well, not quite.)

The *Prince of Grand Street* starred no less than Robert Preston as Nathan Rashumsky, the biggest star of the turn-of-the-century Yiddish theater. Rashumsky was patterned after such downtown luminaries as Boris Tomashevsky and Jacob Adler—and if you doubt that these men were immensely popular with their audiences, take a look at *Jacob Adler: A Life on the Stage*. There's a picture on page 379 that was taken on the day of his funeral, where sidewalks were literally packed from curb to building with fans waiting to see his cortege pass by.

Bob Merrill, whom we met through *Breakfast at Tiffany's* and *Prettybelle*, would do the score—and the book. Like *Fiddler*, *The Prince of Grand Street* was a musical about traditions changing. Here, though, they were theatrical traditions. Should Nathan continue to alter classics such as *Romeo and Juliet* to suit his Russian-Jewish immigrant audience? (He made Mr. Capulet and Mr. Montague business partners who had a falling out over a dry goods shipment.) And should Nathan, now sixty-two, still play Romeo? Nathan insisted all theater was illusion, so what did it matter?

The show begins with that musicalized *Romeo and Juliet*. But at its close, Nathan's producers announce to the audience that Reba Rashumsky, Nathan's wife of forty-seven years, died today—but that Nathan felt that the show must go on. Merrill then takes us backstage to a hardly upset Nathan. "If God summoned her," he intones, "he doesn't know what he's in for. My wife was a disagreeable human being."

That was the show's first big mistake. Merrill should have mentioned then and there that Nathan and Reba met on their wedding day in an arranged marriage; not doing so made Nathan seem callous. If the audience had been immediately told that Nathan had stayed in a marriage that he never wanted, they would have wished him all the best in trying to find the right woman after all these years.

In a second mistake, Nathan's producers plan seven nights of shiva for Reba but Nathan insists he doesn't want them, because he's an atheist. Audiences often find atheism alienating, and Nathan's is hardly necessary here, since it never comes up again in the story. Merrill might have felt that including it would establish that Nathan was his own person, but it didn't help the audience bond with the character.

The show shifted to the shiva and "Fifty Cents," a purposely doleful song that could have just as easily been called "Call the Professional Mourners." Leah Goldfarb (Neva Small) gets there too late to be chosen as one. But she's so desperate for a job to support herself and her grandfather Itzak (Sam Levene) that Nathan hires her. Leah then wildly overdoes the crying, which is supposed to be funny.

Local drama critic Julius Pritkin (Werner Klemperer) comes to the service and asks Nathan, "Is there anything I can do?" Nathan quips, "Write better reviews" and baits Pritkin into an argument the critic doesn't want to have. That Pritkin wanted to take the high road and Nathan the low was the third mistake. How can an audience like a character that always needed to be right, and who used his wife's shiva as a battleground?

Needled by Nathan, Pritkin complains of the actor's "bastardizing of classics into cheap song and dance." Nathan says it's what his audience wants. Pritkin then points out that Nathan takes roles that are far too young for him, but the actor pooh-poohs his objection. So a frustrated Pritkin finally says, "Why don't you just go and play Huckleberry Finn?"—a suggestion he'll come to regret.

Nathan then turns on Leah, firing her for crying much too loudly and getting on his nerves. That was the fourth mistake, for displaced hostility isn't an admirable quality. Leah later goes to Nathan's house and apologizes in a powerful song called "I'm a Girl with Too Much Heart." When she asks Nathan if he is religious, he says he is. That's the fifth mistake, for Nathan is shown to be a person who'd lie in order to impress a young woman on whom he has designs. What made the matter more unsavory was that he was approximately three times her age.

Nathan makes it clear that he'd like to get Leah in bed, while she is (understandably) scandalized that he isn't mourning. "I was forced into marriage when I was fourteen," he tells her. This was the sixth mistake, for in this context Nathan sounds like he's telling Leah (and us) another lie. But if the arranged-marriage information had been in the first scene, the audience would have known Nathan was telling the truth and wasn't just handing the kid a line.

Faced with Leah's resistance, Nathan tells her (the seventh mistake) he can get any woman he wants—"for the honor and the free tickets." He sings, "I'm a Star," his rationalization for any bad behavior he might display. She finally agrees to spend a weekend with him in Atlantic City; once there, he sings "Do I Make You Happy?," a song with the feel of a lovely Yiddish lullaby, to which they dance.

On the very next day comes the eighth mistake: when Leah goes out, a maid comes in, recognizes Nathan, bats her eyelashes—and into bed they go. When Leah returns, she is shocked and hurt, but Nathan matter-of-factly reminds her, "I'm a Star," adding. "Never say you'll be back in an hour and come back in a half hour." But Leah is not going to shoulder the blame for this, and prepares to leave. Nathan implores, "Stay with Me" (a pretty song, recycled from *Breakfast at Tiffany's*), to no avail. Alone, he sings a reprise lamenting, "First she takes my heart / and then she takes the train." While it was a good lyric, no one could blame the lass. No woman expects a new beau to bed someone else on the first weekend she goes away with him.

Nathan returns to New York, desperate to find Leah. He learns from Itzak that she is now working in a sweatshop, and pursues her there (arriving in time to hear "Sew a Button," a mournful waltz). He: "I love you." She: "Will you marry me?" He: "Yes." She: "When?" He: "Eventually." After all, he points out, he'll be in serious trouble with his public if he marries before he's observed a year's mourning.

Leah is mollified for the moment, but Nathan has other troubles: Julius Pritkin has again panned him for "not joining the twentieth century" and taking outrageous liberties with the classics. In a moment of introspection, prompted by Pritkin, Nathan admits to himself how much he needs people to "Look at Me," a jaunty number.

Afterward, he announces to his producers that he plans to marry Leah. They are horrified, convinced that his career (and theirs) will be over if he marries this soon after his wife's death. Nevertheless, at the curtain calls after that evening's performance, Nathan tells his audience that they can hate him if they have to, but he and Leah have already married. They forgive him as the act 1 curtain falls.

The second act begins with Nathan's latest hit, *Young Avram Lincoln*, about "the railsplitter who became president and created a home for the Jews in Illinois." (One of the melodies in this sequence owed a good deal to "Ciao, Compare," another *Breakfast at Tiffany's* song.) Nathan as Lincoln proclaims, "If I'm elected, I will take on the aged, so that no one will ever be a burden to his children." While this is happening, Leah is backstage, where she realizes that she has found "My Place in the World," a ballad that Small sang big.

Pritkin, though, criticizes the play, prompting a challenge from Nathan: "Don't you ever agree with the audience? . . . What do you contribute?" But Pritkin gives him an excellent answer: "I want to elevate our downtown theater. To see that our immigrants are uplifted, and not pandered to." Still, that cuts no ice with Nathan, who brags that his next production will be an adaptation of *Huckleberry Finn*, as Pritkin suggested. If he can't play the teenager to his audience's satisfaction, he says, he'll quit the stage—but if he can, he'll expect Pritkin to quit the paper.

Pritkin—perhaps all too aware that jobs as drama critics are extraordinarily hard to get—makes no such promise upon exiting. But when he leaves, Nathan begins to doubt himself, and asks Leah, "Do they laugh at an old man prancing on the stage like a young boy?" This draws from Leah a very Jerry Herman-ish cheer-up song, called "(You're) The Youngest Person That I Know," which morphs into an enormous production number.

Nathan seeks out Mark Twain himself (Addison Powell), and asks him for the rights to *Huckleberry Finn*. Twain is on the fence about giving them—until Nathan mentions that he plans to play Huck. Then Twain's answer becomes a firm no. Here was the ninth mistake, for Nathan illegally stages his own *Huck Finn*, anyway. Once again—and one time too many—we were shown a guy who simply doesn't believe the rules of the world apply to him. That got awfully insufferable.

When Robert Preston came out dressed as Huckleberry Finn, there was a good deal of laughter from the audience. But all of it was affectionate. With that friendly beginning, it's too bad that Nathan's adaptation retains Twain's use of the N-word (the tenth mistake). However historically accurate that was, it had to turn some of the audience against the show.   Twain sues Nathan, and Pritkin pans him. But in that same column, Pritkin praises an up-and-coming actor—who he says could learn a good deal from Nathan. (Suddenly the drama critic was emerging as the nicest guy in the show. Who'd have expected him to be so gracious after so many bouts with the insufferable Nathan?) Pritkin arranges for Nathan to meet the young actor, and the show ends with Nathan and the kid discussing their first collaboration, in which, Nathan explains, he himself will play the younger part. Curtain.

The "Here we go again" ending was time-honored, but it was certainly threadbare by 1978, and must be considered the eleventh mistake. Granted, Merrill assumed we'd be so in love with Nathan that we'd forgive him everything, but there were too many flaws in the guy for us to embrace him unconditionally. Audiences and critics didn't, and the *Prince* was dethroned before Broadway.

The Prince of Grand Street. March 8, 1978, in Philaldephia–April 15, 1978, in Boston. No Broadway performances.

1978–1979

<small>THE BIGGEST HIT</small>
The Best Little Whorehouse in Texas

Sex does sell, doesn't it?

October 27, 1977. The Actors Studio, New York City—where such names as Elia Kazan and Lee Strasberg helped keep alive the Stanislavsky System of acting.

So what's a musical doing here? And what a scandalous name: *The Best Little Whorehouse in Texas.*

While musicals had been adapted from plays, novels, films, comic strips, and even the Continental Congress's records from 1776, there had never been a musical based on an article in *Playboy.* But Peter Masterson was intrigued by what Larry L. King had written in the April 1974 issue.

It was the story of Edna Milton's brothel, euphemistically called "The Chicken Ranch." It had been quietly operating for decades in LaGrange, Texas, for Sheriff T. J. Flournoy and many lawmakers before him had always looked the other way. But TV muckraker Marvin Zindler, seeking a cause that he could ride to fame, made the whorehouse his new personal crusade—and applied enough pressure to have it closed.

As a Texas native, Masterson had an affinity for the locale. In 1967, he portrayed arguably its most notorious resident as the title character in *The Trial of Lee Harvey Oswald.* The fantasy courtroom drama had lasted a week on Broadway, but Masterson planned to return there, if not as an actor, then as a director or writer.

A stage adaptation of the article would allow him to do both, though he'd collaborate with King on the book duties. He asked fellow Texan Carol Hall—best-known for writing "Jenny Rebecca" for Barbra Streisand—to pen music and lyrics.

Tonight is the first performance. The show's program reveals the real participants' names have been changed to Miss Mona (Masterson's wife Carlin Glynn), Sheriff Ed Earl Dodd (though it's misspelled as Dobb in the program; Henderson Forsythe) and Melvin P. Thorpe (Clint Allmon).

While the program doesn't offer the audience one familiar name, the small studio on West Forty-fourth between Ninth and Tenth Avenues is packed. Who can resist such a title?

After "Twenty Fans" and "Pissant Country Place" musically set the scene, *Whorehouse* delivers surprising impact. It comes after two young women come to the Chicken Ranch in hopes of employment. April (Elizabeth Kemp) has been a prostitute before, but Shy (Joan Ellis) hasn't, and is apprehensive about what she might be getting herself into. That's when Miss Mona sings "Girl, You're a Woman," which puts the most positive possible spin on this lifestyle. The audience is astonished to find itself becoming emotionally involved with both madam and new employee.

After Thorpe reveals to his TV audience that "Texas Has a Whorehouse in It," another emotional thunderbolt lands. April is on the phone talking to her mother, being very vague about her new job in "sales." She asks to speak to her very young son, and tells him that she doesn't think she'll be able to get home for Thanksgiving, but she's sure Santa will bring him some nice Christmas presents. Miss Mona overhears the conversation, and tells April as soon as she hangs up, "We'll see if we can't work it out so you get the curse around Christmas Eve." Now the audience really loves her. So does Stevie Phillips, who had been recently hired by Universal Pictures to scout for properties that would make good movies. She options the property.

That Actors Studio run included the Sheriff's song "Goddam Everything," which was far less benign than the "Good Old Girl" that would eventually replace it. Just as raw was "Two Blocks from the Capitol Building," about the blatant sexual activity that occurred in Austin. The song listing on the original program spent a good deal of ink on the characters involved in that one: Prostitute with Pimp, Cheerleaders, Belly Dancer, Sadist Dancer, Flasher, Hippie Pusher, Businessman, Priest, Marlboro Man, Sailor, Midget, Cop, and Freaked-Out Prostitute.

Both songs were excised after director-choreographer Tommy Tune, a Texan himself, joined the project. He split the directorial duties with Masterson and took over the dances from Christopher "Spider" Duncan. Tune didn't have as many young women on hand as he wanted to play cheerleaders, so he had each young woman wear a yoke on which a mock cheerleader-doll was suspended on either side of her, with balloons in place of breasts and buttocks. A liability became an asset.

The show played better when it moved to the Entermedia, a large but still-considered-off-Broadway theater on Second Avenue, in spring 1978. Pamela Blair came in to play April, though the character's name was now Amber. (Later still it would be changed to Angel.)

Phillips moved the show to Broadway and the Forty-sixth Street Theatre. But the Ash/LeDonne Advertising Agency had a problem. "Whorehouse" had never been part of a Broadway title, and the *New York Times* refused advertising—until management reminded the paper that it had accepted ads for productions of the seventeenth-century classic *'Tis Pity She's a Whore.*

While Phillips entered into a contract with the New York Transit Authority to put "Have Fun at the Whorehouse" on eighty of its buses, Cardinal Terrence Cooke wasn't happy about it. The transit authority reneged, and the media reported it. That helped business.

In 1982, Universal made its film version, which became the sixth-highest grosser of the year. Once again, that title worked wonders. But the film isn't nearly as good as the stage show, for it has less heart and emotional pull. That's what happens when you drop "Girl, You're a Woman" and April-Amber-Angel's telephone call.

But the film was much better than the biggest flop we'll meet in the 1993–1994 season: *The Best Little Whorehouse Goes Public.*

The Best Little Whorehouse in Texas. June 17, 1978–March 27, 1982. 1,584 performances.

The Biggest Flop
A Broadway Musical

Making a mockery of a musical.

As we've seen, at the end of the sixties, out-of-town tryouts were deemed too expensive, so producers opted for previews. Now, at the end of the seventies, one producer named Norman Kean thinks that even previewing at a Broadway theater is too costly.

Instead, Kean decides to mount a glorified workshop—one to which he'll allow theatergoers to buy tickets. He'll rent a theater in the Riverside Church on Riverside Drive at 122nd Street, not far from Grant's Tomb. He'll close his show there if it doesn't go well.

But it should. The last time bookwriter William F. Brown came to Broadway, he had a smash: *The Wiz*. The last time composer Charles Strouse visited, he had *Annie*. The lyricist, Lee Adams, almost did as well on his last time out: *Applause*.

Their Broadway musical is actually called *A Broadway Musical*. It deals with the rigors of producing one of these difficult behemoths from start to finish. Audiences would meet the rookie writer, the cocksure producer, the shyster lawyers, the vulgar theater party ladies, the arrogant black star, and the auteur director. From start to finish, though, the tone was that the average producer who does a musical has no taste and ruins a promising property.

Though Brown is not black but white, this is, like his *The Wiz*, another black-centric show. James Lincoln (Irving Allen Lee) is a young, serious African-American playwright. He's written a drama that indicts the National Basketball Association for taking gifted college players out of school, using them for as long as they are viable athletes, and then discarding them without much thought to their futures.

Lincoln takes his drama to Broadway producer Eddie Bell (Julius LaRosa), who professes to love it—but says he wants to produce it as a musical called *Sneakers*. And then the deluge of problems, especially after black megalomaniac superstar Richie Taylor (Larry Marshall) is signed.

Kean wanted a black man at the helm, and chose George Faison to direct and choreograph; he'd done the latter assignment on *The Wiz*. LaRosa was then a forgotten name, but had been one of the great stars of early TV, and had a million-selling record to his credit called "Eh, Cumpari," in a time when Italian novelty songs sold.

Finally, there was no question whom Kean wanted as Bell's wife Stephanie—his own wife of twenty years, Gwyda DonHowe. This is not as nepotistic as it sounds; DonHowe had already done two musicals and five plays on Broadway.

But the musical almost got buried near Grant's Tomb. Faison was soon fired, and Strouse and Adams begged Gower Champion, who'd directed and choreographed their *Bye Bye Birdie*, to help. He agreed.

For Strouse and Adams, this was their chance to get a little revenge on Sammy Davis, Jr., whom they'd fictionalized as Richie Taylor. Fourteen years earlier, Davis had been difficult all through the Philadelphia, Boston, and Detroit tryouts of their *Golden Boy*. But if this musical was meant to slam Davis, the star got his revenge, for once *A Broadway Musical* moved to Broadway, it lasted 568 fewer performances than the 569 that *Golden Boy* had amassed.

There's an old showbiz adage that if you have three showstoppers in your musical, you'll automatically have a hit. It's another myth that bit the dust with *A Broadway Musical*. While it had those three showstoppers, it couldn't even manage three performances.

The first audience rouser was the title song, in which Eddie tells James all that a Broadway musical can be. The second took place at the top of act 2, when James arrives at the National Theater in Washington. (*A Broadway Musical* couldn't afford a tryout, but apparently *Sneakers* could.) It's hours before show time, and when James walks on stage, he finds janitor Sylvester Lee (Tiger Haynes) sweeping the stage. "But I wasn't always a janitor," he tells him. "I used be a star." And then comes "The 1934 Hot Chocolate Jazz Babies Revue," a number replicating the best of such black revues as *Shuffle Along*, *Blackbirds of 1928*, and, of course, *Hot Chocolates*. The janitor cavorts with every showgirl as he remembers the number in which he starred.

But wait. After the number ends and James is gone, Haynes turns to the audience and confides, "I was never a star. I didn't care. At least I was there" to see such grand shows. (He has a point.)

A Broadway Musical didn't get its third showstopper until it moved into the Lunt-Fontanne. Back at the church, Helen Gallagher, playing Bell's assistant Maggie Simpson, who sees that *Sneakers* is sneaking into oblivion, gave this musical observation to Eddie: "Who Says You Gotta Be Happy?" But once Champion came in—which had nothing to do with Gallagher's leaving and Patti Karr's taking over for her—he pointed out that in any musical comedy, "You Gotta Have Dancing." Adams rewrote the song and suddenly the number became a stroll down Memory Lane, with the dancers offering trademark moves from such choreographers as Kidd, Fosse, Robbins, and, of course, Champion. The cherry on the top of the sundae was one chorus boy's twirling around the stage with his umbrella.

Musical flops often get nicknames. Arguably best of all was *The Prince of Central Park*, which starred Gloria De Haven until she left or was fired; it was then dubbed *Ain't Miss De Haven*. But an even less appealing name greeted *A Broadway Musical*. Wags dubbed it *A B.M.*

Kean (coproducing with Garth Drabinsky, whom we'll run into later) took the failure quite hard. He'd produced the smash revival of *Oh! Calcutta!*, which had garnered him an income but no respect. With the one performance that *A Broadway Musical* amassed, Kean's five productions aside from *Calcutta* had run a combined total of fifty-six performances. Nine years later—with *Calcutta* still running—Kean stabbed DonHowe to death in their apartment, then went to the roof and threw himself off.

No cast album was made, but there is a video of Strouse at the Ninety-second Street Y singing the marvelous title song. Those producing community theater and cruise ship revues should hear it, for it would be an ideal opening number for their own shows. As the concluding lyric goes, "A Broadway Musical / But when it works / Forget the jerks / Who told you it couldn't go / For there's nothing like a Broadway show."

For the most part, that's still true.

A Broadway Musical. December 21, 1978. 1 performance.

3

1979–1989

1979–1980

THE BIGGEST HIT
Evita

When it was okay to like Andrew Lloyd Webber.

A dirt-poor girl rises to greatness? A Cinderella story is always good musical theater fodder.

But *Evita,* the story of Eva Peron, was a tad more sordid than most fairy tales. Eva Duarte (Patti LuPone) was illegitimate as well as poverty-stricken growing up in the not-so-roaring twenties in Argentina. She didn't take long to learn that having sex with men could get her what she wanted, and soon she was a radio celebrity. But that wasn't nearly enough. After she met Juan Peron (Bob Gunton), then Argentina's secretariat of labor and welfare, she decided that she just might do better in politics.

Sam Staggs, in his book *All About "All About Eve,"* says that at a South American film festival, the suggestion was made that Eve Harrington was based on Eva Peron. Even beyond the name, there are similarities: both were actresses who slept their way to the top, albeit a different top.

Though Eva propelled Peron to the presidency and became Argentina's first lady, she wasn't first in the hearts of all her countrymen. This was exemplified by a fictional character based on revolutionary Che Guevara. Che (Mandy Patinkin) is not so easily swayed, and he provides the critical narration in the book and lyrics by Tim Rice and the music by Andrew Lloyd Webber.

If *Evita* can be said to have had a book in the first place. It didn't, not in the way that musical theater had traditionally defined "book"—as a show's non-sung dialogue. In fact, when Rice accepted the Tony for "Best Book," he noted that he and Lloyd Webber had all along planned to write shows with no books.

Though the two would collaborate on a song for the movie version of *Evita*—which took longer (eighteen years) to come to fruition than it took for Mrs. Peron's body to find its final resting place (seventeen years)—Lloyd Webber and Rice never otherwise worked together again. Of the two, need we add that Lloyd Webber emerged as the more successful?

In the thirty-plus years since September 10, 1979, when *Evita* began previews at the Broadway Theater, there hasn't been a day that Andrew Lloyd Webber hasn't been represented on Broadway.

When *Joseph and the Amazing Technicolor Dreamcoat* opened on January 27, 1982, the British composer had two shows running. When *Cats* debuted later that same year—his first Broadway effort without Rice—he had three.

Song and Dance in 1985 and *Starlight Express* in 1987 raised his profile, but it was *The Phantom of the Opera* that took Lloyd Webber to legendary status. He would be the only composer to have two longest-running shows in Broadway history: first *Cats* and then *Phantom*.

And yet . . . and yet . . . in many ways, *Evita* was the high point of Lloyd Webber's career. Not just because his music so well complemented Rice's words. No, the reason is that during *Evita*'s run, Broadway still liked him.

When he was the composer of "only" *Jesus Christ Superstar, Joseph*, and *Evita*, he was applauded and appreciated first for his work, and only second for becoming rich and famous. Few resented *Evita*'s success, or its seven Tonys, including Best Musical. But it "only" ran four years, and finished as the seventeenth-longest-running Broadway musical of all time. Broadway could admire a run like that, without feeling wildly threatened by it.

But after *Cats* opened to its seemingly "now and forever" longest-ever-running success—eventually breaking the beloved *A Chorus Line*'s record—Lloyd Webber became widely loathed for being obscenely rich and famous. Once *Phantom* proved to be more successful still, hating Andrew Lloyd Webber became a knee-jerk reaction and de rigueur.

It's still the same ol' story: Everybody loves an achiever on the way up, but if he achieves too much, people feel the need to take him down to remind themselves that they, not he, has the real power. Many more bristled when Queen Elizabeth II made Lloyd Webber a knight in 1992, and then a lord in 1997.

But wait! Since October 26, 1993, when a revival of *Joseph* began previews at the Minskoff Theater, there hasn't been a day that Tim Rice hasn't been represented on Broadway, either. *Beauty and the Beast* followed a year later, and *The Lion King* three years after that. Granted, Rice only added some lyrics to the former, and wasn't the sole lyricist on the latter. But as long as he continues to rack up performances, he does run the risk of becoming as hated as Lord Andrew Lloyd Webber.

Evita. September 25, 1979–June 26, 1983. 1,567 performances.

THE BIGGEST FLOP
Happy New Year

Shoving songs in a script.

Something old, something new, something borrowed—and the result made those involved mighty blue.

Bert Shevelove, who'd adapted and directed *No, No, Nanette* nine years earlier, announced that he'd do the same for Philip Barry's 1928 high comedy *Holiday*.

Better still, he was bringing back his Tony award-winning choreographer, Donald Saddler, too.

Holiday was a big hit in 1929. It told of Julia Seton and Johnny Case, who met while skiing in Lake Placid and immediately fell in love. Now the animal attraction must yield to real life, and for Julia it's a case of "I love you, you're perfect, now change." She sees Johnny only rising up the ladder at the prestigious firm where he now works; he sees himself taking a year or two off, to the delight of Julia's free-spirited sister Linda.

This time, Shevelove would be "working with" an even higher-regarded songwriter: Cole Porter. That the score would sport both Porter's famous and lesser-known songs would solve the old "They don't write 'em like they used to" problem. And considering that Porter had written lovely songs for *High Society*, the musical film version of Barry's *The Philadelphia Story*, the composer-lyricist had already proved he had the right upper-crust sensibility for the playwright.

Yes, but when *High Society* was being readied, Porter was very much on the scene, getting inspiration from the characters and writing appropriate music and lyrics for them. Now, fifteen years after Porter's death, Shevelove had to select the most apt songs from Porter's catalogue.

The curtain went up. Julia (Kimberly Farr) came in, told everyone what had happened in Lake Placid, and began singing, "Is it an earthquake, or is it a shock?" Unbelievably, the show was already a misfire and a bore.

Why? "At Long Last Love" (originally from *You Never Know*) is a marvelous song—but in context. It's certainly not what Julia would sing—if this character were likely to sing at all. In musicals, people break into song because they get carried away, but, as Barry's play makes clear, Julia is too levelheaded for that. She's the type of person who, when suddenly kissed, chides her fiancé with "Johnny! Mind your manners!" Playwright Barry offers no evidence that she'd be capable of making such witticisms as "Is it the good turtle soup, or merely the mock?" That's the voice of an entirely different character.

To exacerbate matters, Julia was soon singing "Ridin' High" (from *Red, Hot and Blue*) with Johnny (Michael Scot). His singing it could be defended, but Julia's duetting with him seemed out of place. Red wine with fish sometimes works, but rarely.

The other flaw was that songs didn't happen when they should have. When Johnny excitedly tells Linda (Leslie Denniston) that he wants to quit work and live it up, he should be singing. But Shevelove couldn't find an appropriate Porter song, so he had to keep this as mere dialogue. Too bad Porter didn't write the 1939 pop hit "I'm Gonna Live Till I Die."

See how hard it is to find the right old song for an existing script? Writing a song from scratch would ultimately have been easier—and more apt for the situation. The script could even have provided its new songwriter with a title, for Johnny says that he wants to "retire young and work old." That's what he should be singing about.

While Shevelove had beloved old-timers for *Nanette,* he needed a young cast here. He might have cast young stars, but went for young unknowns. Worse, Katharine Hepburn's line readings as Linda from the original *Holiday* film are so ingrained in many minds that poor Leslie Denniston came across as an understudy.

It's the first time in this book that we're seeing an entire score of songs from other shows shackled to a property. It won't be the last. In fact, eighteen years later, Arthur Kopit would take *The Philadelphia Story* and add more Cole Porter tunes to the ones he wrote for *High Society* for a stage adaptation. It remained the story of Tracy Lord, an utterly uptight woman.

And in her first entrance, he had her jubilantly singing "Ridin' High."

Some people don't learn from others' mistakes.

Happy New Year. April 2–May, 10, 1980. 17 performances.

1980–1981

THE BIGGEST HIT
42nd Street

Sweetening a sour novel.

How tempting to say that *42nd Street* was a success because of the drama that surrounded its opening night—when producer David Merrick took the stage after the curtain calls to announce that director-choreographer Gower Champion had died that afternoon.

Merrick, always the hound for free publicity, got more than he ever had—and he didn't have to pull one of his usual big stunts to do it. Champion obliged simply by dying at the right time to make dramatic front-page headlines and a top story on nightly newscasts. Few in the nation can name a Broadway director, but the country knew Champion because he and his once-wife Marge had danced in forties and fifties film musicals. As a result, the populace was made aware of *42nd Street*'s existence in a way that hadn't happened since the demise of *The Ed Sullivan Show* and *Life* magazine.

Almost an afterthought were the rave reviews. Frank Rich started his in the *New York Times* with "If anyone wonders why Gower Champion's death is a bitter loss for the American theater, I suggest that he head immediately to the Winter Garden." People did.

While audiences of course hate paying high prices for theater tickets—and theater tickets have always been expensive, no matter how "low" historical prices may seem by contemporary standards—they don't seem to mind as much if they can see the money on stage. No musical of the one hundred in this book was as quick to show that money had been spent than *42ⁿᵈ Street*, for even before the curtain was all the way up on the first scene, the crowd could see thirty-six dancers tapping their feet in a rehearsal routine. Now the audience was applauding, confident that they were seeing a great big Broadway show. They were soon laughing good-naturedly, too, when the rehearsing dancers were told that they had to be good, because "they're paying $4.40 a seat out there."

Would that they were. Merrick did something unprecedented in raising ticket prices. Not only did he raise the then-current $25 prime orchestra seat to $30, he upped it again soon after to $35. Until now, only a new show had ever broken the price barrier when it first announced a sale of tickets; never in this half-century had one that was already running replaced the new high it had already set.

But whatever the price, audiences came out with plenty of affectionate laughter after all-too-naïve Peggy Sawyer (Wanda Richert) arrives from Allentown to matter-of-factly proclaim that she wants to appear in Broadway musicals. Her new friend Anytime Annie (Karen Prunczik) is squarely on her side, so when *Pretty Lady* star Dorothy Brock (Tammy Grimes) is injured (perhaps because of Peggy), Annie graciously suggests that Peggy take her place. Producer-director Julian Marsh (Jerry Orbach) is dubious, but he gets the performance out of Peggy that saves the show.

It's all so innocent, but the fascinating fact is that *42ⁿᵈ Street*, the original 1932 novel by Bradford Ropes, is actually a hard-hitting look at the making of *Pretty Lady*. While the stage *42ⁿᵈ Street* called musical comedy "the two most glorious words in the English language," Ropes termed it "a bed of roses, thorny side up."

He wrote of chorus girls "who basked a brief moment in the spotlight of Broadway and then hurried onward into the oblivion of marriage." One chorus girl was "just a good mattress for some tired businessman," while another was "one of Broadway's whor-ified girls." As for the chorus boy, he's "pointed out as the degenerate effeminate male whom all normal boys should avoid."

Anytime Annie "was permanently disgruntled unless in close proximity to a gin highball" and was savvy enough to know that "if you have supper with a man, you're his mistress." Her view of her coworkers? "Actors don't take you out to lunch just for the pleasure of watching you eat. I always see the shadow of an abortion over every corsage."

Dorothy Brock is said "to have slept in more beds than George Washington ever did." Though her theme song is "You and Me and a Cup of Tea," one wag says it should be "The Navy and Me and a Quart of Scotch." That's why, in the novel, Dorothy injures herself after drunkenly falling down the stairs. As for Julian Marsh, one *Pretty Lady* worker surreptitiously says that he's "got to be queer" while another calls him "Madame Marsh." His affair with Billy Lawlor corroborates the suspicions.

Would a *faithful* musical adaptation of the novel have done as well? Probably not, for the more stars-in-your-eyes *42nd Street* was Merrick's longest-running production. It bested even his *Hello, Dolly!*, which in 1970 had set the long-run record for musicals, by a year and a half. *4nd Street* would also be the last blaze of glory for Merrick, whose last four productions between 1981 and 1996 would average runs of seventy-one performances.

On *42nd Street*'s opening night, after Merrick came on and made his tragic announcement, Jerry Orbach was the cast member who assumed leadership and demanded that the curtain be brought down. Little did anyone know that *42nd Street* would bring down the curtain on his Broadway career, too. After doing thirteen seasons of TV's *Law & Order*, Orbach died on December 28, 2004.

It was Dick Perry's last production, too. Even staunch musical theater enthusiasts may not know the name, but they certainly have heard his trumpet playing on such cast albums as *Do Re Mi, Funny Girl, Jamaica, Subways Are for Sleeping*, and the notorious *Whoop-Up*, where he provided an obbligato to Susan Johnson's rant about "Men." But most of all, Perry was the trumpeter who stood up during the overture of the original *Gypsy* and played those phenomenal burlesque licks. Nice that he went out with one of Broadway's biggest hits.

When discussion of long-running hits crop up, seldom is *42nd Street* mentioned, because it never held the number one spot. But when it closed, it was no less than the second-longest-running musical of all time; only *A Chorus Line* had run longer.

The 2001 revival ran almost four years, and currently ranks as the third-longest running revival in Broadway history. Gower Champion's death may have provided the initial push, but *42nd Street* became a champion on its own terms.

42nd Street. August 25, 1980–January 8, 1989. 3,486 performances.

The Biggest Flop
Bring Back Birdie

When love turns to hate.

January 26, 1981. The Martin Beck Theater, New York City. The first preview of *Bring Back Birdie*—the sequel to *Bye Bye Birdie*. It's reunited bookwriter Michael Stewart, composer Charles Strouse, lyricist Lee Adams, and female star Chita Rivera.

Some personnel are missing from the 1960 hit. Dick Van Dyke passed on the chance to star, leaving the field open for Hollywood legend Donald O'Connor. Director-choreographer Gower Champion has died, so in his stead is Joe Layton, who's directed ten musicals and choreographed fifteen of them, dating back to *Once upon a Mattress* in 1959.

By seven o'clock, there's already a dense crowd beneath the marquee. There are three reasons why people always turn up early: First, they want to make sure that their tickets are in order; second, they can't wait to get in; third, they're taking no chances on missing even a second of excitement of what is sure to be a hit.

There's a great preponderance of thirtysomethings in the lobby and on the street. They're animatedly chattering and flashing big smiles. *Bye Bye Birdie* was the first musical many of these people saw, when they were teenagers. Some who missed it on stage caught up with the movie version in 1963. While the film is no masterpiece, it did have enough teen-oriented excitement (and Ann-Margret) to get them interested in Broadway musicals.

Finally, the house is opened and everyone pours in, chatting excitedly about the prospect of revisiting Albert, the English teacher; Rosie, his secretary-turned-wife; Conrad Birdie, the king of rock 'n' roll (as that form of music was called before the *'n' roll* was amputated); Kim McAfee, the girl who was chosen to give Birdie one last kiss; and Hugo Peabody, her steady who kept her from doing so.

So every theatergoer is in the highest of spirits as he takes his seat—even though that curtainless stage is flanked by some ugly metallic staging. The sound of happy chattering stops, though, when Layton suddenly bounds onto the stage to say that the show isn't quite ready. Some machinery isn't yet working well, one important cast member has been ill, and other problems are mentioned, too.

This affects the audience not at all. From the crowd comes the unspoken message: "Joe! Calm down! You're worrying for nothing! This is the sequel to *Bye Bye Birdie*, written by the same exact people and starring Chita Rivera! It's gonna be great!"

The show begins, and the usual entrance applause awarded Rivera and O'Connor is substantially sweetened by nostalgia. That Albert and Rosie are breaking into their old office to find a Conrad Birdie contract that will still make him beholden to Albert) does seem a bit bizarre, but the opening song, "Twenty Happy Years," is pleasant enough. Not as good as "An English Teacher" from *Bye Bye Birdie*, but pleasant enough. Then a detective bounds in—not to arrest Albert and Rosie, but to say that Conrad (Marcel Forestieri) is now living in retirement in Arizona.

If that seems strange, what's downright disappointing is the realization that Kim and Hugo will not be part of the story. In their stead are two new teenagers: the Peterson kids, Jenny (Robin Morse) and Albert, Jr. (Evan Seplow). Both are thinking of running away from home, she with her boyfriend, which prompts two pop-rock tunes, "Movin' Out" and "Half of a Couple." The songs are nice enough, but not as strong as "The Telephone Hour," which introduced us to the teens in *Bye Bye Birdie*.

Next, Rivera's Rosie sings about the joys of being a stay-at-home mom who keeps house; then Albert insists that she accompany him to Arizona to find Birdie. The kids stay with relatives, so Rosie takes them to a bus terminal where Jenny meets and joins a cult—not the then-trendy Moonies, but the thinly veiled Sunnies. Meanwhile, Albert, Jr. hooks up with a punk rock band called Filth. Hmmm.

Albert and Rosie arrive in Arizona: She carries the luggage while he sings the ironic "Baby, You Can Count on Me," not nearly as good a song as "Put On a Happy Face" from you-know-what.

By now, everyone is starting to believe Joe Layton's disclaimers. The real knockout punch comes not when they're introduced to a grossly overweight Conrad but when, a bit later, they see and hear Albert, Jr. playing with his band. Each musician is sitting on a toilet, singing: "We are Filth. We are Filth. We are Fil-il-il-il-il-il-il-il, we are Filth!" while flushing in rhythm.

End of act 1. Lights up. Silence from the crowd . . . for a long second, anyway. What comes next is not applause but, from one theatergoer on the left side of the mezzanine, a low-pitched but loud "Booooooo!" What's astonishing is that, like "the wave" in sports, it spreads from the extreme left to the center to the right. The baby boomers become baby boo-mers.

Seven years earlier, a film called *Earthquake* had boasted of its "Sensurround," which simulated the resonance of an earthquake shaking the theater. But it didn't have nearly the surround-sound of this audience response to *Bring Back Birdie*. Has an audience ever gone from blind love to utter hatred more quickly than in that hour-long span at the first preview of *Bring Back Birdie*?

Bring Back Birdie. March 5–7, 1981. 4 performances.

1981–1982

THE BIGGEST HIT
Dreamgirls

A sense of entitlement.

November 2, 1981. The Shubert Theatre, Boston. A new week of performances is about to start for *Dreamgirls*, now in the fourth week of its nine-week tryout. The reviews have been strong, and word has spread, not just because "the new Michael Bennett" musical is good, but also because the cast has a star in the making.

Her name is Jennifer Holliday, and she's playing Effie Melody White, the lead singer and backbone of the Dreamettes, a black girl group just starting out in the sixties, unaware of how far they'll go.

Effie, though, will find that they will eventually go on without her.

Ironically, the trouble for Effie starts shortly after their manager, Curtis Taylor, Jr. (Ben Harney), tells her and her backup singers Deena Jones (Sheryl Lee Ralph) and Lorrell Robinson (Loretta Devine) a heap of good news. Better gigs, better pay, better contracts, better conditions all sound good to her—until he says that she and Deena will be changing places.

How smart of Curtis to give all the good news first before adding, "And Effie, you're singing backup." Getting everybody excited will help short-circuit any rebellion of Effie's.

Or so he thinks. Effie is utterly furious that she won't be the star any longer, and that sends her on a downward spiral where she'll be replaced by Michelle Morris (Terry Burrell). She sure won't go quietly. In what may be the most dynamic first-act closer in Broadway musical history, Effie sings wordsmith Tom Eyen and composer Henry Krieger's "And I Am Telling You I Am Not Going," even though deep in her heart, she knows she is.

Ever since *Dreamgirls* opened here on October 5, this number has often received something that perhaps no other song in the seventy-one-year-history of the theater has had: a standing ovation *during the song*.

There was a time—right through most of the 1970s—when Broadway audiences at a musical showed their appreciation by applauding enthusiastically at the end of each song and at the actors' bows. They stood up only after the curtain had come down for the last time, in order to start their journey home.

No one can say for sure which audience for which show was Patient Zero where standing ovations are concerned, but oral histories have it that *A Chorus Line*—also a Michael Bennett musical—may have been the one that routinely got people out of their seats and onto their feet.

But even those audiences waited until the curtain calls before they decided to stand. No one stands during a song, or even after a song—or even after an act 1 curtain comes down. It just isn't done. It just isn't time.

Until Holliday delivers the marvelous and dynamic "And I Am Telling You I Am Not Going."

The audience adores her, and the funny thing is that she's not even giving a good performance.

Not tonight. Not now. Holliday has been walking through the show for a few performances, because she's unhappy with the way that Bennett has been handling her. He's already fired her once, before an important backers' audition, but had to charm her back, because no one can quite deliver her Act One aria as well as she.

In a few days, Holliday and Bennett will once more declare a truce, and she will be back on track. But this diva-like behavior is right in keeping with the character she's playing. Effie Melody White is not a team player.

When we first meet Effie, she complains about the dressing room and the wigs. Meanwhile, Deena and Lorrell are grateful for the opportunity they've been given, and are instead concentrating on their work.

When Curtis offers the three women the chance to do back-up for star James "Thunder" Early (Cleavant Derricks), Effie snarls, "I don't do back-up." One could applaud her for her vision in knowing that back-up groups have been known to get trapped in that role. (Only the staunchest Elvisholics can tell you that the Jordanaires were Presley's first back-up group.) Still, it's for one night only, so shouldn't she be nice about it? Granted, the Dreamettes DO become Jimmy's back-up group, but Effie's statement that it would be a trap doesn't come to pass.

When Curtis first tells the group of the Deena-Effie switch, Effie, without any finesse or concern about Deena's feelings, blatantly says, "She can't sing like I can." Why can't she say, "Well, Curtis, if you think that's what'll get us to the next level, then I'll certainly go along with it." Any show business enterprise demands teamwork, but that doesn't interest the self-absorbed Effie. Her rebuttal is always that she has the best voice of the three Dreams, but as anyone in show business knows, sheer talent is not enough to succeed. There are many other factors, and if indeed the group needed a glamorous image that only Deena could provide, so be it. Had Curtis' plan failed, that would have been one thing, but when Effie saw that the group was scaling unprecedented heights, she should have realized another well-known show business maxim: 33⅓ percent of something is certainly better than 100 percent of nothing.

After the group is reconfigured and we see the Dreams for the first time, back-up Effie has a couple of solo lines, and sings them too loudly, as if to say, "Hey, audience, I'm the best singer, and I'm going to make sure you know it." How pathetic.

If Lorrell can be happy with her back-up role, why can't Effie? Why must she be the star, and nothing less will do? How can anyone justify this intense sense of entitlement? When Curtis and Effie's brother C.C. decided to revamp the group, Effie was lucky that they didn't dump her right then and there. They could have brought in a new singer, figuring that they'd be safer if they gave audiences three pretty women to look at.

One could argue that Curtis couldn't do that because C.C. would have walked then and there. Perhaps, but the real reason may well be that Curtis cared enough for Effie to give her the chance to stay in a group that could possibly succeed.

Not that Curtis was a great humanitarian. Lord knows he was first and foremost out for himself, and to make a fortune. But Curtis did have genuine feeling for gaining some progress for black entertainers in America. At the time, the harsh show business reality was that blacks weren't welcomed into many nightclubs, let alone living rooms. A black's appearance as a featured performer on national TV would be automatically followed by plenty of hate mail. In *1776*, Benjamin Franklin says to a stubborn John Adams, "How dare you jeopardize our cause when we've come so far?" The same question should be posed to Effie, who is only concerned for herself, and not making life easier for future black entertainers.

Yes, "Great stars have great pride." But look what happened to Norma Desmond who believed that. And look what happens to Effie, too. She leaves show business and takes a long time to make a comeback. How sad that Curtis sabotages it, yes, but sadder still is that Effie couldn't have been a lifelong contributor to the Dreams. At least she could have been cooperative for a while, to buy her time and make enough money to then set out on a solo career. But why be such a poor sport while working for the group? Even if Effie had been treated unfairly—which she had not been—two wrongs don't make a right.

Dreamgirls succeeds wildly anyway. The audience is rapt with attention from the outset—when Early is yelling and screaming that the sandwich he's been given is not correctly seasoned. What a clever way of telling us that he's a star, for only the biggest would dare to complain over such a trivial detail.

People are interested in the story, which has been said to be a thinly veiled expose of the Supremes (Deena = Diana Ross; Effie = Florence Ballard). One difference is that Ballard died at thirty-two from too many pills and liquor, high blood pressure, and a blood clot, while Effie survives. But because act 1 paralleled the Supremes' actual story quite closely, Eyen was wise to mention the Supremes as an existing group midway through the first act, allowing him to deflect any accusation (or lawsuit).

Bennett kept it moving at a fast pace, easily maneuvering though more than three dozen songs, and the music seldom stopped. But the best coup de théâtre occurred when we saw the Dreams on a multi-city tour. The group performed a number, exited behind a tinseled curtain, and as the voice-over stated that they were now in a different city, they immediately returned, only split-seconds later, in completely different outfits. The "ahhhhh!" from the audience was palpable.

Now *that* deserved a standing ovation.

Dreamgirls. December 20, 1981–August 11, 1985. 1,521 performances.

The Biggest Flop
Merrily We Roll Along

A tale of three performances.

Thursday, October 8, 1981. The Alvin Theater, New York City. Much has been said about having your "name up in lights on Broadway," but that rarely happens. Yet the marquee for *Merrily We Roll Along* has been specially outfitted for eighteen letters-in-lights. They flash "Merrily," then "We Roll," then

"Along," and then give the whole title at once. It's worth a visit to Fifty-second Street just to see it.

But there's much more to see inside, because the first preview of the first Stephen Sondheim-Harold Prince collaboration in two and a half years, since their stunning *Sweeney Todd*.

The evening begins with an overture, which has become a rarity in the theater. Its beautiful and brassy sounds hark back to a time when these grandiose medleys knew they were offering wonderful music. When the brass come in for the B-section of a song we'll soon know as "Good Thing Going," they're proclaiming, "Here's the hit song." (Indeed, it was expected to be, for Frank Sinatra had already recorded it.)

The curtain rises on bleachers full of twenty-six young men and women, ages sixteen to twenty-five, all decked out in graduation robes. As the audience cheers for them, their faces, bathed in bright lights, show complete bliss. For months, every one of them has been telling friends and relatives that no less than Broadway's most prestigious producer-director and its most esteemed songwriter has handpicked him or her to be in their new Broadway musical.

In the last eleven years, Prince has produced and directed five Sondheim musicals—and, aside from that pesky year when *A Chorus Line* bested *Pacific Overtures,* the other four shows were the biggest winners at the Tonys. In between, Prince won another for directing the *Candide* revival for which Sondheim provided some additional lyrics. All right, none of the shows was the biggest hit of the season, but each was a piece of choice merchandise.

So twenty-six broad, confident, even cocky smiles say, "This is just the beginning of my brilliant career! In a few weeks, when we open, I'll get great reviews and become—like the show's main character, Franklin Shepard—'Rich and famous and therefore happy, too.' Oh, sure, I'll stay for the length of my contract—well, maybe *most* of my contract—but then I'll move on to bigger and better roles, maybe on Broadway, maybe in feature films, maybe even on TV. Just as soon as this show's finished opening doors for me."

Now comes the show. *Merrily* is the story of the disintegrating friendship of three kids who hope to make it in the arts: Franklin Shepard (James Weissenbach) as a composer, Charley Kringas (Lonny Price) as a lyricist, and Mary Flynn (Ann Morrison) as a novelist. High hopes get dashed as the years progress, a theme that Rodgers and Hammerstein used in their 1947 musical *Allegro*—on which Sondheim had worked as a gofer for his mentor Hammerstein.

Merrily is more palatable than *Allegro,* which got more dour as it progressed. Like the Kaufman and Hart play on which it was based, *Merrily* tells its story in reverse order; thus, the audience gets to see Frank, Charley, and Mary become increasingly nicer to each other, in the throes of early success and loving friendship, as the show continues.

We see them first, though, in the present day, bitter and estranged. In the first scene, where Frank's wife Gussie (Terry Finn) falls into a swimming pool (with water represented by a sheet of light blue paper), we witness Franklin cheating on his wife and not seeming particularly sorry about it. He fights with Charley, who, as we see in the next scene, has recently indicted Frank on national TV in "Franklin Shepard, Inc." (a song that gets Lonny Price a rousing ovation). Meanwhile, Mary drinks like a drunk.

Each actor has a T-shirt that tells the audience who his character is ("Best Pal" says Mary's; "Unemployed Actor" proclaims the one worn by a waiter). A scene set in the sixties has Frank wearing a beard and living in an apartment filled with throw pillows that are shaped like candy bars and adorned with the logos of Butterfinger and other popular treats.

The second act begins with the 1964 opening of Frank and Charley's first Broadway show, *Musical Husbands*. It's such a hit that it's described as "*Funny Girl*, *Fiddler*, and *Dolly* combined." Or, as Sondheim wrote in an early draft of "It's a Hit!," "The songs all have bullets / The theater's so full, it's / A cinch for a Pulitz / er Prize."

At the curtain calls, Price comes out to an explosion of handclapping. Equally loud is the applause for Morrison. But then Weissenbach comes out, and the applause dies seemingly by half. Weissenbach feels it, too—and his face falls considerably. It will fall considerably more in the upcoming days.

Saturday, November 28, 1981. The Alvin Theater, fifty-one days later. Fifty-two previews have gone terribly, and the opening was postponed more than once. Twelve days ago, the critics finally came; few had anything good to say, headed by the *Times*'s Frank Rich, who used such words as *shambles, fatuous, facile, labored, unfortunate, wasted,* and *upsetting.*

Earlier this week, Prince announced that *Merrily* will close tonight after sixteen performances—by far the shortest run any of the twenty musicals he's produced. To quote one of Sondheim's lyrics for Mary, "God don't answer prayers a lot."

The curtain comes up on these same kids in those same graduation robes, but the expressions on their faces are markedly different. Now they offer glazed, shell-shocked smiles, ones that are unable to mask their totally broken hearts.

One face is completely missing from the original twenty-six, for Weissenbach was replaced in previews by Jim Walton. The kids also saw choreographer Ron Field give way to Larry Fuller, and Judith Dolan redesign the costumes and minimize the T-shirts.

A poignant moment comes early in the second act, when *Musical Husbands* is opening. Producer Joe Josephson (Jason Alexander) has come out into the lobby for a break while the show is concluding. He talks to a friend for a while, then tells him, "I gotta get back in for the closing"—meaning the closing number—when the other theatrical meaning of that word strikes him. "I didn't mean the *closing*," he says. The audience reacts with a swoon of sympathy.

Then, suddenly, what had given these kids bragging rights all year long is over. Those invitations to seasons-long parties and awards ceremonies won't happen.

They can forget about those backstage visits from casting agents who think they'd be good for the lead in the next big Hollywood blockbuster, or the powerful writers who want to write a musical just for them. On Monday, they'll have "Unemployed Actor" metaphorically written across their T-shirts as they apply for jobs as waiters.

Yet, to quote a line from the second act, "True greatness is knowing when to get off." That's what Sondheim and Prince know. Okay, they seemed to say, you think we're that bad? We know when we're not wanted. We'll leave.

Once it was gone—and once the sterling cast album was made—people started hungering for *Merrily We Roll Along*. Regional, college, and high school productions abounded day after day after day after day after day after day. How many two-week flops yield three cast albums?

But would it ever come back to New York?

September 30, 2002. LaGuardia High School, New York City. Lonny Price has become the artistic director of Musical Theatre Works, a company devoted to developing new musicals. When the time came to stage a benefit, Price decided on the *Merrily We Roll Along:* The Original Broadway Cast Reunion Concert.

The evening's host is Jason Alexander, whose big credit *Seinfeld* is so well known to all of America that he didn't even bother listing it in the program. He jokes that this reunion was held in a high school auditorium "because *Merrily* starts at a high school graduation, and this makes it an environmental setting"— before he shrugs and concedes, "And we got a helluva break on the place."

Alexander has a good deal of tenderness to dispense, from mentioning that "We've all been trading pictures of our children" to admitting to both Sondheim and Prince, sitting in the audience, "We want to say what we didn't know enough to say twenty-one years ago. You brought this group together," he says, his voice breaking with emotion. "You never disappointed us. We hope we didn't disappoint you, and hope we don't disappoint you tonight."

They don't. After he mentions (most accurately) that we're about to hear "one of the most kick-ass overtures in Broadway history," the overture offers even more than the audience has memorized from the recording; the LP couldn't include the extra sections of "Now You Know" and "Good Thing Going" that were heard at the Alvin (now the Neil Simon Theater) in 1981.

As the twenty-piece orchestra plays, the audience sees on a back wall screen the slide of that glorious marquee that had crowned the theater for the last few months of 1981. But that slide is soon trumped by pictures of the production, and those kids aged sixteen to twenty-five.

Then, to tumultuous applause, adults from thirty-six to forty-six years of age file on stage, garbed in red graduation gowns. All but Sally Klein, the original Beth (Frank's first wife), are here. Some of the men have lost hair, but none of the cast has lost any of its spirit.

Right from their beautiful harmony on "The Hills of Tomorrow," the audience knows all will be right. And everything is. The chorus occasionally uses books, but the principals dispense with them, and never miss a word or cue. Even now, the 1981 *Merrily* was one of the most important events of these actors' lives, so many of them remember word for word what they did more than two decades ago.

Geoffrey Horne, who in the original production was brought in during previews to portray an older Franklin, was not needed, for Walton had aged enough to play the role. What a galvanizing performance he gives. Walton has been around plenty since *Merrily,* and now knows what he might not have then: he can carry a show—and he does.

In "It's a Hit!" when Price sings the lines about "selling out," he looks squarely at Alexander, who enjoys the good-natured jibe along with the audience, as visions of his fried chicken commercials dance in their heads.

Morrison, now totally devoid of her baby fat, is galvanizing in her numbers, be they as plaintive as "Like It Was" or as no-nonsense as "Now You Know." Those who have heard the cast album know that all the voices have of course aged, but for the better. The fizz of Coca-Cola has become the richness of cognac.

After singing "Old Friends," they all collapse to the floor, possibly out of exhaustion, or possibly to kid us that they're bushed. But when they get up and give a group hug, the audience knows their affection for each other is profoundly real.

Alexander proves he's a good team player, staying in the back row of the opening number. But his just getting up to start "Now You Know" gets him laughs. Such is the benefit of superstardom. He tears down the house with his section of "Opening Doors," where, as producer Joe Josephson, he complains, "There's not a tune you can hum." (Oh, yes, there is.)

Liz Callaway, subbing for Klein, sings "Not a Day Goes By"—for Klein, not Walton, originally sang the song in previews. By the time she gets to the fifth syllable, the recognition applause starts, thanks to all those renderings the song has since received in recordings and cabarets. Callaway also joins Walton and Price for some Irish step-dancing in "Bobby and Jackie and Jack" (a lighthearted spoof about the young Kennedys set in the early days of JFK's presidency), which gets cheers, as does their throwing around a football to mock the First Family's penchant for touch football.

All the principals perform while the chorus sits stage left and right on—yes, once again—rows of bleachers. There's the lagniappe of songs not on the cast album ("Growing Up" and "The Blob"). For the final scene, the cast comes out in the T-shirt costume scheme originally employed, and that gets a big hand, too. Walton's in a red "Frank" shirt, Price in a "Best Friend" blue, and Morrison in a "Pal" green. (Now Tony winner Tonya Pinkins has "Inquiring Reporter" on hers.) And as soon as they finish "Our Time," the whole house stands, even though many attendees know there's still a "Hills of Tomorrow" reprise to go. But the audience can't wait to let the players know just how much it loves them.

Once the cast finishes the school anthem, the crowd is on its feet once again.

For those who, like Mary, want it the way that it was, this is the closest thing they'll ever get. So many of the show's lines and lyrics register on so many different levels: *Some things you don't forget. Time goes by. Party! Playing host to the very best. It was good, it was really good. I want it back. You and I get continued next week. It's not that nothing went wrong. What a time to be alive! Being what we can. Years from now, we'll remember, and we'll come back.* But one lyric that a young Franklin Shepard matter-of-factly sang could never apply to this night: "I sort of enjoyed it."

It gets better. The cast turns around and looks at the enormous picture hanging from the rafters—of all of them in 1981 in their graduation gowns in a show that ran a shorter time than *A Family Affair* or *Hot Spot*. Had Prince in 1981 defiantly told the press, "We're going to fight!" and held on for four, six, or nine months, there wouldn't be this sorry-grateful sadness-joy rocking La Guardia High School tonight.

After a reprise of "Old Friends" has the crowd clapping in rhythm, old friends Stephen Sondheim and Hal Prince are brought to the stage. At this point, they haven't worked together since *Merrily We Roll Along*, possibly because each needed to try something—and someone—new after a decade of dazzling creations. They still have one more collaboration left in them—*Bounce*—but this will be their final moment of glory.

David Loud, who by this night has become the musical director of six Broadway musicals including *Ragtime*, harks back to those days between October 8 and November 28, 1981. Says Loud, "It was so painful to see and hear an audience hate so much what we loved so much. Now, to have people love it the way we did was so wonderful."

Merrily We Roll Along. November 16, 1981–November 28, 1981.
16 performances.

1982–1983

THE BIGGEST HIT
Cats

Taking a posthumous honor to a new height.

It was a tiny little article tucked at the bottom of the page in the October 15, 1980 edition of *Variety*: "*Cats* Dance Musical from T. S. Eliot Verse," its headline read.

The three-paragraph story said the show "is scheduled for West End presentation next spring" though "no cast has been set and no theater designated." It went on to mention such names as producer Cameron Mackintosh, director Trevor Nunn, and choreographer Gillian Lynne—before citing its composer, adding "Webber, in collaboration with lyricist Tim Rice, has composed several pop operas for legit, among them *Jesus Christ Superstar, Evita,* and *Joseph and His Amazing Technicolor Dreamcoat.*"

Even after *Evita,* the *Variety* reporter felt that Andrew Lloyd Webber needed to be identified?

Who knew that from this little squib that one of London and Broadway's most famous hits would be born? One must credit Lloyd Webber for seeing a musical in the fifteen poems that T. S. Eliot wrote in 1939: *Old Possum's Book of Practical Cats.* Lloyd Webber set thirteen of the poems virtually verbatim. ("The Naming of Cats" had all of six extra words.)

The biggest change for the American production—which opened seventeen months after the London debut on May 11, 1981—was thirteen new lines. When director Trevor Nunn discovered that performer Stephen Hanan, who'd play Gus the Theater Cat, could sing opera bouffe, he and Lloyd Webber created a new section for him in "Growltiger's Last Stand."

As for the hit song "Memory," it was not part of Eliot's collection, but came from one of his unpublished works. So did the character of Grizabella, the woebegone doomed-to-death cat who'd sing it. ("You know what people always came backstage to tell me?" asked Loni Ackerman, who played Grizabella for years. "That I should have come back at the end of the show looking like a million bucks. After all, cats are said to have nine lives.")

Hanan kept a journal during rehearsal, which was later published as *A Cat's Diary: How the Broadway Production of "Cats" Was Born.* During rehearsals, he wrote with relish about the score, the set, and his fellow feline performers; during previews, he admitted that "Much of the 'plot' is incomprehensible, but it doesn't seem to matter to the audiences."

Eventually it did. With the great, record-breaking, eighteen-year run came the inevitable backlash. Jokes and snide remarks showed up everywhere from dinner tables to national TV. "It's better than *Cats*" became a *Saturday Night Live* cliché. But *Cats* was just what the veterinarian ordered for a starting-to-sag Broadway that desperately needed a smash hit to show it could still entice customers.

Cats received ten Tony nominations, including the most curious one for Best Book. Never before had a nominee been dead for eighteen years, with no idea that the musical was happening, let alone the opportunity to actually work on it. More to the point, as was the case with Lloyd Webber's previous show, *Evita,* *Cats* had no book—which has traditionally meant a show's non-sung dialogue.

As Tony time approached, some thought *Cats* might not win for Best Book. But among its competition were two also-rans: *Merlin,* which had played an inordinately long sixty-nine-performance preview period before it dared to open (to unenthusiastic reviews), and *A Doll's Life*, which had played five performances and called it a life. Though neither had a chance, they at least had genuine books, filled with dialogue that led in and out of songs.

Perhaps *My One and Only* would win. It was a revisal of *Funny Face*, a fifty-six-year-old musical. And while Timothy S. Mayer's adaptation had had terrible trouble in Boston, veteran Peter Stone came in, doctored it and saved the day. *My One and Only* was now a bona fide hit—not as big as *Cats*, to be sure, but a hit. Would it take the Best Book prize?

No, it wouldn't. When *Cats* won for Best Musical, Actress (Betty Buckley as Grizabella), Costume Designer (John Napier), Director (Trevor Nunn), Lighting (David Hersey), and even Best Score—though T. S. Eliot had done his work in 1939—no one much complained. But Best Book? It was another lowering of the bar for the Broadway musical.

Cats. October 7, 1982–September 10, 2000. 7,485 performances.

The Biggest Flop
Dance a Little Closer

Oh, how the mighty have fallen.

March 11, 1983. A small, makeshift theater at Michael Bennett's Studios at 890 Broadway. Potential investors are at the workshop of a new musical. If enough of them believe in what they see, the show will wend its way to Broadway.

But confidence is not instilled by the show's bookwriter-lyricist, who walks shakily to center stage. Perhaps he's just worried that he'll slip on the sheet of plastic that covers much of the floor. *Dance a Little Closer* will have some ice-skating in it, and, for today anyway, that plastic will have to pass for ice.

The writer has on his trademark white gloves, which he often wears to hide his inveterate nail-biting. The gloves, though, can't disguise that his hands are shaking.

He is Alan Jay Lerner, who wrote all the words for *My Fair Lady*, *Gigi*, and *Camelot*. But the now sixty-four-year-old Lerner is nervously eyeing the eighty or so assembled. Finally does he dare to say something. It turns out to be one of dramatic literature's most famous lines: "I have always depended on the kindness of strangers."

How fast a legend can sink! Lerner's two previous new musicals have *together* amassed only twenty-five performances. The one before that, *Lolita, My Love*, as we saw, closed out of town twice. He hasn't had a hit since *Camelot*.

At that moment, Lerner might have wished that he'd instead worked on *Merlin*, about King Arthur's favorite magician. Though it probably wound up as that season's biggest money-loser, it did run 199 performances, thanks to producers who were reluctant to throw in the towel. As *Merlin* cast member Nathan Lane still likes to say, "It was the musical that wouldn't disappear."

But as facile a lyricist as *Merlin*'s Don Black is, he's no Lerner. And Elmer Bernstein, *Merlin*'s composer, is no Charles Strouse—the music man behind *Bye Bye Birdie*, *Applause*, and *Annie*, and now Lerner's partner.

However, Strouse's last three musicals have amassed even fewer performances (twenty-two) than Lerner's previous two. But this time, they had adapted *Idiot's Delight*, Robert E. Sherwood's 1936 Pulitzer Prize–winning play. Maybe that would make a difference.

Lajos Egri, in *The Art of Dramatic Writing*—an invaluable guide for playwrights—could have told them it was a bad idea. He comes down quite hard on *Idiot's Delight*: "It is far from being a well-constructed play," he wrote. "The characters had nothing to bind them . . . there are no people in his play, no people who really matter."

They included Harry Van, a second-rate entertainer who gets stuck in the Italian Alps in 1936, when the government won't allow anyone to leave the country. At his hotel arrives Irene, a former Russian aristocrat, or so she claims. But Harry thinks she's an impostor—that he had a torrid one-night stand with this very woman in Nebraska ten years ago. He—and we—spend the whole play wondering and trying to glean the truth. All this is played out around the other hotel guests—a doctor, a munitions merchant, a Fascist, a Communist, et al.

Wrote Egri, "Characters wander in and out with no particular motivation. Characters, instead of engaging in conflict, tell us about themselves." If the authors had asked Egri's advice, he might have quoted one of their song titles back to them: "It Never Would Have Worked."

But Lerner wanted to update the play into what he called "the avoidable future," upping the ante to the threat of nuclear war. He changed Irene into Englishwoman Cynthia Brookfield-Bailey, probably so Liz Robertson, a British star—and his eighth wife—could play her. Len Cariou, in his first Broadway appearance since *Sweeney Todd,* would portray Harry. But the musical repeated a crucial mistake that the film version had also made: it let the audience see that the two principals have indeed met before.

In retrospect, Lerner may have been ahead of his time in one move he made: he changed *Idiot*'s married couple, the Cherrys, into two gay men (Brent Barrett and Jeff Keller) who want to marry. (In 1983, this was not yet the much-talked-about issue it would become.) When a minister was asked whether such a union could or should be sanctioned, he could have simply said, "I don't know." Instead, he started what would be a four-minute song called "I Don't Know." Lerner wrote it to a melody that Strouse had composed as "The Well-Wishers," then the opening number of *Applause*, more than a decade earlier.

Perhaps *Idiot's Delight* had been overestimated, but it would run literally three hundred times longer than *Dance a Little Closer*, which closed after its opening night on Broadway. That meant twenty-six performances total for Lerner's last three shows, and twenty-three for Strouse's last four. What a sobering reminder that success, however spectacular, is never guaranteed to last —and that you can't depend on the kindness of anyone.

Dance a Little Closer. May 11, 1983. 1 performance.

1983–1984

THE BIGGEST HIT
La Cage aux Folles

Drag in the clowns.

While *La Cage aux Folles* was the surprise movie hit of 1978—no foreign film had ever grossed better in America—its success was not what prompted producer Allen Carr to buy the rights for musicalization. Long before the film, Carr had been in Paris and had seen the play version.

What he also saw was a musical in this story of Albin, whose alter ego is Zaza the drag queen, her lover Georges, and "their" son Jean, the result of Georges' one-night stand of heterosexual promiscuity.

Carr's original plan was to have Mike Nichols and Tommy Tune codirect, Tune choreograph, Maury Yeston do the score, and Jay Presson Allen do the book. The team had the idea to Americanize the property, moving it from St. Tropez to New Orleans.

Would *The Queen of Basin Street* have been as successful as *La Cage aux Folles,* the musical that did wind up on Broadway for almost fifty-one months? As one of Jerry Herman's songs goes, "Who knows? Who knows? Who knows?" But *Queen* was dethroned when Carr didn't want to pay Nichols what the director thought he was worth; once Nichols left, Tune and Allen soon followed. Yeston was willing to stay, but because Carr wanted to start clean, Yeston was instead given a percentage of the show—which turned out to be a tidy sum—in exchange for his work on *La Cage* to that point.

Enter Jerry Herman, who'd had three flops in ten years before doctoring a hit *(A Day in Hollywood / A Night in the Ukraine)*. He returned the action to France, and once he saw Harvey Fierstein's *Torch Song Trilogy,* he thought the playwright would have the right sensibility for the material. Arthur Laurents as director and Scott Salmon as choreographer completed the all-gay creative team.

Herman gets a great deal of credit for writing the gay anthem "I Am What I

Am," but his greatest masterstroke was musicalizing Albin's male-to-female transformation into Zaza. That was missing in both the original play and the film, for watching it in those media would have been as boring as watching his make-up dry. But in a musical, Albin could sing "A Little More Mascara" to himself during the transformation, making for a fabulous five minutes. (Herman had written the melody for this song more than two decades earlier. It had a different lyric, was called "Beautiful," and came from his 1961 off-Broadway flop *Madame Aphrodite*.)

George Hearn, who'd win a Tony as Albin/Zaza, says,

For my audition, the producers offered to provide a dress and heels for me. I was surprised that Boston, long known as a blue-nosed town, embraced the show during our tryout there. One woman there was waiting in line at the Colonial Theatre to buy tickets, but she suffered a heart attack. Still, she wouldn't leave in the ambulance until someone promised to keep her place in line.

The management was so pleased with the reception in Boston that when the cast album was issued, all copies distributed in Massachusetts bore a little round white sticker that said, "Thank you, Boston!" They should have offered their thanks to Broadway, too, for once the reviews were published, the lines for tickets at the Palace Theater were equally long and dense.

Herman provided a jaunty song 'n' dance for Jean-Michel (John Weiner) and his fiancée (Leslie Stevens) in "With Anne on My Arm," but there was literally more to this number. Soon after, we heard the melody reprised, but this time Albin and Georges (Gene Barry) were singing "With You on My Arm." Having a familiar melody helped eased resistant heterosexual audiences into the gay romance.

And it worked, too. As the show's press agent Shirley Herz noted, Jerry Herman was the first composer-lyricist to have three shows that ran over 1,500 performances: *Hello, Dolly!* (2,844), *Mame* (1,508), and *La Cage* (1,761).

Actually, *La Cage* would have run even longer had the Palace not been forced to close; the office building that housed the theater was being refurbished as the Embassy Suites Hotel. Management announced that the show would move to the nearby Mark Hellinger Theater, with Lee Roy Reams taking over as Albin. Then the move was deemed too costly, and the musical instead closed. (So would the Hellinger a few years later.) Twenty years earlier, even an also-ran such as *Bajour* could find the money to switch theaters during a less-than-seven-month run. Now, though, unions made a move prohibitively expensive.

It was Herman's last musical, though he would be given a chance to write another blockbuster. Around the turn of the new century, Mel Brooks asked him to write the score for *The Producers*, which would become the biggest hit of

2000-2001. Herman told Brooks that he should write the score himself, and that's what he did (though he got by with a "little" help from his friend Glen Kelly). Would *The Producers* have been even better with a Jerry Herman score? Once again: Who knows? Who knows? Who knows?

La Cage aux Folles. August 21, 1983–November 15, 1987. 1,761 performances.

THE BIGGEST FLOP
The Human Comedy

The off-Broadway hit that became a Broadway flop.

When we last left Galt MacDermot, he'd had two of the biggest flops of the 1972–1973 season. Not until the 1983–1984 season would he have his next musical on Broadway. This time, though, instead of writing an original musical, he made life easier for himself by doing an adaptation: a musical version of William Saroyan's *The Human Comedy*.

Though the financial outcome wasn't any different, at least this time the reviews would be good.

MacDermot recalls,

> It started when I was asked by someone at Banff Cultural Center of Canada to write an opera. I said, "Sure, but on what subject?" The man said, "Choose one." Well, at the same time, someone had told me to read Saroyan's *The Human Comedy*, which I did, and wound up really liking. So I called Bill Dumaresq and asked if he'd like to do it with me. He knew the movie version and loved it, and said yes right away.

The two had collaborated on *Isabel's a Jezebel*, a musical produced in London in 1970 that lasted a mere sixty-one performances—probably because its subject matter involved abortion. The cast album had no liner notes at all, which suggested that the record producer wanted to keep the controversial subject from the public.

The Human Comedy, though, was quite different. The story follows Homer Macauley (Stephen Geoffreys), a fourteen-year-old boy who's dealing with a number of hardships. First, it's 1943—which means wartime. With Homer's father dead and his older brother Marcus drafted and overseas, who's going to bring home the bacon? Not Homer's widowed mother (Bonnie Koloc), or his younger brother Ulysses (Josh Blake). His sister Bess (Mary Elizabeth Mastrantonio) could, but she's studying in college—where the family wants her to stay.

In the excellent film, Homer (a never-better Mickey Rooney) is seen just having landed a job at a telegraph office. His boss is telling him to "Be polite to everybody. Take off your cap in elevators, and above all things, don't lose a telegram. And if anything comes up that you don't understand, just come to me."

In fact, Homer does question his own ability with singing telegrams. His boss says that it's no big deal to deliver one, immediately assuming that the boy has a good voice. He does say, "Let's see how you'd do it," and Homer delivers a perfect rendition of the famous "Happy Birthday" song. "That's fine," says the satisfied boss.

It's a nice enough scene, but not nearly as good as what happens in the musical. Here, Homer has not yet landed the job—so there's much more at stake for him. What's worse, one of his would-be bosses says, "You're a little bit young for the job," making us worry that he won't get it. Then another boss demands, "Can you sing? Sometimes we have a telegram requiring you to sing. Can you carry a tune, or do you sing flat?"

Now Homer must audition, and if he doesn't come through, he'll fail his family. The boy then goes into of MacDermot's most felicitous melodies, "I Can Carry a Tune," as he insists, "I can carry a tune while on the run / Howl at the moon, sing at the sun . . . I can carry a tune at the drop of a hat / At weddings or funerals, just like that . . . I can make up tunes like the rest of them / Do-re-mi with the best of them."

Yes, he desperately wants the job, and he's so endearing that the audience just as much wants him to get it. But then a boss says, "Do you know how to sing 'Happy Birthday'? / We'll see if you can carry a tune."

And now Homer sings the famous song—terribly. God-awfully, in fact, nowhere near the melody (which smartly saved the production for paying royalties to the tune's composer. Yes, all these years later, the estates of the writers are still collecting). But, oh, does Homer throw his heart and soul into it! When he gets to the name of the person who's having the happy birthday— "Methuselah"—he really knocks himself out, stretching the name over measures of music—always atrociously, never on pitch, which is the fun of it. Yet while we're laughing, at the same time we're concerned he won't get the job.

But the moment he finishes, the bosses look at each other and, each knowing that the kid wants it so bad, say, "That's good!" The kid's hired, and we breathe easier, both because we're happy for him and because we've finally stopped laughing at how poorly he sang.

Of course, be careful what you wish for. By getting the job, Homer soon finds himself delivering telegrams that don't sing—ones that pass on the painful message that young men have been killed in action. Hardest of all, of course, will be the one he reads that says his brother Marcus has died, too.

MacDermot reports that after he and Dumaresq had written about a quarter of the first act, they went to Banff to show the impresario what they had.

> I don't think the guy liked it, but what he said was, "We need a subject that's Canadian." He hadn't said that before. So I said, "We can't set it in Canada, so, okay, we won't do it for you." Bill and I spent the rest of the year finishing it, and when we played it for Joe Papp (the first producer of MacDermot's *Hair*), he agreed to produce it. And Banff never called me back.

Though the collaborators wrote it to be staged conventionally, director Wilford Leach, who just come off that famous *Pirates of Penzance* revival, saw it as an oratorio. In the intimate Anspacher Theater, actors would stand at music stands. It worked well enough there, but on Broadway, the same approach looked cheap.

"At the Public Theatre," says MacDermot. "It was lovely to watch those kids from ten feet away. There, you didn't mind that there was no action or choreography. But on Broadway you did."

So *The Human Comedy* played more previews (twenty) than actual performances (thirteen) during its ten-day April 1984 Broadway run. Interesting footnote: future star Mary Elizabeth Mastrontonio's understudy was a performer who's an even bigger star today: two-time Tony winner Donna Murphy.

"The other thing," says MacDermot, "is that the *Times* wouldn't re-review it. So we didn't have that added push of a new set of reviews. I sometimes think that if the Internet had been in existence then, Frank Rich's rave would have remained there for everyone to see day in, day out—and we would have made it."

The Human Comedy. April 5–15, 1984. 13 performances.

1984–1985

THE BIGGEST HIT
Big River

Let's pretend.

Saturday, April 20, 1985. The Eugene O'Neill Theatre, New York City. The final Saturday night preview of *Big River*, a new musical by Roger Miller.

Yes, the same Roger Miller who wrote the music and lyrics for those funny and funky country songs in the sixties—including "Dang Me"—and the more serious "King of the Road."

A musical version of Mark Twain's *The Adventures of Huckleberry Finn* would seem to require a country sound. But if someone even a decade earlier had predicted that the writer of "You Can't Roller Skate in a Buffalo Herd" would be in the same theater where the authors of *She Loves Me, The Waltz of the Toreadors,* and *A View from the Bridge* once toiled, he would not have been believed.

And yet, on this Saturday night, a number of celebrities are entering the theater, dressed to kill. Three of them have Best Musical Actress Tonys, and all expected to be at a theater tonight—but performing, not watching. Alas, all their shows have closed prematurely, so what else do they have to do tonight?

Two Tony-winning director-choreographers are here, too. They would have rather been out of town with tryouts, but the money wasn't forthcoming for their new shows. So they're here to see this one.

They and so many other Broadway professionals are here wearing not only fancy clothes, but also glassy smiles. Because everyone knows the harsh reality: *This is the last musical of the season, and if this show doesn't make it, there really can be no Best Musical Tony Award this year.*

It's been a God-awful season. This week alone, a revival of *Take Me Along* closed on opening night, while *Grind* debuted to terrible reviews. A week ago, *Leader of the Pack* actually asked Broadway to accept a show where new songs were not written for the book (about songwriters Ellie and Jeff Greenwich's life together and apart). Instead, their hit songs (and misses) were plugged into the story here and there. A revue is one thing, but who'd ever have imagined that a book show could stoop so low?

As for the others, add up the runs of *Harrigan 'n' Hart, Andre DeShields' Haarlem Nocturne, The Three Musketeers,* and *Quilters,* and all together they didn't run as long as *Flora, the Red Menace,* Harold Prince's shortest-running musical in the first quarter-century he was producing.

Still, Broadway must hope and pray. Fourteen months earlier, *Big River* was produced at the American Repertory Company in Cambridge, Massachusetts, where the reviews and audience response weren't that strong. Perhaps, though, Miller and his bookwriter William Hauptman— never before represented on Broadway and barely off-Broadway—have come through.

They have to! Otherwise, we'll have to give "No Award" for Best Musical! How will that look on national TV?

From the orchestra back rail, in the standing room position, one can see the many celebrities taking their seats. Nice and close. There's been no demand for tickets, so good seats are easy to come by.

The curtain rises on Gordon Connell dressed to look like Mark Twain. A coo of recognition greets him, and then a nice laugh after everyone reads a sign: *Persons attempting to find a motive in this narrative will be prosecuted; persons attempting to find a moral in it will be banished; persons attempting to find a plot in it will be shot.* And while those are the words Twain chose to start his novel, here they almost seem to mean, "Don't expect too much."

The audience won't. There's a sprightly opening number in which Huck (Daniel H. Jenkins) is harassed by his aunts, who ask him, "Do You Want to Go to Heaven?" You'd think by the end of the number he'd make a decision one way or another, but the song just ends without advancing the action. Still, the celebrities lead the applause and the cheers, looking at the musical glass as half-full; it was a catchy tune, anyway, wasn't it?

There will be more of them. Soon Tom Sawyer (John Short) and his pals bound on to sing "(We Are) the Boys"—equally tuneful but dramatically inert. The audience is starting to suspect that this could be the pattern all night long—tub-thumpin' country songs that do nothing for the book. And when Huck finishes his balled, "Waitin' for the Light to Shine"—a pretty tune that also goes nowhere—they're sure of it.

Nevertheless, they continue to applaud enthusiastically. The next song scores especially high. It's sung by John Goodman, who won't be famous as Roseanne's husband for a few years. Now he's playing Huck's father, and he sings about his dissatisfaction with the "Guv'ment." The heavyset actor pours himself into such standard-issue Miller lyrics as "Well, you dad gum, dad gum, dad gum guv'ment."

One section of the song has Goodman rant increasingly higher . . . and higher—before he suddenly drops a couple of octaves and resumes the song down there. The three Tony winners burst out into gleeful laughter and throw their heads back in sheer delight. Never mind that a singer's going low when he's expected to go high is not worthy of such a response. These celebrities would never do such a thing or allow it in one of their shows. They know it's a cheap and dishonest way of getting a laugh. But tonight, with the stakes so high, they've got no choice but to pretend that it's *funny*.

After Huck kills a hog and spills his blood everywhere—all in hopes that the authorities will assume it's his blood and that he's been killed—Tom Sawyer comes out to sing the comic "Hand for the Hog." This isn't a scene that needs such a moment, and perhaps some in attendance are starting to the think that this one—and maybe for that matter "Guv'ment" and even "Waitin' for the Light to Shine"—have been unearthed from Miller's trunk. Were songs not deemed strong enough for the pop marker in Miller's late-sixties heyday now being recycled on Broadway?

People always applaud where a car is driven on stage, so they're going to clap at a moving raft, too. "Muddy Water," the song that follows, has seven sections, five of which offer the exact same lyric. Perhaps Miller himself is speaking through Huck when the lad proclaims that he "hereby declares myself to be nothing ever other than exactly what I am."

Credit where it's due, *Big River* is a well-meaning show, one that might be nice for kids to see. So the audience laughs uproariously when a shady character who claims his name is Bridgewater is called Bilgewater by someone who doubts him. They also applaud enthusiastically when the act 1 curtain comes down, not on a cliffhanger, but just after an arbitrary song ends.

And so it goes all night long, with songs that have a pop but not theatrical sensibility. But persons searching the narrative for musical theater craft will be deemed troublemakers. Don't they understand that Broadway needs to show the nation in that two-hour infomercial in June (otherwise known as the Tonys) that it has a quality product?

Big River winds up winning seven Tony Awards in a year so putrid that three categories are eliminated: Best Choreography, Best Actress in a Musical, and Best Actor in a Musical. Too bad for Jenkins, whose Huck Finn grows from a racist teen to a sensitive and smart young man; he might have won in that category had it existed. But the Tonys couldn't possibly give someone an award without putting him in competition with anyone, could they?

No—not for ten more years.

Big River. April 25, 1985–September 20, 1987. 1,005 performances.

The Biggest Flop
Grind

The end of a producing era.

Grind was the twenty-second Broadway musical that sported Harold Prince's name as a producer—and the last.

As a producer, Prince had started off very well. In his first twelve years (1954–1966), he had five smash hits—*The Pajama Game, Damn Yankees, A Funny Thing Happened on the Way to the Forum, Fiddler on the Roof,* and *Cabaret.* But Prince had often said over the years that he preferred directing to producing; hence, he hired himself to stage twelve of his musicals. Not that it was the only way he could get a directing job; four other managements had hired him to stage their musicals, too.

Yet in following eleven years (1967–1978), while he'd won four Best Director of a Musical Tonys for shows he'd produced, none had been a financial gusher. (Yes, he had won for *Sweeney Todd* and *Evita,* but he hadn't produced them.)

For *Grind,* Prince was listed seventh among the nine producers above the title. But he certainly was the one and only director in the piece, and at this point in Prince's career, that mattered more.

Producing—meaning raising money—was getting harder, and not just because producing a musical was far more expensive and a longer time was necessary before recoupment. Rarely did Prince appear on a panel or lecture hall where he didn't mention that he and his original partner had only had to raise $250,000 for *The Pajama Game* and had brought it in for $162,000. *Grind* wound up costing $250,000 short of $5 million—and would lose every cent.

What's more, even the most loyal of Prince's investors must have raised an eyebrow or two at his having four disasters thus in the eighties: two musicals (*Merrily We Roll Along* and *A Doll's Life*) and two non-musicals (*Play Memory* and *End of the World*). As a director, Prince knew what stimulated him, but as a producer, did he no longer know what people wanted to see?

Actually, from the outset, Prince was attracted to dark musicals. In 1957 alone, he coproduced both *New Girl in Town*, about prostitute Anna Christie, and *West Side Story*. Since then, he'd been drawn to musicals that involved everything from Nazis (*Cabaret*) to cannibalism (*Sweeney Todd*). But *Grind* may have been the bleakest of them all.

Though it took place in 1933—the same year in which *Annie*'s story was told—it was hardly a fairy tale. It was set in Chicago, at Harry Earle's Burlesque Theatre, called "the garbage can of show business." There were a few homages to burley-q gags (Straight man: "How long can a juggler keep his balls in the air?" Top banana: "Just as long as he can stand on his head.") But for the most part, this was a woefully serious story.

That it dealt with show business segregation was the least of it. Harry (Lee Wallace) insisted, "We got no mixing. Coloreds and whites ain't on stage together. They got separate acts, separate dressing rooms. Everybody knows their place." *Grind* reminded audiences what a terrible time this was for blacks. The irony was that Earle's was only a stone's throw from the "Century of Progress," the 1933 World's Fair that celebrated Chicago's one hundredth anniversary.

Leroy (Ben Vereen) was the black top banana who had a thing for Satin (Leilani Jones), the lead black stripper. That she wasn't interested didn't lead to too many dynamic plot twists.

Playing Gus, the white top banana, was Stubby Kaye. He was still fondly remembered for his Nicely-Nicely in *Guys and Dolls* (1950) and his Marryin' Sam in *Li'l Abner* (1956). Audiences who got to *Good News*' fifty-one previews and sixteen regular performances in 1974–1975 probably enjoyed seeing his exuberance as a football coach, too. But here a gaunter and less able-looking Kaye played a character who was going blind—which was far less fun. In a medical sketch, Gus played a doctor who'd inject his stooges with a long needle. The stooges, though, complained that he was hurting them because he couldn't see where to put the needle or how to keep it from causing pain. (What a convoluted plot turn!)

Gus picked up a bum in the alley to be his latest stooge. What he didn't know was that Doyle (Timothy Nolen) was dutifully committing a slow suicide by drinking himself to death. Once he'd been an Irish terrorist, but when his wife found out that he was planning a bombing, she left him and took their son with her. The train on which they traveled turned out to be the one on which Doyle had planted a bomb.

Doyle sang about these incidents in two different Irish-tinged songs, one with a "lu-tara-lee-a-lay" lyric and the other with a "a bomb-bomb, bombity bomb." While anything can be set to music in a musical, the more difficult the subject, the greater the songs must be. Composer Larry Grossman and lyricist Ellen Fitzhugh didn't rise to the occasion.

The songwriters failed in their opening number, too. The first lyrics were "This must be the place you heard about. The word about town is out." The interior rhyme was too clever, especially when set to Grossman's lickety-split melody. It was a "What is he saying?" moment for the audience—and if there's one thing an opening number must be, it's crystal clear.

Other moments were too sad. Satin's nine-year old brother was so looking forward to getting his first two-wheeler, and minutes after he did, some white toughs grabbed it and destroyed it. Leroy's defense was to laugh it off, but Satin couldn't. Not long after Doyle and Satin dared to consider romance, they were assaulted by white thugs, too. Harry eventually fired Gus, who then committed suicide.

Fay Kanin's book didn't spare us the funeral, or two racial epithets that a 1985 Broadway audience didn't want to hear. Sure, there was a semi-happy ending where we learned that show business helped integration move forward, but that message offered little consolation after all the tragedies.

Still, this would be the last time that producer Prince would have to tell his disappointed cast members that they would soon be out of work. From now on, Prince could leave the money matters in other hands, and just concentrate on the artistic side. He must have been glad he hadn't seduced investors into pledging money for his next musical—*Roza,* which, under his direction, ran all of twelve performances. But there must have been many, many times when Prince and his investors must have wished he'd produced as well as directed his subsequent new musical: *The Phantom of the Opera.*

Grind. April 16, 1985–June 22, 1985. 71 performances.

1985–1986

The Biggest Hit
The Mystery of Edwin Drood

Audience participation.

No one person had ever won Tonys for both Best Book and Best Score—until this season. Rupert Holmes accomplished the feat for adapting *The Mystery of Edwin Drood,* Charles Dickens' last—and unfinished—novel. His show wound up winning Best Musical, too.

Given that Dickens died before he could disclose whom he believed to have murdered Edwin Drood, Holmes had what seemed an inspired notion: to have the audience pick the perpetrator from the information he gave them.

Holmes said he first got the idea for the show on a train trip in 1971.

I pondered how one might end a story whose author had given it no ending. I thought about all the times in theater when something went wrong, when an actor went up on his lines, an expected entrance wasn't made—causing another actor to ad lib to cover the moment. If a prop fell and an actor neatly picked it up and made some clever comment, the audience would wriggle with delight or even applaud, knowing "That doesn't happen every night." Not only does the performance suddenly feel special, but the audience feels special as well, as part of a select club or inner circle. And I wondered if there was a way that this highly theatrical effect—which acknowledges the difference between a live performance and a pre-recorded one—could be built into something as imposing and seemingly un-malleable as a Broadway musical.

So Holmes decided to create a variety of confessions that would give the audience the feeling that it was truly determining the outcome of the piece. He says,

To some degree it was, although only from scripted options they'd been given. It was a tremendous amount of work, because I had to write (and orchestrate) a third act's worth of music, lyrics, and dialogue, most of which would go unheard at any given performance. But I loved the sense of event that it gave the proceedings. I loved making the audience feel as if the actors considered them to be the most important people in the world at that particular moment.

The suspects included John Jasper, the choirmaster at Cloisterham Cathedral, as well as Helena and Neville Landless, the brother and sister from Ceylon. While Helena didn't seem to have much motivation, Neville was scandalized to hear that Drood planned to go to Egypt and build a commercial road made from the bricks taken from the pyramids (in those days before national landmarking).

Certainly the murderer couldn't be the Reverend Mr. Septimus Crisparkle, religious man that he is—though his neglected assistant Bazzard could be responsible. What about Princess Puffer, who was no stranger to illegalities, given that she ran the local opium dispenser? Or Rosa Bud herself? Sure, she was Edwin's Drood's betrothed, but she didn't seem to want to marry him, just as he seemed to not want to marry her.

Or was the crime an accident? After all, John Jasper did give his coat to Drood to protect him from the cold he would encounter when leaving his house. The murderer, seeing Drood in it, could have believed (s)he was killing Jasper.

So Holmes wrote many different confessions, just in case the audience inferred that Bazzard did it because he needed to be in the spotlight. Or that Neville and Jasper each wanted Rosa and would kill Drood to get her. Or that Helena hated Edwin for being so terrible to her beloved brother.

The other three, though, might have thought they were killing Jasper. Rosa Bud was so abnormally frightened of him that she might have been moved to murder. Princess Puffer had been Rosa's nanny, and might have wanted to protect her from him. Reverend Crisparkle once wildly loved Rosa's mother, and eventually transferred that ardor to the daughter. And what about a strange detective named Datchery who shows up late in the show? Is he one of the other characters in disguise?

"The voting for each performance was legitimate," insists Holmes. "It was done by acclamation, so there was no way to rig that, except if an actor packed the house with his relatives and friends."

The voting for the murderer was overseen by cast ensemble members who ventured into the audience, which they divided into districts. Each district was asked to vote by showing their hands as a candidate's name and number (ranging from 1 to 6, held in the hands of the performers on stage) was called out by the vote taker. Says Holmes,

> The reason for dividing the audience into districts was so that, amid the cacophony and the varying pace of voting from section to section, it would be impossible for the audience to accurately gauge for whom the various districts are voting. Thus, we'd keep the identity of the "elected" Murderer a surprise until the moment that he or she was revealed.

When the ensemble members finished tallying their district's votes, they would rush backstage with the note pad on which they'd written, say, "Jasper 3, Rosa 14, Puffer 2," etc., and turned it over to the assistant stage manager. He then added the results from each district to determine which person was the "winning Murderer."

Holmes explains why:

> The news was then given to an actor backstage who joined the scene in progress—so that he could relay this information to the winning murderer so he'd have a minute to both brace himself for the scene ahead and slowly move to center stage for the big reveal. At the same time that the performer was notified of his or her selection, the stage manager was telling the conductor by headset the identity of the killer; the conductor then held up a chalkboard for the orchestra to see, so they the musicians would know to which section in their music they should next turn.
> During the Broadway run, Holmes noticed certain trends.

The most obvious suspect,, and the person I think Dickens likely had in mind all along, is John Jasper, the crazed choirmaster and protagonist. In the preamble to the voting, I intentionally emphasized to the audience what an obvious solution this would be. Of course, the audience rarely took the bait and voted for Jasper, which is precisely what I wished. Neville usually had a poor showing, too. Because he was hot-blooded, had a dreadful temper, and had threatened Drood on numerous occasions, those qualities ironically made him the second-likeliest suspect. And Puffer was seldom chosen because she's a lovable character, especially when she's played by a beloved star such as Cleo Laine. The audience generally had difficulty in considering someone so dear to them as a killer."

However, he says, when Puffer is portrayed by an unknown—or played ineptly—she stands a better chance of "winning."

That leaves Rosa, Helena, and Crisparkle as the most usually accused. Holmes says,

The fair, virginal Rosa Bud seemed too good to be true. Helena Landless was a tempestuous Dragon Lady, with shades of (moody forties film actress) Gale Sondergaard. As for the kindly Reverend Crisparkle: what trumps a lunatic choirmaster? A lunatic priest! But Rosa tended to be victim more than a third of the time. Then, after a few months, Helena was taking these honors. Finally, the Reverend Crisparkle found a way to advance to the front disproportionately to the others. So if any of these three ended up in first place with the other two relatively close behind, I felt the audience was responding as expected.

However there was no way anyone could predict with certainty the outcome at any performance. We also discovered that when the murder suspects stood in a row numbered 1 to 6, the voting was weighted more toward the higher numbers than the lower. This was in part, I think, because the audience was still getting its bearings when the voting began, and often didn't fully understand what it was supposed to do until the first one or two candidates had been passed by. It's also human nature not to say "Yes" to the first choice offered. When a waiter tells you the specials of the day, rarely do you stop him after the first item and say, "That's exactly what I want; don't tell me the others." However, with our election you couldn't go back and vote for choice one or two; the way we sequenced the voting, if you didn't vote for Number 1 when his or her name was offered, you'd lost your chance. So we found the 4, 5, and 6 slots were "power positions" while 1 and 2 were weak, and 3 was neutral.

With that information in hand, Holmes adjusted.

In order to keep the endings—and the cast—fresh, I suggested that anyone voted Murderer at a performance should be relocated to the number 1 slot at the next performance, and that the remaining actors would all move up one slot. This meant that favorites would be bumped back to the weaker slots each time they won, whereas all others would move inexorably toward those premium power positions. This constant shifting of sequence (and 'penalizing' the previous performance's winner by making him climb the ladder from the lowest rung again) kept the choices diverse throughout the show's run.

Holmes also reports that

As the rivalry and the quest for the final confession compounded itself over a long run, actors would try to find ways to sway the voting within their own performance. When Helena Landless started winning a lopsided share of the elections, we watched Jana Schneider from the back of the theater and discovered that during the dinner scene, she was quite blatantly slipping a prop carving knife up her sleeve, making sure it reflected an overhead light so that the audience would take note. She was asked to cease and desist. Likewise, with the rigors of an extended run, one performer developed a murderous hatred of another cast member and became, frankly, a little loony. During this time, the audience consistently swerved toward that slightly crazed performer. They sensed that there but for the grace of Equity went a maniac.

And Bazzard? Says Holmes,

Before the audience voted on the Murderer, they voted on the identity of "the Detective in Disguise named Datchery." Bazzard was the overwhelming favorite—not because the audience used its deductive powers, but because he had so little to do, and this way, they could give him his share of the spotlight, if only for a moment. Each audience has this opportunity to be generous and good-hearted to an unsung thespian, and on the average of 80 percent of the time, they seized this chance to show their kindness. That also meant that much of the time, Bazzard wasn't a candidate for Murderer. But on those 20 to 25 percent of occasions when Bazzard wasn't picked as Datchery, he was thrust into the Murderer's Lineup—which also meant that someone else (usually Helena or Rosa) was pulled—making the voting quite different. The audience sometimes realized it had lost its opportunity to give Bazzard his big moment and compensated here. Sometimes it just considered him the least likely suspect, or it picked

Puffer or Neville for Murderer, because suddenly those characters weren't in competition with such stronger candidates as Helena or the Reverend.

"But the ultimate factor that makes the voting unpredictable," says Holmes, "is simply the audience itself." He continues,

Every audience is an organism newly created at each performance. There are two sides to every theater curtain; for the actors, it rises on the audience as much as it rises on them. The voting at *The Mystery of Edwin Drood* is, for me, a lighthearted but formalized acknowledgment of the conspiracy between actors and audience that occurs at every performance of every stage musical or play.

Ten years later, someone did manage to match Holmes' triple crown. Jonathan Larson won for Best Book of a Musical, Best Score of a Musical, and Best Musical, too, for *Rent*. Holmes sadly remains the only such winner who could go up to the stage and accept his awards; Larson tragically died before his show's first off-Broadway preview.

And yet, if Best Orchestrations had been a category in 1985–1986—it wouldn't be for eleven more years—Holmes probably would have won yet another Tony, for he'd charted his own music. Even Jonathan Larson didn't do that.

The Mystery of Edwin Drood. December 2, 1985–May 16, 1987. 608 performances.

THE BIGGEST FLOP
Big Deal

A great talent who's wrong for the show.

Happy New Year's failure taught us that adding existing songs to a property leads to a synthetically unexciting show. But what if an "insert-old-song-here" musical were to be staged by Broadway's most exciting director-choreographer, Bob Fosse?

Of the artists who doubled as both directors and choreographers, no one had aggregately won more Tony Awards than Fosse, who, as of this season, had won seven. Granted, six of them were "only" for choreography, while there was but one for direction—for *Pippin* in 1973. But that year, Fosse won two other directorial prizes: the Emmy for *Liza with a "Z"* and the Oscar for *Cabaret*. Here, then, was a living legend.

Director Bert Shevelove and choreographer Donald Saddler couldn't make

Happy New Year work—but betting against Bob Fosse to achieve what they couldn't was not necessarily wise.

His source was the 1958 Italian film *Big Deal on Madonna Street.* Fosse's desire to do a musical version of this crime caper dated back more than twenty years. In the mid sixties, he thought of doing an evening's worth of two musical one-acters based on Italian films. The first would be called *The Small World of Charity,* based on Fellini's *Nights of Cabiria*; the second would be *Big Deal on Madonna Street,* which would culminate in a robbery from which the thieves would escape by helicopter. (Yes, long before *Miss Saigon*'s authors thought of it, Fosse did.)

The one-act *The Small World of Charity* became, of course, the two-act *Sweet Charity.* One must wonder, though, whether *Charity*'s bookwriter, Neil Simon, got one of his best jokes from *Big Deal on Madonna Street,* because that film's director was Mario Monicelli. Remember that Simon had not-too-bright Charity tell foreign film star Vittorio Vidal of her admiration for Monica Monicelli—which she pronounced as "Mon-IK-a Mon-IK-a-lee" before he corrected her.

With *Charity* expanding, Fosse put *Big Deal on Madonna Street* on the back burner. For 1985–86, he'd finally move it to the forefront.

Big Deal on Madonna Street dealt with thoroughly incompetent thieves who plan their "perfect crime" imperfectly. They want to rob a person's apartment, and expect to rent the vacant apartment next door to bore through. By the time they get around to renting, it's already occupied by two elderly women and their maid. So the criminals choose the best-looking among them to romance the maid, so he'll eventually be able to get into the apartment.

He does get her to be his girlfriend—but the day before the robbery, she quits, and they're flummoxed again. Add to this one criminal's breaking his arm, and another having to watch his infant child because his wife is in jail, and it's nonstop hilarity.

Fosse wrote the book for the musical, and while he followed the screenplay rather closely, he moved the setting to 1930s Chicago and changed the crooks to African-Americans. This unfortunately reinforced the prejudices and stereotype that blacks are both dishonest and inept.

A bigger liability was that Fosse's murky sensibility and Jules Fisher's much-too-dark lighting were wrong for the lightweight show. Starting with "Life Is Just a Bowl of Cherries" might not have been such a bad idea. ("Don't take it serious," is, after all, one of its lyrics.) But Fosse directed Loretta Devine to sing it in sultry fashion. Ralph Burns also provided hard-hitting brass orchestrations with twangy bass guitars, and some songs were delivered as rap. The promise of a smarmy evening, and not a funny one, was set.

And yes, the aspect of recycled songs did make the show boring. There was a scene in which a judge listened to a defendant's spurious testimony, looked askance, and then sang the title line of the song, "I've Got a Feeling You're

Fooling." That got a laugh, but then audiences had to sit through the whole song.

Fosse gave "Everybody Loves My Baby" a different meaning. Though the 1925 song's original meaning for "baby" was "girlfriend," here the father (Alan Weeks) of that infant meant "baby" literally. In the original film, that baby was an obstacle to his father; here, having the man pay tribute to the kid was not what the show needed. Just as *Fiddler* was about tradition, *Big Deal* was about incompetence. But *Fiddler* has many songs that deal with tradition; Fosse couldn't find any old songs that dealt with lack of ability.

The production numbers worked, and Fosse received his eighth Tony for Best Choreography. But *Big Deal* would have been a better show in 1966 if Neil Simon had written a lightweight but funny book to tuneful Cy Coleman music and lyrics by Dorothy Fields that would have been right for the action. That musical might well have become a big deal. As it was, critics used the title against this show to say that it was no big deal at all.

Big Deal. April 10–June 8, 1986. 69 performances.

1986–1987

THE BIGGEST HIT
Les Misérables

Broadway's critics dare to disagree with London's.

With reviews like these, you'd think this would have been the biggest flop of the season:

"Melodrama, contrivance, and artifice . . . lacking the power to move . . . the shell of theatre . . . not the bones of drama."—Suzie MacKenzie, *Time Out*

"As sanctimonious as it is melodramatic . . . the book declines into a crude cops-and-robbers epic and drips with sentimentality . . . a turgid panorama . . . it left me doubtful."—John Barber, *Daily Telegraph*

"Little to grip the ear and still less to trouble the mind . . . We're kept waiting for ages for out-and-out melody. A show that's all singing needs fresher words than this."—Jim Hiley, *Listener*

"The spectacle tells us nothing much . . . the songs are unmemorable . . . the story is sentimental and melodramatic . . . told by the writers with great sententiousness."—Christopher Edwards, *Spectator*

"It is all curiously remote."—David Nathan, *Jewish Chronicle*

"They have been seduced down the primrose path of spectacle . . . reduced to the trivialising and tearful aesthetic of rock opera . . . Come back, Sigmund

Romberg and Rudolf Friml; all is forgiven . . . notes tumbling and scampering after a tumult of words without ever quite catching up . . . all too frequently fall[ing] into the pretentious and the banal . . . melodies plummet dispiritingly . . . this witless and synthetic entertainment."—Michael Ratcliffe, *Observer*

"Middlebrow entertainment rather than great art . . . often seems to consist of nothing but narrative climaxes . . . sinks into utter banality."—Michael Billington, *Guardian*

"The reduction of a literary mountain to a dramatic molehill . . . unfortunate . . . a lurid Victorian melodrama."—Francis King, *Sunday Telegraph*

"This anguished version of intertwining destinies turn [the author's] tidal wave of emotions into ripples of cheat sentiment . . . little verbal excitement or novelty . . . it leaves one curiously uninvolved."—Jack Tinker, *Daily Mail*

"It is almost a pleasure to be bored by it. And that—despite some tenderly affecting romantic moments after the first hour or two, [it] is exactly what you may be. Watching it is rather like eating an artichoke: you have to go through an awful lot to get a very little."—Kenneth Hurren, *Mail on Sunday*

"A load of sentimental old tosh. A sticky mess. I'd forget about a West End transfer."—Lyn Gardner, *City Limits*

Producer Cameron Mackintosh didn't take Gardner's advice after reading her review in October 1985. For one thing, the public was flocking to see *Les Misérables* at the Royal Shakespeare Company's Barbican Theatre. So despite the many lethal responses from the critics, Mackintosh moved *Les Miz,* as it came to be chummily known, to the Palace in London's Theatreland on December 4, 1985, so that more could be moved by the story of Jean Valjean (Colm Wilkinson) and his unstinting nemesis Inspector Javert (Roger Allam). While it has since moved to a smaller theater, it is, as of this book's writing, still playing— and has lasted thousands of times longer than the French Student Rebellion of June 5–6, 1832, that it dramatizes.

Oh, the reviews weren't all bad. Though Benedict Nightingale in the *New Statesman* thought "one tender death scene came blasting through the auditorium like a force-ten fart," he also concluded that "gradually Trevor Nunn and John Caird's production increased its hold." Michael Coveney in the *Financial Times* said it was "an intriguing and most enjoyable musical." Sue Jameson of *London Broadcasting* stated that it was "an evening of the best British theatre." Clive Hirschhorn exclaimed, "What a consummate pleasure it is to find a musical in which the music is not only worth singing, but it is exceptionally well-sung . . . bold and frequently exciting . . . I left the theater impatient for a cast recording." Sheridan Morley in *Punch* exclaimed, "We have the musical of the year, if not the half-decade . . . There is an energy here that exists in the work of no British composer, past or present . . . that score surges through the theatre . . . *Les Misérables* is everything the musical theater ought to be doing."

But by and large, the reviews were not commensurate with the more-than-quarter-century run in London. Little did Barber, Hurren, Tinker, and Morley know that *Les Miz* would easily outlive them. By the time an American edition of *Les Miz* was being readied, its older brother had become London's town's hottest ticket, selling out at each and every performance, for a solid year and a half.

So were the reviews from the American critics similar to the ones that their fellow wizards gave the show in London?

No. Odd how that works.

When the $10 million production opened its pre-Broadway tryout at the Kennedy Center on December 27, 1986, the *Variety* critic (bylined simply "Paul") had a markedly different opinion. "*Les Misérables* is exactly what the slumbering musical stage has been waiting for—a smash hit of the highest caliber with a dynamic score . . . a treat to the ears . . . a wide variety of compelling numbers [that] tug at every emotion."

Had the score been changed? Had the show been rewritten? Well, a tiny bit. Among the nips and tucks, Gavroche, the little revolutionary, lost the first (and larger) section of his song "Little People." But that couldn't have made that much of a difference, could it?

When *Les Miz* opened on Broadway *at* the Broadway (the second-biggest theater in town), *Variety*'s New York critic Richard Hummler—"Humm"— wrote, "It's a smash, all right. Magnificent stagecraft is joined to an uplifting theme . . . and to stirring music. The show's narrative propulsion, sensual scenery, organized staging and outstanding singing gives the $47.50 public its money's worth and then some."

But in those days, Frank Rich in the *New York Times* counted most. His review began, "The contemporary musical theater can flex its atrophied muscles and yank its audience right out of its seats." If that didn't grab one's attention, perhaps this would: "The ensuing fusion of drama, music, character, design and movement is what links this English adaptation of a French show to the highest tradition of modern Broadway musical production." He also cited the show's "conviction, inspiration and taste" as well as its "profligately melodious score."

Rich wasn't alone. Clive Barnes in the *New York Post* called it "the stuff of theatrical legend. This is red-blooded, two-fisted theater. Start fighting to see it."

In short, the *Les Miz* New York reviews were almost the exact opposite of the London ones. *Variety* tallied twelve favorable, six mixed, and four unfavorable. The naysayers were headed by Howard Kissel in the *New York Daily News*: "Most of Claude-Michel Schonberg's music is drivel—singsong, repetitious, emotionally dead [with] unbelievably simple-minded lyrics." But John Simon of *New York* magazine began his review with something closer to truth: "There is no way a critic can affect a popular hit of two continents with an $11 million advance sale in New York alone."

So perhaps the better reviews in New York were a response to the success of the enterprise rather than to the show itself. Critics in New York had been in agreement with their London colleagues about *Cats,* but the public didn't care a whit. Now that *Cats* was still selling out nearly five years after it had opened—no Broadway show had ever done that—should New York critics let their readers see once again that they were in disagreement with the public? There was a good chance that critics who were critical of *Les Miz* might not hurt the show, but might hurt themselves and their own credibility.

Not that every American theatergoer responded to *Les Miz,* of course. Take popular game show guest Bruce Vilanch, who said, "It's a show where a person sings a ballad with a certain light on him—and then he dies."

But the show certainly hasn't.

Les Misérables. March 12, 1987–May 18, 2003. 6,680 performances.

THE BIGGEST FLOP
Smile

Getting attention on the nation's number one news show.

The ad campaign went, "From the bookwriter of *Fiddler on the Roof* . . . the composer of *Annie* . . . the lyricist of *Godspell.*" Sounds great, doesn't it?

But *Rags*—which honored our great-grandparents who courageously left their homes, families, friends, and languages for an unknown land, people, and tongue—would run four performances. More than eight months later, it received five Tony nominations. No show had ever received more nominations than performances. Says Stephen Schwartz. "All you had to do to back then was *open* to get a Tony nomination."

One went to bookwriter Joseph Stein, while Schwartz and composer Charles Strouse shared another. That *Rags* didn't score in the direction department surprised no one; the show went through (at least) four directors. Choreographer Ron Field, though, was recognized for his flavorful ethnic dances.

The other Tony nod went to producers Lee Guber, Martin Heinfling, and Marvin A. Krauss. Bad call. Smart producers would have made certain that *Rags* opened on Broadway on the Fourth of July—and not just because that's a particularly patriotic day. For on July 4, 1986, the one hundredth birthday of the Statue of Liberty was celebrated in grand fashion. After five years of refurbishment and tons of scaffolding surrounding the twelve-story statue, Miss Liberty reopened for her centennial. It became a national event, shown on television, with fireworks happily exploding in the background.

So *Rags,* whose logo was the Statue of Liberty, should have opened that same weekend, for it would have shared in the media attention and greatly benefited. But *Rags* didn't have its first preview for more than a month later, wouldn't officially open for two more weeks, and closed two days later.

Still, five Tony nominations count for something, and it's four more than *Smile* received. Only bookwriter Howard Ashman was recognized; even the superb score he wrote with composer Marvin Hamlisch was snubbed.

So though it played twelve times as long as *Rags, Smile* is the biggest flop of the season, because, in a sense, it failed twice. The musical about the few highs and many lows of the Young American Miss Pageant originally had a book by Jack (*Vanities*) Heifner and lyrics by Carolyn Leigh. If Leigh was being counted on to bring a female sensibility to the project, she was surely also chosen for her trademark earthiness. We've already seen it in *Wildcat* ("Don't thumb your nose, bub"), but it had also appeared in *Little Me* ("You ain't no Eagle Scout") and *How Now, Dow Jones* ("Watch your bloomers, Mabel.")

Leigh sure didn't characterize many of the sixteen Young American Misses as sweet innocents. To begin with, they're unimpressed with Santa Rosa, where the pageant is held—saying that the biggest noise in town is "the flushing of the chemical johns / For seven thousand mobile homes" in "horny Californee-ay." One girl sings, "Me, I had to sell myself to pay the rent," while another remembers "one whole season laying a jock." Another lass sings that the contest is "every man for himself . . . so man the lifeboats, and let all the women and children die."

What does choreographer Tommy French think of the girls? Leigh brought out the animal imagery in him: "These sows / Ain't none of them Juliet Prowse." He tells his struggling dancers, "The local zoo has a hippo who does it better on all fours." The girls drive Tommy to such distraction that he tells them not just to "Take five" but to "Take five *years*."

Of course, the time comes for the pageant itself, when the girls pretend to be the sweet things they believe the judges want to see. Hence, Hamlisch wrote the happy-go-lucky "Walking in the Sunshine," a nifty soft-shoe. The girls sing, "A song in my heart / My heart in a song / My days are no longer lightning- and-thunder-ful / Isn't is it wonderful?"

Yet when *Smile* opened on Broadway in 1986, neither Heifner nor Leigh was with it—and the only music left from Leigh's tenure was the title song. One might assume Leigh's death three years earlier was the reason, but there may be more to it than that. In his memoir, *The Way It Was*, Hamlisch doesn't even mention that Leigh ever worked on the show, but cuts right to Ashman—and then metaphorically cuts into him, too, for taking on three jobs: bookwriter, lyricist, and director. Perhaps he's still angry with Ashman for talking him into dropping all but one of his previous songs and coming up with more than a dozen new ones.

The night before *Smile* officially opened on Broadway, *60 Minutes*, which had been following the show's genesis for three years, aired its findings. In allowing the investigative reporting, *Smile*'s producers were taking a big risk. Getting coverage on one of the nation's top-rated shows could prove a boon to business, but if *60 Minutes* came to frown on *Smile*, the national audience would hardly be inclined to buy tickets.

The November 23, 1986 segment sure didn't start off optimistically. *60 Minutes* anchorwoman Diane Sawyer stated, "American musicals are in big trouble" and that "So many recent ones have flopped, hardly anyone wants to gamble on them anymore."

Sawyer turned back the clock a year to the $250,000 workshop performance on December 11, 1985, when David Geffen, the Shuberts, and many others attended to see if they'd invest. Hamlisch was confident: "This show is begging to be a musical." Sawyer said of Ashman, "This is his first and maybe only shot at the big time." In a way, she was correct; while Ashman's stage adaptations of his films *Beauty and the Beast* and *The Little Mermaid* respectively reached Broadway in 1994 and 2008—and his off-Broadway *Little Shop of Horrors* arrived there in 2003—Ashman lived to see none of them; he died of complications from AIDS in 1991.

Geffen refused to take *Smile* to Broadway, and while Sawyer noted that "The Shuberts wouldn't talk to us," she reported that they wouldn't invest. Their refusal made Hamlisch bitter, for the Shuberts had made plenty from his *They're Playing Our Song* and, much more to the point, his still-running *A Chorus Line* at their flagship theater.

But two others stepped forward: Sidney L. Shlenker, owner of the Denver Nuggets basketball team, and Richard Kagan, who admitted that Hamlisch is his "best friend and godfather to my children." Schlenker had no problem providing $2.5 million of the $4 million needed; "The fun that goes with it," he explained, "beats the devil out of government bonds."

Kagan had to rely on backers' auditions to get the other $1.5 million, but he managed it, and soon *Smile* was auditioning for theater party and group sales agents. When one agent described the show as "cute," Sawyer opined, "But at $47.50 an orchestra seat, 'cute' may not be enough."

Peppered throughout the segment were snippets of songs from *Smile*, including one that was dropped: Doria Hudson (Jodi Benson), the most savvy beauty contestant, sang, "Back home in Waco, Texas, I was voted Miss Teenage Complexion / It was run by a horny old skin doctor / Twenty-five girls for his private inspection."

Hamlisch also demonstrated how he'd come up with the tension-filled music for the act 1 finale. He started singing "Until Tomorrow Night," in which the contestants panicked about the next day's competition, before the camera cut to an actual performance in progress. In this snippet, the competing young women engaged in a pillow fight—to show that they were still just little girls at heart.

Sawyer stood in front of the marquee of the (now-defunct) Mechanic Theater in Baltimore before moving inside to ask twenty-four-year-old Benson and eighteen-year-old Anne Marie Bobby—who portrayed Robin Gibson, the most naïve contestant—how they judged their show's chances. Offstage, Bobby wasn't so starry-eyed, and it was Benson who offered a more optimistic "8 ½" to Bobby's "8." Shlenker may or may not have been quoting *Guys and Dolls* when he said "it's better than even money."

Finally, Sawyer went to the opening night party in Baltimore, where everyone cheered Kagan as he read a review that said, "*Smile* has already won the regional finals and is ready to compete in the big leagues." But Sawyer added, "Not all the reviews were glowing. Will *Smile* be a hit? Tomorrow night, the show finds out. A week from tonight, we'll let you know."

The reviews were dreadful. So a week later, *60 Minutes* broadcast its three standard subjects (and Andy Rooney, too) without offering any mention of *Smile*. Was the program reneging completely in light of the show's bad reception? Near broadcast's end, longtime host Mike Wallace took a few seconds to clean up odds and ends from previous weeks; the broadcast was wrapping up, and *Smile* had missed its chance. But then Wallace said, "Last week, we promised to tell you what the critics thought of the Broadway musical *Smile*," before pausing and adding unemotionally, "Not much."

Smile. November 24, 1986–January 3, 1987. 48 performances.

1987–1988

The Biggest Hit
The Phantom of the Opera

"My show never stops."

The *Phantom of the Opera*'s first entry in the Guinness Book of World Records states that it's Broadway's longest-running show. As of this writing, more than twenty-two years' worth of playgoers have seen that chandelier descend.

(Slowly. Very slowly. Too slowly, in fact, and not commensurate with the panic of the people on stage who are just about to be smashed by it. Surprising that crackerjack director Harold Prince didn't think to make his actors on stage move in slow motion so that chandelier and cast would be in sync.

Nevertheless, this oversight obviously hasn't hurt the $8 million production from grossing more than $715 million on Broadway alone, and $3.2 billion worldwide.)

But *Phantom* has another World Record in the Guinness book. George Lee Andrews has been recognized, too, for doing more performances in a Broadway show than any other performer ever has.

Those familiar with other performers' long-running records may be surprised that Carol Channing doesn't hold the title for *Hello, Dolly!* or Yul Brynner for *The King and I* did more. No. In fact, add her 4,500 performances as Dolly Levi to his 4,626 outings as the King of Siam, and they amount to only a few more performances than the total George Lee Andrews has amassed in *The Phantom of the Opera*. Putting it into perspective, such teen idols as Miley Cyrus and Vanessa Hudgens have never lived a day when *Phantom* and George Lee Andrews have not been on Broadway.

"Everyone knew it was going to be a huge hit, so at the auditions, I saw every character man in New York auditioning, too," Andrews says. His eyes sparkle as he adds, "This show was obviously going to run for at least two years—maybe even five."

Of course, Andrews had a leg up because he had a history with the Prince. Of the three Broadway shows in which Andrews had appeared, two—*A Little Night Music* (1973) and *On the Twentieth Century* (1978)—had been staged by Prince. (The other, *Merlin*, was our biggest flop of 1982–1983.) And though Andrews had been the butler in the original *Night Music*, he was promoted to the lead, Frederick Egerman, for the national tour that starred Jean Simmons as Desiree and Margaret Hamilton as Madame Armfeldt.

Andrews still vividly recalls what happened after his final *Phantom* audition. He stayed on stage while Prince went to the back of the house to sit and discuss him with composer Andrew Lloyd Webber and producer Cameron Mackintosh. As he says,

> I could overhear that Hal wanted me to do Don Attilio, the singer who appears in *Il Muto* [the opera-within-the-play]. Andrew and Cameron, though, were pointing out that the actor who plays Don Attilio in London also understudies the Phantom—which everyone knew I couldn't do because I'm a bass baritone. Though the Phantom is said to be a baritone, he's a really baritone with tenor chops—which I don't have.

So Andrews was worried. Then, he says,

> I overheard Hal tell Andrew and Cameron that I could instead understudy both of the managers, Monsieur Firmin and Monsieur André. And while they were arguing, Hal suddenly got up and came trotting down to the front of the stage. He told me, "I really want to get you in this show." And I relaxed, because I believed that he would.

No one can say that Andrews hasn't paid Prince back with his loyalty. "At first," he says, "I figured I'd do it for two years. But then I got bumped up to play Monsieur Firmin, the manager, and I said, 'Okay, I'll stay another two years.'"

Two years passed, and Andrews discovered reasons to stay on:

The security is important. At that time, I had two kids who were ten and fourteen. This would give me the means to pay for any future schooling they'd want. But that wasn't the only good thing about it. So many actors have to go out of town very often and they wind up not even getting to know their kids. This show let me be there for them when they needed me.

Andrews played Monsieur Firmin for eleven years. Since then, he's played the slightly larger role of Monsieur André. But over these twenty-two years, Andrews has every now and then flirted with leaving.

I auditioned for other shows. Then I'd hear some songs or read the script and know they weren't going to be around very long. Doing the occasional reading and workshop keeps my creative juices flowing, and I have taken some time off every now and then to do a limited run of a show. But I know I've got a nice part right here in *Phantom*, and a good paycheck, too.

In other words, the Angel of Music you know is better than the devil you don't. While many actors in long-run shows rationalize by saying, "Every performance is different because the audience is different," Andrews claims that almost every performance is different because he's not always playing with the same actors. "When you figure in vacations, replacements, subs, and sicknesses, the show itself doesn't change, but the connections on stage do. And that's fun. As corny as it sounds, I always try to give a better performance from the one I did the previous night."

Of course, Andrews hasn't been there for every performance. He does take his two-week vacation every year, often to return to his native Milwaukee. "I don't miss the show when I'm away, but I'm not unhappy to get back. It's nice to know that it's still there. I will say that if I were on vacation and didn't want to go back, then I'd really have to leave."

Not yet. He's uncertain if his retirement or the show's closing will come first. "I'm sixty-seven," he admits, "so people are always saying, 'When are you going to retire?' That does get me thinking, but I always come to the conclusion that I'll worry about it some other time."

He does occasionally get tuckered.

Appearing in a Broadway show is hard work, because it's physically and mentally involving and tiring. But I know that I'm in better physical and mental shape than I would have been had I not been doing this eight times a week with no real layoffs. [Dressing room–mate] David Cryer figured out that we climb more than three hundred steps a performance. No matter what else I do Sunday through Saturday, I get quite a workout eight times a week.

There are more stairs, too, when he goes to his third-floor dressing room.

"Most of the time there I read, but out of one ear, I can hear the show through the speaker system. By now, there's a certain cue that automatically goes off in my head when I know I have so much time to get back downstairs for my next entrance. That's been ingrained for a while."

Actually, Andrews isn't that surprised that he has this talent for longevity. "When I was in high school, I got a perfect attendance medal. And when I started acting in Milwaukee, a writer for a local paper described me as the workhorse of the group."

In the past twenty-two years, he's seen the musical go from a white-hot ticket to a staple at the "pushcart," as the industry calls the TKTS discount booth.

Around two years in, the laughs either got smaller or disappeared all together. I wondered if we were doing something wrong, but I finally realized that we weren't playing to the tri-state audience anymore, but for many foreign people who don't know English. But I don't believe we've ever had a performance when the house was any less than two-thirds filled. In recent years, the movie helped us rather than hurt us. People who saw the movie suddenly wanted to see it live, and we got a whole new generation in here.

But it's been a few years since anyone saw more than one original cast member on stage. Andrews reports that in 2005, when Mary Leigh Stahl, who played both the Wardrobe Mistress and the Confidante in the opera-within-a-play, left the cast, he then became the sole original cast survivor. Before her, Andrews reports that Richard Warren Pugh, the original Auctioneer, left for a very different reason: "He passed away."

No one can accuse Andrews of not being sentimental about them and all the others.

After the first year, people whom I'd enjoyed were leaving, people with whom I'd gone through that exciting opening together. I started thinking, "The rest of us are going to forget them, and I don't want that to happen." So I asked everyone who left for an eight-by-ten glossy, and I started a wall where I put their pictures so we could always see them. Even if people came back—and plenty have—their pictures stayed on the wall.

Eventually, though, the walls were filled. "So," says Andrews, "I took them all down, scanned them, and reduced them to four-by-sixes. Now I put about fifty on a poster-sized sheet, and frame them." Over 250 actors are on the basement walls.

Mishaps in the twenty-two years?

There are scenes where I must read letters, and occasionally the prop people give you the wrong one. You look at the letter you're supposed to be reading, and you see words you're not supposed to be saying. So you look away from the letter, but then you remember that you're supposed to be reading, so you look back at the words you're not saying. It's very easy to get confused.

Most of all, Andrews especially remembers a Wednesday in 1990:

During the matinee, I was playing Firmin, but the actor playing André fell ill, and at intermission decided he just couldn't continue. Because I was his understudy, I took over for him, and my understudy took over Firmin. And because I'd taken some time off to do the City Opera production of *A Little Night Music*, I wound up playing Frederick Egerman that night. Three roles in one day!

(Perhaps the Guinness Book of World Records needs to hear about this, too.)

But by and large, *Phantom* is a well-maintained machine, and mistakes, Andrews reports, have been minimal.

Considering it's a gothic type of musical, you'd think it would be haunted at least a bit, but it's not. My daughter [Jennifer Lee Andrews] played Cosette in *Les Miz* for a while, and said, "We have so many turntable problems, and we have to stop the show pretty often. Do things like that happen in your show, too?" I told her, "My show never stops."

And has he become at all chummy with Lord Andrew Lloyd Webber? Says Andrews, "I think he probably does know who I am."

The Phantom of the Opera. January 26, 1988–. Over 9,400 performances.

THE BIGGEST FLOP
Chess

The-about-to-be period piece.

The obvious contender for biggest flop of the season would be the five-performance *Carrie*. Too bad, for, as *Wicked* proved many years later, there was a market for a musical about a teenage girl who feels unpopular.

But few Broadway observers thought that the musical version of Stephen King's horror novel had much of a future. And while the songwriters had won an Oscar for the title song to *Fame*, one song doth not a score make.

There was, though, one atypical bit of hoopla surrounding *Carrie*. Not that often does a mass-market paperback book sport the logo of a Broadway musical. But in early 1988, Signet re-released King's novel with the musical's stylistic three-red-line, two-white-line, one-red-teardrop logo. "The 4-million copy bestseller is now an electrifying musical," said a banner at the top of the book. The back cover promised—and truer words were never spoken—"There's never been a musical like *Carrie*," then listed the credits for the show. So while most book collectors always want the first edition of any tome, musical theater enthusiasts only want the sixty-first edition of Stephen King's *Carrie*.

In case anyone's wondering . . . after Linzi Hateley, who played Carrie White, was drenched in "blood" just before show's end, was she able to get it off in time for her curtain call? In fact, no. She didn't even try, but emerged still bloodied, looking like the wrath of God.

But the biggest flop of the season was really *Chess*—the musical in which Anatoly, a Soviet chess champ (David Carroll) was to do battle with Freddie, the American challenger (Philip Casnoff). Of course, romance would cause a minor war, too, as Freddie's manager, Florence (Judy Kuhn), fell in love with Anatoly, which brought his wife, Svetlana (Marcia Mitzman), no pleasure. Needless to say, the show made use of the Cold War rivalry between the U.S. and the U.S.S.R., and of the symbolism offered by the game, in which human beings could be seen as pawns to a political power.

Carrie lost $8 million to *Chess*'s $6 million, but the expectations for the former were far lower than the latter. *Chess*'s music was already known to millions because of its concept album with music by Benny Andersson and Bjorn Ulvaeus (of ABBA fame) and lyrics by Tim Rice (of *Jesus Christ Superstar* and *Evita*).

Besides, while both musicals had previously been produced in London, *Carrie* was a failure that had limped to Broadway, with the legendary Barbara Cook deciding not to repeat her role as Carrie's mad mother, Margaret. *Chess*, though, opened on Broadway boasting that its London edition had just celebrated its second anniversary in the West End. It was destined to run yet another year.

The two shows dovetailed through their directors. *Carrie*'s director, Terry Hands, and *Chess*'s, Trevor Nunn, were once co-artistic directors of the Royal Shakespeare Company. Though both had green-lit the wildly acclaimed *The Life and Adventures of Nicholas Nickleby* and *Les Misérables*, Nunn had codirected with John Caird, while Hands had "only" produced. What's more, Nunn had directed *Cats*, too.

So Broadway was looking forward to Nunn's *Chess* more than Hands' *Carrie*. While Nunn hadn't had a hit with his last Broadway outing—*Starlight Express*—he still was about to have his name on four musicals on Broadway.

But only for two months. A song in the show claimed, "One night in Bangkok makes a hard man humble;" so did the Broadway reception of *Chess*.

To be fair, the passage of time had dealt a blow to the musical. *Chess*, which had opened in London on May 14, 1986—more than a year before President

Reagan told Mr. Gorbachev to tear down that wall, reached Broadway only as the Cold War was melting. While the Soviet empire did not officially fall until Christmas Day, 1991, the handwriting was on the wall that the U.S.S.R. was doomed. Despite the change in the political climate, the London *Chess* had momentum that kept it going for another year; *Chess* on Broadway seemed to be dealing with old news.

Yet, had the production that had opened in London been replicated here, the reception would have been better. While *Cats* and *Les Misérables* had taken every precaution to make the Broadway versions look exactly as it had done in London, *Chess* in New York had a completely new look. Robin Wagner, the designer of the London set, redesigned it for Broadway, adding enormously tall towers that looked as if they were about to tip over and end any chess match right then and there.

Worse, though, was the decision to have Richard Nelson add a genuine book. The libretto didn't illuminate the story, but slowed it. Many musical theater enthusiasts believe the score to *Chess* is marvelous; the last thing they wanted to see on stage was Nelson's turgid book interrupting the segue of one memorable song into the next.

Had an exact replica of the London *Chess* opened on Broadway, the results certainly would have been better. But "what might have been" will always haunt *Chess*. Michael Bennett was originally signed to do it, and while some of his ideas wound up in the London production, he had to bow out long before it even reached rehearsals. No one can say for sure how much *Chess* lost because of Bennett's contracting AIDS, but one can assume that it was one of musical theater's greatest casualties.

Chess. April 28, 1988–June 25, 1988. 68 performances.

1988–1989

The Biggest Hit
"My Marriage to Ernest Borgnine."

So who won the Pulitzer Prize for drama in 1919, 1942, 1944, 1947, 1951, 1962, 1963, 1966, 1968, 1972, 1974, 1986, and 1997?

No one, that's who. The Pulitzer committee decided that no author of a play or musical merited an award that year.

Similarly speaking, we can't name a biggest hit of 1988–89, because there wasn't one.

Jerome Robbins Broadway ran 633 performances, and *Black and Blue* amassed 829, but both lost money, so they can't be counted as hits.

The highlight of the latter show came not during a performance, but at the Tony Awards, when Ruth Brown accepted her Best Musical Actress Tony: "It took me forty-two years to climb those eight steps." Even years later, Brown remembered something wonderful that happened after the ceremony: "Angela Lansbury, a real Broadway lady," she said, "came over and told me it was the best thing anyone had ever said in any of the awards ceremonies she'd seen. And she'd been to the Oscars, too!"

Ethel Merman, in her 1978 autobiography, had a chapter entitled "My Marriage to Ernest Borgnine"—which was simply an empty page, for the star did not want to discuss her thirty-two-day union with him. We must put an almost empty page here, too, except to ask, was there ever a season that more suggested that Broadway was in serious trouble?

The Biggest Flop
Legs Diamond

Never have there been more serious contenders.

Which to choose?

There was a revival of *Chu Chem*—pronounced not "Choo Chemm" but "Hucchum." (It's a Yiddish term meaning "wise man.") Had *Breakfast at Tiffany's* not been such a disaster during 1966–1967, the original *Chu Chem* would have been our biggest flop of that season; it closed in Philadelphia. Former Broadway press agent Joshua Ellis is still talking about Yiddish legend Menasha Skulnik's coming out before the show to say, "Ladies and gentlemen, you and I have spent wonderful times together in the theater"—before implying that this would not be one of them.

Says Ellis,

> Skulnik had to stop the show to remind the orchestra that had just started to play the vamp to a song that the tune had already been cut. He also told the audience, "It was a terrible song." Later he began the second act by telling the crowd "that I must beg your indulgence one last time," because he had to deliver the news that Molly Picon, his costar, wouldn't be able to continue with the show. He did keep from us, though, that she had quit for good during intermission. So he introduced her understudy, Henrietta

Jacobson, who was about twice Picon's size. As a result, she couldn't get into Picon's costumes, but simply pinned them on what she'd happened to wear to the theater that day

The 1989 *Chu Chem* didn't encounter this much chaos, but at sixty-eight performances, it was far from a hit.

Welcome to the Club was set in "A New York City jail exclusively for alimony delinquents." We met five incarcerated divorced husbands and three of their unhappy ex-wives. By the end of the show (with book by Hemingway scholar A. E. Hotchner, music by no less than Cy Coleman, and lyrics by both) most of the couples get back together. But if the conflict between husbands and wives had reached the stage where the men were jailed, there'd better be darned good reasons for these happy endings. The authors couldn't find them. *Welcome* outwore its welcome after twelve performances.

Starmites, which took place both "on earth and inner space," lasted sixty performances. Liz Larsen portrayed Eleanor, a young teen who loses herself literally in comic books, morphing into Bizarbara. Inner space is also where she meets such women as Canibelle (Gwen Stewart) and Balbraka (Freida Williams), as well as a lizard named Trinkulus (Gabriel Barre).

Shortly after *Starmites* closed, Barre saw Jason Alexander on a talk show. After the host congratulated the star for his *Jerome Robbins' Broadway* Best Musical Actor Tony, Alexander said it wasn't such a big deal because he'd beaten a guy who played a lizard.

And then there was *Senator Joe* (based on Wisconsin's McCarthy, of course), which played its first preview on Friday, January 6, 1989, and its last ones on Saturday, January 7, 1989. Not only did it not have the money to open, but it also didn't have enough to put up its marquee. Those who attended any of its three previews entered a theater that still said *Kenny Loggins on Broadway*, even though that show had closed more than two months earlier.

Senator Joe's failure to open deprived the world of knowing what the critics would have said about the scene that took place in McCarthy's stomach. The stage was flanked by grisly red drops, while two characters—one named "Enzyme" and the other tabbed "Fatty Deposits"—did a dance designed for them by Wesley Fata.

But the biggest flop of the season had to be *Legs Diamond*.

Every year, the editors at *New York Magazine* face a conundrum. Who should grace the cover of the Fall Preview issue? With the hundreds if not thousands of entertainment options that Manhattan and the four other boroughs offer every autumn, the editors must decide which personality will be of the most interest to New Yorkers, and which has the most potential to deliver a memorable evening.

So the *New York Magazine* Fall Preview on September 12, 1988 featured Peter Allen, the star of the upcoming Broadway musical *Legs Diamond*. That's how big a hit the show about a Roaring Twenties gangster was expected to be.

Allen was pictured sitting with his back to a piano on which two chorines sat. He was grabbing one's left leg, while yet a third pair of upside-down legs were poking up from the bottom of the cover.

Legs would be expected to abound in a musical called *Legs Diamond*—though the character Allen would play wasn't called Legs because he had a penchant for female gams. Womanizer though he was, this gangster got his name for running out on his friends. Would that seem to be a character in which audiences would take much interest?

From the moment he saw the 1960 film *The Rise and Fall of Legs Diamond*, Allen thought they would. He planned not only to star as the hoodlum, but to write the music and the lyrics. He'd show Broadway just how magnificent he was.

Allen (1944–1992) had an ego the size of Rhode Island—which may not be big for a state, but certainly is for an ego. Notice that none of our biggest hits of the season have had a composer-lyricist-star. One of those jobs is hard enough; two may be manageable with only the greatest talents; someone who did all three hadn't happened on Broadway in a long time. Even Anthony Newley, who starred in both *Stop the World—I Want to Get Off* (1962) and *The Roar of the Greasepaint—the Smell of the Crowd* (1965) had his longtime collaborator Leslie Bricusse help on each. Granted, George M. Cohan did all three tasks (and more), but musicals were more primitive in the early part of the twentieth century.

Allen's writing a number of pop hits didn't mean he could write a Broadway score. He should have left the lyrics to theater wordsmiths who know how to pick good spots for songs, and how to dramatize them. His song "Speakeasy" stressed that such an establishment was a den of iniquity. Given that most people today think of Prohibition as a bad idea, he would have made a more refreshing choice by writing a song called "All We Want Is a Little Drink."

At a nightclub, a singer sang a lyric, "If you love me, let me hear your applause / If you love me my song is yours." Legs interrupted her, sat at the piano, and began singing different lyrics to the melody: "If you love me, let me see your knockers / If you hate me, put your knockers away." Allen was so secure that his fans unconditionally adored him that he believed they would forgive the lapse of taste because the song and the performance were his.

Legs Diamond's chorus girls sounded squeaky and silly. The show taxed its drummer, because he constantly had to tap out a rat-tat-tat-tat sound to emulate machine gun fire. The audience had to be annoyed by plenty of police whistles, too.

Who came up with the line, "Okay, girls—here comes A. R.! Let's show him the new number"? Original bookwriter Charles Suppon? His successor, Harvey Fierstein? Doctor Bruce Vilanch? Whoever did can't be too proud of such an obvious song cue.

The worst flaw, though, was choosing a property about an unworthy character. When Legs realizes that he can fix the World Series, he gets excited and starts singing, "Life's getting better every day." This is a character we cannot get behind.

Allen was also unconvincing as a gangster who strung along three women (Randall Edwards, Brenda Braxton, Julie Wilson). Vilanch says, "I told Peter that no one would accept him in this heterosexual role after he'd outed himself so vividly. I also told him that he was only attracted to the show because of the spats-and-tux duds he'd get to wear. I warned him never again to do a show just because of the costumes."

Vilanch says that neither he nor the first two librettists came up with the show's most memorable line. For after Legs had seemingly been killed in the first act—only to appear very much alive in the second—he yelled, "Only a critic can kill me!" Allen himself came up with that one.

That, didn't make him a bookwriter, though Allen probably believed that he could do that, too. The irony is that if Allen had been able to settle solely for writing the music for the show, he would have at least been applauded for a job well done. If this had still been the era when Broadway musicals got albums recorded by jazz and instrumental artists—such as *Lester Lanin Plays "I Had a Ball"*—*Legs Diamond* would have sounded very good. "When I Get My Name in Lights" was a snazzy opening number; "Cut of the Cards" was a rhythmic winner; and "The Man Nobody Could Love" was a second act success that many people would have hummed coming out of the theater—if they'd only stayed for the second act.

Actually, the critics weren't brutal. Frank Rich in the *New York Times* said it best when he called it "a sobering interlude of minimum-security imprisonment that may inspire you to pull out a pen and attend to long-neglected tasks." That, though, did keep the box office from keeping busy.

And yet, *Legs*'s last days saw rabid musical theater enthusiasts hoping that it would run forever. For in early 1989, the Nederlander Organization first leased, and then sold, the Mark Hellinger Theatre to the Times Square Church—but stated that the new owners couldn't take possession until *Legs* closed. Even having this Peter Allen atrocity on the boards was preferable to losing one of the town's most beautiful theaters.

But finally, this Australian's show went down under, with a loss of nearly $6 million. At the closing performance's curtain call, Allen remained on stage to show his gratitude to the many who'd got him this far. "We might as well thank these people now," he said. "I mean, we ain't gonna see ya at the Tonys."

And, for that matter, the Hellinger, which had played host to five Tony Awards, would never see another. The Nederlander Organization didn't take the advice that its tenants *1600 Pennsylvania Avenue* had given thirteen years earlier: "Take Care of This House." The theater was lost to Broadway for at least the next two decades to come—and probably for many more.

Legs Diamond. December 26, 1988–February 19, 1989. 64 performances.

4

49TH ST. N.Y.C.

T MISBEHAVIN

SAT SEP 10 1988

MAJESTIC THEATRE
245 W. 44TH ST. N.Y.C.
THE PHANTOM
OF THE OPERA
2:00P SAT DEC 10 198

VIR
245 W

RMEZ40
LOCATION
Z
F I
$20.00
M/BOX
F

M 109

IMPERI
249 WEST
The Shubert Organization

IRLS

8:00F

8:046448

26
3:0
D 11

ganization

EC'8R 27

STREET THEATRE
HESTRA $15.0
TICKET COMPANY.

IMPER
249 WEST 4
BILLY
THE MU
7:00 PM
APR 28,

2609
RCHO
SEC
B

*INCLUDES $0.00 FACIL
MAIMP2108-0426-M23

9E
09.
MP
ORCH*
SECTION/BOX
ORCH CENTER
G 1
ROW S

2x
G 102
ROW SEAT
PAL400C
24MAR94

NO REFUNDS/N

BEAUTY AND
///
THE PALACE
1564 BROADWA
THU APR 21, 190

JAMES
246 WEST 447
"GOOD N
EVENINGS AT

FEB'RY
14
1975

FRI
PRICE
Maximum
Mezz.-Balc.
resale restri
to support
License gran
refunding pu

ROUNDABOUT THEATRE COMPANY PR

CABARET
AT STUDIO 54
Mon, January 14, 2002 8:00
Doors Open 1 Hour

3B 105 ORCHESTR

THE
457
ND

NOV 02 1990
10/1
$40.0

ORCH
K 10
245.0
K

CQ0127E ORCH
EVENT CODE
$ 0.00
PRICE & ALL TAXES INCL
ORCH CENTER

G 111
ROW SEAT

COMP
All Taxes Incl. If Applicable
ADM.$

NO REFUNDS/NO EXCHANGES

THE CAPEMAN
* ** *
MARQUIS THEATRE
211 W. 45TH, NYC
TUE JAN 27, 1998 7:00PM

ORCH
SECTION/BOX
CO 1X
G 111
ROW SEAT
MAR601C
10JAN98

NEDERLANDER

THU DE

MINSKOFF TH
ORCHESTRA

1989–1999

1989–1990

THE BIGGEST HIT
Grand Hotel

Old musicals never die—or even fade away.

April 2, 1992. BMG Studios, 110 West Forty-fourth Street, New York City. Recording session for the original cast album of *Grand Hotel*.

For a Broadway musical to be recorded three weeks after opening isn't unexpected—but for a show to do it three weeks before *closing* is another matter—especially when the show is just about the celebrate its one thousandth performance. Never has a still-running show taken longer to be recorded. But in these days when cast albums cost hundreds of thousands of dollars and can really only be certain of selling a few thousand copies, companies aren't in a rush. (When the recording is released, the back of the box—since in 1992 CDs still come in long boxes—will proudly proclaim, "At last!")

So much time has passed that many of the original cast members have left the show: Michael Jeter, who played dying bookkeeper Kringelein; Liliane Montevecchi, who portrayed fading ballerina Grushinskaya; Karen Akers, who was her devoted secretary Raffaela; Jane Krakowski, who created ambitious typist Flaemmchen, and David Carroll as penniless Baron Felix von Gaigern. Only Timothy Jerome, portraying desperate businessman Preysing, is still with the production.

So it's a warm reunion for many—but not everyone. David Carroll isn't here, which is all the more poignant when the time comes to record "We'll Take a Glass Together." It's the show's highlight, a tribute to money in which the ailing but suddenly wealthy Kringelein celebrates with the Baron by throwing himself on, above, below, and across a bar.

It's also the number that changed Michael Jeter's life, for it helped to get him the Best Featured Musical Actor Tony. Though the awards traditionally air on CBS, the Friday after the June 3, 1990 broadcast, ABC News named Jeter the Person of the Week, and replayed his acceptance speech: "If you've got a problem with alcohol or drugs, you can't stop, you think life can't change, and that dreams can't come true, then I stand here as living proof that you *can* stop. It changes a day at a time, and dreams come true."

Now Jeter must do the number with Brent Barrett. The latter succeeded Carroll two years ago, when Carroll was losing his bout with AIDS. Three weeks ago, RCA producer Bill Rosenfield called Carroll to the studio to lay down his tracks in advance, for word had it that Carroll was not doing well. Says Akers, "It was so sad to watch someone who was so angry and frightened of dying. When I'd go to his apartment, I'd see the eighteen bottles of pills in his bathroom."

As it turned out, Carroll was more seriously ill than Rosenfield realized. He died that day in the studio bathroom before he could sing at all.

But, as *Grand Hotel* insists, life goes on. At one table are two elderly men, Robert Wright and George "Chet" Forrest, two lifelong friends (but never lovers, they've always said). Their first Broadway credit was *Song of Norway* in 1944. But their first film credit was much earlier: *The Man in Possession* in 1931.

At the table next to them is a songwriter who wasn't even born when *Song of Norway* opened. He's Maury Yeston, who, in 1982, beat out Stephen Sondheim for the Best Score Tony, as he saw his *Nine* win the Best Musical Tony, too.

Wright and Forrest didn't quite collaborate with Yeston on *Grand Hotel*. After the show opened in Boston to some negative reviews, director-choreographer Tommy Tune asked Wright and Forrest for changes. When they were slow to come up with new material, Tune brought in Yeston to beef up the score. (Interesting that this should happen to a show with a plot point involving a "Boston merger.")

Yeston came up with a new song for each main character: "At the Grand Hotel" for Kringelein; "Bonjour, Amour" for Grushinskaya; "Everybody's Doing It" for Preysing; "I Want to Go to Hollywood" for Flaemmchen; "Love Can't Happen" and "Roses at the Station" for the Baron and "Twenty-two Years" for Raffaela. They are important components of *Grand Hotel*'s two-plus-year run.

But Tune wasn't just performing a charitable act by keeping Wright and Forrest's "Who Couldn't Dance with You," a fox-trot for Kringelein and Flaemmchen. He wasn't merely placating them, either, by retaining their "Maybe My Baby Loves Me," the scat-sensation done by two bellboys (David Jackson and Danny Strayhorn). And last but hardly least, he did himself and theatergoers a favor by keeping "We'll Take a Glass Together." It's the Broadway musical's most exciting production number since "Who's That Woman?" in *Follies*. Yes, Tune's magnificent staging was a great part of the success of these numbers, but all three are excellent songs.

Tune also called in Peter (*1776*) Stone to add some book material, though original librettist Luther Davis staunchly resisted. Said Davis, "When Tommy told Wright and Forrest, 'I'll walk if Maury doesn't come in,' they caved in. When he tried that on me, I told him, 'Go ahead and walk if anything is put in the book by anyone but me.'"

For while Yeston's name appears officially on the window cards and playbills—and will be on this cast album—Stone's is nowhere to be found. Said Stone many months earlier, "I didn't take credit, because the people who know Broadway know that I did it, and the people who don't know Broadway don't care who wrote a musical's book anyway."

Davis, after hearing this, countered with

The reason Stone's name isn't anywhere is because he didn't do anything. When Tommy said he wanted him, I said no, because I knew everyone would say he'd written the whole thing. Tommy insisted, but I called Peter and said, "I don't want you here." He was president of the Dramatists Guild then, and very sensitive to the rights of writers, so he said, "I wouldn't think of coming if the author didn't want me."

Three days later, I come to the theater, and there's Peter. I said, "What the hell are you doing here?" and he told me, "Tommy says he won't do *The Will Rogers Follies* (on which Stone was writing the book) if I don't at least show up." Peter wanted to add jokes like having Kringelein say that there was this wonderful extra toilet in his room, and I said, "That's something only an American would say. Europeans know about bidets, and Kringelein does, too." It went in, but I eventually took it out.

It was yet another adventure for the project. *Chu Chem*, last season's flop, took almost twenty-three years to get to Broadway after its 1966 closing on the road. That was officially the longest time between an out-of-town closing and a Broadway resuscitation. But only eight months later, the torch was passed to Davis, Wright, and Forrest for a thirty-one-year span. For their musical *At the Grand*, based on Vicki Baum's *Grand Hotel*, opened July 7, 1958, in Los Angeles, but closed September 13, 1958, in San Francisco. It never made it to Broadway's Forty-sixth Street Theater on September 25 of that year.

Said Davis,

I originally wanted to do a musical that didn't have its hand out for laughs, like tips. I mean, there are even laughs in "Poor Jud Is Dead." What property had serious characters that could be musical? In getting the rights, I had it in the contract that if we ran sixty-four performances, the rights would be mine forever. Then I started work, changing the location from Berlin to Rome. Back then, Berlin was still thought of as a war zone; Rome, on the other hand, was now a hot spot with sex and beautiful people. And because (director) Albie Marre was married to Joan Diener, who had a big booming voice, I changed Grushinskaya from a ballerina to an opera singer.

Marre brought the show to Oscar winner Paul Muni in hopes that he'd play Kringelein, the meek bookkeeper who goes to the Grand Hotel for one last fling before he dies. Said Davis, "Muni's wife was greatly responsible for his doing it. She asked me, 'Would he be able to wear a top hat, tux, and tails if he did this show?' When I said yes, she told him to do it—'because I've been dying to see him get all dressed up properly.'" But, Davis reported, Muni didn't get along with Marre, Diener, and most everyone else, and lead producer Roger L. Stevens closed the show.

Decades later, musical and vocal director Jack Lee happened to mention *At the Grand* to Tommy Tune, who was intrigued enough to get in touch with the three creators for the materials. He liked what he read and heard; so did Marty Richards and his wife Mary Lea Johnson (heiress to the Johnson & Johnson fortune), who put up $200,000 for a workshop at the Diplomat Hotel at 108 West Forty-third Street. The three-sectioned ballroom in which they worked actually inspired Tune and set designer Tony Walton.

Said Davis,

> In what I thought was a big and brave gamble, Tommy after weeks of preparation said, "I just saw *Our Town*, and I want to do *Grand Hotel* without any scenery, too." I didn't think that would be what people would expect of the title, but he had wonderful ideas for tying the scenes together and musicalizing the show. He heard the show as a continual piece of music, unlike what we were used to—talk, song, talk, song—and we thought what he did was brilliant. The idea of putting the orchestra above the action was another great idea that came from his wonderfully creative brain, too.

But Davis felt that Tune was less than brilliant for wanting Peter Stone. Wright and Forrest had to feel some animosity toward Tune, Stone, and Yeston, for when the time came for the show's vocal selections to be published, they insisted that the book not include anything but their songs. As a result, musicians who want to play the score have to buy two books, one with their songs, and one with Yeston's.

That's why *Grand Hotel* took so long to be recorded. Yeston says,

> Wright, Forrest, and I were always on great terms because I never did anything without their express consent. Everything had to be at their invitation. They were great troupers who insisted I stay on and do anything to keep the show from closing.
>
> But once the show opened and was running, they genuinely expected BMG to record their original score and not the opening-night show. They wanted their original work, of which they were proud, to be recorded and printed for posterity. Who could blame them? They'd been working on it since the early fifties.
>
> But BMG would do no such thing. Finally, after more than a year, they relented and did the practical thing. So in the studio that day were very deep emotions: The loss of David Carroll, the waste of a year, Luther Davis' anger, and Tommy Tune's exasperation. It took a lot of character for them to finally go along with the cast album.

Grand Hotel. November 12, 1989–April 25, 1992. 1,017 performances.

THE BIGGEST FLOP
Annie 2: Miss Hannigan's Revenge

The sun doesn't come out.

Charles Strouse, as we saw, didn't succeed with his *Bye Bye Birdie* sequel. How would he fare with his *Annie* sequel?

Worse.

Annie 2 was only part of the title; *Miss Hannigan's Revenge* was the other.

The show begins in "1934," as the first song goes, at the Fifth Avenue mansion of Oliver Warbucks (Harve Presnell). But, the Depression being what it is, things are financially tough even here. "Rubber's really on the skids" is one nifty Martin Charnin lyric, though an even better one has Warbucks insisting that his staff "Learn to turn your paper over so you've written on both sides." Charnin also wrote a couple of cute in-jokes that refer back to the source material. The first has Annie (Danielle Findley) bravely accept the new austerity measures by saying, "One red dress is all that I'll ever need"—which in fact was all she ever wore in the funnies. Similarly, Warbucks later says, "This is hard-boiled economics; this is not, my friends, the comics."

Annie and Warbucks have another problem when Marietta Christmas (Marian Seldes), a representative for the "United Mothers of America," arrives. She says that Warbucks isn't capable of raising a little girl alone, and that he must marry so that Annie will have a mother; otherwise, the organization will take her away from him.

Warbucks reluctantly agrees and says he'll start a nationwide search for a wife. But Annie says she doesn't want a mother in a "1934" reprise that regrettably sounds as if it's a Nazi anthem instead of a tender song in which Annie fears someone new coming into her life. Charnin offers a number of small things that irritate a kid—"Mommies make you eat things like squash"—instead of including what made *Annie* great: genuine emotion.

Meanwhile, Miss Hannigan (Dorothy Loudon), now released from prison after having served her time for trying to extort money from Warbucks, hasn't learned her lesson. She approaches old pal Lionel McCoy (Ronny Graham) and insists that he help her kidnap Annie and split the ransom. "How Could I Ever Say No?" he sings, with the wonderful trademark "Strouse bounce" heard in "It's the Hard-Knock Life," "The Telephone Hour," "It's Superman," and dozens of others).

Warbucks is too busy to court anyone, so finding the future Mrs. Warbucks falls on the ever-dependable shoulders of secretary Grace Farrell (Lauren Mitchell). Soon she's complaining in song that Warbucks is always saying, "Grace, take a memo! Find my reading glasses! Get me a wife," which she followed with, "He doesn't know I'm alive." A better lyric would have had her say that Warbucks only knows she's alive when he needs something.

Still, Grace does her job and starts interviewing potential candidates, asking them some rarefied questions to test their cultural mettle. Charnin got in some good jokes about Edgar Allen Poe, Vincent van Gogh, Bela Bartok, Lillian Hellman, and Dostoevsky in a pleasant enough ditty, "The Lady of the House."

But a creaky plot device had a disguised Hannigan come in and prey on Warbucks' sympathy with a terrific song, "But You Go On," written during the Washington run; in this working-class woman's "I'm Still Here," Hannigan tells of one tragedy after another in her life. Nevertheless, bookwriter Thomas Meehan gilded the lily by having Hannigan choose as her alias "Charlotte O'Hara." That no one sees through that name makes everyone seem stupid, and now the audience can only laugh at both the characters and the authors.

Hannigan gets an unexpected break in the kidnapping plot because she finds a street urchin named Kate who is a dead ringer for Annie (Findley played her, too). If Hannigan and Lionel can switch her with the real Annie, they'll be far away with the ransom by the time Warbucks notices that the real Annie is still missing. Hannigan sang to Kate, "You! You! You! can be Annie, too!"—a nice pun on the show's title. (Much of Strouse's melody came from "Love Comes First," Margo Channing's original eleven o'clocker when *Applause* tried out in Baltimore.)

Hannigan and Lionel tail Daddy Warbucks when he goes to—and sings about—"Coney Island." That may sound too much like *Annie*'s "N.Y.C.," but Strouse's wonderful, ragtime-tinged melody excused the similarity. The song begins, "You never know what'll happen to you in Coney Island," and ends, "You'll never come back the same." That latter line was not merely a celebration of Coney Island, but offered a second layer of meaning: Annie wouldn't come back the same, because the kidnappers would switch her with Kate, who'd then return to the Warbucks mansion. While the nine-minute number continued with heavenly Peter Howard dance music, Hannigan and Lionel were seen trying to capture her.

They got Annie, too, through another smart move the authors devised: Annie wants to go on a carnival ride, and when Grace says she'll go with her, Annie says she wants to go alone. Which of us didn't feel the same way in our youth after years of riding with our parents? Grace lets her—which gives the ne'er-do-wells the chance to make the switch.

Even after the closing notice had been posted, Charnin took one Strouse melody, "All I've Got Is Me," and rewrote it as "I Guess Things Happen for the Best"—and then again as "My Daddy." (All dealt with Annie's feelings once she was kidnapped.) Charnin has said that the third song allowed Annie to "get closer to Daddy Warbucks, which is what *Annie 2* should have been about all along." No, she was close enough to him, and no audience member ever left *Annie* doubting that the two loved each other. There was no need to reiterate emotions that were already so well established.

Annie 2 should have been the story of a girl who wanted her new father to marry Grace Farrell—not necessarily because she needed a mother, but because she felt that Grace really loved him, and she wanted to see them together. The cue that Grace wanted Warbucks was clear in the original *Annie*; late in the show, there was a moment when Annie and Warbucks embraced, and Grace instinctively went to join them—and then just as quickly backed off, waving her arms back and forth while mouthing, "No, no, no, no, no"—knowing her place and staying in it.

So *Annie 2* should have had Annie juggling two struggles: First, she'd try to get this nice young woman to admit she loves Warbucks and not worry that he'll just think she's out for his money. Second, Annie would get this hesitant, older man to admit his feelings and not fear he'd be spurned because he's older, fatter— and certainly balder—than the men to whom Grace would more easily be attracted. A few misadventures along the way prior to a happy ending would have made for an audience pleaser.

Because *Annie 2* had booked the Marquis Theatre, *Me and My Girl*, which had been ensconced there for more than three years, was to be evicted. By then, moving a show even around the corner was prohibitively expensive, costing in the neighborhood of $1 million. That would have been too much money for a show in its fourth year to make up, so it closed. Had *Annie 2* booked another theater, *Me and My Girl* could have lasted at least another year.

After the shuttering, the authors returned to work, and created a semi-new show called *Annie Warbucks*. But that's another story.

Annie 2: Miss Hannigan's Revenge. December 22, 1989–January 20, 1990, in Washington. No New York performances.

1990–1991

The Biggest Hit
Miss Saigon

And you thought the falling chandelier was something.

November 2, 2000. The Broadway Theater at Fifty-third Street, New York City. While *Miss Saigon* has been playing to so-so houses for a while now, every seat is taken tonight. Producer Cameron Mackintosh and everyone else on hand are celebrating performance #4,000. Only *A Chorus Line*, *Cats*, and *The Phantom of the Opera* have achieved that pinnacle.

The crowd is clapping and roaring as soon as the house lights dim, and the sounds increase as the curtain rises. Audience members go wild as the Engineer (Luoyong Wang), Kim (Melinda Chua), Chris (Michael Flanigan), John (Charles E. Wallace), and Ellen (Margaret Ann Gates) each make an entrance. What must this response be like for these unknown actors? For months, maybe even years, they'd become accustomed to playing to tourists and procrastinating New Yorkers, all of whom greeted them with silence.

Tonight, the heat is on at *Saigon*, the crowd is hotter than hell, and the first-act curtain gets sustained cheers, too. Near the end, the eleven o'clock number "The American Dream" gets decibel-breaking applause, too.

But what gets neither entrance nor exit applause? The helicopter.

And to think it was once the show's most famous calling card.

Mackintosh even decreed back in 1991 that because the front mezzanine seats were the best from which to see the helicopter, he'd charge $100 for them, while orchestra seats would be $60. (Less than a year after opening, when *Miss Saigon* was shown not to be a kill-to-get-a-ticket hit, the $100 seat quietly disappeared.)

But long before this four thousandth performance, Broadway had admitted that the special effect wasn't so special after all. When musical theater enthusiasts first heard that the show had a helicopter, they must have assumed that they would see an entire chopper, shown from fore to aft, fly across the stage. Instead, they simply got the front of a helicopter going up into the rafters.

That the helicopter didn't get any appreciative applause at performance #4,000 may have been a surprise, but everyone expected a titanic explosion of applause the moment that Jonathan Pryce—the original Engineer—came out after the curtain calls to do a reprise of "The American Dream." And instead of singing the lyric "There I will crown / Miss Chinatown / All yours for ten percent down," Pryce sang, "Four thousand down / *Miss Saigon* takes the crown!"

Not quite. In less than three months, *Saigon* was gone. Since that night, *Beauty and the Beast*, the *Chicago* revival, *Rent*, and *The Lion King* have eclipsed it (and *Mamma Mia!* and *Wicked* undoubtedly will).

Ironically, that helicopter may well be why *Miss Saigon* didn't run even longer than it did.

For *Miss Saigon* did not tell its story chronologically. The show started in April 1975, Vietnam, when G.I. Chris (Willy Falk) met and fell in love with Vietnamese prostitute Kim (Lea Salonga). All of a sudden audiences were whisked three years ahead to April 1978, where a woman named Ellen (Liz Callaway) suddenly became an issue in the town that had been renamed Ho Chi Minh City.   Act 2 began a few months later in Atlanta, then segued to a month later in Bangkok. Then audiences were returned to Saigon in April 1975, when the city fell—and the helicopter flew.

Director Nicholas Hytner could have made matters easier by having projections that said, "Saigon, 1975" and "Ho Chi Minh City, 1978," but he expected theatergoers to figure out the switch on their own. Many didn't. Many couldn't.

But why did the authors and directors use this confusing back-and-forth plan?

Perhaps they feared that if they'd told the story in chronological order, then the helicopter would have appeared in act 1—and act 2 wouldn't have been as spectacular. But the creators underestimated the pull of their story—a darned good one; it is, after all, based in part on Puccini's *Madama Butterfly*—and their solid score. *The Phantom of the Opera* dared to play its big card—its falling chandelier—in act 1, and certainly didn't suffer. Perhaps *Miss Saigon*, which ran less than half as long as *Phantom*, would have held on longer had it told its story sequentially.

After Pryce finished "The American Dream," he thanked New York, "where everyone made me feel incredibly welcome." That got a laugh, as many in the house remembered the strife that Pryce had endured ten years earlier, when he was ready to repeat his acclaimed London *Saigon* performance in the Broadway company. David Henry Hwang, the author of *M. Butterfly*, and B. D. Wong, the Tony-winning star from that show, had initiated a protest against the casting of Pryce as the Engineer, a Eurasian character. They wanted an actor of Asian descent, which Pryce definitely was not.

No matter. Hwang and Wong held firm, and brought many to their side. That's when Mackintosh simply said that Pryce was essential to the show's success, and that he wouldn't do the show without him. He cancelled the $6.5 million Broadway production.

That caused substantially more commotion. Fifty performers expecting to work for years in *Miss Saigon* (thirty-four of whom were members of minorities), suddenly had no jobs—not to mention the jobs and money lost by the behind-the-scenes workers. A $25 million advance sale—the largest ever—would have to be refunded.

As Wayman Wong, a reporter for the *New York Daily News*, said,

The issue was equal opportunity, not about being politically correct. Cameron Mackintosh and casting director Vincent Liff claimed that Jonathan Pryce was the best choice to play the Engineer because they made a worldwide search and couldn't find a single Asian or Asian-American actor who could play the role. After Equity eventually approved Pryce, only then did Liff admit that the worldwide search they had made was not actually for the Engineer, but for an actress to play Kim. In reality, they weren't interested in anyone other than Pryce to play the Engineer.

Yes, it was Mackintosh's prerogative to cast whoever he wanted, but why slander the talents of many fine Asian and Asian-American actors who might have played the Engineer? One of the arguments that Mackintosh made was that no comparable Asian male star could be found to play the Engineer. Well, the role of the Engineer was a star-making part, the way Kim was a star-making part for a then-unknown Lea Salonga. If you don't give

Asian men the opportunity to originate a lead on Broadway, you won't have any Asian male stars. After Pryce left the Broadway show, that role was played by nothing BUT Asian-American actors.

Eventually, the show proceeded with Pryce, who won a Tony. In retrospect, Asian actors greatly benefited from getting jobs for ten years' worth of performances. But most of those four thousand performances—including this one, with Louoyong Wang—proved that many capable Asian actors could play the Engineer.

This reprise of "The American Dream" got everyone in the house clapping in unison—and laughing hard when Pryce concluded, while pointing to the cast, "They're overjoyed / Not unemployed!" before a barrage of balloons, confetti, and streamers poured from the ceiling. The helicopter didn't make an appearance, and wasn't missed at all.

Miss Saigon. April 11, 1991–January 28, 2001. 4,092 performances.

THE BIGGEST FLOP
The New Musicals Project

A new idea doesn't get much of a chance.

Ever since the wildly successful *A Chorus Line* had been developed through a workshop, producers had embraced this new—and less costly—form of developing a show.

But in the past fifteen years, what was supposed to be the new panacea had proved to be as flawed as the old tryout or preview system. Because workshops were only performed for industry insiders and friends, they couldn't show what a true audience would think—and that turned out to be a fatal omission. As Peter Stone liked to say, "If you asked each member of an audience what's wrong with your show, few people would be able to tell you anything constructive. But the audience as a whole watching a show lets you know when they're engaged, amused, or bored by their attention, laughter, and applause—or lack of it."

So with the workshop-originated *Runaways, Dance a Little Closer, It's So Nice to be Civilized, Legs Diamond*, and plenty of others failing, was there another way that a producer could eat his cake and have it, too?

Martin J. Bell thought so. What about going only slightly out of town—say, to Purchase, New York, only twenty-eight miles from Broadway? What if subscriptions were sold to lovers of musicals who'd be willing to see works in progress?

The State University of New York in Purchase had a commodious performing arts center there where a musical could try out in peace. And that was key: no reviews. Call it an out-of-town glorified workshop with an average audience to contribute its collective opinions.

Seats would cost $24–$32 on weeknights, $32–$39 on weekends—two-thirds the cost of the then-current $60 Broadway top. As the *Times* reported, "The program's budget for the first year was $10 million, of which investors contributed $2.5 million. The remaining 75 percent was to have come from ticket sales ($6.4 million), corporate sponsorship and the transfer of musicals to commercial venues."

Producing artistic director Bell enticed exciting artists for his first show: *Kiss of the Spider Woman* had bookwriter Terrence McNally adapting Manuel Puig's novel to music by John Kander and lyrics by Fred Ebb, under Harold Prince's direction. It would run from May 1 to June 24, 1990, and then undoubtedly move to Broadway.

Next would be *The Secret Garden*, based on Frances Hodgson Burnett's beloved children's novel. It would have a book and lyrics by Pulitzer Prize winner Marsha (*'night, Mother*) Norman, and music by newcomer Lucy Simon. Susan H. Schulman would stage the work for an October 23–December 23, 1990 run.

Then would come *My Favorite Year*, based on the 1982 film of the same name, adapted by Joseph Dougherty, an Emmy winner for *thirtysomething*. The music would be by Stephen Flaherty and the lyrics by Lynn Ahrens, both of whom had just had a nice off-Broadway hit with *Once on This Island*. As soon as it moved to Broadway in October, 1990, they'd prepare the new show for a Purchase run from January 8 to March 2, 1991.

The final selection of the first season would play from March 19 to May 18, 1991. *Fanny Hackabout Jones* would have Erica (*Fear of Flying*) Jong adapt her own novel. The aforementioned Lucy Simon would again compose to lyrics by Susan Birkenhead.

Nine thousand subscribed, and everything looked good. For *Kiss of the Spider Woman*, Tony winner John Rubenstein played Molina, the Latino homosexual window dresser who had been incarcerated for a trumped-up morals charge. Kevin Gray portrayed Valentin, the political activist who has nothing but loathing for the gay man who's obsessed with Aurora (Lauren Mitchell), a minor movie star. But the two men being thrown together yielded unpredictable results; each made the other a better person.

But then critics both important (Frank Rich of the *Times*) and negligible (Leida Snow of WINS Radio) came to see *Kiss of the Spider Woman*, even though they hadn't been invited. As Rich explained in *Hot Seat*, a collection of his reviews, he didn't feel bad about doing so, for the show was "a for-profit venture with Broadway prices that did not advertise itself as a work in progress." Negative reviews caused single ticket sales to dry up. Only twenty-two thousand attended *Kiss of the Spider Woman*, which producer Bell estimated to be less than 40 percent of capacity. None of the other three shows would debut in Purchase.

"I overestimated the box-office income and undercapitalized the operation," said Bell told the Times. "We failed, but I hope this does not discourage others from trying."

So far, it has.

New Musicals opened with *Kiss of the Spider Woman on* May 1, 1990. It ran until June 24, 1990, and the operations for the organization ceased on July 31, 1990.

1991–1992

THE BIGGEST HIT
Crazy for You

The reviews are in—and out of this world.

February 20, 1992. The Shubert Theater, New York City. Just before eight o'clock in the evening.

Audiences are about to see the second official performance of *Crazy for You*, the "new" Gershwin musical. Ken (*Lend Me a Tenor*) Ludwig has provided a new book to George and Ira's 1930 hit *Girl Crazy*. He's taken a few songs from that musical, adding others from less famous shows, and has seen it all put on stage with Mike Ockrent's direction and Susan Stroman's choreography.

Ludwig could have done better. He included "They Can't Take That away from Me," whose lyrics tell why Bobby (Harry Groener) is so smitten with Polly (Jodi Benson): "The way you wear your hat. The way you sip your tea . . . the way you sing off-key . . . the way you hold your knife . . . the way we danced till three." But he hadn't shown Polly doing any of these things. The musical would have been stronger if he had in advance of the song.

No matter. This morning, the cast was able to pick out a number of wonderful nuggets from Frank Rich's review in the *New York Times*: *Riotously entertaining. The American musical's classic blend of music, laughter, dancing, sentiment and showmanship. A long-awaited shift in Broadway fortunes. Makes everything seem young again, the audience included. Reclaims the Gershwins' standards in all their glorious youth.*

Rich had the most praise for "An extraordinary choreographer named Susan Stroman." Stroman must have enjoyed reading such lines as *a model of old school musical comedy instruction. Bursting with original talent. Miracle. New and thrilling ideas. It is the big numbers in* Crazy for You *that people will be talking about. Short of George Balanchine's* Who Cares? *I have never seen a more imaginative response to the Gershwins onstage.*

Rich was hardly alone. Scanning Clive Barnes in the *New York Post* yielded these goodies: *The brass and the gold of Broadway are back. Will doubtless have audiences crazy for it through the blissfully indefinite future. A considerable Broadway hit. Stroman's scintillating choreography. The dancing is wonderful. It glows from top to tap. It should remain for quite a while.*

Howard Kissel in the *New York Daily News* wrote the shortest of the three reviews, but still the cast was able to find *something scrumptious. A host of exhilarating dance numbers. An explosion of joy.* And "delicious" was the adjective he chose when he cited seven performers by name.

One of them was Beth Leavel, who played the modest role of Tess, one of the showgirls whom Bobby imports to Deadrock, Nevada, where he plans to produce a show. Leavel only had a few lines, and soloed a couple of lyrics in "Slap That Bass."

But she was working. Almost a year ago, she'd appeared in *An Unfinished Song*, a low-profile off-Broadway musical that had lasted a month. She hadn't appeared either off- or on Broadway since. Up till now, her only Broadway credit was becoming an Annie in *42nd Street* when the show was on its last legs in the last of the three theaters it played.

Of all the performers who roared onto the stage of the Shubert Theater for its second performance, Leavel appeared to be having the best time. Her face showed the relief of "Yes! I've finally originated a role in a hit! I don't have to go looking for work tomorrow! Or the day after that! Or in the foreseeable future!"

Leavel also appeared to be the one who most believed in what she was doing. She was almost defying anyone not to like the show, with her face showing "There! Wasn't that wonderful? You know it was wonderful! I know it was wonderful! And it's going to be wonderful for a long, long time. I'm not worry about you getting your money's worth, because that's just what you're getting!"

And at the finale, the wide-armed gesture she gave after she sang, "Who could ask for anything more?" definitely said, "And, really, who could?"

Leavel stayed with *Crazy for You* for two years. She'd eventually go on to play the lead in the 2001 revival of *42nd Street*, and would win a Tony from her stint in the title role of *The Drowsy Chaperone*. But there's a good chance she was never happier than she was on the night when she knew that unemployment insurance was no longer in her immediate future.

Crazy for You. February 19, 1992–January 7, 1996. 1,622 performances.

THE BIGGEST FLOP
Nick & Nora

The reviews are in—and out goes the show.

December 9, 1992. The Marquis Theater, New York City. Just before eight o'clock in the evening.

Audiences are about to see the second official performance of the musical that opened last night. But, as Frank Rich mentioned in this morning's *Times*, there have already been "100,000 customers who paid full price to see *Nick & Nora* during its nine weeks of previews."

That's not all Rich had to say about this new musical with book and direction by Arthur Laurents, music by Charles Strouse, and lyrics by Richard Maltby, Jr. Rich commented on a remark he heard from a patron leaving the after the show—"Well, it's not as bad as they said it would be." He agreed before adding, "Which is not to say it's good. Like the less gifted celebrity who's famous for being famous, this musical will no doubt always be remembered, and not without fondness, for its troubled preview period, its much postponed opening, its hassles with snooping journalists."

One of them, in fact, was Alex Witchel, the *Times* gossip columnist who'd married Rich six months earlier.

Rich went on to call the show "an almost instantly forgettable mediocrity" that "was probably doomed before it played its first preview." He especially took to task the leads who'd each won a Tony for a past effort: Barry (*The Robber Bridegroom*) Bostwick as Nick Charles, suave detective, and Joanna (*Into the Woods*) Gleason, as his sophisticated wife, Nora. Rich felt, "Neither of these talents has the larger-than-life personality or all-round musical comedy pizzazz it takes to ignite a star-centric Broadway musical." Later in the review, he decided that the two "have limited warmth and cannot really dance. The heart sinks from the opening number."

(Actually, choreographer Tina Paul wanted that look. As she said of Bostwick and Gleason in an interview with *Theater Week* magazine, "They have to be at ease with each other, but they mustn't look like professional dancers. They can't be doing 'steps.' I want a lot of continuous motion while they're having a conversation and acting out a scene, not a dance break in the middle.")

Rich concluded, "All the other failures in *Nick & Nora* are secondary to its inability to deliver the glamorous stars and atmosphere promised by its title."

Oh, well. At least before he unleashed his heavy artillery, Rich referred to Bostwick and Gleason as "talents."

Frederick Winship in UPI gave the musical a positive notice. No other critic did. How would Bostwick and Gleason go out and face the world tonight?

And what a long journey it had been. Already the show was a full season late.

Fifteen months earlier—on August 22, 1990—in the small theater space underneath City Center, *Nick & Nora* did a staged reading in hopes that the rest of the $4 million could be raised right there and then. Bostwick and Gleason were there, as were Christine Baranski as Tracy Harding, the movie star who went to school with Nora; and Keene Curtis as Max Bernheim, her director, who's been arrested by Lt. Wolfe (Michael Lombard) for murdering bookkeeper Lorraine Bixby (Faith Prince).

But as events unfold, there'll be ample reason to suspect union president Victor Moira (Chris Sarandon); ex-con Spider Malloy (Jeff Brooks); nightclub singer and Lorraine's girlfriend Maria Valdez (Valarie Pettiford); or even the blueblood Bostonians Edward J. Connors (Kip Niven) and his wife, Lily (Debra Monk), patterned after Joseph P. and Rose Kennedy. As it turns out, Tracy herself and Yukido (Thom Sesma), ostensibly her houseboy but really her lover, turn out to be responsible. (The show's theme: Everyone has something that he'd kill for.)

At the backers' audition, these twelve performers showed that the Strouse and Maltby score nicely replicated a 1937 sound. But the way the mystery played out wasn't as satisfying. Ideally, when a mystery is solved, everyone in the audience is swatting his forehead with the palm of his hand, saying, "Awwwww! I shoulda seen that coming! They gave me the important clue, and I was too dumb to notice!"

Yes, there was something about blue and gold being the official colors of the posh school that Nora and Tracy had attended—and a scarf was found at the murder scene sporting the same colors. That's not enough to make an audience chastise itself for missing a clue.

What the staff also hoped the money men in the audience would respond to was the relationship between Nick and Nora. Certainly they were in love, but when Nick refused to take Tracy's case, Nora stepped forward to do it in his stead. The issue of whether or not the hotshot detective's inexperienced wife could solve the mystery became a bone of contention for them, a possible source of wounded pride for him, and resentment from her that he might not want her to succeed.

But the producers didn't get the money from that room that day, and spent the next year searching and scrounging for it.

Finally, the producers raised enough to start rehearsals, but the tryout that they'd already booked for the Mechanic Theater in Baltimore had to be scrapped. Hence those aforementioned previews. They didn't expect to do a whopping seventy-one of them, but after the opening was postponed from November 10 until December 8, they did them.

Nick & Nora shows the difficulties actors have in finding jobs. Fifteen months after that reading, ten of the twelve performers were still available. Josie de Guzman replaced Pettiford, and Remak Ramsay took over for Curtis. (Baranski stayed in place, but her character's surname changed from Harding to Gardner.)

En route, de Guzman lost her job and was replaced by Yvette Lawrence. (As if Maria was the problem with the show.) But de Guzman wound up having the last laugh; less than four months later, she joined the *Guys and Dolls* revival during previews, taking over for Carolyn Mignini as Sarah Brown and getting two years' work out of it.

Meanwhile, the creators didn't sit still. They replaced the songs they'd written for Tracy ("Now You See Me" became "Everybody Wants to Do a Musical"), Max ("Not Me" gave way to "Max's Song"), Lorraine ("Hollywood"/"Men"), Maria ("The Road to Guadalajara" / "Boom Chicka Boom") and Lily ("Battlecry" / "People Get Hurt"—which had been a song for everyone called "People Like Us").

Nick and Nora's songs were the most changed. "Cocktails for One," Nick's first-act closer, was dropped in favor of "Look Who's Alone Now." Nora's "A Dangerous Man" was spelled by "Let's Go Home." Their duet "It's Easy" became "As Long as You're Happy." With Victor and Spider, they had sung "Quartet in Two Bars," but that was replaced by the duo "Swell." Their finale, "Time to Go" morphed into "Married Life."

But all the work was for naught. So now that Bostwick and Gleason had to come out and do the show, would they walk through it? Many times, actors who've received bad reviews retreat from the audience as if behind bulletproof glass.

Not these two. Each delivered rip-roaring performances that showed—or seemed to show—that they were having barrels of fun. If someone had come to the show not knowing about the nine weeks' worth of troubles—and not knowing anything about musicals—he would have thought he was at the town's biggest hit. That's how committed they were.

When the Tony nominations were announced, though, Bostwick and Gleason weren't on the list. But *Nick & Nora* wasn't entirely shut out. Strouse and Maltby were nominated for their score. This made Strouse the only composer nominated for two shows that didn't reach double figures in performances: *Rags* (four) and *Nick & Nora* (nine). He is also the only composer to have three nominations for shows that ran under twenty performances, thanks to his 1981 nomination for *Charlie and Algernon* (seventeen performances).

Gleason may well have been in good spirits for that second performance because she was deeply in love—with fellow cast member Chris Sarandon. As of this writing, they're still a couple, and presumably glad they did the show. What made Bostwick so happy-go-lucky at that second performance might well have been that the whole damn thing was coming to an end. Or maybe both stars were simply ultra-professional.

Years later, Arthur Laurents would say, "I've come to the conclusion that there *was* no Nick and Nora. It was William Powell and Myrna Loy who had all that chemistry." They certainly did have that, but those two fine actors had good characters to play and witty repartee to deliver (at least in the first classic film *The Thin Man*).

Nick & Nora. December 8–15, 1991–December 9, 1991. 9 performances.

1992–1993

THE BIGGEST HIT
Kiss of the Spider Woman

If at first you don't succeed . . .

When we last saw *Kiss of the Spider Woman*, it was closing in ignominy along with New Musicals, its sponsoring organization. But, just as courageously as the characters they musicalized, bookwriter Terrence McNally, composer John Kander, lyricist Fred Ebb and director Harold Prince faced the situation head on, and wouldn't give up. They went back to work.

Their revisions caught the interest of up-and-coming producer Garth Drabinsky and his Live Entertainment Corporation of Canada. Since his theater in Toronto needed a tenant, Drabinsky chose *Spider Woman* for a June–August 1992 run. Then he took it to London, where it opened on October 20, 1992 for nearly a year's run. Then it was off to Broadway.

How close was the original production in Purchase, New York to the Broadway version?

Dropped from the score were three songs for Aurora. Even during the Purchase engagement, "Man Overboard" ("The second afternoon at sea she gave a sailor such a wink / that he lost his equilibrium and fell into the drink") had given way to "Sailor Boy." The other two were "I Don't Know," in which Aurora asks Molina why he's frightened of her; and "Never You," a duet with Armando, a passionate admirer in one of her films ("Other loves might tell some easy lie / Say 'Forever!' when they mean 'Goodbye!'").

Armando also lost "Everyday," an appealing song in which he admits that his commoner status puts Aurora out of his reach. "An everyday man wants an everyday wife," he sings, but can't force himself to forget that "You don't find love like this every day."

Other excisions included the second-act opener "Good Clean Fight," a revenge fantasy march for the prisoners. ("You can amputate his arm as he's snoring in the night / You can booby trap his mess hall and destroy his appetite."); "Cookies," in which Molina and Valentin fantasized about food; and "Lucky Molina," in which the other prisoners reacted to his release.

Kander and Ebb then added "Bluebloods," Molina's first attempt at engaging Valentin in conversation; "Dressing Them Up," his statement on how seriously he took his job as a window decorator; "I Draw the Line," Valentin's insistence that Molina not invade his space; "Marta," his song of longing for his beloved; and three new numbers for Aurora: "Where You Are," her song of support for Molina; "Russian Movie / Good Times," which she shared with him, and "Anything for Him," in which Valentin joined them, too.

The same week that *Kiss of the Spider Woman* opened, *Ain't Broadway Grand* was closing. A look at the March and April playbills shows how little work was done on the latter show in a month's worth of previews. The scene-and-song list for *Ain't* was exactly the same for both months, aside from a change in act 2, scene 5. In March, the scene was set at the "Rehearsal backstage at the Winter Garden Theater." In April, it was set at the "Rehearsal backstage at the Alvin Theater." That was the total of the ostensible work that the staff did on the show.

Ain't Broadway Grand lasted twenty-five performances. *Kiss of the Spider Woman* would run more than thirty-six times as long.

But, of course, *Kiss* also made an important casting change: Aurora, the Spider Woman, was now played by Chita Rivera. It's astonishing that the Puerto Rican-American legend wasn't asked to play the Spanish star in the first place. Kander and Ebb had written for her twice before, in both *Chicago* and *The Rink*; the latter resulted in her first Tony. Her being on board apparently inspired the collaborators to write substantially better songs for Aurora.

Molina was now played by Brent Carver, and Valentin by Anthony Crivello. Virtually the entire cast was replaced; only Philip Hernandez, who'd played the small role of Marcos in Purchase, was retained, but was reassigned to the small role of Esteban.

Not to be underestimated were the contributions from Jerome Sirlin, who provided a completely new set design and some dynamic projections. While Thomas Lynch's original design in Purchase had been grey-walled and dreary—which, of course, was accurate for a South American prison—Sirlin's relied on bars that were geometrically more arresting to the eye.

So, in less than three years, the out-of-town closer turned into the winner of eight Tonys, including Best Musical. Winning the top award wasn't the biggest surprise that night, though. Who in the world of Broadway—or the world of rock— ever would have thought that John Kander and Fred Ebb and Pete Townshend one night would all be honored with the same award? But that's what happened on June 6, 1993, when the team and Townshend, the composer-lyricist of *The Who's Tommy*, tied for the Best Score Tony. The old guard from Broadway met—let's face it—the old guard from rock.

Producer Garth Drabinsky was hardly drab. The quintessential showman—the most dynamic one since the days of David Merrick and Alexander H. Cohen—was high tech. He liked to have focus groups assess the possibilities of any show he was thinking of producing. Little did he know that another kind of focus group—called a jury—would in 2009 focus on him and find him guilty of financial improprieties. The man who produced a musical set in a prison was eventually sentenced to seven years in one himself.

Kiss of the Spider Woman. May 3, 1993–July 1, 1995. 904 performances.

THE BIGGEST FLOP
The Goodbye Girl

A small thing comes in a big package.

Five of the most important people a musical has on its staff—the leading lady, bookwriter, composer, lyricist, and director—had all won Tonys. The first three of them—Bernadette Peters, Neil Simon, and Marvin Hamlisch—had already reached legendary status. Director Gene Saks had steered three Broadway musicals to runs over five hundred performances. And while David Zippel was only known for *City of Angels*, his sharp lyrics made clear that Broadway would hear from him again and again.

That they chose a beloved property made the enterprise more promising: Simon's own 1977 film, *The Goodbye Girl*. Peters would play Paula McFadden, who's looking forward to tomorrow, when she and her young daughter Lucy will move to California with Paula's actor-boyfriend Tony. On the eve of the move, though, Paula comes home to find a letter from Tony saying that he's already gone without them. Worse, Tony has sublet the apartment to an actor named Elliot Garfield. When Elliot arrives, he feels bad for Paula, and though he has title, he allows her and Lucy to live with him. Plenty of hard feelings emerge before the two—no, three—fall in love.

Playing Elliot was a Broadway neophyte, but a name known and cherished by much of the American public: Martin Short, veteran of dozens of TV shows and a few films, too. But he was no theatrical virgin; Short had been on many stages in his native Canada, starting with *Godspell* in 1972 with fellow neophytes Eugene Levy, Gilda Radner, Andrea Martin, and Paul Shaffer.

Trouble was apparent when Saks left during the Chicago tryout—even though he and Simon had already collaborated eight times. Saks' replacement was Michael Kidd, who'd first stepped on a Broadway stage in 1939. In his first decade of choreographing (1947–1957), Kidd's seven shows included *Finian's Rainbow*, *Guys and Dolls*, *Can-Can*, and *Li'l Abner*. In his next decade, his seven shows yielded no hits at all. As Kevin Kelly reported in the *Boston Globe* when *Ben Franklin in Paris* was trying out, "The direction and choreography are by Michael Kidd, but who is Michael kidding?"

The Goodbye Girl would be Kidd's first Broadway directorial assignment in thirteen years—and that previous one had merely been a restaging of *The Music Man* that had lasted all of twenty-one performances.

Maybe it all went wrong from Peters' opening number. "No More" was a harangue in which Paula insisted that she would never again let herself be victimized by a man. Getting to know a character in a musical through an angry song is off-putting; the opening number should have been a sunny one—perhaps Paula is having fun doing some last-minute shopping, looking forward to the trip to

California and a new life. Let the devastation be handled in the dialogue afterwards.

No one can claim that the songwriters took an easy route. The film has a scene where Lucy is ill, so Elliot rushes to her bedroom with his guitar and begins playing and crooning softly to her. Lesser talents would have put a song there, and made it a treacly moment.

The film only fleetingly shows Mrs. Crosby, the landlady. The musical did substantially more, as Hamlisch and Zippel gave her (Carol Woods) a song to herself. Nothing was wrong with Woods' performance, but audiences just weren't interested in spending time with her.

Especially failing the production was another Tony winner, set designer Santo Loquasto. He may not have been given much of a budget with which to work, but the black backdrop with squares of different colors dotting it looked utterly cheap.

What no one realized is that *The Goodbye Girl* is a very small movie. Much of it takes place indoors (as the vast majority of Neil Simon's work does). This is rarely more than a three-character tale, and whether or not Simon likes to work off-Broadway, that's where this mini-musical belonged. A scene where Elliot is playing Richard III in a terribly misconceived production takes two quick minutes in the film; it became a bloated five-minute song in the script, and wasn't necessary.

Peters and Short did not sign very long contracts, and management did consider replacing them when those contracts were up—but then decided the added cost wouldn't be worth it.

By then, the Tony Awards had treated *The Goodbye Girl* about the way Tony had treated Paula. While there were nominations for the two leads, Kidd, and choreographer Graciela Daniele and the musical itself, Hamlisch and Zippel weren't nominated for their score—while the fledgling songwriters for the forty-six-performance *Anna Karenina* were. The songwriters didn't throw themselves in front of a train, but they had to be disappointed.

The Goodbye Girl. March 4–Aug. 15, 1993. 188 performances.

1993–1994

THE BIGGEST HIT
Beauty and the Beast

Anaheim beats Sondheim.

Decades ago, many a producer had put his own name on his productions: *The Ziegfeld Follies. The Earl Carroll Vanities. The George White Scandals. Ned Wayburn's Gambols.*

But never had a corporation made its own brand name a part of its title.

Oh, people kept calling the biggest hit of the 1993–94 season *Beauty and the Beast*—but the official title was *Disney's Beauty and the Beast*. And while there had been a person named Walt Disney, he had died in 1966, twenty-eight long years before *Beauty and the Beast*—no, *Disney's Beauty and the Beast*—arrived at the Lunt-Fontanne Theater. So it was the corporation and not the man that was being celebrated in the musical's title.

As Tevye said in *Fiddler on the Roof*—which was never called *Harold Prince's Fiddler on the Roof*—"It's a new world."

Yes, a corporate one. In 2000, a little less than halfway through the run of *Disney's Beauty and the Beast*, the Roundabout Theatre Company was opening a new facility, which would include the word "American" in its name. Patriotism was not the motivation; "American Airlines" was the full name that would be placed on the newly refurbished Selwyn Theater, thanks to a generous "donation" from the airlines.

Similarly, the theater that had been known as the Winter Garden since its opening in 1911 was in 2002 suddenly rechristened the Cadillac Winter Garden—not, say, out of a new and urgent appreciation of the French explorer Antoine Laumet de La Mothe de Cadillac, but because General Motors had paid to have its Cadillac brand put before the public. If this continues, Broadway may yet see plays and musicals produced in the Kaopectate Theater.

Disney's Beauty and the Beast didn't get much respect from Broadway; the Best Musical Tony went to *Passion*, Sondheim's fourth such prize. But Anaheim beat Sondheim: *Disney's Beauty and the Beast* certainly captured the public's attention; it would run almost twenty-two times longer than *Passion*'s 250 performances, which still represents the shortest run for any Tony-winning musical.

Despite its $12 million budget, *Disney's Beauty and the Beast* wasn't as handsome as one might have expected. Ann Hould-Ward's costumes were impressive (and won the show its only Tony out of ten nominations), but the dullish backdrops looked as if they'd been taken from the warehouse that had stored Shubert operettas since the thirties.

But the show succeeded because parents could take their children, who'd see some nice lessons validated on stage. The story started centuries ago, with a prince who was said to be "selfish and spoiled," two words to which children could relate, for they often heard them applied to themselves.

An old woman comes to the Prince's castle and asks for a night of shelter in exchange for a rose; when he denies her, she gives him a second chance, which ends the same way. Actually, this is a case of entrapment, for the crone is really an enchantress, though she isn't so enchanting when she changes the Prince into a snarling, raging, panting jungle beast.

The curse will only be reversed if the Prince/Beast can learn to love selflessly—

and if someone can love him equally—before the petals fall off a certain rose. Rather unfairly, the enchantress also casts a spell on the Prince's household, slowly turning each member into an inanimate object. Only if the Prince can break his own enchantment will they be restored. (But kids in the audience could relate to this, too: They'd all been in classrooms where one kid did something wrong, and the teacher punished everyone.)

The scene switches abruptly to a nearby village, where Belle (Susan Egan) is smart enough not to fall in love with Gaston (Brent Moses) simply because he's tall, dark, and handsome. His utter conceit bothers her. Though Belle is always polite to him, Gaston will learn that love cannot be forced. To Belle, inner beauty is more important than outer beauty (even though Belle is pretty pretty herself).

Belle can only imagine herself falling in love with someone who shares her love of reading. No one in town does, but she is strong-minded enough to dare to be different. And even though her father, Maurice (Tom Bosley), is the town eccentric, she loves and defends him against the more conventional townspeople.

How deep is her love? When Maurice is captured by the Beast (Jeff McCarthy), she offers to take his place. The beast accepts, unaware that she's going to make him into a better man. She teaches him how to be polite and sincere, and how to control his temper, for might does not always make right. "Please" and "thank you" become part of his vocabulary. At one point, Beast does fail Belle, but she gives him a second chance. The Beast begins to act in gentlemanly fashion, and learns to say he's sorry when he does something wrong—even when he does it inadvertently. He also learns the famous lesson "If you love someone, set her free"—and that leads him on the road to getting the curse reversed, and making him a happy and loved prince, and his household very happy, too.

With such good feeling streaming through the theater, who could resist coming out of *Disney's Beauty and the Beast* and not buying the T-shirt that read "*Disney's Beauty and the Beast*: My First Broadway Show"?

One more question, though: after the two title characters come to love each other and the spell is broken, the Beast is transformed into a handsome Prince. So why, when the title song is reprised, does the chorus look at the happy couple and still sing the lyrics "Beauty and the Beast?" Shouldn't they be singing "Beauty and the Prince?" Or at least "Beauty and the Prince formerly known as Beast"?

Let's be thankful, though, that the last lyric of the show isn't "Disney's Beauty and the Beast."

Disney's Beauty and the Beast. April 18, 1994–July 29, 2007.
5,461 performances.

THE BIGGEST FLOP
The Best Little Whorehouse Goes Public

So let's try an infomercial.

Now comes the third rhinestone in the triple crown of musical sequels.

As was the case with *Bring Back Birdie* and *Annie 2*, the original team was back in place for *The Best Little Whorehouse Goes Public*: Producer Stevie Phillips, bookwriters Lary L. King and Peter Masterson, songwriter Carol Hall, and, of course, Tommy Tune, who'd choreographed and codirected their previous biggest hit of the season, *The Best Little Whorehouse in Texas.*

This time, Phillips would promote her show via a media device that didn't exist when the first *Whorehouse* debuted in 1978. President Reagan's signing the Cable Communications Policy Act that deregulated television in 1984 led to the birth of the infomercial—an *info*rmative com*mercial* of an inordinate length that appeared to be a TV show, too.

Phillips enlisted Bob Schapiro as writer-director and Jim Caldwell as emcee, and spent $350,000 to make the infomercial for *Goes Public* and $150,000 to air it. Caldwell first took us to Lyon County, Nevada, "where prostitution is allowed by law," and where "the United States government has tried to run a whorehouse like it's running a widget factory."

In the infomercial, King explained why:

> We start with the Internal Revenue Service seizing a brothel in Nevada for not paying its back taxes. What's the IRS gonna do? The Internal Revenue Service man doesn't want to come there and run this. It'd be bad for his image. So they appoint a young woman tax agent whom they more or less throw to the wolves to go out and collect the back taxes by operating this brothel in the name of the Internal Revenue Service. So she's wise enough to get Mona Stangley, the original Chicken House madam, and makes a deal to run it for her.

(Notice that King called Mona's old stomping grounds the "Chicken House" instead of its actual moniker, the "Chicken Ranch." One would think that after this author's twenty-year acquaintance with it, he'd know its actual name.)

The infomercial introduced us to Jerri Coppa, the actual tax agent on whom this story was based. To establish her wholesomeness, she was shown playing a board game with her husband and two children. Coppa recalled that "A senator was screaming on the phone, 'Why the hell is the federal government running a brothel?'"

King set up the show's villain—"Senator A. Harry Hardast, a Southern fried politician, [who] takes great moral umbrage and great indignation at the fact that stocks are going to be sold in a common whorehouse to the great American public." Ronn Carroll, as Hardast, got into God-fearing, scripture-spouting activist mode and delivered a minute-long harangue that ended with "So help me God, and Robert E. Lee."

Dee Hoty, who'd play Mona, recited one of her lines: "You're sayin' Uncle Sam will pay me to do in Nevada the same thing that Texas locked me up for? One of these days, I gotta read the Constitution."

Hoty sang some of "I'm Leaving Texas" in a recording studio. When she reached the lyric "Chili always gave me gas," an unnamed man gave Carol Hall an admiring look, which she just as proudly returned. Caldwell described Hall as "perhaps the best American songwriter on Broadway today." (And most of us mistakenly thought it was Stephen Sondheim.)

We also went "behind the scenes to feel the emotion, the thrills, and the challenges of bringing a hit show to Broadway." Bob Mackie's colorful sketches came to life as costumes. "They're hardly dresses," Mackie asserted. "They just barely cover their crotch." He later asked a chorus girl, "Do you want to show us your shining crotch?"

The dresses' upper regions had flesh-colored fabric covering breasts to trompe l'oeil–suggest that we were seeing the genuine articles. (Vertical ribbons were strategically placed.) Mackie admitted, "I can be a little trashy" and said the dresses offered "every man's fantasy"—a cheerleader, a perfect little chef, Nefertiti, and Lolita."

Masterson and King admitted going to the actual Nevada brothel for research purposes. Said King, "What passes for romance there may not exactly be love, but may not be too bad." He was, however, careful to make clear that the musical had hired "actresses, not real-life prostitutes." He also mused, "There are probably twelve, fourteen young women chorus girls in there that'd make an old man like myself leave home."

Ganine Giorgione, who'd double as a "Street Whore" and "Working Girl," diplomatically remarked, "Larry King is playful, and he does like his ladies." Lanie Sakakura, who was to portray "Showroom Patron," said "Larry King is a great screenwriter [sic]," but was more frank when adding, "And he has a mouth on him like you wouldn't believe." To counterbalance that charge, Caldwell quickly added that King was a Lyndon B. Johnson speechwriter, while the screen showed an august picture of the White House.

Jim David, who'd been cast as "Comedian" and "The President's Hairdresser," was introduced. Caldwell said he "explains the action, helping to advance the story, sometimes thumbing his nose at everything that's going on." (David wouldn't turn out to be the only one who did that.) Tune said, "We call him 'The Joke Slave,'" but King's opinion was more pronounced: "If you watch Jim David deliver his material and don't laugh, hell, I got bad news for you: You've been dead about six months."

Caldwell also had much to say about "the renovation of an historic Broadway landmark," referring to the Lunt-Fontanne Theatre—"the home of "*The Ziegfeld Follies, Peter Pan* and even *The Sound of Music*." Yes, but the *Peter Pan* that played there was the 1979 revival, not the 1954 original. Schapiro could have mentioned Richard Burton's 1964 *Hamlet*, but probably thought that wouldn't interest his target audience.

"Even the great shows have had some pretty crummy seats," Caldwell confessed, before showing workmen taking out the theater's old seats and replacing them. The new seats were to be "staggered and raked, so you can see over people's heads," with "cushions with all the bounce," and "no gummy bears underneath."

Of course, the main motivation was to sell tickets, so occasional messages flashed, "Stay tuned for a special Broadway discount!"

"Often you can only get the best seats from scalpers," Caldwell said, before letting us eavesdrop on telephone calls where tickets were sold for $325.50 a pair (at a time when box-offices were charging $65 for the best seats). Caldwell then offered a 25 percent discount via Ticketmaster, with tickets at a mere $48.75, with a 40 percent reduction on the service charge, and only $2.50 in shipping and handling. To get this generous deal, though, a ticket buyer was forced to say "the secret code phrase" of "Tommy sent me."

The upshot? Tune said, "I haven't created a flop Broadway musical yet, and I don't intend to start with *The Best Little Whorehouse Goes Public*."

But he did. What the sequel needed was not an infomercial, which was found wanting and only aired twice. It needed the ingredients found in the first show. *Texas* elevated the characters, made them real, and made us care about them. Instead, the sequel put stereotypes in a dirty cartoon. Granted, the name chosen for the moralist in the original—Melvin P. Thorpe—sounded ridiculous, but it was Woodrow Wilson compared to A. Harry Hardast.

Worse, one song had women in glass cubes, spreading their legs wide as they engaged in phone sex. While Hall provided a fetching boogie-woogie melody, the men who called sang, "I've cleaned the lint between my toes, I've trimmed the hair in my ears and nose." In a courtroom scene, Hal's lyrics referred to the lawyer's "big subpoenas" and the judge's "tiny gavel."

The infomercial did not, of course, give away the show's ending in which Mona is elected—yes—president of these United States. And to think that in *The Will Rogers Follies*, the title character was aghast to hear that an actor would someday become chief executive.

And yet, Scott Holmes, who'd play Mona's old beau Sam Dallas, said in the infomercial, "I can feel it in my bones that this thing is gonna take off. If you don't get your tickets now, you're gonna be waiting for years."

Well, yes, in a manner of speaking. Caldwell was equally inaccurate in predicting that *The Best Little Whorehouse Goes Public* "was bound to be an award-winning hit show." Hoty did get a Tony nomination as Best Actress in a Musical, while Mackie and orchestrator Peter Matz had to settle for Drama Desk nominations. None won.

The Best Little Whorehouse Goes Public. May 10, 1994–May 22, 1994. 16 performances.

1994–1995

The Biggest Hit
Smokey Joe's Café

Saved by the Tonys.

June 4, 1995. The Forty-ninth Annual Tony Awards, New York City. Richard Frankel, the lead producer of *Smokey Joe's Café,* has high hopes for tonight. Considering that his show will lead off the annual broadcast, perhaps some of the millions upon millions of viewers will be moved to buy tickets for his faltering musical revue based on the songs of Leiber and Stoller.

"If the show were only novelty songs like 'Yakety-Yak' or 'Charlie Brown,' it wouldn't have appealed to me," said Frankel. "But songs made famous by the Drifters are markedly different, as are Peggy Lee's hits, and country-and-western songs, too. Add in 'Spanish Harlem,' and you've got a pretty wide range for a Broadway show."

But the critics didn't quite agree. Though the March 3 reviews for the show weren't putrid, they weren't money notices. When the *New York Times* calls a show "a strangely homogenized tribute to one of popular music's most protean songwriting teams," theatergoers don't say, "Wow! I'd better call Telecharge now!"

"And we'd spent all our money," recalled Frankel that night. "Four million. Even a little more."

But Rocco Landesman, then president of Jujamcyn Theaters (owner of the Virginia, where *Smokey Joe's* was shakily ensconced) took a meeting with the producers. Said Frankel, "He said, 'I know the reviews are mediocre, but I believe in the show, and my checkbook is on the table.' Then he left."

Frankel and his partners were astonished. For a moment. Then they were off and calculating.

"We figured we needed $1.2 million from him, to do ads—and to cover losses—and that's precisely what we borrowed. And now we were hoping that the Tony Awards would help the nation see we had a good show. Each show was entitled to 2.5 minutes," recalled Frankel, "so we decided to split it up. First we'd provide the opening number with the men, and then we'd come back later with the women doing another song."

On the monitors inside the Minskoff, Frankel watched Adrian Bailey, Ken Ard, Victor Trent Cook, and Frederick B. Owens in front of the side marquee of the Virginia Theater on Fifty-second Street. The sign "7 Tony Nominations, Including Best Musical" was easily seen as the men sang and strutted to "They say the neon lights are bright / On Broadway / They say there's always magic in the air." By then, they'd swerved around to the front of the marquee, where the words "Stunning!" "Blissful!" and "Tuneful" were featured for all the nation to see. (What's more, would-be tourists had to be impressed at how clean Fifty-second Street looked.)

This part of the sequence had to have been taped in advance, for only a moment later, the *Smokey Joe*'rs were seen literally on Broadway in front of the Marquis Theatre, continuing their walk and their song. Their destination was the Minskoff, where *Sunset Boulevard*, their only competition for the Best Musical Tony, was playing. Eager crowds behind blue police sawhorses wildly cheered their every move.

The quartet then entered the actual packed auditorium itself, walked down the right aisle, and stormed onto the stage. "They say that I won't last too long on Broadway," the lyric went, but Frankel started to believe that with the sharp way the number was playing, the cheering crowds, and the dynamic entrance, that lyric wouldn't turn out to be true.

Two hours later, Frankel and his coproducers were in misery—and not just because *Smokey Joe's* failed to win even one award. What had happened was that the Tonys weren't going to make the eleven o'clock cutoff that CBS imposed. Executive producer Gary Smith made the executive decision: *Smokey Joe's* second number, "I'm a Woman," featuring the four female cast members, wouldn't be broadcast at all.

"Brenda Braxton, B. J. Crosby, DeLee Lively, and Patti Darcy Jones were standing in the wings waiting to go on," said Frankel immediately following the broadcast. "To put it mildly, I'm very upset. It's unfair of them to go back on their agreement with us."

But they didn't need the extra number. The dynamic "On Broadway" was enough to cause a surge in business the very next day. Within weeks, Frankel and partner paid off their loan to Landesman. Fifteen months after opening, the show had paid back the entire $5.2 million, and opened companies in London and Japan.

One can't argue with success. *Smokey Joe's* continued to make money the old-fashioned way—by earning it. "The only thing that really counts is word of mouth," said Frankel. "Between winter sales and direct mail, we made profitable grosses. Broadway is mostly a tourist business and we benefited by that. Between the foreign and North American visitors, 60 to 70 percent of our audiences were tourists, with the rest coming from New York City suburbs."

He wasn't complaining. "People recommend *Smokey Joe's* genuinely and enthusiastically—just like with *Cats*, which a lot of people sneer at. I hate that. Shows like this speak to people and get them to respond."

Just as they did after seeing *Smokey Joe's Café* on the Tonys.

Smokey Joe's Café. March 2, 1995–January 16, 2000. 2,036 performances.

The Biggest Flop
Sunset Boulevard

And you thought the helicopter was something.

And while the biggest hit of the 1994–1995 season lost the Best Musical Tony, the biggest flop of the 1994–1995 season won it: *Sunset Boulevard*, the story of faded film star Norma Desmond (Glenn Close), her former husband and now butler (George Hearn), and her kept lover, the failed writer Joe Gillis (Alan Campbell).

Some may say that a musical boasting a run of more than two years can't be the season's biggest flop. But considering that it was one of only two new musicals produced the whole season—and *Smokey Joe's Café* was the other— what choice do we have? While many Broadway producers and writers would have killed for *Sunset*'s twenty-eight-month run, its losses have been estimated from $2.5 million to $20 million.

The musical, adapted from the famed 1950 film, was the latest Andrew Lloyd Webber musical. The book was by Christopher Hampton, the lyrics by Don Black. But ever since the composer ended his association with Tim Rice, every show with music by Lloyd Webber has been known simply as a Lloyd Webber show.

Sunset came to New York with a black mark against it, thanks to what became known as "The Patti LuPone Factor." In London, she'd played Norma, but Lloyd Webber wasn't impressed enough to allow her to play the role on Broadway. When he announced that Glenn Close would be his new Norma, LuPone didn't say anything like "Well, Andy, if you don't want me, I understand; let's shake hands, and no hard feelings."

LuPone wouldn't settle for less than a million-plus settlement, which she used for a home improvement: a swimming pool. That was a fascinating purchase, given that both the original film and the musical version of *Sunset Boulevard* open with a dead man at the bottom of a swimming pool. How many times has LuPone envisioned Lloyd Webber at the bottom of her pool? We'll never know.

Nevertheless, the musical was expected to be a Broadway blockbuster. Just think of all the faded female stars of yore who could play Norma. Seven actresses played Dolly during *Hello, Dolly*'s Broadway run; with shows now running around twice as long as they used to, much of Broadway could look forward to more than a dozen grand theatrical dames at the Minskoff in the next ten to fifteen years. (Not everyone felt this way; as *New York Daily News* writer Wayman Wong liked to say, "Perpetual *Sunset* is rather an unsettling thing.")

That seemed possible at the Tonys, where seven trophies, including Best Musical, went to the show. But it was an imperfect year. Matters were so bad that no one—*no one*—was nominated against Lloyd Webber for Best Score. So he won unopposed.

One song was slightly recycled. The melody for the B-section of the dramatic "As If We Never Said Goodbye," where Norma returns to the studio after years of missing it, was not created for *Sunset*. Lloyd Webber had originally composed it as the B-section of "Half a Moment," a song from his then-forgotten 1974 flop *Jeeves*. When that show was refurbished for Broadway as *By Jeeves* in 2001, Lloyd Webber had to write a new B-section for "Half a Moment."

Much of the money went to John Napier's set. Certainly Norma had to live in a splendor, but did her mansion really need to rise and fall so that a scene set in another location could be played under it?

Phantom's story required its chandelier to fall. *Miss Saigon*'s required that a helicopter get people out of Vietnam. But mansions are famously sedentary, and making the one at 10086 Sunset Boulevard float was unnecessary grandstanding. A 2008 London revival without any special effects was much more praised.

On the other hand, that revival ran only six months. Was the reason that people really did want spectacle—or had the show returned too quickly? (The original production had closed less than a decade earlier.) Was it *Sunset*'s tainted reputation? Some will tell you the simple reason is that the show is not very good.

Actually, in some ways, the musical improved on the movie. In the film, Joe escapes from Norma's clutches on New Year's Eve by going to a party. He then calls Max to say he won't be returning, only to be told that Norma has attempted suicide. He rushes back to her, and only then does the stroke of midnight turn New Year's Eve into New Year's morning.

But in the musical, when Joe calls from the party and Max tells him about Norma's slashing her wrists, the other party guests are counting down to "Happy New Year!"—showing a dramatic and sharp contrast between his and Norma's misery to their happiness.

The film has a scene in which Norma pretends to be Charlie Chaplin for Joe's amusement. While the writers did create a song for this moment—and LuPone played it for some London previews—they were wise to drop such an obvious moment.

But that wasn't their smartest omission. The movie included a scene in which Norma plays bridge with her fellow forgotten movie stars. Director Billy Wilder hired Anna Q. Nilsson, who'd started her film career in the title role of *Molly Pitcher* in 1911; H. B. Warner, who appeared in forty-five silents between 1914 and 1929; and, most recognizable of all, Buster Keaton, who starred in fifty silents, directed twenty-eight, and was involved in the writing of twenty-two. All their careers either had come to an end or were virtually over, and they knew it. Joe callously called them "the Waxworks."

Had this scene been retained for the stage version, how much more embarrassing it would have seemed. Imagine three true theatrical has-beens on stage feeling the pity of from the audience eight times a week. That's something Nilsson, Warner, and Keaton didn't have to feel night after night. The musical's creators mercifully dropped it.

The anticipated parade of divas in the role didn't quite happen. Close was succeeded by Betty Buckley, and then British star Elaine Paige came in. But by then, *Sunset* was on the Boulevard of Broken Dreams, and walked, rather than ran, to the finish line.

Sunset Boulevard. November 17, 1994–March 22, 1997. 977 performances.

1995–1996

THE BIGGEST HIT
Rent

First come, first served, first class.

There are many reasons given for *Rent*'s runaway success.

This rock musical version of *La Bohème*—which traded nineteenth-century Paris for late twentieth-century East Village—received some unexpected nationwide publicity. Even those in the hinterlands with no real knowledge of musical theater became aware that Jonathan Larson, *Rent*'s bookwriter, composer, and lyricist, had suddenly died from an aortic aneurysm before the musical's first official off-Broadway preview. He was not quite thirty-six years old.

The music Larson wrote for *Rent* didn't sound much like Broadway, but it was melodious enough to appeal to traditional theatergoers. In turn, the book and lyrics caught the fancy of the younger generation because it showed kids their own age dealing with parents whom they thought were morons. Of course, the parents in *Rent* were the kids shown twenty-eight years earlier in *Hair*, when they were just as annoyed by *their* parents. Larson apparently believed that the more things change . . .

As much as the critics and the public liked *Rent*—it won the Pulitzer, Tony, Drama Desk, New York Drama Critics Circle, and Outer Critics Circle Awards— Larson probably would have improved it had he been able to work on it.

Obviously the book was a little muddled, for not long into the run, one page of the Playbill was devoted to a "Note about the Plot of *Rent*." That four-paragraph explanation was followed by a page sporting the "*Rent* Family Tree." This schematic offered inch-square pictures of (going clockwise) landlord Benny (Taye Diggs) and Bohemians Mimi (Daphne Rubin-Vega), Roger (Adam Pascal), Collins (Jesse L. Martin), Angel (Wilson Jermaine Heredia), Joanne (Fredi Walker), Maureen (Idina Menzel), and Mark (Anthony Rapp). Next to their names were one-sentence descriptions, such as "Benny is married to Alison Grey of Westport, whom we never see." Printed synopses in programs were usually only the province of dinner theaters, in case patrons had had one too many drinks and were unable to follow what was going on. Did it happen with *Rent* because some theatergoers were just plain confused as to what was going on in this multi-prize-winning show?

Many have alleged that *Rent* garnered its smash-hit status partly because of Larson's unexpected death and the ensuing media circus. Says Rapp, who'd played Mark in readings and workshops dating back to 1994, "I can tell you that back then after any performance we did, people would come up afterwards and just swarm around Jonathan. That doesn't often happen to authors, but it sure did in his case. They weren't coming up because they thought he was going to die."

Even President Clinton made time to see the show. Menzel, who played Maureen—the performance artist who insisted that the audience moo like a cow—recalls the night she spotted the president in the audience. She looked right at him, and didn't let him off the hook, but demanded that he moo. And, she says, he did.

But one factor that was vital to *Rent*'s success hasn't been much discussed. Perhaps reacting to Ben Brantley's review in the *Times* that "the top ticket price for *Rent* is a whopping $67.50, a figure that would feed most of its cast in an Avenue B restaurant," the management decided to offer $20 tickets to the first twenty people who showed up at the box office.

Such deep discounts weren't uncommon, but they were always for the seats far in the upper reaches of the mezzanine or balcony. *Rent*'s management, though, was offering $20 tickets for the first two rows of the orchestra. First come, first served, first class.

One week after the show opened, Justin Plowman was hired as "The Line Guy." That means he'd supervise those who'd stand in line waiting to buy the $20 tickets.

Easier said than done. Many showed up several hours before the performance, often with blankets, sleeping bags, or cots—to ensure a place in line, and to be one of the chosen twenty.

"On weekends, it got very difficult," says Plowman. "People would show up ready to sleep on the street not just for the Friday night show, but for both Saturday performances and the Sunday matinee, too. I'd have four lines going at once, and there were times they spread all the way down Forty-first Street till they reached Eighth Avenue."

Though more people tended to wait in line on sunny spring or cool fall days, Plowman recalls plenty of hopefuls joining the line in the dog days of summer and the dead of winter. "One terrible, snowy and cold winter night, I arrived to find three people in a tent. They were using one car battery to fuel a heater they had, and another to provide a current to a TV so they could watch *Seinfeld*."

While camping out would seem to be something that teens would perversely enjoy, Plowman reports that plenty of people long past their twentieth birthday joined these crowds. That more mature types were on hand didn't make Plowman's job any easier, for unethical line-cutting knows no age barrier.

Word spread, and the lines got longer. After a long, frustrating year in which Plowman felt he was losing the battle, he went to management and told them another solution had to be found. "Allan S. Gordon (one of *Rent*'s producers) and I came up with the idea of a lottery," he says.

Now people in line would have to arrive two and a half hours before the show, write their names on cards, and put them in a bucket. Then, two hours before the performance, a drawing was held. Each winner could buy two tickets. Plowman returned to the line with a shiny new bullhorn and made the announcement.

"Because the theater was so close to the Port Authority Bus Terminal," says Plowman, "people would just drop by on their way home, figuring, 'Well, let me enter the lottery, and if I win, I'll just stay in town and see the show. And if not, I'll just go home as I planned.'"

Eventually, of course, those who lost on a daily basis accused Plowman of rigging the lottery. "And there were about two dozen people who showed up almost every day for six years or so. One day, when I was pulling out names, one guy was really obnoxious about it," he says. "So I challenged him with 'Okay, why don't *you* pull out the next card?' And he did—and it was his. Boy, did that backfire."

The management was losing all of $950 a week at first, but never more than $1,700 a week as price increased. That's not much of a loss leader, and the publicity was worth so much more. Plowman says there were times when four hundred people entered the lottery in hopes of buying a pair of the twenty allotted tickets. Some who didn't win would bite the financial bullet and buy regular-price seats.

But the lottery kept *Rent* in the public eye long after the initial flurry of excitement and activity abated—and long after Larson's death was news. Later, Larson's struggle to get a musical produced was dramatized in the 2001 musical *tick, tick . . . BOOM!* Here we saw Larson (Raul Esparza) as a young composer-lyricist who sometimes feels he's getting nowhere. Part of his angst comes from turning thirty. That may sound young to many of us, but Larson turned out to have a point, for when he reached that age, his life was actually five-sixths over.

Ironic that in *tick, tick . . . BOOM!* Larson is shown to be consumed with Stephen Sondheim's opinions of his work. He especially admires Sondheim's *Sunday in the Park with George*. Could Larson have ever imagined that his show would receive the Pulitzer Prize as *Sunday* had done a dozen years earlier? Actually, Larson trumped Sondheim's ace by winning the Tony, too, which *Sunday* did not. (When *Rent* started advertising in the *New York Times* ABC ads, more often than not, it didn't even bother to list that it had won the Tony, but preferred to stress its Pulitzer.)

As for the *Rent* actors, playing to those first two rows of $20 ticket-holders who attended time and time again could be problematic. Both Rapp and Daphne Rubin-Vega rued the incessant attendance of someone they came to call Lippy— "because he was lip-synching and contorting himself through each and every lyric," says Rapp.

Nevertheless, it's a rare Broadway show today that doesn't offer some sort of lottery for its less well-heeled (or more tight-fisted) patrons. In the long run, that will be *Rent*'s biggest legacy.

Rent. April 29, 1966–September 7, 2008. 5,123 performances.

The Biggest Flop
Big

Time doesn't heal everything.

Big's producers had all their money and were ready to open in the 1994–1995 season. But Andrew Lloyd Webber had announced he was bringing his *Sunset Boulevard* to Broadway that same fall. Suddenly, *Big*'s powers-that-be decided to postpone by a year. They reasoned that they'd never win the Best Musical Tony with another surefire Lloyd Webber smash as on the scene. The following season, they decided, they wouldn't face such formidable competition.

But as we've seen, the reception for the British megamusical wasn't as strong as expected. So had *Big* gone toe-to-toe with *Sunset*—whose competition for Best Musical was only *Smokey Joe's Café*—many critics and voters might well have said, "Oh, *Big* is a good ol' fashioned American musical! Give it the Tony!"

Instead, in 1995–1996, not only did *Big* lose in every one of its (only) five Tony categories, but it wasn't even nominated for Best Musical. In the nominations it did receive, *Big* wound up facing much stiffer competition, from both *Rent* and *Bring in 'da Noise, Bring in 'da Funk*. Many critics—especially the younger ones—embraced the new wave, and delighted in the signs that the sound of musical was inexorably changing. The show struggled through less than six months of half-filled houses before losing over $10 million, then the highest deficit a Broadway production had ever endured.

Ironically, *Sunset Boulevard* did wind up hurting *Big*, but in an unexpected way. Throughout May, 1996, despite its Tony snubs, *Big* was holding its own. It wasn't making much of a profit, but it was at least making expenses, thanks to all that business from TKTS—the half-price booth in Duffy Square.

But then one day in June, the producers noticed that they'd suddenly sold far fewer tickets than usual. The reason: for the first time, *Sunset Boulevard* wasn't doing enough business and had to start using the TKTS booth itself. *Big,* which had often been TKTS patrons' first choice, no longer was.

Big wasn't perfect, but its heart was in the right place. The show, based on the hit 1988 movie of the same name, told the story of Josh Baskin (Patrick Levis), who wanted to grow up fast—until he suddenly did through a magical machine. Then he wanted to become a kid again.

But when bookwriter John Weidman turned screenplay into musical, he was intrigued by one issue that the film overlooked. If indeed Josh (Daniel Jenkins) fell into a great job at a toy company with a big salary where Mac (Jon Cypher), his boss, loved him—and got a sophisticated and sexy girlfriend, Susan (Crista Moore), to boot—why would he want to return to uncertain pre-adolescence? He'd lose the wealth, power, and love that he'd accumulated. How could returning to the oppression of teachers and parents seem a better option?

Some may answer, "Oh, but you've got to go through a complete childhood and adolescence; if you don't, you're missing something." Granted, but that's a realization that comes with the wisdom of age. Josh still had his thirteen-year-old mind, so he wouldn't sense that—especially with his clearing more than a grand a week (as the script stated) and enjoying a great sex life, too.

Weidman decided to change a scene in which Josh met Susan's friends at a dinner party. In the film, he wound up helping the son of one friend to learn algebra, to the admiration of all. Weidman dispensed with the son, and soon had Josh in over his head with adult conversation and interaction. He didn't have the sophistication in food, drink, culture, and behavior to make the social grade. He could fake his way through the work day, where he had to test toys, and he had no problems in bed—but he couldn't cope or compete during the hours between quitting time and hitting the hay. That's good reason to want out of his wish.

Alas, Weidman's solution carried with it one liability. Many theatergoers, seeing the logo of a pair of sneaker-clad adolescent feet on the trademark oversized piano keyboard, assumed that *Big* was a family show. Hence, plenty of parents brought their offspring—and the children did giggle delightedly during the second scene, where a suddenly big Josh awakes in his small bunk and struggles to put on the jeans an finds he's literally too big for his britches. But for the rest of the show, the kids rarely laughed again.

Perhaps lyricist Richard Maltby, Jr. and composer David Shire, each approaching sixty, weren't the logical team for this contemporary tale. For "Stars"—in which Josh creates constellations for Susan on his apartment walls and ceiling via a light-projection toy—they wrote a waltz. A thirteen-year-old, late twentieth-century kid does not think in three-quarter time. For "Coffee Black"—which Josh sang the morning after he lost his virginity—they wrote forties boogie-woogie instead of nineties rock.

Worse, they never managed to write an arresting song for the moment in the movie that everyone most fondly remembered—when Josh and Mac meet in a toy store and dance on an oversized piano. "Fun" should have been the score's best number and a memorable showstopper, but instead, it was melodically one of the weakest. Orchestrator Douglas Besterman did what he could by using Dixieland—certainly the most fun-filled styles of music. But choreographer Susan Stroman could never make "Fun" build properly, either.

Worst of all, while Jenkins and Cypher danced on that keyboard, the pianist in the pit played the notes they were hitting. Instead of stepping on a silent keyboard, the boys should have been challenged to hit the notes themselves on a live keyboard. The number came off as artificial and at odds with what we expect to see live on stage.

Similarly, when Josh envisions his thirteenth birthday party, a friend carried out a cake with thirteen candles on it—but each "candle" had a light bulb on top, and they weren't "lit" until the kid carrying the cake pulled a switch that illuminated them all at once.

While Stroman never conquered "Fun," she did produce a marvelous moment in the second act where Josh watches a young boy shyly come on to a young girl, whom he teaches how to skateboard. This was a fine way of showing Josh what he'd lost by growing up too fast. And Stroman, famed for her use of props, gave a unique sound to one number when she had kids at the mall play with the straws tightly stuck in their plastic-lid-covered drinks. That squeaky sound they make when you pull them up and down? It was great fun when set to music.

Big took a severe beating, first in Detroit, and then on Broadway, Even Stroman got lukewarm reviews for the first time in her career. Still, as much pain as *Big* brought to Stroman and Weidman, it couldn't have been that bad an experience for them; they'd re-team in 2000 on *Contact*—one of the biggest hits of its season.

Sure, *Big* had problems, but had it opened in the post-9/11 era of feel-good, traditional-sounding musicals *(The Producers, Mamma Mia,* and *Thoroughly Modern Millie)*, it would have had an easier time of it. It was too early for 2001–2002, and too late for 1995–1996. It might have been right on time in 1994–1995.

Big. April 28, 1996–October 13, 1996. 193 performances.

1996–1997

The Biggest Hit
Chicago

Everything comes to those who wait.

The Tony-winning Best Musical *Titanic* was not the biggest hit of the season. It barely made back its $10 million cost (which was, incidentally, $2.5 million more than was needed to build the actual ocean liner *Titanic* in 1912).

The biggest hit of 1996–97 was the Tony-winning Best Revival, *Chicago*—the cynical 1975 musical about Roxie Hart, who murdered the lover who was about to abandon her, and convinced her husband Amos to raise thousands of dollars so shyster (but effective) lawyer Billy Flynn could keep her from prison. To date, *Chicago* is the only show to win more Tonys for its revival (six of eight nominations) than for its original production (none of nine nominations).

Actually, the original *Chicago* probably would have come home with one Tony when it was first eligible in the 1975–1976 season, had that Tony scandal over William Daniels' Featured Actor nomination not erupted in 1969. If Daniels had been correctly placed in the Best Musical Actor category, he would have easily bested Jerry Orbach for his role in *Promises, Promises*. Because Daniels wasn't, many Broadway observers felt that Orbach's win was tainted.

So when Orbach was nominated as Billy Flynn, voters may well have felt that he'd won his Tony already, and gave the prize to George Rose in *My Fair Lady*—not for playing Henry Higgins, but in the clearly supporting role of Alfred P. Doolittle. Had Daniels won in 1969, voters would have probably given the previously unrewarded Orbach the Tony in 1976.

While the original *Chicago* was a money-making hit—only thirty musicals had then ever run longer than its 898 performances—it played second-class citizen to *A Chorus Line* all through its run. Besides, wasn't Gwen Verdon, at fifty, too old to play the irresponsible Roxie? Her falling ill merely two months into the run only underlined that she was getting older. When Liza Minnelli came in to rescue her, she was an age-appropriate twenty-nine—and business soared. When Verdon returned, the signs of age returned with her, and business was never again quite as strong.

Besides, *Chicago* was charging an all-time high of $17.50 for an orchestra seat, while *A Chorus Line*'s top was the standard $15.

In 1996, though, *Chicago* was leading a charmed life. In May, it started out as the ninth presentation of Encores!, a staged-reading series that was originally designed to rescue forgotten musicals. (That itself tells much about *Chicago*'s reputation.) *Chicago* was such a surprise sensation that it was immediately picked up for Broadway with the Encores! cast—including Ann Reinking as Roxie. She'd played it midway through the original run, and though she was now only three years younger than Verdon had been in the role, she seemed younger—partly because Verdon's voice turned prematurely old by the late sixties.

Reinking was well accompanied by Bebe Neuwirth as fellow murderess Velma Kelly and by James Naughton as Flynn. Neither he nor she was as impressive as Chita Rivera and Orbach had been in those roles. But now that *A Chorus Line* wasn't blinding everyone to *Chicago*'s worth, even Reinking got a Tony for her choreography, which was just her watered-down recollections of what original stager Bob Fosse had done in 1975.

Fosse had originally lost Best Director of a Musical and Best Choreographer Tonys to Michael Bennett and his *Chorus Line* juggernaut. Yet no one could have accused Fosse of a lack of imagination. For Roxie's trial scene, twelve jurors would obviously be required. The production couldn't pay that many actors to just sit around, so Fosse turned the liability into an asset: have one performer sit in the jury box, and with facial putty, change his look to represent our seeing one juror at a time.

But more to the point, when Fosse was cowriting *Chicago*'s book (with its lyricist, Fred Ebb), he or they soon came to an important conclusion: if this story were done as a realistic musical, audiences wouldn't be able to root for this common criminal. So Fosse and/or Ebb created a concept musical, where vaudeville would be the overriding metaphor. Roxie could sing a Helen Morgan song on a piano. When Flynn wanted her to keep quiet and let him do the talking, they'd do a ventriloquist act with her playing the dummy on his knee. Another murderess would do a "high-wire act"—meaning that she'd hang. Fosse and/or Ebb were also smart to make her a Hungarian who knew no English besides "not guilty." With the language barrier between her and the audience, the crowd couldn't become emotionally involved with her.

Female impersonators were always a part of vaudeville, so the bookwriters decided to have Mary Sunshine, a sympathetic reporter, played by a man—though that would be kept a secret from the public, using the actor's first initial (M. O'Haughey) to mask his sex. When the ruse was revealed in the second act, the 1975 audience squealed in pleasure and surprise. But drag was infrequent back then. In the ensuing years, it had become a mainstay of our culture. So in 1996, when D. Sabella entered as Mary Sunshine, many audience members were heard to whisper to their companions, "That's a man."

Chicago, under the auspices of Barry and Fran Weissler, made great hay out of stunt casting—the practice of putting performers in roles because they're first and foremost famous; if they had the ability to do the show, so much the better. But that wasn't a prerequisite. Robin Givens, Melanie Griffth, Marilu Henner, and Brooke Shields portrayed Roxie. Jasmine Guy played Velma. But the Billy Flynns included Maxwell Caulfield; Louis Gossett, Jr.; George Hamilton; Harry Hamlin; Huey Lewis; Jerry Springer; Usher Raymond; Patrick Swayze; Alan

Thicke—not to mention the two original "Dukes of Hazzard," John Schneider and Tom Wopat.

What the *Chicago* revival also did was revive the moribund Broadway musical movie. The only stage musical that took longer to get to the screen was *The Bohemian Girl*, filmed in 1935, ninety-two years after its premiere—but for good reason, since movies had not been invented when that show opened in 1843. Putting it another way, When *Chicago* first opened, the stars of its eventual film, Renée Zellweger and Catherine Zeta-Jones, were respectively six and five years old.

The 2002 film was the first musical since *Oliver!* (1968) to win the Oscar for Best Picture, and Hollywood executives began to think that the time might have come to revive the Broadway musical on screen. *The Phantom of the Opera*, *Rent*, *The Producers*, *Mamma Mia*, and *Nine* followed (for better or worse).

Some of *Chicago*'s success was linked to O.J. Simpson's sensational 1995 murder trial, for he, like Roxie Hart, was acquitted. How sad that this media circus was a component of *Chicago*'s getting its long-overdue due. Yet Simpson and the musical continued to have a strange symmetry. On November 14, 2007—the day on which *Chicago* celebrated its tenth anniversary—news broke that Simpson had written a book about the murders called *If I Did It*. Whether he did or not, *Chicago* sure did become the longest-running revival in Broadway history.

Chicago. November 14, 1996–. Over 5,500 performances

The Biggest Flop
Whistle down the Wind

An American fiasco becomes a solid London hit.

Six years into the run of *The Phantom of the Opera*, Davis Gaines assumed the title role. It was certainly was a good job, but, by 1994, not one for which an actor received much notice. As far as the press was concerned, it was Michael Crawford's hand-me-down role, and there was no big news in who was now playing the Phantom.

By then, composer Andrew Lloyd Webber rarely showed up at the Majestic Theater, and director Harold Prince not all that much more. Now, however, Gaines would see substantially more of them—for they had chosen him to be the leading man of their new musical, their third collaboration after *Evita* and *Phantom*: *Whistle down the Wind*.

Gaines had to be the happiest man on Broadway—until he got a look at the script. Not that the story isn't intriguing. The musical was based on Mary Hayley

Bell's 1958 novel that deals with three children growing up in rural England. Swallow (a girl) is twelve, Brat (a girl) is ten, and Poor Baby (a boy) is seven. They find a sleeping man, awaken him, and ask him who he is. When he says in irritation, "Jesus Christ," they take him literally, and believe him to be the Son of God. Little do they know that he's a much-wanted fugitive from justice.

Gaines would play this man (known simply as The Man), who's escaped from a prison in Louisiana (where the action was reset). Now he's been on the run for days, and is tired and injured when he shows up in the barn owned by the widower Boone, the children's father.

Yet his character's exhaustion meant Gaines would speak little, and in short sentences. While the Phantom doesn't have more than a half-hour's stage time, his few appearances count dramatically. In the new show, much of Gaines' time would be spent sleeping, while the children stood near him and offered their own theories about God.

The Phantom also was involved in six songs in the first act, including the show's biggest hit, "The Music of the Night." The Man in *Whistle* had just one song in the first act, "Annie Christmas," delivered when the children begged Jesus to tell them a story. Given that it was a narrative, it had no chance for hit-tune popularity.

Playing Swallow was Irene Molloy (not to be confused with the character of the same name in *Hello, Dolly!*). The day the reviews came out, she reached her eighteenth birthday, but probably wasn't celebrating, for the reviews weren't good. Compare Molloy to Hayley Mills (Bell's daughter), who was fourteen during the filming of the 1961 movie version. Mills conveyed the naïveté that could have allowed a twelve-year-old to believe that this ragtag bum was actually Jesus Christ. Washington audiences couldn't swallow that Molloy's Swallow would swallow that this man was Jesus Christ.

Actually, Bell's novel has another point to make: people need to believe in something, anything, and will often let their faith get in the way of their reason. Once they commit themselves to a god, they can't easily let him go. Molloy's Swallow was in for a pound long after she'd realized that The Man wasn't worth a penny. But Harold Prince's direction didn't make that clear.

With an unconvincing leading lady and a static leading man, no wonder *Washington Post* critic Lloyd Rose called *Whistle down the Wind* "just dull." The real Jesus Christ brought Lloyd Webber career-starting success, but this fake Jesus Christ wasn't helping at all.

Andrew Jackness' designs were simple, featuring a clapboard house, a clapboard church, the barn interior, and a roadside inn. As for the special effects that Lloyd Webber fans had come to expect, the second act had a bright light representing an oncoming train on suddenly lowered train tracks; the closest thing the first act had was a baptism in which an actor was fully immersed in genuine water.

Management first said that it would postpone the April 17, 1997 opening at the Martin Beck Theater to June 15. Then it announced the musical wouldn't open at all, but would be repaired and later show up in London.

Such promises are usually made to save face and are rarely kept, but Lloyd Webber, his lyricist Jim Steinman, and bookwriter Patricia Knop did go back to work. Obviously, Lloyd Webber thought he had some solutions, for his name wound up on the book, too, as did Gale Edwards'. One smart move they made was eliminating the role of Boone's sister, Dot; with one fewer set of eyes watching the kids, they had more opportunities to tend to The Man.

Edwards also directed the new production that opened on July 1, 1998 at London's Aldwych Theatre—where it didn't close until January 6, 2001, 1,040 performances later. Never had a bound-for-Broadway out-of-town closing done this well in London. While Americans might have overdosed on the foreign-born Lloyd Webber, he was still much welcomed at home. He and Steinman even got a hit song out of the show; "No Matter What," was, for the wildly successful Irish group Boyzone, their most popular-ever single.

If Irene Molloy seemed too old for Swallow, she was a child compared to the new Swallow: thirty-four-year-old Lottie Mayor. What may have helped was that Londoners were more familiar with the novel and film. (The latter has never been released here either on VHS or DVD.)

Yet the London version wasn't markedly different. Two of the children's songs ("Spider" and "Grownups Kill Me," an expression much used in Ball's novel) were dropped and replaced with "I Never Get What I Pray For" and "Home by Now"—which served pretty much the same function. Three other songs were repositioned, but the profound difference was that The Man (Marcus Lovett) finally got a big song in act 1 ("Unsettled Scores") and another in act 2 ("Try Not to Be Afraid"). What's more, Peter J. Davison set much of the show near a highway that moved up and down. Lloyd Webbers fans expected at least that much scenic dazzle.

But when *Whistle down the Wind* came to America for a national tour, designer Paul Farnsworth returned to the simplicity of Jackness' originals. The tour opened September 9, 2007, in Houston, the first stop of the forty-four weeks it would be out on the road. But five months later, on February 17, 2008, the show ignominiously came to a close in Norfolk, Virginia. Even with the new songs for The Man, Americans weren't having *Whistle down the Wind*, no matter what Londoners thought.

Whistle down the Wind. December 12, 1996–February 9, 1997, in Washington. No Broadway performances.

1997–1998

THE BIGGEST HIT
The Lion King

Style over substance.

There's that old theatrical idiom that if a musical has a marvelous opening number, it can coast for quite some time on it. *The Lion King* did just that.

This new product from Disney surprised quite a few people who'd seen their *Beauty and the Beast* three years earlier. While the look of that hit was standard-issue Broadway, this production was very different. Director and (almost equally important) costume designer Julie Taymor started the show with a genuine pageant. She turned dozens of actors into stylized animals through headpieces or appendages. They came down the aisle and/or bounded onto stage while the sun rose to start the morning—and the show.

Taymor would be the second female director ever to win a Tony Award—and only by three minutes and thirty-four seconds; since the Tony powers-that-be had arranged that the prize for Best Direction of a Play would be bestowed just before Best Direction of a Musical; thus, Ms. Garry Hynes won first for staging *The Beauty Queen of Leenane*.

The book by Roger Alles and Irene Mecchi shares some similarities with some lofty properties. As in Genesis, a son (here, the lion cub Simba) disobeys his father (the lion king Mufasa) by going into forbidden territory. As in *Hamlet,* the prince's uncle (Scar) is responsible for the king's death, usurps the throne—and then must face the son when the lad finally understands what happened. The musical could even be said to borrow from *The Wizard of Oz,* for when the wicked potentate is killed, the soldiers who once served loyally aren't at all sorry.

Alles and Mecchi included a smart and strong line after Simba takes a foolhardy risk and Mufasa chastises him; the cub defends himself by saying that he thought his father wanted him to be brave—to which Mufasa sternly answers, "I'm only brave when I have to be."

But this can't make up for the fact that so much of the dialogue in the musical is inane. There are punny jokes about a "cub" sandwich and such toss-offs as "That looks like a shower curtain from the Guggenheim." Granted, animals in Africa don't speak English in the first place, but if they did, they wouldn't be using it to cite a museum on Fifth Avenue and Eighty-ninth Street.

The hoariest type of jokes abound. When Pumbaa the warthog says, "Maybe he'll be on our side," Timon the meerkat sneers, "That's the stupidest thing I ever . . ." before interrupting himself with "Hey, maybe he'll be on our side," as if it had been his idea all along.

"He looks blue" is taken literally by the listener, who says in all innocence, "I'd say brown and gold." At one point, the word "motto" is dropped into the action and someone asks "What's a motto?" before someone else quips, "Nothing; what's a motto with you?" Then there's the character who laughs wildly at something he's just said, and, when no one else responds, suddenly stops as if he hadn't found anything funny in the first place. And wouldn't you know that the line "What do you want me to do, dress in drag and do the Charleston?" is followed by the character dressing in drag and doing the Charleston?

To be sure, *The Lion King* was aiming for children, but it needn't have sunk to the level of jokes about flatulence. In the late seventies, comedian George Carlin did a routine wherein he complained that there were no fart jokes on TV. Be careful what you wish for, George.

What would Walt Disney, the company's founder, have thought of this attempt at humor? Worse, how would he have felt about Scar's saying, "I need to be bucked up," only to have Timon answer, "You've already bucked up royally." That joke depends on one's knowledge of the word "fuck," and Walt Disney, ever the champion of decent entertainment for children, wouldn't have wanted to see little kids turning to their parents and saying, "I don't get it"—forcing either an explanation or a finesse.

Most scores written by committee don't score, and there are seven writers listed for *The Lion King*. Elton John and Tim Rice did most of it and get larger billing than the other five. But why couldn't they have written all of it? Having two collaborators keeping an eye on what a show needs is better than having a bunch of writers doing things piecemeal. Maybe that's why so many of the show's lyrics are prosaic, such as "Nobody loves me / There's the rub / Not even the cub."

But oh, those first few minutes of style over substance. They may be the reason why *The Lion King* was the first American musical to pass over 50 million in worldwide attendance.

The Lion King. November 13, 1997–. Over 5,500 performances.

The Biggest Flop
The Capeman

It's a crime.

August 29, 1959. New York City, Forty-fifth Street, between Ninth and Tenth Avenues. The street gang known as the Vampires shows up at a schoolyard, headed by their leader, to fight the Norsemen. But the Norsemen don't show, and the Vampires either mistake a group of kids for them, or are simply out for a fight, and anyone will do.

Sixteen-year-old Salvador Agron, who wears a dramatic black cape, and gang leader Luis Hernandez, who wields an umbrella with a knife at its point, wind up killing two young men. For Mayor Robert F. Wagner, it's the last straw in a year that's seen much too much teen violence. He puts fourteen hundred additional police on streets, and two days later Agron is captured. His statement to the press: "I don't care if I burn. My mother could watch me." Agron would be the youngest person ever sentenced to death, though after spending three years on death row, his sentenced was reduced to life in prison by Governor Nelson A. Rockefeller.

Agron didn't waste his incarceration. He found God, learned to read and write, received a high school equivalency diploma, and actually started taking classes at a nearby university. In 1976, Governor Hugh Carey decided Agron would be eligible for parole in 1977.

But Agron foolishly couldn't wait. When he saw a chance to escape, he took it—though he stayed out only two weeks before he voluntarily returned to prison. Thus, his parole didn't come until 1979. Once he got it, he spent the last seven years of his life telling inner-city youths not to make the mistakes he did. In 1986, after contracting pneumonia, he died two days shy of his forty-third birthday.

Does this story sound as if it should be musicalized? Twelve-time Grammy winner Paul Simon thought so, and had Nobel Prize–winning poet Derek Walcott to help him write both book and lyrics to his words and music.

Before the show, the announcement that told an audience us not to take pictures, make recordings, or unwrap candies later was not only given in English, but also repeated in Spanish. One can applaud the management's attempt to make a whole new audience feel welcome on Broadway. But the Latino audience could be excused for not wanting to see a show in which one of their own is shown to be a heartless murderer.

"That's just the first act," *Capeman* defenders will say. And while that's true, there's nothing inherently dramatic about watching a man learn to read and write in prison, or even accept Jesus Christ as his Lord and Savior. The most interesting conflict that Simon put to song was a conversation a prison guard had with Agron, in which he effectively argued that he had to struggle to send his children to college, while a murderer was getting to attend free of charge.

Agron's escape wasn't even made dramatic; indeed, his cross-country journey to Arizona couldn't have been, because he had to be quiet and blend in with the crowd. Songs dealing with that condition could have made for some tension, but couldn't have provided much conflict.

So no wonder that director Susana Tubert, an Argentinian protégée of Harold Prince, couldn't fix the show. Subsequent directors Eric Simonson and Mark Morris, as well as play doctor Jerry Zaks, were flummoxed, too.

One could argue that Salvador Agron was not nearly as bad as Sweeney Todd, and that killer became the central figure of an acclaimed, even beloved musical. But Sweeney is considered to be a fictional character. There are those who say he did exist, but if he did, he lived long ago and far away, more than a century earlier and in a foreign country. We don't bear any responsibility for him. For Agron, growing up in the midst of poverty, prejudice, and hatred, we might.

Of course, *West Side Story* had a hit 732-performance run (which ended, coincidentally, a month before Agron and Hernandez's actual crimes). But there too, the characters were fictional. We saw the Jets and the Sharks reluctantly and accidentally brought to the breaking point; Agron and his henchmen seemed to have killed time by killing people. The Norsemen didn't show up? Well, there are some other kids, so let's take out our hostility on them. As the *Daily News* headline would state, "Slew 2 because 'I felt like it' says Cape Man." Too many theatergoers in 1998 still remembered that, as well as Agron's cocky interviews. Even four decades later, that wound was still too raw.

How sad that of all the projects Paul Simon could have chosen to musicalize, *The Capeman* was his choice. Perhaps he was attracted to the inner-city music of the fifties, those street-corner symphonies that yielded doo-wop and a cappella harmonies, as well as double-time rhythms. The sounds of drumsticks thumping on guitar cases, a chance to write in the *aguinaldo*, *bomba*, and *plena* styles of Latin music proved irresistible to him—but not to theatergoers, because of that subject matter.

Surely Simon could have found a property that could have used those sounds and that music, and yet glorified the achievements of Latinos and Latinas. A musical about the Vampires didn't do that—though, as we'll soon see, this wouldn't be the last unsuccessful musical to deal with vampires.

The Capeman. January 29–March 28, 1998. 68 performances.

1998–1999

THE BIGGEST HIT
Fosse

Components, not characters.

June 6, 1999. New York City. The home office of author Ken Bloom, who's written a dozen books about Broadway. For years, he's hosted a party on Tony Awards night. Coming early are those who don't have tickets to the actual event at the nearby Gershwin Theater; arriving late are those tuxedoed types who attended the ceremonies.

The place is still packed at one in the morning, two full hours after the Tonys have concluded. The conversation remains animated, as it always is when musical theater enthusiasts get together. These are the people who know that Charles Nelson Reilly replaced Victor Spinetti in *Skyscraper*, that *Pacific Overtures* played its two out-of-town tryouts in Boston and Washington, and that RCA Victor would have recorded *Foxy* in 1964 if the damned thing had run longer.

Suddenly, when there's a conversational lull, Michael Zande, the company manager for City Center Encores!, scrunches up his face, as if trying to remember a fact. Then he says, "What won Best Musical tonight?"

And for a long moment, no one makes a sound.

For no one can remember.

Eventually, Bloom recalls "*Fosse!*" and everyone laughs in embarrassment. Two hours later, we've already forgotten?

It's been that kind of season. The other three Best Musical nominees *combined* ran a *total* of 430 performances: *It Ain't Nothin' but the Blues* (284), *Parade* (85), and *The Civil War* (61). And *Blues* wouldn't have run that long if it had had more than eight performers sitting on chairs and singing songs; running costs were pretty cheap.

Up till that point in Tony history, seventy-four Tony-*losers* had run more than 430 performances all by themselves. In fact, in the forty-five seasons where the Tonys had announced Best Musical nominees (they didn't for the first seven years of the awards), there were eight years (1959, 1962, 1973, 1980, 1982, 1991, 1992, 1995) when *every one of the losing nominating musicals* ran more than 430 performances.

What's also interesting is that for the fifth time in a decade, a Tony-winning musical didn't garner a single award in any of the four performing categories. No one from *Fosse* went to the Gershwin stage to claim a Best or Featured Actor or Actress prize. In the nineties, this had also happened with *The Will Rogers Follies*, *Crazy for You*, *Titanic*, and *The Lion King*; for most of those, the directors were the real stars.

In the first quarter-century of the Tonys, Best Musicals also meant Best Performances. Not until *Company* in 1971 and *Two Gentlemen of Verona* in 1972 was a single performer unrewarded in a Best Musical. After that, almost a decade passed before another musical (*42nd Street* in 1981) would yield no best starring or featured actor or actress prizes. But then the deluge in the nineties.

Fascinating, though, that the two Fosse retrospectives—both this eponymous homage mounted nearly a dozen years after his death, and *Dancin'*, the 1978 revue that he both conceived and staged—each ran over a thousand performances. Most Fosse shows hadn't run nearly that long—because, it's been said, most Fosse shows were cold in an era when musicals had been warm. With his two revues, though, audiences didn't have to bond with characters or worry what was to happen to them; they could just enjoy the skill of everyone involved.

During *Fosse*'s run, a theatergoer could, for the first time in Broadway history, see two different versions of three numbers in two different theaters. The revival of *Chicago* that had opened more than two years earlier had already been offering "Razzle Dazzle," "Hot Honey Rag," and "Nowadays," that were also chosen for *Fosse*.

Fosse set another record of sorts. No other Best Musical had won so few other awards, and only in the so-called minor categories. Aside for Best Lighting (Andrew Bridge) and Best Orchestrations (Ralph Burns and Douglas Besterman), *Fosse* went home empty. It was darned lucky to open in the wan season that it did.

Fosse. January 14, 1999–August 25, 2001. 1,093 performances.

THE BIGGEST FLOP
The Civil War

A short-lived triple crown.

March 24, 1999. The St. James Theatre, owned by Jujamcyn Theatres. Rocco Landesman, Jujamcyn's president, is seated on stage. But aren't those two people sitting next to him Gerald Schoenfeld, chairman of the Shubert Organization, and James M. Nederlander, chairman of the Nederlander Organization?

Douglas (*The Scarlet Pimpernel*) Sills, acting as emcee for today's event, points to the trio and likens their being together to the Potsdam Conference of 1945 when Stalin, Churchill, and Truman met. It's a good joke, for it contains some truth; these three rival moguls aren't often on the same stage at the same time.

They have one commonality: each has a musical by composer Frank Wildhorn in one of his theaters. Schoenfeld has been the biggest beneficiary, for *Jekyll & Hyde* has been at his Plymouth Theater for almost two years. Nederlander has been collecting rent sixteen months, ever since *The Scarlet Pimpernel* landed at the Minskoff. Landesman is the new kid on the Wildhorn block; last night, *The Civil War* played its first preview here.

So Frank Wildhorn has three shows running on Broadway. "And who was the last American composer to do this twenty-two years ago?" Sills asks the crowd, getting a response from a few musical theater enthusiasts who cry out, "Stephen Schwartz." Wildhorn is then announced, and offers an "Aw, shucks" smile as he goes to shake hands with everyone.

But there's a profound difference between Schwartz's achievements and Wildhorn's. For one thing, Schwartz wrote all the lyrics for *Pippin* and *The Magic Show,* and most of them for *Godspell*. Though Wildhorn claims an "additional lyrics" credit for *Jekyll & Hyde*, he had a lyricist on all three shows. More importantly, all of Schwartz's shows were certifiable hits; at this point, Wildhorn's two long-runners had not paid back, and the financial fate of *The Civil War* was yet to be seen.

As it turns out, *The Civil War* was less a genuine musical than a glorified concert with some pretty songs ("Virginia") and some stirring ones ("Sons of Dixie"). The show offered singers rather than characters. If there's one thing that the real Civil War had, it was drama. There wasn't much here, because the book (by Wildhorn and director Gregory Boyd) didn't strive for much.

One week before the 1998–1999 Tony Awards were announced, Wildhorn was suddenly reduced to two shows on Broadway, when *The Scarlet Pimpernel* went on a summer-long hiatus. One week *after* the Tonys were dispensed, Wildhorn was down to just *Jekyll & Hyde,* for *The Civil War* had closed. And while it ran only one-sixth as long as *The Scarlet Pimpernel,* and clocked only one-twenty-fifth of *Jekyll & Hyde*'s 1,543 performance count, *The Civil War* would be the only one of the three for which Wildhorn would be nominated for Best Score.

The Civil War. April 22, 1999–June 13, 1999. 61 performances.

5

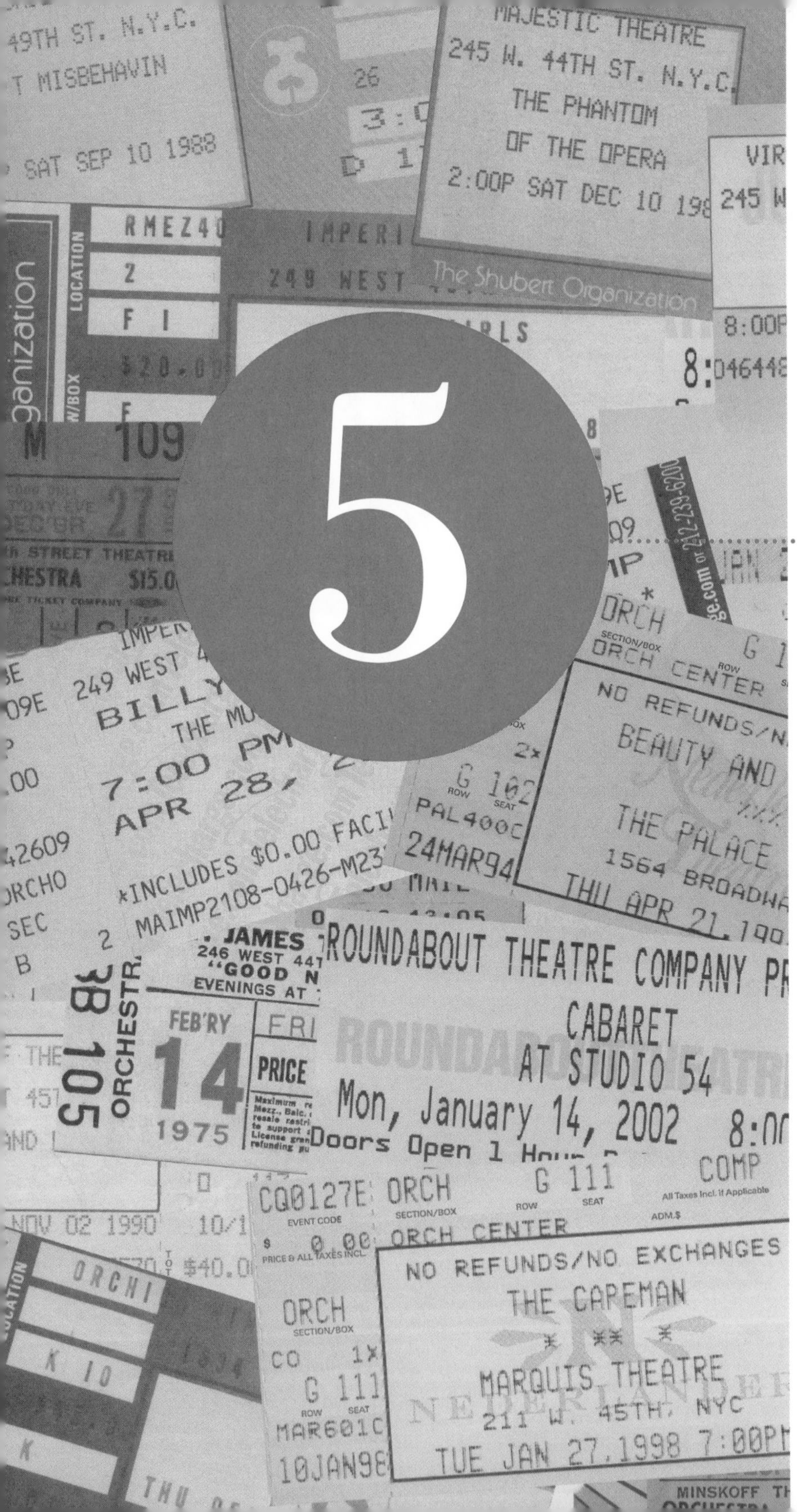

MAJESTIC THEATRE
245 W. 44TH ST. N.Y.C.
THE PHANTOM
OF THE OPERA
2:00P SAT DEC 10 19
The Shubert Organization
SAT SEP 10 1988
249 WEST
BILLY
7:00 PM
APR 28,
*INCLUDES $0.00 FACI
NO REFUNDS/N
BEAUTY AND
THE PALACE
1564 BROADW
THU APR 21,
24MAR94
ROUNDABOUT THEATRE COMPANY PR
CABARET
AT STUDIO 54
Mon, January 14, 2002 8:0
Doors Open 1 Hour
COMP
CQ0127E ORCH
ORCH CENTER
G 111
NO REFUNDS/NO EXCHANGES
THE CAPEMAN
MARQUIS THEATRE
211 W. 45TH, NYC
TUE JAN 27,1998 7:00PM
10JAN98
246 WEST 44
"GOOD N
EVENINGS AT
FEB'RY
14
1975
PRICE
ORCHESTRA
NOV 02 1990
$40.0
MINSKOFF TH

1999–2009

1999–2000

THE BIGGEST HIT
Aida

The virtual composer.

Back in 1956, when *Bells Are Ringing* was trying out in Boston, things weren't going well. Star Judy Holliday and bookwriters-lyricists Betty Comden and Adolph Green had been friends for almost twenty years, but at the moment, Holliday wasn't happy with them. She desperately needed an eleven o'clock number, and they and composer Jule Styne hadn't yet come up with a song she liked—or even one they liked.

According to Styne biographer Theodore Taylor, everyone was pretty miserable until Styne called Comden and Green into hotel suite one night. He had an idea for a song, went to the piano, and sang eight bars: "I'm goin' back where I can be me, to the Bonjour Tristesse Brassiere Company." Green screeched, "Yeah!" All three went to work and finished the song in an hour.

It happened because Styne had noticed during the New Haven and Boston tryouts that the audience always laughed at a first-act joke that Comden and Green had written, where Holliday said that she once worked for the Bonjour Tristesse Brassiere Company. Had Styne not been on the scene night after night to watch the show and observe the audience's delight in the idea of a brassiere company named Bonjour Tristesse, one of Broadway's greatest eleven o'clock numbers wouldn't have been written.

Composer Elton John wouldn't have been able to do something similar for his *Aida*. Not just because he doesn't attend every performance; he doesn't attend *any* rehearsal or *any* performance until opening night. He's just too busy with his lucrative concert tours or, to be fair, his charitable trusts into which he puts a good deal of time and effort.

Still, can't a man who's interested enough to sign on for a Broadway musical deign to spare a couple of months to help make it a success? Granted, he takes phone calls from his lyricist Tim Rice, hears what he needs, and soon faxes him back a melody which Rice then sets to words.

Nevertheless, John's lack of involvement would seem to hurt a show. With *The Lion King*, at least there were other songwriters ready to write new songs as needed. For *Aida*, though, John was the one who was supposed to provide the entire musical score.

On the other hand, John could argue, the wildly successful results for both *The Lion King* and *Aida* show that there's nothing wrong with the way he operates. Once can't help wondering, though, how much better these shows could have been artistically had he been there to study what was working, what was not, and why.

Aida might well have got away with it because the book by Linda Woolverton, director Robert Falls, and David Henry Hwang was so strong. The audience's interest was grabbed in the second scene: Aida (Heather Headley) is just another Nubian slave being herded from ship to shore—or so the audience believes. Suddenly, she is able to escape, grab a soldier's sword, and hold it at her enemy's throat, ready to cut. Attention must be paid be such a woman—and Radames (Adam Pascal), the captain of the Egyptian army, does just that. He decides to assign her as handmaiden to his betrothed, the noblewoman Amneris (Sherie Rene Scott).

But Amneris is a bubbleheaded bimbo. No wonder Radames comes to prefer Aida. But by show's end, Amneris acquires many strong qualities—partly because of Aida's influence on her. Amneris takes an emotional journey; she goes from a self-obsessed person who believes that clothes are, as her song goes, "My strongest suit," to one who holds attitudes worthy of a female pharaoh. When she discovers that Radames and Aida are lovers, she is responsible for enforcing Egypt's laws, which doom them to death by suffocation. But Amneris is gallant enough to show some mercy, and allows them to die together in the same tomb. She doesn't allow her own hurt to blind her into a full-blown revenge.

Aida is one of musical theater's best heroines, not only because she's smarter than many people she meets, but also because she improves them. Headley did a solid job with the character and won the Tony—but she essentially had it weeks before the ceremony, when *New York Times* theater critic Ben Brantley raved about her. (Voters tend to believe when a *Times* critic raves.)

This wasn't the first Broadway musical based on the famed Verdi opera. *My Darlin' Aida* opened on October 27, 1952 and closed on January 10, 1953 after merely eighty-nine performances, at a complete loss of $300,000—which, as Daddy Warbucks says in *Annie*, was a lot of money in those days.

My Darlin' Aida is a title that gets our guffaws, but there was a little method in that show's madness. Given that Verdi's *Aida* takes place around Memphis, director Charles Friedman thought to set a new musical version in Memphis, Tennessee. The war that's so important to the plot could be changed to the American Civil War. Radames became Raymond Demarest, Amneris became Jessica, and Aida stayed Aida. Friedman then put his own lyrics to Verdi's score.

So twice in Broadway history the *Aida* story became a musical in which the composer was nowhere near the premises. Verdi, though, had an excuse. He'd been dead for fifty-two years.

Aida. March 23, 2000–September 5, 2004. 1,852 performances.

The Biggest Flop
Wise Guys

Dying is easy; musical comedy is hard.

In 1994, after decades of pushing the proverbial envelope and repeatedly breaking the musical theater mold, Stephen Sondheim announced that that his next venture would be a musical comedy.

Not since 1962 had Sondheim had written one. *A Funny Thing Happened on the Way to the Forum*, not so coincidentally, turned out to be the longest-running show in his career. While none of the seventeen musicals that carried Sondheim's name had ever cracked the thousand-performance plateau, *Funny Thing* came closest with 964.

Sondheim teamed with John Weidman, his *Pacific Overtures* and *Assassins* librettist. They'd tell the rollicking story of the irrepressible Mizner Brothers. Addison (1872–1933) was a self-trained architect who was at the right place (Palm Beach and Boca Raton, Florida) at the right time (the mid 1920s)—or so he thought. His grandiose schemes resulted in financial disaster, but also in some arresting buildings that are now on the National Register.

Wilson Mizner (1876–1933) wrote three now-forgotten Broadway plays, none of which ran more than four months. But that was just one of his careers. Alaskan prospector, Manhattan merchant, boxing manager—not to mention fortune-hunting husband—were some of the others. One of the reasons that brother Addison went broke is that Wilson was handling their finances—and mishandling investors. Cocaine didn't help matters.

As Sondheim himself wrote in an article for the *New York Times*, the Mizners "represent(ed) two divergent aspects of American energy: the builder and the squanderer, the visionary and the promoter, the conformist and the maverick, the idealistic planner and the restless cynic, the one who uses things and the one who uses them up."

Sondheim says that he and Weidman eventually noticed something else

> *Our* Mizners, were in many ways the Bob Hope and Bing Crosby of the *Road* movies—Wilson as Crosby the manipulator, Addison as Hope the patsy, two conniving rivals who would stop at nothing to ruin each other, but partners and soul mates in the face of the world. And vaudeville to the core.

Because there was more than a little Pseudolus and the Devil in these guys, the show would star performers who'd already done those roles. Nathan Lane, who'd won a Tony for the 1996 *Funny Thing* revival, would portray Addison. Playing Wilson would be Victor Garber, who'd had a 1994 Tony-nominated success as the devilish Mr. Applegate in the *Damn Yankees* revisal.

Sounds like fun, though the director chosen wasn't known for laugh-fests. Still, the up-and-coming, no-stopping-him Sam Mendes had, a few years earlier, delivered exciting London revivals of Sondheim's own *Assassins* and *Company*. Then he'd stormed Broadway with a sensational revisionist *Cabaret* that was headed for a six-year run. Maybe all he needed was a chance to show that he had a sense of humor, too.

Mendes certainly knew enough to fill out the cast with some of Broadway's funniest young men (Brooks Ashmanskas, Kevin Chamberlin, and Christopher Fitzgerald) and equally funny young women (Candy Buckley and Nancy Opel). So, after an October 1999 workshop at New York Theatre Workshop, Broadway would receive this joyous and joyful entertainment on April 27, 2000.

It had been a long journey for Sondheim. In 1952, when he was twenty-two, he was so intrigued by the Mizners that he wrote a musical about them. Then he learned that one of the Mizners' old friends—one Irving Berlin—was working with esteemed playwright S. N. Behrman on their own musical based on Alva Johnson's biography *The Legendary Mizners*. Ambitious producer David Merrick held the rights. Sondheim realized that he had better find another subject to musicalize.

Berlin and Behrman never finished the show, so six years later when Sondheim worked with Merrick on *Gypsy*, he asked if the producer still had an option on the biography. When Merrick said he'd dropped it, Sondheim thought he'd return to the project.

But in the next thirty-five years, Sondheim always got to a different musical first: *Funny Thing, Anyone Can Whistle, Do I Hear a Waltz?, Company, Follies, A Little Night Music, Candide, The Frogs, Pacific Overtures, Sweeney Todd, Merrily We Roll Along, Sunday in the Park with George, Into the Woods, Assassins* and *Passion*.

Then, in 1994, when the Kennedy Center in Washington, D.C. said it wanted to commission a work from Sondheim, a Mizner Brothers musical was the one he chose to do. *Wise Guys* would have a workshop in autumn 1995, followed by a full production in early 1996.

When that date rolled around, a new announcement was needed: A fall 1996 workshop would precede a full production opening on June 30, 1997.

Fall 1996 brought only the news that the *Wise Guys* workshop was rescheduled for January 1997, and the actual production slated for fall 1997.

As it turned out, the best the show could do was a March 27, 1997 reading in New York. A full script was in place, but only two rather lengthy musical sequences were offered. While Garber played Wilson, Patrick Quinn played Addison. All that happened for the rest of the year was a second reading on November 8, where Lane first played Addison. At least that long-postponed Kennedy Center production is scheduled—*tentatively* scheduled, of course—for sometime in 1998.

"Tentatively" is right. In spring 1998, the announcement was made that the show would now open in February 1999 at the Kennedy Center, with Mendes attached to the project for the first time.

October 1, 1998 brought the third reading of the script and much of the score, directed by Mendes. But the Kennedy Center powers-that-be were not impressed, and decided to let the project go. Scott Rudin, who'd already been a producer of Sondheim's *Passion* and the 1996 *Funny Thing* revival, signed on. He, Sondheim, and Weidman hoped for a commercial production for the 1998–1999 Broadway season.

But that season was almost over on April 30, 1999, when all Mendes could do was stage a fourth reading. By that fall, though, everyone involved felt that a Broadway opening on April 27, 2000 would happen, since a full workshop with Lane and Garber was scheduled for October 1999.

Mendes, though, could only offer the first act. By the closing four weeks later, the second act was staged, though the best the actors could do for the final twenty minutes was read from scripts. In between, on November 10, 1999, Rudin decided the show wasn't ready for Broadway, so April 27, 2000 came and went without *Wise Guys*. The show died on East Fourth Street.

Never had a show with so many wonderful names attached been so close to Broadway—forty streets and a few avenues away—and not made it in.

But the show did contain some wonderful material. Sondheim came up with a snazzy vaudeville-styled soft-shoe opening ("Wise Guys") and Weidman contributed a de rigueur New Jersey joke followed by a rim shot.

But then the action switched to the Mizner brothers' boyhood home in Benecia, California, where their father gave them some advice from his deathbed. Did he have to be in the last moments of his life? Polonius gave Laertes plenty of advice when he was alive and well; couldn't Mr. Mizner have done the same?

There was plenty in the show about the lads' strong feelings for their mother, down to a very sincere "A House for Mama" that Addison planned to build. Such sincerity is not the hallmark of either vaudeville or musical comedy.

For a show that was supposed to be funny, there were precious few jokes. Though Neil Simon had had four consecutive flops after his Pulitzer Prize-winning *Lost in Yonkers*—including one musical, *The Goodbye Girl*—maybe this would have been the time for him to finally collaborate with Sondheim.

On the other hand, chicanery strikes audiences differently when it's for real. There was no Harold Hill and no River City. But there was a Palm Beach and a Boca Raton. These real-life tricksters might not have been best served by out-and-out musical comedy.

Also odd was that Lane was playing the less eccentric and more honest of the two brothers. The previous season, he'd had a success playing sharpie Hubie Cram in *Do Re Mi* at Encores! Garber seemed the more likely of the two to be on the up-and-up.

In the next eight years, the musical would go through four titles *(Gold!, Strike It Rich, Bounce,* and *Road Show)*, many directors (Hal Prince, Eric Schaeffer, John Doyle), many Mizners (Richard Kind, Howard McGillin, Marc Kudisch, Michael Cerveris, Alexander Gemignani), and one lawsuit (between the authors and Rudin, who claimed he still held the rights while they were engineering a deal with the Goodman Theatre in Chicago). The closest the musical ever came to Broadway was the Public Theatre on Lafayette Street in fall 2008.

Maybe Sondheim just wasn't meant to do a conventional musical comedy at this point in his career—or maybe critics and audiences had come to expect so much more from his art that this show seemed slight.

Perhaps Sondheim, who had been used to tryouts in a city or two—or even Broadway previews—couldn't adjust to the vagaries of workshops that don't offer as much trial by fire. Parkinson's Law states that "Work expands so as to fill the time available for its completion." No question that with all the fluid deadlines and workshops, Sondheim didn't get it done quickly. When he was writing *A Little Night Music* in the early seventies, he went into rehearsal with six songs not yet written. All were in place for the Tony-winning score when the tryout began in Boston.

What *Wise Guys / Gold / Strike It Rich / Bounce / Road Show* proved was that Sondheim wasn't God after all. Though for many decades, he sure seemed to be.

Wise Guys. October 29–November 20, 1999. 22 workshop performances.

2000–2001

THE BIGGEST HIT
The Producers

You can't fool all of the people all of the time.

Sunday, November 30, 2003. The Canon Theatre, Toronto. A preview performance of *The Producers* before it officially opens next month. The house is filled with theatergoers who know that two and a half years ago, this was *the* show that Broadway embraced. Now it's their turn to see the musical version of Mel Brooks' 1968 film about Max Bialystock, the desperate producer who acts upon an offhand remark made by accountant Leo Bloom: one can make more money with a flop than a hit. If a producer raised much more money than he spent, he could keep that money once a show flopped, because the investors wouldn't expect anything back.

So of course Bialystock and Bloom purposely choose the worst play they can find—*Springtime for Hitler*, by Nazi sympathizer Franz Liebkind. (Marc Miller, in his Theatermania review of the cast album, wittily asked, "Why don't they just produce *Follies?*"—which always winds up losing money.)

Bialystock and Bloom also hire Roger De Bris, the town's worst director, to stage it with a little help from his paramour Carmen Ghia. Alas for them, when audiences and critics see *Springtime for Hitler*, they assume it's a spoof, and welcome it as a hit. How can Bialystock and Bloom pay back all the investors now expecting vast sums of money?

The film has become such a classic in the thirty-five years since its release that the Toronto audience might feel it knows what to expect. But no one can say that the film's auteur, Mel Brooks, threw in a few songs and called it a musical. Along with his co-bookwriter Thomas Meehan, he greatly deepened Leo's character and expanded his role. Leo became a person with a goal: he genuinely wanted to be a producer. En route, he fell in love with office receptionist Ulla, who betrayed and abandoned Leo, then returned and repented. Another nice detail had Max telling Leo that he would have to earn a certain hat that only a producer would wear. Credit Brooks, too, for not just sitting pat on his famous "Springtime for Hitler" number, but instead greatly expanding it.

How, then, did the capacity Toronto audience take to the show? If a theatergoer had closed his eyes and simply gauged by the applause, he would have assumed that there were 150 people in the house. Not until Franz Liebkind showed up did they really start laughing, especially when his pets—mechanized pigeons—began flapping. But they gave out an offended "Oooh!" when Franz produced the swastika armbands.

They laughed a bit at Roger De Bris and Carmen Ghia, but something fascinating happened when the latter made his first exit: Carmen's body exited quickly, but his extended right arm did not; as he left, he waved it ever so slowly behind him, only inching it offstage long after the rest of his body was out of sight. It's the type of move that always gets applause—except here it didn't. Maybe after Carmen re-entered, re-exited, and did the same gambit again—but milked it even more—he would get some handclaps. But though the Toronto audience chuckled, they didn't applaud.

Scott, Roger's resident choreographer, made a big entrance, put his arms akimbo, and posed to show off his astonishingly overstuffed crotch. Here was another moment engineered for applause, but none came. A full hour and fourteen minutes passed before the audience would applaud a line—after Ulla did her erotic dance, and Max told her, "Even though we're sitting down, we're giving you a standing ovation." The Toronto theatergoers would applaud only one other time, when they saw the *Springtime for Hitler* dancers reflected in a tilted upstage mirror forming a swastika.

At the end of the show, most theatergoers were indeed standing—to put on their coats. After the orchestra finished playing the last note of the out-music, a couple of people applauded. As the crowd filed out, some faces looked content at best, while others showed great disappointment. No one could be heard complaining about Sean Cullen as Max or Michael Therriault as Leo, but no one could be heard raving about them, either. "It was okay," opined one woman. "It was funny," replied a man, but he said it unenthusiastically, after giving a shoulder shrug. Said another, as he made his way up the aisle, "This won eleven Tonys?" He was more aghast when he was told *The Producers* actually won twelve.

That's more than twice as many Tonys as *My Fair Lady*'s five (though there were far fewer categories in the fifties). Yet on Broadway, *The Producers* didn't run as long as *Fair Lady*, even in an era where runs have been inflated because of a doubled population, an explosion of tourism, and the number of seats in Broadway theaters basically staying the same.

That's what comes from selling a show as a star vehicle. Though in 2001 director-choreographer Susan Stroman gave the show a super-slick production, once Tony-winners Nathan Lane (as Max) and Matthew Broderick (as Leo) left, there was much less interest in *The Producers*. Worse, the show's producers made no effort to get stars remotely of Lane and Broderick's caliber.

First came Henry Goodman as Max, who was fired for not being funny enough. And then the deluge, including Fred Applegate (who?) as Max. Perhaps he was actually *Damn Yankees*' Mr. Applegate, to whom Mel Brooks said, "Listen, fella, if you can get Nathan and Matthew to return around New Year's Eve, I'll let you play the lead for a few months."

Indeed, on December 30, 2003, Lane and Broderick came back for a three-month run, and the show returned to capacity and scalpers. When they left on April 4, 2004, the show returned to playing to hundreds of empty seats.

Every one of our biggest hits of the season, after it lost is original stars (if it had any in the first place), fared better than *The Producers*. Why? The signs outside the St. James in New York still trumpeted, "The Best Musical Ever!" and "The Most Tony Awards in Broadway History." But the public only thronged to it when Lane and Broderick were on the premises. It might have stayed at capacity had Brooks got Jason Alexander and Martin Short, two household-name stars, in New York instead of Los Angeles.

Ironically, Short was Brooks' first choice for Leo. In 1999, Brooks appeared on *The Martin Short Show*, on which Lane was also a guest, and offered both contracts to do *The Producers*. Both declined then, though Lane would soon sign on, and Short would take a few years.

The eventual lackluster attendance at *The Producers* suggest that the $10.5 million musical was overpraised when it opened. Brooks' music was simplistic, and his song titles sounded dull. The first three were "The King of Broadway," "We Can Do It," and "I Wanna Be a Producer." The last-named was a good example of his lyric predictability: "I wanna be a producer / With a hit show on

Broadway / I wanna be a producer / Lunch at Sardi's ev'ry day." In a later song, "Argentine" was pronounced "Argentyne," and was then asked to rhyme with "Brilliantyne" and "Listeryne." Yet Brooks' score won one of the twelve Tonys.

When Max and Leo sang about *Springtime for Hitler*—"It was so crass and so crude"—they actually had a better description of *The Producers* itself. Witness Bialystock's claim that "I always had the biggest hits / The biggest bathrooms at the Ritz / My showgirls had the biggest tits." Had he said, "My showgirls had the biggest *breasts*," theatergoers would have laughed harder, because the joke would have been on them and their expectations.

Perhaps another problem was a severe lapse in logic, one the movie didn't make. In the film, Franz was furious, on opening night, to see hippie Lorenzo St. DuBois (L.S.D.) playing his beloved Hitler in a ridiculous way. Obviously, Franz had never sat in on one rehearsal, and while that's hard to believe, we've seen with Elton John that such a situation can happen. So film audiences could buy that plot twist.

In the musical, however, Franz was *cast* in the role of Hitler. So why, the day after opening, was he out to kill Bialystock and Bloom for ruining his show? During four weeks of rehearsals, Franz supposedly learned such lyrics as "I'm the kraut who's out to change our history," "Every hotsy-totsy Nazi," and "I'm the German Ethel Merman." Why only on opening night, after he broke his leg and couldn't perform, did he suddenly notice what kind of show he was acting in and become furious, yelling at Max and Leo, "You made a fool out of Hitler!"

The gaffe could have been easily avoided. Roger DeBris could have decided that there were no good auditionees, and he'd just have to play Hitler himself. Or, if Franz did get the part, Bialystock could have said to him after the opening, "Franz, why didn't you say anything before?"—allowing the author to look embarrassed and meekly answer, "Vell . . . you know, when you see it from out front, it looks different . . . " That would have been believable; what they wound up with wasn't.

As for the Toronto production, it lasted nine months, six fewer than *Les Misérables*, and 123 fewer than *The Phantom of the Opera*. Just as on Broadway, no smash-hit musical of the past quarter-century fell from so high a perch to so low a rung in so short a time.

The Producers. April 19, 2001–April 22, 2007. 2,502 performances.

THE BIGGEST FLOP
Seussical

There is life after Broadway.

November 27, 2004. The James Street Players, Babylon, Long Island. Fifty-eight performers—count 'em, fifty-eight—are on stage doing a musical. The completely packed theater for this Saturday matinee includes quite a few children, so there's that special kind of laughter one doesn't often hear on Broadway: The adult theatergoers laugh, and after they've finished and quieted down, a delicious giggle comes from a little kid who just needed a moment longer to get the joke. That prompts the audience to laugh again—because they're so taken with the kid's enjoying himself. Two laughs for the price of one.

At the end of the show, the applause is long and loud. Of course it often is in community theater, but who would have expected it from the show that was the biggest flop of the 2000–2001 season?

Usually, it's only the Broadway hits that stock and community theaters want to do. Up till now, if a musical was tainted by a massive Broadway failure—and *Seussical* certainly was—very few little theaters and their directors wanted to go near it.

And *Seussical* was a flop right from its tryout. Its troubles in Boston became so well known that even *Saturday Night Live* took a swipe at it—joking that a *Seussical* spokesperson had said, "We'll work out the kinks. We'll work out the glitches. We'll work out the shneezles and beezles and squitches."

And how did *SNL* know? Broadway was now well connected to the Internet, where posters would routinely (and sometimes maliciously) give their opinions. As a result, too many theatergoers learned in advance that *Seussical* was struggling. Many went into the Richard Rodgers Theater with low expectations—including the critics. They complained that there were too many stories, characters, and elements, taken from no fewer than nineteen of Dr. Seuss' books.

But much of the blame was placed on David Shiner, a nimble clown who certainly had the physicality to play the Cat in the Hat. But the Cat was asked to emcee and sing, and Shiner was shown to have very few musical theater genes in his limber body. By the time he was replaced by Rosie O'Donnell and then Cathy Rigby, the poisonous advance word-of-mouth could not be stopped.

There was difficulty in finding the right child actor to play JoJo. Here was a character whose vivid imagination is nurtured by the Cat, allowing him to meet Horton the Elephant (Kevin Chamberlin) and plenty of inhabitants of a brave new small word called the Jungle of Nool. But finding an ideal JoJo wasn't easy. Anthony Blair Hall was replaced after three months with semi-teen idol Aaron Carter. The move to spur the box office didn't help nearly enough; *Seussical*'s reputation was just that bad.

And it would get worse. While Lynn Ahrens and Stephen Flaherty's previous Broadway outing—*Ragtime*—had won them a Best Score Tony, they would not be nominated for *Seussical* in either the book or score categories. The only nomination thrown *Seussical*'s way was for Chamberlin. With his main competition being Nathan Lane, the producers closed *Seussical* before the awards were even dispensed.

But the nation knew that Dr. Seuss and his work would seem to be a natural for musicalization. Never has a property that has lost nearly $10 million done so well in the high school and community theater market. For once, people in the hinterlands said, "So what it flopped on Broadway? We like it, and we're doing it." Says Russell Ochocki, a director of licensing at Music Theater International, "*Seussical* has become one of our biggest shows for the amateur market."

The odd name's inclusion of "Seuss" certainly helped, for it immediately suggests a kid-friendly show. It was also one that contained many positive messages: *A person's a person, no matter how small. It's possible. Anything is possible.* Most of its characters are honorable, as is witnessed by what they say: *I won't let you down. Please believe in me. I meant what I said. I won't break a promise. Faithful—100 percent. This time I'll do better than try. We're gonna get there. Sooner or later we'll find it. Thanks in advance.* The show also teaches that kids need to express their individuality, and that outcasts can find kindred spirits, each of whom will make the other feel better.

There's also a reminder that parents make mistakes—even when they're sure they're right. That occurs when JoJo's mother and father send him to a military school, where General Genghis Khan Schmitz chides kids who have "an imagination out of control," ones "who don't color between the lines," and "who have an opinion." Good thing that the authors show the General as awfully silly—and that they included JoJo's rebuttals, too: *This is no time for war. This war makes no sense. I don't think it's right to teach kids to fight.*

In addition, there's the tale (and tail) of a bird named Gertrude McFuzz. Although she's told that "your tail is right for your kind of body," she doesn't think so—and so she takes steroid-like pills to help build it up. Indeed they work, but she's eventually sorry that she took them. Gertrude learns to be herself, and finds that she's worth liking—just as kids should in these days when they're inclined to give so much attention to body image.

The musical also has a line about "your kind and powerful heart," which is fitting, for that's precisely the kind of heart that *Seussical* has. When Mayzie LaBird wants an hour's break from sitting on her unhatched egg, Horton volunteers to do it not only "for an hour" but for "maybe two"—showing a wonderful generosity of spirit in giving Mayzie what she asked for and then some.

Alas, Mayzie takes advantage of him, eventually giving up her own egg and trusting that Horton will do right by it. Indeed he does. It's a nice scene that adopted children should see, for it reinforces that even if your original mother may not have been ready to take care of you, you can find a new parent who is.

Meanwhile, Gertrude takes on a task that will take her seven arduous weeks, but she doesn't care, because she wants to do it for Horton. *Seussical* creates situations where we see what good individuals are willing to do to help good individuals. Kids need to learn that.

But ultimately it's the messages that make Seussical a special musical. *Follow your hunches. I've got someone to believe in.* And my own personal favorite, *How lucky to be in the theater.*

Indeed. Ahrens and Flaherty's quality work lives on. When *Seussical* opened on Broadway, some of the nation's hit tunes were "Gansta! Gangsta! How U Do It" and "Shake Ya Ass." While they were more popular than *Seussical* at the time, they'll never be again.

Seussical. November 30, 2000–May 20, 2001. 198 performances.

2001–2002

The Biggest Hit
Mamma Mia!

What people need after 9/11.

Who uses the word "jukebox" anymore?

People on Broadway, that's who.

Though fewer and fewer coin-operated music machines can be found in the cafes, diners, and taverns where they used to flourish, the term "jukebox" is alive and well on Broadway. Now, though, it's gone from a noun to an adjective in order to describe a certain type of musical—one that borrows already-existing songs.

But there are subdivisions of the jukebox musical genre. One species has the secondhand tunes simply performed one after the other with no words to interfere, as we saw with *Smokey Joe's Café.*

The other type of jukebox musical takes old songs and puts them in a new book. That's a much harder task.

Nevertheless, *Mamma Mia!* managed to succeed—though its listing its songs alphabetically and not scene by scene showed that it was more interested in creating a concert than a genuine musical.

Still, there is a story. Sophie (Tina Maddigan) is getting married, and wants her father to attend the ceremony. But just who is he? A look at her mother's diary from way back when only shows that Donna (Louise Pitre) was sleeping with Sam (David W. Keeley), Bill (Ken Marks), and Harry (Dean Nolen). So Sophie invites them all to her wedding, and all three attend. None quite understands why he received an invitation, but each one shows.

In Greece, yet.

That's where Donna and Sophie live, and that's where this trio travels from various American cities to their taverna. Why would they do this for someone they don't know? Traveling that distance is hardly a hop-skip-and-a-jump, and involves no small expense. Maybe one guy would come for a lark, maybe another if he could parlay it with a business trip, but all three? Highly unbelievable.

Back in 1979, Broadway had another musical with a similar plot: *Carmelina*. During World War II, its eponymous Italian heroine had affairs with three different American servicemen. After the war, they went home, and Carmelina found that she was pregnant. Because she didn't know which one was the father, she told each that he was. For eighteen years, Carmelina has collected three child support checks each month, telling her neighbors in San Forino that she's the widow of American soldier Eddie Campbell, who died soon after they were married, and whose family has subsequently supported her. That explains the lavish lifestyle she and her beloved daughter Gia have always enjoyed.

Truth to tell, *Carmelina's* co-bookwriter Joseph Stein (1912–), co-bookwriter and lyricist Alan Jay Lerner (1918–1986), and composer Burton Lane (1912–1997) failed to acknowledge the 1969 film whose plot they even more slavishly copied: *Buona Sera, Mrs. Campbell*. But both that film and *Carmelina* chose better than *Mamma Mia!* in having all three possible fathers return to San Forino for a nostalgic reunion of war veterans. For that, all three would conceivably return, and each would welcome the chance to finally meet his daughter. But would three relative strangers spend much time and money to get to a wedding in Greece of their old girlfriend's daughter, unaware of any closer tie? Plenty of people won't go to their own relative's wedding if it's held even a state away. Yet Sophie gets perfect attendance from her request.

Neither *Buona* nor *Carmelina* was a box-office hit; the latter ran all of seventeen performances. (*The Village Voice* called the 1979 show "the best new musical of 1954.") Meanwhile, *Mamma Mia!* became the most successful musical of 2001, which was a greater achievement, for that was the same year of *The Producers*. Mel Brooks' hit has long since closed, while *Mamma Mia!* continues to routinely sell out more than eight years into its run. It's already passed *The Producers* to become Broadway's eleventh-longest running musical.

Certainly, there is an emotional pull in Sophie's wanting her father—whoever he might be—at her wedding. If she can't discover which is the one, then who'll give her away at church? Despite the implausible plot point, it's affecting, but Sophie's story is not what fills the theater night after night. The force behind *Mamma Mia's* success is the music of ABBA, that mid seventies / early eighties Swedish group—and the enthusiasm of those baby boomers who adored them.

Not that *Mamma Mia!* wanted to notice *Carmelina* in any way, but it inadvertently if slightly does by having Sophie mention 1979—as "the year she got pregnant with me." Since Sophie is twenty years old, keeping her year of conception in the script means the story, whenever we happen to see it, is taking place in 2000—making *Mamma Mia!* a period piece, set in the last year of the last millennium.

The show starts with Sophie doing a ritual-like cheer with her three closest friends (who then disappear until the final curtain). There's a nice symmetry here, though, for Donna will soon be doing her own ritual-like cheer when her two old friends arrive. Rosie (Judy Kaye) and Tanya (Karen Mason) used to sing with her in their group, "Donna and the Dynamos." But Rosie can now be best described as The Fat Person Who Makes a Fool of Herself, finessing the moves she could routinely do years ago.

Tanya still looks good, but the joke is that the multi-married beauty is incompetent at even the most rudimentary tasks. That leaves us to center on Donna and Sophie.

Of course, if the former Weismann Girls can do a nostalgic number, Donna and the Dynamos can, too. Comparing "Who's That Woman?" though, to either "Dancing Queen" or "Super Trouper" demonstrates how much Broadway has devolved. When six do-ragged men pop their heads over the set to join in the title song—and have no business being there—the crowd greets them with delight instead of asking, "Who the hell are those guys, who have nothing to do with what's being said or sung?" *Mamma Mia*'s audiences think musicals are essentially silly, anyway, so this gives them a chance to laugh at the art form.

The other songs are better shoehorned in, though there is the second-act time waster "Take a Chance on Me" for minor characters Rosie and Bill. Sam must stomp around the room saying nothing as Donna sings "The Winner Takes It All," because ABBA never wrote any lyrics to fit his emotions.

But what's strangest of all is that never has so big an audience pleaser had so few applause buttons for its hit songs. It's sheer bad showmanship when a line of dialogue or a quick entrance time and time again short-circuits applause on a recognizable song. To make matters worse, librettist Catherine Johnson goes for the hoariest theatrical convention: Overhearing the Conversation That Shouldn't Be Heard. Here, Sam is the eavesdropper who learns what he shouldn't when sneaking around where Sophie and her beau are talking.

A little later, Sophie is astonished when Donna says, "My mother disowned me." Why hasn't this come up before? Does Sophie's curiosity about her father not extend to her grandparents?

And then there's the set. Sam, an architect, takes a look at Donna's taverna and fondly says, "I designed this place twenty-one years ago." it's nothing to boast about; aside from *A Chorus Line*, which isn't supposed to have a set, never has an original production of a smash musical offered such woebegone scenic values. Two small-sized units were all the audience saw.

Mamma Mia! has surpassed *Grease* as the longest-running show to fail to win even one Tony. To say that a post-9/11 need to be entertained at any cost is responsible for its success would be unfair; after all, it had been running successfully for two and a half years in London before the terrorist attacks.

But the megamix that ends the musical displays what the baby boomer audience really wants: songs they already know and love, sung by people dressed in the disco-era clothes they once wore. *Mamma Mia!* gives them the opportunity to say, "Yeah, we were silly back then. We admit it. But we were young, alive, and well. That means something to us now when we're facing retirement, social security, and health issues."

Historians note the irony that the French Revolution, which eliminated a despot and established democracy, took place in 1789—only fifteen years before Napoleon for all intents and purposes eliminated democracy and established himself as a despot. The British musical took a few more years than that to come full circle. From the infancy of the art form and right through the 1960s, the British musical was a pale imitation of the American one. Not until Andrew Lloyd Webber and Tim Rice decided to eliminate book and downplay choreography in the seventies did the British musical find its own unique style.

And yet, *Mamma Mia!* returned the British musical to its American-styled roots. Songs and book lived together in peaceful coexistence, while many a dance took over when people finished singing. The more things change, the more they stay the same.

Mamma Mia! October 18, 2001–. Over 3,500 performances.

THE BIGGEST FLOP
Sweet Smell of Success

What people don't need after 9/11.

"Although it is expertly done, can you draw sweet water from a foul well?"

It's one of the most famous quotations from a review of a musical: The last line of *New York Times* critic Brooks Atkinson's appraisal of *Pal Joey*, on December 26, 1940. He didn't much enjoy spending time with Joey Evans, the low-level entertainer who tries to sleep his way to the top while stringing along a lovely girl whom he claims he loves. Remember, too, that those were simpler times for the American musical; the show that opened before *Pal Joey* was *Meet the People*, while the one that opened directly after it was *All in Fun*.

Imagine what Atkinson would have thought of *Sweet Smell of Success*, whose leads could have made Joey Evans seem as innocent as a rose. J.J. Hunsecker

(John Lithgow) was a 1950s syndicated columnist who enjoyed treating everyone else as if they were bugs on the sidewalk. (Read: Walter Winchell.) Sidney Falco (Brian d'Arcy James) was a press agent who would lie, cheat, and pimp if he thought it could help him with J.J. in any way.

And even though Sweeney Todd and Mr. Hyde had been musicalized on Broadway in recent years, they were characters in musicals set in a long-bygone era. J.J. and Sidney were kept in their fifties milieu, but their gambits were, of course, similar to ones that contemporary men and women do every day.

Ernest Lehman's original seventy-two-page novella *Sweet Smell of Success* led to a much-acclaimed 1957 film. A look at each proves that bookwriter John Guare, composer Marvin Hamlisch, and lyricist Craig Carnelia made the characters much more compelling than they were in the source materials.

Both of the previous properties told about all-powerful gossip columnist J.J. Hunsecker, his aberrant love for his sister Susan, and their interaction with a hungry publicist Sidney Falco. Herre in the musical, the publicist starts out as Sidney Falcone, but in act 1, scene 1 J.J. suggests he change his name to the more pungent Falco (claiming that the ending "o" sound that well served Harlow, Garbo, and Monroe). And Sidney agrees! What a mighty way of showing us J.J.'s all-encompassing influence: with one offhand suggestion, he even has the power to change people's names. There's nothing in either the novella or the film that more strongly suggests that Falco would do *anything* to please J.J.

Neither the novella nor film has the scene where J.J. is in St. Patrick's Cathedral—after hours, for, as J.J. offhandedly tells Sidney, Cardinal Spellman lets him drop in when he wants. (Another indication of J.J.'s power.) But being in church doesn't keep J.J. religious; instead, he uses the opportunity to make Sidney swear that he'll keep his eye on his half-sister Susan (Kelli O'Hara) and make sure nothing bad happens to her. And the operative word is "swear." J.J. literally has Sidney make the oath while Hamlisch's religious-tinted music makes it all the more eerie.

The musical greatly enhanced the character of Susan. Originally, J.J. Hunsecker's sister was a "late baby" to his father and mother—but in the musical, she's the product of his father's second marriage. Not that lusting for one's half-sister instead of your full-blooded sister is only half as bad, but the choice to make the two characters half-siblings is a more compelling one. The world has come to see plenty of children whose parents have endured multiple marriages, so a number of half-siblings have complicated feelings for their half-siblings. Here's a musical that brought up the subject.

And while all three properties showed that J.J. is much too enraptured with Susan, the musical's collaborators offered another improvement from the novella and the film: J.J. doesn't try to keep her for himself, but tries to fix her up with someone else—no less than Senator John F. Kennedy. This does make J.J. a bit better, for he wants the best man for Susan, and knows that it's not necessarily himself. (There is a nice irony, too, in J.J.'s thinking that JFK would be a good husband, now that we've since learned he wasn't the most faithful of spouses. The collaborators obliquely showed us that J.J. doesn't necessarily have everybody pegged.)

In the film, Susan is shy and retiring, and admits, "I'm weak. I can't change." That often true of people with powerful siblings. She is stronger in the novella, where she enacts revenge on Falco. But in the musical, she is stronger still. So while the film pitted a strong J.J. against a weak Susan, and the novella offered the strong J.J. vs. a stronger Susan, the musical went for the strongest J.J. vs. the strongest Susan—which always offers the best dramatic possibilities.

That the film's shrinking violet was replaced by the musical's confident young miss was more realistic. If J.J. were the terror of the town, the apple of his eye would surely be the object of rapt and fawning attention from everyone else. This was well dramatized in the song "For Susan." J.J showed Sidney all the letters, postcards, and souvenirs from the celebrities—Gary Cooper, Humphrey Bogart, et al.—who paid Susan great attention over the years. That could make a girl feel good about herself, and make her strong enough to do what Susan did at the end of the show: bring down her brother.

Not everything that the collaborators invented for the musical was dead-on correct. Making J.J. an ex-vaudevillian did seem to be an unconvincing and unnecessary stimulus for a song. But there's no question that the three collaborators made *Sweet Smell of Success* their very own. They didn't just cut a bit of dialogue and replace it with a song, as so many (dull) writers of (dull) musicals have.

Too bad that actor Jack Noseworthy was terribly wrong as Susan's boyfriend Dallas. An audience had to be on the side of these lovers, but Noseworthy seemed to be a street punk, a sewer rat, so that J.J.'s not wanting his sister to hang out with the likes of him made sense—though it wasn't supposed to. Martin Milner in the movie seemed like a genuinely nice guy, and J.J.'s not liking him seemed wrong and misguided.

To be fair to Noseworthy, the authors changed his character to be more worldly-wise; now he's an already-divorced father. Still, if someone similar to Milner had been cast, he would have made us think that his previous marriage was a youthful mistake. Noseworthy was so repugnant that we started to suspect that the breakup of the marriage was his fault and that his wife was well rid of him. And while the novel specified that Dallas had a crew cut, Noseworthy retained the anachronistically long hair style that he wore in real life. He also ruined his two important songs by overdoing them with the amateurishness of a high-school boy who'd been cast in the annual musical because no other boy had showed up.

That was a shame, for the songs, like all the others, were strong ones. Guare and Carnelia wrote with one voice, so that the work remarkably seems to be from one bookwriter-lyricist. The language was always imaginative and in keeping with the harsh world of New York nightlife in the fifties.

Director Nicholas Hytner made a mistake from the outset: he allowed too long a time to pass in the opening number without letting the audience applaud. A theatergoer needs to hear everyone around him applauding to reinforce that what he just heard was terrific, and that everyone appreciated it. Pop operas can go for scenes without applause and not be hurt, because they play more like operas. But traditional musicals need an audience to applaud early and often to set the tone of excitement. Without that validation, audience members begin to wonder if the people around them are enjoying themselves. Such a situation often gets a musical off on the wrong foot.

But the main reason that *Sweet Smell of Success* did not catch on with the public may well have to do with the incident that took place six months earlier: the September 11, 2001 bombing of the World Trade Center. Now, more than ever, people needed sheer escapism. Hence *Mamma Mia*'s sweet smell of success.

Sweet Smell of Success. March 14, 2002–June 15, 2002. 109 performances.

2002–2003

The Biggest Hit
Hairspray

A tall—and fat—tale.

Twenty-five full years after *Annie* opened, another fairy tale debuted at the same theater.

This one was called *Hairspray*.

It's true. What was the real likelihood of heavyset Tracy Turnblad (Marissa Joan Winokur) auditioning and getting accepted for *The Corny Collins Show*, Baltimore's hippest dance TV program in 1962? What also seemed a stretch was that Corny (Clarke Thorell) cared only about how Tracy danced and not about how she'd look on TV.

Even if such an overweight kid did make the cut, what were the odds that the ever-so-handsome and hunky Link Larkin (Matthew Morrison) would fall in love with her? (Just ask Neil LaBute, author of *Fat Pig*, in which a charming woman loses her boyfriend because he's embarrassed to be seen with her.) But Link liked Tracy's "way of putting things" and felt that "getting to know you is the beginning of a whole lot of adventure."

Most kids in Link's position would feel that big Tracy was beneath his lofty station. Seeing such a character and scenario was refreshing, but it was also unrealistic. Bookwriters Mark O'Donnell and Thomas Meehan were mocking Tracy's arch-enemy Amber Von Tussle (Laura Bundy Bell) when they had her say, "You people are ignoring the laws of nature," but she wasn't all that far from the truth.

Meanwhile, there was another fairy tale going on in the Turnblad household. Would a wildly overweight housewife retain the lust of a still-skinny husband a couple of decades into the marriage? But Edna Turnblad (Harvey Fierstein) certainly did, as husband Wilbur (Dick Latessa) couldn't help putting his arms around as much of her body as he could. "I think of her as prime real estate," Wilbur says.

Tracy and Edna's good fortune didn't stop with love. Both got a ton of free clothes, because a merchant of plus-sized stores wants them to endorse his products.

Certainly there was much to admire in Tracy. She was able to stand up to her enemies ("Amber Von Tussle, you have acne of the soul!"), believe in herself ("You've got to think big to be big"), and was surprised when she was rebuffed ("Is there no pity for a teen who's just trying to fit in?").

Most admirable of all, Tracy went up against racism. She not only fought for herself, but also waged war with bigoted TV show producer Velma Von Tussle (Linda Hart) and anyone else who'd limit her black friend Seaweed J. Stubbs (Corey Reynolds), his mother, Maybelle (Mary Bond Davis), and any other African-American to one day a month on Corny's show.

Her stand against racism landed her in jail. But Link got her out by blowtorching away the bars on her jail cell—making a Tracy-sized hole, just as in cartoons when a character breaks through a wall. Thus *Hairspray* added a cartoon ingredient to its fairy-tale scenario.

In the midst of this came a wonderful early-sixties pastiche score. Too bad that from the B-section of "Mama, I'm a Big Girl Now"—Tracy's plea for independence—composer Marc Shaiman and lyricist Scott Wittman early on dropped an especially smart line. Tracy sang to Edna, "Mom, you're always telling me to act my age, well, that's just what I'm trying to do." Don't we all wish that when we were teenagers, we'd had the presence of mind to say that to our mothers when they levied that charge against us? The problem is usually that parents expect their teens to act years beyond their age. (But if Shaiman and Wittman dropped the line because they felt it was too smart for a sixteen-year-old, they very well may have had a point.)

In the final fairy-tale action of the night, Maryland's governor so enjoyed seeing Tracy on TV that he gave her a pardon. All this was as unlikely as—well, as Annie's getting the world's richest man to adopt her.

But if you can't have fairy tales in musical comedy, where can you have them?

Hairspray. August 15, 2002–January 4, 2009. 2,642 performances.

The Biggest Flop
Dance of the Vampires

Don't change musicals in midstream.

The show began on a dank, dark set of the forest primeval with eerie lighting that flashed over the audience. Onto the stage walked Sarah (Mandy Gonzalez), along with two other equally innocent-looking actresses, who pretended to be genuinely afraid. Given the phantasmagorical beings that were slithering out of the set, the kids had every reason to be. But the scary mood was not sustained. Suddenly there were jokes, with the preponderance involving mushrooms, but one establishing that the year is "eighteen-eighty-something."

That the characters didn't know what year it is shows that the authors didn't know the time of day—and the audiences weren't going to give it to them. For even this early in the show, it was already too late for jokes, because the sets, costumes and staging (which looked like act 1, scene 2 of *The Tempest*) had already prepared us for a serious musical.

So had the logo, which suggested a dark and stormy night.

So had the title, which sounded earnest.

Given that much of the first act of *Dance of the Vampires* was out for unmitigated laughs, it should have used the subtitle that its source, the 1967 film *The Fearless Vampire Killers*, originally employed: *Pardon Me, but Your Teeth Are in My Neck*. That line would have let people immediately know they were in for a spoof. But because the audience didn't know, the jokes struck theatergoers as inadvertently incompetent dialogue, making the crowd primed to laugh at the show, and not with the "funny" lines: "God has left the building." "I've been looking for an original sin." "I once danced the polka in Cupid's beer garden." "Sucked as dry as a mummy's scrotum," not to be confused with "Sucking for dummies." Harvard freshmen write such gags for Hasty Pudding Shows—only to be told by the seniors that they must do better.

Jim Steinman's lyrics included such less-than-poetic phrases as "I used my body just like a bandage." His "rhymes" included a father's singing to his daughter, "You're not ready. Don't leave Deddy." And John Carrafa's choreography truly appeared as if it belonged in *The Tall Guy*, that movie that spoofed musicals and offered a musical version of *The Elephant Man*.

Dance of the Vampires switched its style in midstream, going from the serious pop-opera that it was in Europe to the retro-chic musical comedy that was, after 9/11 and *The Producers*, suddenly again in style on Broadway. That must be why the "Creatures of the Night," as the program derivatively identified them, came out in pants that seemed to be discarded overalls from Dogpatch. The dance they did wasn't at all scary, but instead resembled something from a sixties variety show that was desperately trying to be *au courant*. Comedy is best served by bright lighting, but vampires can only exist in the dark, so most of the show was set at night—and that dim lighting undercut whatever comedy was attempted.

Then a character in a black cape headed down the aisle to the stairs leading to the stage. That seemed to be an effective entrance for Michael Crawford, whom audiences were rabidly anticipating. Here would be the star's triumphant return to Broadway. But this was actually an usher who was seating latecomers; all ushers here were forced to wear capes to add to "the experience."

Actually, Crawford got a much better entrance as Count von Krolock, emerging, of course, from a coffin. He'd been forty-six when he opened *Phantom* in London—and was now about to turn sixty-one. Those fifteen years in any man's later life make him perilously prone to additional poundage, and Crawford turned out to be no exception.

Worse, Crawford was made up as garishly as Liberace in Las Vegas but only succeeded in resembling an entertainer who plays a side lounge. He gave his last name as Krolock—in an Italian immigrant's accent, though only his middle name (Giovanni) was Italian. Later he'd admit to more Italian middle names—Capellini and Trovatore, derived from pastas and operas. At the end of his first number, there was not a smidgen of applause. Some return to Broadway.

"Garlic" was a song in which a bunch of peasants waxed rhapsodic about the foodstuff in front of a set straight out of a Shubert road operetta. "Garlic, garlic! The secret of staying young," they sang, before adding, "Garlic, garlic! It's why we're so well hung!" Lest anyone doubt the singers were peasants, René Auberjonois, playing Professor Abronsius, soon emerged to blithely say, "Greetings, gentle peasants!"

The show could have solved its problems by the same means that Jerome Robbins fixed *A Funny Thing Happened on the Way to the Forum*. That 1962 musical wasn't working in Washington because it didn't have the right setup at the top of the show; it needed "Comedy Tonight" to inform the audience that this would be a fun-filled musical.

In Europe, *Tanz der Vampire* had been a serious musical, but once it became *Dance of the Vampires* and decided to morph into musical comedy, it needed an equally droll opening number to set the tone and let people know what kind of evening it would be.

Of course, *Funny Thing* was a much better show, without a single anachronism. *Dance of the Vampires* certainly embraced anachronisms: *Bela Bartokovich. Come up and see me sometime. Shake and bake. Wagner's Greatest Hits.* A "Do Not Disturb" sign on a coffin. References to bodily fluids, coffee bars, exercise, and dental work may technically not have been anachronistic, but each had a contemporary ring.

A musical with a few first-act problems usually has a murderously awful second act. But this musical's act 2 let audiences finally see and hear some of the show that had been enchanting Europe. For suddenly the jokes were kept to a minimum and the heartfelt songs were sung to the max. But 2003 was a little late to hear a juvenile would-be hero (Max Von Essen) sincerely sing, "There's a dream known as home." Imagine *The Boy Friend* with a score that suddenly turned serious. *Dance of the Vampires* was a dish of meatballs topped with whipped cream.

And then there was Steinman's interpolated pop hit, "Total Eclipse of the Heart." In hopes of setting it up, the first act sported three mentions of a "total eclipse." When the hand-me-down song finally was sung, Crawford said, "No! No!" as part of the dialogue—but the effect seemed to be that he was inadvertently commenting on the authors' decision to include it.

That wasn't the only time Crawford provided unintentional humor. At one point he said, "Sometimes I look in the mirror and wonder, where have I gone?" The audience didn't immediately laugh, but when it did, there was a mocking quality, for the crowd had found another meaning: How could Michael Crawford look at himself in the mirror each morning, given how he's chosen to spend his stage time? He even had to don drag for a joke that never paid off. Credit where it's due, though, Crawford could still sing, and he held one note so long that he made Ethel Merman sound like the King in *Once upon a Mattress*. (Of course, there are those who say the note was pre-recorded.)

René Auberjonois, who once won a Tony for singing a song called "Fiasco," now found himself in one. ("This looks pretty cryptic," he had to say when he came across a couple of crypts.) While Crawford and Gonzalez were busy singing "Total Eclipse of the Heart," was Auberjonois humming to himself an older pop song, "Walk Away, Renée"?

Ron Orbach played a character who was eventually supposed to be dead, but director John Rando contorted him into a terribly awkward position where the actor had to keep his right leg up in the air—so while the character's wife was saying how stiff he was, the poor soul really had to struggle to hold a position that neither he nor anyone else could sustain. (Orbach was, of course, a poor soul in another way, for during the tryout of *The Producers*, he was the original Franz Liebkind. But he endured a knee injury, so Brad Oscar had to take his place—and then Nathan Lane's. This was the year that Orbach should have become incapacitated.)

There were visual jokes about sponges, but no jokes in a woeful list song about books. A gay character suddenly emerged to do a seduction scene with Our Young Juvenile Would-Be Hero. A comic number had a bunch of zombies sing, "Eternity isn't what it's cracked up to be"—though everyone else who'd become dead seemed very happy about it, so Steinman just went for a cheap anachronistic joke. Crawford's death scene was technically impressive, but again there was no applause, because the audience was long lost by this time.

At this point in his career, John Rando should have told his producers early in the game that if they suddenly wanted a laugh-fest instead of a serious musical,

Dance of the Vampires should at best be ninety intermissionless minutes and not a two-act extravaganza that got out well after ten-thirty.

Although Crawford's character died, the vampires did wind up taking over the world. Audiences were shown the Times Square of the future, where signs proclaimed the availability of Bloodweiser Beer and that tasty orange powdered drink Fang. A show called *Bats*, which had a logo uncannily like a Lloyd Webber show of yore, said the show was now in its thirty-ninth year. *Dance of the Vampires* barely made it past thirty-nine days.

Even in that time, a cast member made a serious breach of theatrical etiquette, according to make-up artist Angelina Avallone. "One ensemble member came out in red make-up when everyone else was in green," she recalled. "And when I asked why after, the actress admitted that her parents were seeing the show today, and she wanted them to know which one she was."

Dance of the Vampires. December 9, 2002–January 25, 2003. 56 performances.

2003–2004

THE BIGGEST HIT
Wicked

Bring on the girls.

You run 2,526 performances, you win the Tony for Best Musical, and you're *still* not the biggest hit of the season?

'Tis true. *Avenue Q* was on Broadway for more than six years. But the biggest hit of the season—and for many seasons to come—was *Wicked*—*The Wizard of Oz* from the vantage point of the Wicked Witch of the West.

Gregory Maguire, who wrote the novel on which the musical is based, was intrigued by something he noticed in the classic 1939 film version: the Wicked Witch's green skin. Wouldn't you turn out to be antisocial, too, if your face looked like that?

"I love when someone takes a famous story and sees it in a completely different way," says Stephen Schwartz, *Wicked*'s composer-lyricist.

But Schwartz claims that when he and bookwriter Winnie Holzman were writing the show, neither he nor she ever said to the other, "And you know, this musical is going to be a phenomenon with teenage girls!'"

"That never occurred to us," he says. "Obviously we thought the show could be good, and the subject matter would interest audiences. The only person who understood its appeal to that demographic was Nancy Coyne," he says, referring to the chief executive of Serino Coyne, Broadway's foremost advertising agency. "She envisioned early on that teenagers, girls in particular, would respond as much as they have."

Wicked's lead producer, David Stone, doesn't much care for the theory that he has mostly young girls to thank for the show's success. "This is not just a show for teenage girls," he says, "but for everybody."

Stone has a point, even though *Wicked*'s two witches-in-training meet as teenage girls, allowing the thirteen-to-nineteen set to identify with them. The luckier few of them identify with beautiful G(a)linda (Kristin Chenoweth) who is, as she sings in the score's most bouncy tune, "Popular." More identify with her roommate Elphaba (Idina Menzel), who has that skin condition much worse than acne. It's not easy literally being green.

While high schoolers wrestle with popularity issues on a daily basis, their parents' teenage years aren't so far behind them. Mothers and fathers easily remember when they worried about being in the in-crowd—or being out of it. And who grows out of issues with their bodies—especially as they tend to get worse with time?

Of course, *Wicked* has other assets. When theatergoers entered the Gershwin Theater, they saw the entire proscenium arch covered with objects that showed the inner workings of the Land of Oz, all topped by a dragon's head, dead center. Soon after the scrim went up, G(a)linda, the "Good" Witch, entered in the same type of bubble that Billie Burke used for transportation in the iconic 1939 film.

Holzman did a stunning job of condensing Maguire's long explanation of how Baby Elphaba was born green. If for some reason we didn't feel immediate sympathy for her, we certainly did when she sang "The Wizard and I"—a bolt-of-lightning moment where we immediately and squarely took her side. No one had to wait until "Defying Gravity," her dramatic first-act ending aria, to care about her.

That Idina Menzel delivered both songs so dynamically only added to the glorious experience. She earned her odd billing over the title: it was over Chenoweth, but only to the right, where one's eye might not immediately take notice. It was a nice metaphor for a character who's an outsider.

Chenoweth had an entrance after Menzel finished "The Wizard and I," and obviously had a hard act to follow. But this Tony, Drama Desk, Outer Critics Circle, and Theatre World Award winner wasn't worried. She knew that she had quite a bit to bring to the stage—including that astonishing four-octave range belied by her petite body.

They went off to meet the Wizard (Joel Grey), who, oddly enough, deftly mentioned "philanthropists." Frank Morgan, the 1939 film's title character, famously said, "Back where I come from there are men who do nothing all day but good deeds. They are called phil- . . . er . . . phil- . . . er . . . er . . . good-deed-doers." Why did this "same" Wizard not have trouble with that word?

In the language category, though, Holzman worked so hard (and successfully) to give Oz a distinctive language, including a number of made-up words, as well as known words with added syllables. What a shame that choreographer Wayne Cilento couldn't find an equally distinctive style in how Ozians move.

But the score had a life outside the show. According to Brian Drutman, vice-president of the Broadway and Soundtrack Division of Decca Label Group, *Wicked*'s original cast album has sold upwards of two million copies—and that doesn't count the German and Japanese-language recordings. Aubrey Berg, the chairman of the Department of Musical Theater at the College-Conservatory of Music at the University of Cincinnati, auditions thousands of high schoolers each year who want admission to his program. He says, "There hasn't been an audition song as popular as 'Popular' or 'Defying Gravity' since 'Corner of the Sky.'"

Interesting that all three are Schwartz compositions. By June 2007, when *Wicked* played its 1,500th performance, Schwartz had had three Broadway musicals that had run that long, only the second composer-lyricist (after Jerry Herman) who could make that boast. Now Schwartz can claim the title as the only composer-lyricist who's had three shows run longer than 1,900 performances. What's more, each of his—*Pippin*, *The Magic Show*, and *Wicked*—was the biggest hit of its season.

Wicked. October 30, 2003–. Over 2,800 performances.

The Biggest Flop
Taboo

Location, location, location.

Yasmina Reza's comedy *Life (x) 3*, about an unsuccessful dinner party, ended its Broadway run on June 29, 2003.

Bryony Lavery's *Frozen*, about a kidnapped child who is murdered, began its Broadway run on April 28, 2004.

And what relevance do these two well-received plays have to *Taboo*, the biggest flop of the 2003–2004 season?

Quite a bit, in a manner of speaking. Both plays were ensconced at Circle in the Square Theatre, the cozy, 776-seat playhouse that's a unique Broadway structure. While it isn't quite a circle in a square, it is an oval in a rectangle—and it's a great little space for atypical shows.

And that's what *Taboo* was. The life and times of one George O'Dowd—better known as eighties pop music sensation Boy George—was less of a musical and more of, to use a word first coined in the sixties, a happening.

Young Londoners who were raised on eighties music didn't much go to the theater, so *Taboo*'s producers did what they could to make them comfortable. Though they chose a space near Leicester Square—the heart of London's Theatreland—they didn't opt for a stately home such as the Wyndham's or even the intimate Arts Theatre.

Instead, they chose a crypt in a church, transformed it, and renamed it The Venue. The playbill proclaimed that *Taboo* took place at "an abandoned London warehouse, which formerly was the location of the hottest club of the eighties." That's what The Venue looked and felt like—which is what *Taboo*'s audiences wanted.

So when TV host and earnest Broadway cheerleader Rosie O'Donnell announced that she'd put up the entire $10 million to bring *Taboo* to New York, she made her first mistake by choosing the ornate Plymouth Theater with a proscenium arch.

Sad. Do a hundred episodes of a TV series, and you're an enormous hit, with enough episodes to strike gold in syndication. Do a hundred performances of a Broadway musical, and you lose $10 million.

But O'Donnell might not have, had she chosen Circle in the Square, which would have merged the club and theater world into an exciting and atypical space.

Taboo. November 13, 2003–February 8, 2004. 100 performances.

2004–2005

The Biggest Hit
Monty Python's Spamalot

The Hasty Pudding Show goes to Broadway.

February 18, 2005. Cambridge, Massachusetts. The Hasty Pudding Theatre. *Terms of Frontierment* is the 157th musical written by Harvard collegians. This one takes place in the Wild West, where Luke N. Forglory, a Daniel Boone type, winds up meeting Western dance hall entertainer Chicksie Dix, as well as whorehouse madam Iona Brothel, Chief Lester Thamohicans and his daughter Pocahotness. The Chief, faced with the prospect of Pocahotness' marrying another woman, says, "This isn't Massachusetts!" When a stupid person is discussed, Chicksie Dix says, "Is his middle initial W?" in reference to a then-sitting president.

Terms of Frontierment doesn't neglect the time-honored Pudding formula of puns ("Play Keno, Sabe!"), double-entendres ("She loves to pet her beaver"), anachronisms ("Life sans moi is duller than Chanel without Coco"), and homages to musicals of yore (a character called The Gay Caballero sings a bit of "Don't Rain on My Parade.") And, in a nod to Erich Segal's 1970 novel *Love Story*, which took place at Harvard, Hindu Indian Sam Osa says, "Love means you never have to wear a sari."

The Hasty Pudding Show is the one place on the planet where you're guaranteed to hear show music that most sounds like the Golden Age of Broadway. Derrick Wang acknowledged that by including a nice Richard Rodgers "wrong note" in the title song. Add in intentionally cheesy choreography (in "Manifest My Destiny") and, of course, men dressed as women, especially for the de rigueur kick line, and you've got a Hasty Pudding Show.

That same night New York City, another Hasty Pudding Show is being performed, albeit by professionals and Tony winners. At the Shubert Theatre, *Monty Python's Spamalot* is playing its sixth preview.

Eric Idle, who wrote the book and lyrics—and even some of the music with lead composer John DuPrez—offers the same ingredients found in Cambridge. Puns include one where chopped-off arms are said to be "Alms for the poor." One double-entendre has a knight make a gesture that suggests breasts as he says, "She's got huge"—before he completes the sentence with "tracts of land," making it seem as if we're the ones with the dirty minds.

Anachronisms? King Arthur asks, "Why do they call this 'The Middle Ages' when nothing comes after us?" Homages to musicals of yore include the knights purposely aping the dance moves of the Jets in *West Side Story*. Pastiche music comes in with "Always Look on the Bright Side of Life," a song that's meant to mock the upbeat melody and philosophy found in the best show songs. (Indeed, despite the winking, it almost passes muster as a genuinely wonderful theater song.)

Add in intentionally cheesy choreography (twice, there's a silly chorus of tap-dancing knights) and, of course, men dressed as women, though not necessarily or solely for the de rigueur kick line.

Of course, *Spamalot* is more polished and performed by a more seasoned cast. But it's still a spoonful of the same pudding. Flatulence jokes? Of course there are some in each. But *Spamalot* does *Frontierment* one better—or worse, depending on your point of view—by including many jokes about incontinence as well.

Performers don't just break wind; they break the fourth wall, too. On three separate occasions, a character chides the orchestra conductor. Later, a spectator is dragged out of the audience and brought on stage.

Show business in-jokes abound, too. Sara Ramirez, playing the Lady of the Lake, does a Liza Minnelli impersonation before segueing into playing the white performer who soulfully sings like a black one, right down to offering a pain-filled grimace when she delivers a particularly difficult passage. Later, Ramirez gets angry when the spotlight operator is late in illuminating her; even after he gets on the ball and bathes her in white, she still holds a grudge and glares at him with hatred. (She'll win a Tony for her trouble.)

And how about this show-biz joke? When Arthur mentions "Excalibur," an unseen chorus sings the word over and over again, as everyone on stage looks confused, and starts searching to see from where the sound is emanating. As Ethan Mordden wrote in *Open a New Window*, when discussing this same formula joke that was used in the 1962 musical *A Family Affair*, this is "a musical comedy jest so old that your great-great grandmother fell out of her cradle laughing at it." And that was forty-three years before *Spamalot* opened.

Yet the audience at the Shubert almost fell out of their seats at this tidbit and plenty of others. And why did everyone laugh like seals all night long, from the first hint of a joke till the last? Perhaps people saved up their laughter for decades when Broadway was overwhelmed by the megamusical. How many jokes did they hear during the British invasion? There's one funny lyric in *Cats* ("let the cat out of the bag"), one funny line in *Sunset Boulevard* ("Did he read the script?"), one amusing song in *Les Miz* ("Master of the House"), one somewhat comical song in *Miss Saigon* ("The American Dream")—and none at all in *The Phantom of the Opera*.

Audiences had been so starved for laughter that they were now roaring at any attempt at humor—including laughing at the once-beloved megamusical. One song begins, "Once in every show, there's a song like this," in the style of the power ballad that audiences endured and all took all too seriously—and all too recently—in *Jekyll & Hyde* and *Jane Eyre*. So when Arthur is told, "You must put on a musical—but not an Andrew Lloyd Webber one," the line gets even more applause that the George W. Bush quip got in *Terms of Frontierment*.

So Broadway has another post-9/11 mindless entertainment. The average Hasty Pudding Show runs six weeks. *Monty Python's Spamalot* ran almost four years and won the Best Musical Tony.

Monty Python's Spamalot. March 17, 2005–January 11, 2009. 1,575 performances.

The Biggest Flop
Chitty Chitty Bang Bang

A very different kind of star gets the final curtain call.

Raul Esparza and Marc Kudisch were Tony nominees, while Philip Bosco was a Tony winner. All had significant parts in *Chitty Chitty Bang Bang*, but none got the last bow.

One might assume that the gentlemen were being gentlemanly, and allowing Erin Dilly or Jan Maxwell, also in important roles, to get the last bow. Or, in an equally grand gesture, what about all Henry Hodges or Ellen Marlow, who played the children who propelled the story?

No. The last bow went to the automobile known as Chitty Chitty Bang Bang.

Say what you will about *Phantom*'s falling chandelier or *Miss Saigon*'s helicopter, at least they knew their place. The former appeared at the beginning and end of the first act, while the latter showed up in the second act. Then both retired for the night.

But technology had become so important to the Broadway musical that the car took center stage at *Chitty Chitty Bang Bang*'s end, while twenty-two actors stood to its right, twenty-three to its left, each one extending an arm to display the reason the show was done in the first place.

Perhaps it was the right decision, given the dull and misconceived book from Jeremy Sams and his "additional material collaborator" Ivan Menchell. (Of course, screenwriters Roald Dahl and Ken Hughes, who penned the awful 1968 movie, had to bear some responsibility, too.) Let's also indict those Sherman Brothers for providing another sugar-sweet score.

The book was smart, though, to have Jeremy and Jemima Potts, the two kids, establish early on that "We hate school"—for that line would make most every kid in the audience bond with them. There is something, too, in having the kids love a wrecked car and wanting their daddy, Caractacus (Esparza), to buy it for them. But it was too expensive for this failed inventor, who nevertheless said optimistically, "One of these days, one of these inventions is going to work." What was curious is that he said this line after one of his inventions had indeed been shown to work, delivering a hearty breakfast.

Also after the car were Goran (Chip Zien) and Boris (Robert Sella), two villains from Vulgaria. (We knew they were villains because they laughed maniacally after they divulged aloud their sinister plot.) They then sang a song about how they'd "Act English." It was a reasonably quick patter song, and because Zien and Sella sang with thick Vulgarian accents, the allegedly witty lyrics couldn't be easily understood. Soon after, the kids become acquainted with a woman whose name was actually Truly Scrumptious (Dilly).

Caractacus demonstrated a hair-cutting machine at a fair. It dismally failed, and his now-bald victim chased him all around the place, perhaps to get some laughs from the kids in attendance. Caractacus ran onto a stage where a group of entertainers were doing their act, which seemed to be a tribute to bamboo. Every now and then, the entertainers suddenly stopped singing so that Caractacus could have the song's punch line all to himself. What wasn't explained was how they knew enough to stop just in time for Caractacus, who knew precisely when to sing. That was especially impressive, given that he'd stumbled into the number.

Goran and Boris followed Grandpa Potts (Bosco), but they got too close, and when he sensed that someone was behind him, a Vulgarian let out a "Quack!" in hopes that the old man would assume a duck was behind him. He didn't, but said, "It's only an owl"—allowing the kids in the audience to feel superior to the old dolt.

The kids felt more superior still when they met the real villain, the Baron Bomburst (Kudisch), who carried a stuffed animal with him at all times. The Baron in fact prohibited children from his kingdom so that the Toymaker could make toys for him and him alone. His wife, the Baroness (Maxwell), then had a line that had the ring of double entendre: "I should have never allowed toys in our marriage."

To ensure that the kingdom remained childless, a Childcatcher (Kevin Cahoon) was engaged, as expressed in his song "Kiddy-Widdy-Winkies." He did catch Jeremy and Jemima, and when Caractacus heard about it—and found other kids the Childcatcher has captured—he didn't spring into action, but sang a song with the kids called "Team Work Can Make a Dream Work." One would have expected that he'd immediately rescue his children.

Of course, the plot all worked out splendidly. The Childcatcher was captured, put in a net, and raised all the way up to the balcony out of everyone's sight. Still, he wouldn't go quietly, but gave a snarling laugh that echoed through the auditorium. So Truly Scrumptious took out a rifle and shot twice. Should a "kids' show" have included a premeditated murder?

When Scrumptious fired her gun, she was in that aforementioned car. (Guess she was riding shotgun.) The car did a nice trick by lifting up and circling around in the air, though when it repeated the move—the only one it performed all night, in fact—the audience might have started to become a little bored. In the history of transportation, cars did replace horses, but now we were back to having a one-trick pony.

Perhaps *Chitty* died for another show's sin: after *Miss Saigon* opened in London, Broadway heard about the helicopter ad nauseam, so when it showed, many were disappointed that it didn't do more than it actually did. But both *Phantom* and *Miss Saigon* were much worthier musicals, so that's the ultimate reason they ran. *Chitty* instead ran out of gas long before its producers expected it to.

Chitty Chitty Bang Bang. April 28, 2005–December 31, 2005.
285 performances.

2005–2006

THE BIGGEST HIT
Jersey Boys

It's smarter to be lucky than it's lucky to be smart.

Branch Rickey, once the general manager of the Brooklyn Dodgers (and a character in the 1981 flop musical *The First*), famously said that "Luck is the residue of design."

But in the case of *Jersey Boys*, its design was the residue of luck. Bookwriters Marshall Brickman and Rick Elise were very fortunate that way back in the early sixties, four young singers chose a certain name for their singing group.

Tommy DeVito, Bob Gaudio, Nick Massi, and Frankie Valli went through quite a number of names: the Variety Trio, the Variatones, and then the Four Lovers were among the first, while Frankie Valley and the Travelers, Frankie Valle and the Romans, the Village Voices, and the Topics were among the last.

But the group's auditioning to appear at a bowling alley changed the course of their history—and the course of the musical about them. The name of the establishment was the Four Seasons, and even though the group failed to impress the owners there, the foursome nevertheless thought they'd found the ideal name for their group.

Such songs as "Sherry," "Big Girls Don't Cry," and "Walk Like a Man" were of course more responsible for cementing their success in the early sixties. With both the unique vocal blend and these solidly pulsating songs, the Four Seasons undoubtedly would have succeeded if they'd called themselves the Lennon Sisters.

Without that name, however, Brickman and Elice probably would not have thought of the excellent and unique structure of splitting the book to *Jersey Boys* into seasons: spring, when the lads were just starting out; summer, when they began to succeed; fall—not autumn, because the group did take a fall here; and winter, which showed their various states of discontent.

As we've heard over the years, in every marriage, there are three sides of the story: his story, her story, and the truth. Using the same principle, Brickman and Elice gave us everyone's side in *Jersey Boys*. The street-smart (and stupid) De Vito (Christian Hoff) told of spring; the charmingly naive Gaudio (Daniel Reichard) filled us in on summer; the ever-irrelevant Massi (J. Robert Spencer) took the fall, while the best was saved for last: Valli (John Lloyd Young) went with winter.

While that structure became an important component of the show's success, Brickman and Elice get credit for making a decision that had nothing to do with luck. In the show's first ten minutes, they showed us one of the Seasons-to-be going to jail, as well as another one committing the crime of breaking-and-entering. Because the writers stressed the life and crimes of Tommy DeVito and the actual incarceration of at least two individuals, audiences got the impression they were telling the plain, unvarnished truth.

Jersey Boys may not have been 100 percent honest; few biographies are. What really happened in these four lads' lives may be far more sordid. But the authors sure weren't trying to hide the boys' mistakes and law-breaks. That gave us every confidence that they were telling us the inside story, and not offering a whitewash or a hagiography. More miraculously still, despite all the guys' wrongdoings, they got us to care about them.

When the show began its life at the LaJolla (California) Playhouse in October, 2004, John Lloyd Young was not with it. Though he had auditioned, director Des McAnuff instead chose David Norona to play Frankie. The run sold out and was extended three times, and plans were made to bring the show to Broadway—but Norona decided not to come with it. He opted to do a TV series called *Inconceivable*.

So Young—who not long before had been ushering at the Paper Mill Playhouse in Millburn, New Jersey, where he also appeared in one small role and understudied another—got the part. What he also got was the Outer Critics Circle Award, the Theatre World Award, the Drama Desk Award, and the Tony Award for his riveting performance. As for *Inconceivable*, the series lasted ten episodes. How unlucky for Norona. How lucky for Young.

Jersey Boys. November 6, 2005–. Over 2,000 performances.

The Biggest Flop
Lestat

A type of musical the public doesn't want.

Actually, *Lestat* was best damned vampire musical Broadway had seen in years.

Granted, that wasn't saying much, considering that Broadway's most recent vampire musicals—*Dance of the Vampires* (2002) and *Dracula: The Musical* (2004)—had been atrocities. *Lestat* was certainly not a great show, but it was an occasionally good one. It had a few intriguing ideas and ingredients, two wonderful lead performances, and plenty of good supporting ones.

When we first meet the earnest Lestat (Hugh Panaro) in the early nineteenth century, he's just slaughtered some pesky wolves—which he enjoyed doing more than he'd expected. (Foreshadowing!) He returns home to what many sons have experienced: a father who criticizes, and a mother who encourages. She was played by Carolee Carmello, who seemed as stiff as her starched costume, but there was a reason: her character was ill. "You must live the life I never could," she tells Lestat, so he goes off to visit old pal Nicolas, who's working at a theater. Backstage, the chorus girls ogle Lestat with great interest. (In real life, they'd snub him with the imperious indifference that those in the theater give to unknown backstage visitors.)

Lestat goes home with Nicolas (Roderick Hill), who is sexually interested in him. Though Lestat does a bit of flirting, he soon says he needs "some air." During his walk, he gets attacked by Head Vampire Magnus. (Is the message that he should have just opted for gay sex?)

Now Lestat is a vampire, too. That was predictable, but the story improves when Lestat arrives home, and lets his mother see who he's become. She then says, "Make me as you are"—perhaps out of motherly love, perhaps feeling that the eternal life of a vampire must be better than death. That led to a different kind of Oedipus complex, as Lestat became a mother-sucker.

Savvy audiences would have expected this, because an actress of Carmello's stature surely wouldn't have agreed to die and disappear in act 1. Yet it appears that she did, for she vanished for virtually all of act 2. Carmello had more right to sing "What Happened to My Part?" than Sara Ramirez did in *Monty Python's Spamalot.*

But Carmello did have a scene in which she saw a passerby, screamed with hunger, and pounced on the poor live bait. Perhaps a healthy laugh was the intention of bookwriter Linda Woolverton, lyricist Bernard Taupin, and/or director Robert Jess Roth. (Elton John, who doesn't take a hands-on interest in the show he's writing, probably had no opinion.)

Whatever the case, humor cropped up, but much of the laughter sounded superior, rather like the response to *Dance of the Vampires.*

Lestat spends his time biting necks and making converts. (Vampires, it seems, are bi; any neck in a pinch.) "Forgive me," he says to the first person he kills, who can't comment one way or another.

When Nicolas learns about Lestat, he decides he wants to be a vampire, too. But while Lestat's mom loves her new role, Nicolas doesn't. (Apparently, the bite affects each victim differently.) Lestat wants Nicolas cured, but the Vampire of Vampires isn't around, so Lestat euthanizes the lad. And wouldn't you know that that's precisely when the Vampire of Vampires shows up? (Well, vampires do sleep late.)

The story takes a few odd turns. Some vampires start a theater troupe (no kidding), and, in a welcoming speech, tell the audience that those who feel unnerved are free to leave. Is this warning intended for those seeing *Lestat*, too? Perhaps, for what the Vampire Theatre Company presents could be best described as a choreopoem, where dancers in masks cavort between brightly colored sheets that horizontally span the stage. Very artsy.

Woolverton's bookwriting becomes pedestrian when Lestat and his mother enter a church and he says, "I wonder if we'll be struck down." But there's a nice moment after Mom says she wants to see the world and Lestat discourages her: her excellent rebuttal is that as a mother, she's always known that he'll leave her—so what's the problem with her leaving him?

Lestat goes overseas, ostensibly to open an American franchise of vampires, and meets Louis (Jim Stanek). It's another scene that reads as a gay man's attempts to seduce a straight one. That these two become domestic partners and parents of a girl named Claudia is equally unexpected—as are the problems they have dealing with a prepubescent. Poor Lestat! When he came across Claudia, she was a dying consumptive, so he figured he'd "save" her. This short-term solution became a long-term problem.

Too bad that Elton John and Bernard Taupin never joined the BMI-Lehman Engel Workshop. They would have learned that when a scene switches to Paris, and later to New Orleans, they don't have to write a song that lists the generic charms of each city. Taupin may have been the season's greatest creator of mis-rhymed and mis-accented lyrics. John's music came off better, but what was passable in the theater wouldn't get many spins on a CD player. Still, a song in which Lestat proclaimed, "The thirst! I feel it coming on!" got cheers (and could have got a soft drink commercial).

Panaro and Carmello both threw themselves (okay, sank their teeth) into their roles. When each took center stage to sing, a galvanizing moment followed. Allison Fischer was atmospheric as Claudia, so the audience might not have minded that she was characterized in too-contemporary language and demeanor for 1828. Her anachronistic country song was also ameliorated by her doing it so well.

Set designer Derek McLane saved the splendor for the second act. Susan Hilferty's costumes were rich and evocative. Kenneth Posner had one terrific lighting effect where sunlight slowly but surely sneaks across the stage, and you know what that does the vampires. Or do you? Woolverton and Rice gave us new information and rules about the life and times of vampires: pshaw on crosses and stakes in hearts; garlic wasn't even mentioned.

By the way, after thirty years pass, the action returns to the Vampire Theatre Company, and it's still going strong. *Lestat* didn't do as well. In a time when the world seems consumed with vampires in *Twilight* and Anne Rice's own *The Vampire Chronicles*, the Broadway musical remains the one arena where vampires haven't made a killing.

Lestat. April 25–May 28, 2006. 39 performances.

2006–2007

The Biggest Hit
Mary Poppins

Practically imperfect in every way.

In 1941, Boston Red Sox outfielder Ted Williams won the American League Batting Crown with a .406 batting average—the highest ever.

In 1968, Boston Red Sox outfielder Carl Yastrzemski won the American League Batting Crown with a .301 batting average—the lowest ever for a champion.

One needn't know a thing about baseball to infer that Williams' accomplishment was substantially better than Yastrzemski's—yet both won the same prize. Yastrzemski simply did it in a poor year for hitters.

2006–2007 was a poor season for musicals on Broadway. By default, *Mary Poppins* wound up as the biggest hit of the season.

Spring Awakening was expected to be. The rock musical version of Frank Wedekind's 1891 play—about adolescents coping with sexuality and suicide—received raves from the critics and eight Tony Awards, including Best Musical. Yet its 859 performances represented the shortest run that a Tony-winning musical had seen in a decade.

What's more, *Spring Awakening* played the Eugene O'Neill Theater, one of Broadway's smallest houses, with only 1,108 seats. And yet, during *Spring Awakening's* 114 weeks on Broadway, it sold out only five of them. The rock score was at odds with the 1890s German setting, and the lyrics made little effort to rhyme. Without rhymes, an audience has a harder time understanding the words, and eventually becomes less engaged than it would if it could comprehend what's being sung.

Much less heralded by the critics was a musical that dealt with two substantially younger children: Jane and Michael Banks, the preteens who request a nice new nanny—and get one in Mary Poppins.

It's the role that got Julie Andrews a 1964 Best Actress Oscar. But that may well have been her consolation prize for her not getting to reprise her Eliza Doolittle in the *My Fair Lady* film that same year. Look carefully at her Mary Poppins, and you may well see that this haughty woman is simply not that demanding a character to play.

The film is beloved, despite some lapses in logic. In one scene, Mary, her friend chimneysweep Bert, and the two Banks children magically enter a new world through a sidewalk painting. Once they're there, Bert is quick to send the kids off to a fair, and for the next nine solid minutes, he spends a "Jolly Holiday" with Mary. Some nanny she is, letting kids go off unattended. Good thing this isn't the musical in which the Childcatcher appears.

If that's not bad enough, at day's end, when the kids want to reminisce about all the fun they had, Mary pretends it didn't happen. What kind of nanny plays such a head game with little kids?

The next day, Mary, Bert, and the children visit Uncle Albert, who "loves to laugh." He laughs so much that he rises to the ceiling as if he were helium-filled. Bert and the kids find him hilarious, but Mary Poppins is not amused at all. What a pill!

Indeed, a case could be made that the movie should have been called *Bert*. He's the one who tells the children that they should better appreciate their father. Later he advises Mr. Banks to not neglect his children because of work. Mary does very little.

However ordinary the stage musical was, at least these flaws disappeared from it. Julian Fellowes' book still told of busy Mr. Banks (Daniel H. Jenkins), who's concentrating more on his job than on his family. He does eventually come to the tender-hearted and warm conclusion that there's no place like home. In the mid sixties, when the *Mary Poppins* film debuted, this was an issue that was just starting to be discussed. By the time that the *Mary Poppins* musical debuted, it was an idea that had been examined ad nauseam. (Many an audience member laughed upon hearing the line "There are more important things than making money." This coming from Disney!)

Half the Sherman Brothers' film score was retained, while the talented George Stiles and Anthony Drewe made some solid contributions. "Practically Perfect" was an excellent song by which to introduce Mary. It also included a nifty in-joke, when Mary sang about her "forte" and pronounces it "for-tay." Most etymologists say that the word should be pronounced "fort." But if she's erring, well, that does make Mary not perfect, but practically perfect, doesn't it?

As Mary, Ashley Brown had to hit the heights—literally—flying up to the upper rafters of the New Amsterdam Theatre, defying gravity more than Elphaba does. She also sang the role beautifully, and had a pleasant demeanor. As Bert, Gavin Lee had great charm, sang well, and moved like the wind. But when new stage performers take on famous roles originally played by stars, they always come across as understudies.

Directors Richard Eyre and Matthew Bourne provided the entire enterprise with little soul. A Tony-winning musical of fifty years earlier insisted that "You gotta have heart," but there wasn't an iota of an aorta on the New Amsterdam stage. For a big production number inspired by that thirty-four-letter non-word "supercalifragilisticexpialodocious," Bourne provided a distinctive gesture for each note and syllable. That took the focus off the lyric which is, to quote the song itself, "quite atrocious."

Bob Crowley's giant dollhouse of a set overwhelmed what is essentially a small and quiet story. It didn't stop him from getting the only Tony Award that the show would snare.

Still, *Mary Poppins*, which ran three years in London, wound up running longer on Broadway. One must wonder, though, what the score would have been like had Stephen Sondheim written it. That may seem to be an impossible scenario, but in the late forties and early fifties, Sondheim, of all people, actually started work on musicalizing *Mary Poppins*. Had he continued, would he have had what's always eluded him: the biggest hit of the season?

Mary Poppins. November 16, 2006–. Over 1,600 performances.

The Biggest Flop
The Pirate Queen

Familiarity indeed breeds contempt.

Assistant conductor Joshua Rosenblum remembers it well. One day when he went to rehearsals for *The Pirate Queen*, his percussionist Dave Roth made a bold prediction. Recalls Rosenblum, "He told me I'd better get used to spending a lot of time away from my wife and kids, because the show was going to run twenty years."

Roth was only off by nineteen years and ten months.

The Pirate Queen represented the next step in a law of diminishing returns for Alan Boublil and Claude-Michel Schonberg. Their first Broadway musical (*Les Misérables*) effortlessly won the Tony and ran sixteen years. Their second (*Miss Saigon*) lost the Tony but ran ten years. *The Pirate Queen* didn't get a single Tony nomination, and couldn't run ten weeks. (In between was their *Martin Guerre*, which flopped in London and then toured to a few American cities before it tried to wend its way to New York—which it never did.)

But what a dynamic opening *The Pirate Queen* had. The curtain rose on a scrim, lit from behind, so that the audience could see a person steering the wheel of a ship. The scrim was then released from the top, allowing it to fall to the stage floor, and making for a magnificent and unexpected *coup de théâtre*: A man wasn't at the wheel; a woman was.

Granted, the show was called *The Pirate Queen*, so a woman at the wheel should have been expected. But audiences could be excused if they'd automatically assumed that a male was in command. Each theatergoer had had a lifetime's experience of seeing men run ships in books and films. Such a supposition isn't easily whisked away.

The woman at the wheel is Grace O'Malley (Stephanie J. Block), or Grania, as her father Captain Dubhdara (Jeff McCarthy) calls her. When Grace sees any ship, "it is almost sexually arousing," says a stage direction. But we're in Ireland in 1550, when "everyone knows that a female brings a ship bad luck." Even

Grace's beloved beau, Tiernan (Hadley Fraser), wants her to "Be that woman who stands fiery and unbowed who waits home for me on the shore."

Before Tiernan's ship leaves, Grace sneaks on, and when the ship is suddenly in danger, she acts so heroically that she became immediately beloved—until her cap falls off and everyone sees her "flaming red hair." (Rather than rely on this all-too-convenient accident, Boublil, Schoenberg and co-bookwriter Richard Maltby, Jr. would have done better to have someone see through Grace's disguise. But characters in musicals seldom do.)

Tiernan has mixed feelings about Grace's being there. When he says he wants to ask her father for her hand, Grace says he needn't, for he already has it. She is also quite potent in the battle that follows. So far, Grace is a very interesting character—especially to female theatergoers who currently work in what many still perceive to be a man's world.

But she loses some of their sympathy in the next scene. Dubhdara tells her that she must marry Donal (Marcus Chait) to merge two warring families. Tiernan is scandalized, but Grace adopts a still upper lip and agrees, even though she suspects Donal is worthless. (He is.)

Grace, though, knows something that the audience doesn't: a marriage in those days and in that culture merely meant "a trial period of three years and a day." (The writers should have had her bring that up to Tiernan in advance.)

In the next battle with the British, the Irish women pretend to be interested in seducing the English soldiers—before they kill them. Grace spares the life of her prisoner, though, the Queen's emissary Richard Bingham (William Youmans, who played effete so audiences would automatically hate the character).

Grace says she's sparing Bingham so that he can "go tell your queen that you were bested by a woman." That's worth more than killing him? Grace would seem to have made an egocentric mistake, one we don't want a leader to make. It will come back to haunt her.

First, though, she must deal with Dubdhara's dying. Donal was looking forward to inheriting his title of Chieftan, but Dubdhara gives it to Grace instead. That would have made a solid first-act ending, but the creators wasted time by showing us Dubdhara's funeral before the curtain came down.

In act 2, Grace gives birth to a boy, but she gets no maternity leave, because she has to fight the British again. Bingham arranges to have the unhappy Donal betray his wife, and though Tiernan kills Donal, Grace spends seven years in prison before Queen Elizabeth (Linda Balgord) takes pity on her because Grace hadn't seen her child all in that time. No sooner is Grace home, though, than she engineers another charge against the Queen.

Perhaps *The Pirate Queen* didn't sail through the choppy Broadway waters because it sounded too much like *Les Misérables*. Julian Kelly's orchestrations, aside from including an Irish piper, had the same soft string accompaniment on the ballads. Worse, the singers were apparently instructed (perhaps by director

Frank Galati, more likely by Boublil and Schonberg) to sing the songs in the *Les Miz* manner, in a let-me-take-you-into-my-confidence voice.

Even the placement of the songs seemed close to *Les Miz*'s blueprint; Donal's raucous "Boys Will Be Boys" took place around the same time that the Thénardiers had done the same-sounding "Master of the House."

One could argue that more than twenty years had passed between *Les Miz* and *The Pirate Queen*, while two very similar songs from Rodgers and Hammerstein—"You'll Never Walk Alone" from *Carousel* and "Climb Every Mountain" in *The Sound of Music*—were only separated by fourteen years. Why didn't many complain about the same sentiments and sound in each of those shows?

Because audiences knew *Les Miz* too well from its sixteen-year run. They had ample opportunity to see it again and again—and many took it. *Carousel* wasn't around nearly as long to underline the similarities. It got a movie in 1956, sure, but after a few months it was gone from the theaters, and it was only available through the occasional limited re-release and TV airings; its video would only be issued decades after its original run.

Even when *Les Miz* wasn't on Broadway, it was available through an anniversary concert on tape and DVD. And a mere five months before *The Pirate Queen* made its Broadway debut, a revival of *Les Miz* had opened, reminding audiences once more of its score and sound.

W. S. Gilbert had told the world more than a hundred years earlier that it was "a glorious thing to be a Pirate King," but it wasn't nearly as glorious to be a Pirate Queen, at least not on Broadway.

The Pirate Queen. April 5, 2007–June 17, 2007. 85 performances.

2007–2008

The Biggest Hit
South Pacific

The full sound of music.

"If you've got it, flaunt it" was the mantra of *The Producers*, and the producers of the 2008 *South Pacific* revival took that to heart. They put thirty musicians in the pit, but didn't rely on theatergoers' ears to discern that. Because they'd put the immense orchestra under the stage, they had the front of the stage retract so we could see each and every musician—even the harpist.

Broadway orchestras routinely included a harpist back in *South Pacific*'s original day—in 1949. Now Broadway orchestras—nay, Broadway pit bands, really—don't. How nice to see that golden instrument poking its head out of the pit. How wonderful Richard Rodgers' music sounded, even before we heard a word of Oscar Hammerstein's lyrics.

The poetic ones were brought to life by Paolo Szot as French expatriate Emile de Becque; Kelli O'Hara as his love, Navy nurse Nellie Forbush; Matthew Morrison as Princeton-educated Lt. Joseph Cable; and Li Jun Li as Liat, the young Polynesian woman he came to love. Hammerstein's earthier lyrics would be sung by Danny Burstein as Luther Billis, the Seabee who's always trying to make a buck out of World War II.

And yet, in this acclaimed revival, once again *South Pacific*'s two nagging flaws weren't noticed. Emile, who admits to Nellie that he once killed "a bad man" in self-defense, isn't the only one who gets away with murder. The musical itself figuratively does, too.

The first flaw appears after the Navy brass call in civilian Emile to their office and ask him to take on a dangerous spying mission. He refuses, causing Cable to snort, "Aren't you just a guy in love with a girl, and you're putting her above everything else in the world?" Emile answers, "Yes, I do care about my life with her more than anything else in the world. It is the only thing that is important to me."

"It is the only thing that is important to me." His two children, Ngana and Jerome, wouldn't be happy to hear that. Over the centuries, many children have feared that if their father remarried, his new wife would usurp their place in his heart. If Nellie is "the only thing that is important to me," Ngana and Jerome have good reason to worry.

That Emile and Nellie fall in love and become engaged so quickly isn't particularly problematic; a quick proposal is a time-honored musical theater convention. What Emile hasn't bothered to mention to Nellie, though, is that he has that son and daughter. Any father of two *must* tell his girlfriend before he pops the question that if she becomes his wife, she'll inherit two stepchildren. Emile, though, only trots out his kids days after Nellie has accepted his proposal.

What's even worse is the way he tries to charm his way out of it. "Nellie, I have a surprise for you," he says, as if he has a present that will thrill her. "You sit over there—something I've been preparing for two days to tell you. Close your eyes. No peeking," he insists.

So while this little girl from Little Rock may be expecting a big rock, she is shocked to learn that her intended has two children by a Polynesian woman. Nellie had previously stated that she is "naïve as a babe to believe any fable" she heard "from a person in pants." Her naïveté seemed to be betraying her once again.

Given the success of the show, few if any in the audience apparently cared, probably because the score and production of *South Pacific* were so heavenly.

But an interesting point about each production: This revival began previewing on March 1, 2008 and opened thirty-three days later on April 3. The original 1949 production, however, opened in New Haven on March 10, 1949, traveled to Boston for a March 14 opening, and debuted on Broadway on April 7, 1949— only twenty-eight days after that first-ever performance.

Why would a set-in-stone revival need five days more to ready itself than did the original production? What's more, the original used its four weeks to restage a major number, cut two songs and some dialogue, and create a new song ("This Nearly Was Mine?").

Theodore S. Chapin, the president and executive director of Rodgers and Hammerstein, provided the answer: "Computers."

South Pacific. April 3, 2008–. More than 600 performances.

THE BIGGEST FLOP
Cry-Baby

Hoisted on their semi-sequel petard.

We've seen three sequels emerge as the biggest flops of their seasons: *Bring Back Birdie* (1981), *Annie 2: Miss Hannigan's Revenge* (1990), and *The Best Little Whorehouse Goes Public* (1994). In 2007–2008, a semi-sequel snagged the "prize."

After *Hairspray* emerged as a mammoth hit—only fourteen musicals had ever run longer in their original productions—three of its producers, Adam Epstein, Allen S. Gordon, and Elan V. McAllister, decided that what the public wanted was another musical of a John Waters movie. So did Waters himself.

And so, *Cry-Baby*, adapted from the 1990 Waters film of the same name, started its march to Broadway.

But there was a world of difference between the two. In 1988, the *Hairspray* movie was on its way to grossing $200 million. Two years later, the *Cry-Baby* film took in only $8 million. Granted, *Oklahoma!* was adapted from a play that ran only seven weeks. But the great disparity between public interest in *Hairspray* and *Cry-Baby* should have been some cause for concern.

Nevertheless, *Hairspray*'s bookwriters Thomas Meehan and Mark O'Donnell signed on. But Margo Lion, who'd initiated *Hairspray* and was its lead producer, passed. Instead of asking Marc Shaiman and Scott Wittman to do the score, Waters and the producers opted for Broadway newcomers David Javerbaum and Adam Schlesinger. The former was a writer for *The Daily Show* and *The Onion*, while the latter was a bassist and songwriter for the rock group Fountains of Wayne.

When auditioning for the show, each writer had submitted his work separately. The producers suggested they try writing together. And while every song eventually had both their names on them, Javerbaum admitted to playbill.com that "the majority of the lyrics are mine, the majority of the music is his."

The curtain went up on an "Anti-Polio Picnic." There, a bright-eyed teenage victim of polio was rolled out in an iron lung. He bravely smiled and said, "I sure wish I could have gotten that shot!" That *Cry-Baby* stems from a John Waters movie does mean that bad taste will be the order of the day, but asking an audience to laugh at an affliction is about as low as writers can go. What's more, it wasn't the type of visual gag that audiences had ever seen in *Hairspray*—so now the memory of the previous hit was working against *Cry-Baby*'s success, and not for it.

A black kid was happily partying with white kids at the picnic. But *Cry-Baby* was set in 1954 Baltimore, the same city where *Hairspray* had already shown us that such integration hadn't even happened by the early sixties. So how could we believe what we were seeing when the other (superior) musical had taught us otherwise?

Maybe it was just nontraditional casting. If so, that explained why so many of the cast members were too old to play teenagers. Elizabeth Stanley played one named Allison, but seventeen months earlier, she'd played flight attendant April in the Broadway revival of *Company*.

Allison was one of the "good" kids who proudly proclaimed, "What a wonderful time to be what's known as a square," in one of Javerbaum or Schlesinger's all-too-knowing lyrics. These kids should have been *taught* the term "square" when the "bad" kids came in, headed by their leader, the very strangely named Cry-Baby (James Snyder).

For a while, *Cry-Baby* seemed to be making a point about the nation's fear quotient in the early fifties. By its mentioning Safety Awareness Day, gas masks, and air raid alarm systems, the musical appeared to show how the nation in those days was concentrating on playing it safe—but that Americans weren't way-down-deep *really* worried or *that* fearful. After all, the United States was still the big kid on the planet's block, a country no other would dare to attack, with a stable economy that was constantly improving. Still, that didn't excuse that Allison sang a lyric with wordplay far too deft for a mere teen, that "Everyone's so full of false alarm."

But *Cry-Baby* soon dropped the social commentary and settled in simply to tell its story about adolescent rebellion, how it really didn't do any harm, though adults needlessly worried about it. In the process, it did reiterate that the new music united kids to rebel against adults, and changed the world in the process.

Those two offshoots of the rock 'n' roll revolution, though, were more significant than the songs themselves. So when Schlesinger and Javerbaum's score aped the era of lousy songs, it simply offered different lousy songs. *Hairspray* offered much better pastiches.

The lyrics in *Cry-Baby* were admittedly smarter than the average song of the early rock 'n' roll era, but they often showed the lyricists speaking, and not the characters. Meehan and O'Donnell's stage directions made a point of saying that the hero was "a James Dean-like figure." But would anyone who's "James Dean-like" use such words as "misconstrue" or such phrases as "Life's a trumped-up charge" or "Here's a brief memo you may not have got"? Worst of all was Cry-Baby's singing, "I'm in complete command of my lachrymal gland." If a gang leader had ever said that to his gang, every hood he knew would have sneered, "Talk English, will ya?"

All-too-lofty language spread to the other teens. Allison sang, "They made sure my status was perfectly quo." A "bad girl" crooned, "One look my way can make an angry mob disperse." All the kids joined in to refer to something "ripped from the world's most depressing thesaurus." Then there was Cry-Baby's simile, "We're like switchblades laughin' at a butter-knife."

Cry-Baby also sounded anachronistic when he sang "Nobody Gets Me"— meaning "No one understands me." That expression came much later. "Pervs," "open mike," and "state-of-the-art" sounded much too ahead-of-their-time for 1954, too. Then there was "Girl, Can I Kiss You . . . ?"—whose ellipsis stood in for "with Tongue." After two A-sections, each of which ended with that line, the B-section began with "I've been cursed with a thirst no one else can quite quench." Needless to say, the word "quench" was chosen so it would rhyme with "French."

There was also little inspiration from O'Donnell and Meehan's book. The moment a priest came on stage, another character made a reference to molestation—which would *never* have happened in the 1950s. There was also the device of someone (Allison's aunt) walking in just in time to overhear a piece of information that had been a secret, for if she hadn't, the plot couldn't have resolved itself affirmatively. And considering that *Hairspray* got away with unbelievable bending of the law, *Cry-Baby* thought it could do that, too, all in the cause of a happy ending.

But it wasn't so happy. The closing number, "Nothing Bad's Ever Gonna Happen Again" was going affably along until the iron-lunged lad was rolled out once again from the stage left wings for all to see before he rolled off again, stage right. A distinct silence often met the boy's second appearance. The crowd was in essence saying, "Gee, we were starting to enjoy ourselves there, and you had to remind us of that polio-afflicted kid and ruin it."

There was also an in-joke that cited a much different musical from *Hairspray*. When Cry-Baby was incarcerated in act 2, his prison uniform bore the number 26401—the same number that prisoner Jean Valjean had worn in *Les Misérables*. Of course, only those who were sitting close could see it, but that turned out to be a substantial number of people who attended *Cry-Baby*. After all, good seats were easy to get throughout the two-month run.

Cry-Baby. April 24–June 22, 2008. 68 performances.

2008–2009

THE BIGGEST HIT
Billy Elliot

More success when the dances aren't done by vampires.

How modest of *Billy Elliot: The Musical* to say that it won ten Tony Awards, when it could have said it had won twelve.

A quick look does support the total of ten: Best Musical, Best Actor, Best Book, Best Featured Actor, Best Choreography, Best Direction of a Musical, Best Orchestrations, Best Set Design, Best Lighting Design, Best Sound Design. Ten, count 'em, ten.

But one could effectively argue twelve, because twelve people took home Tonys on June 7, 2009. For the first time in Tony history, three people shared the Best Actor prize: David Alvarez, Trent Kowalik, and Kiril Kulish, each for playing the role of Billy Elliot in repertory.

The decision made sense. Any kid who plays Billy is certainly going to have to dance, because, of course, a good part of the story involves this young lad's discovering the world of ballet. He must go from literally putting his toe in to slowly but surely committing to a way of life that confounds his working-class father and brother. But each of the boys was able to show that Billy's passion and ability for dancing would grow and grow, so that each dance piece the kid did was more sensational than the one before it. Not long after Billy was told that dance isn't just "a technical exercise" but also "a very personal expression from within," each of the boys achieved the latter in a most dramatic first-act curtain.

Because of that family conflict, there were plenty of scenes where the Billys had to act, too, and they shrewdly built from a "what's-the-use" funk to plenty of backbone-resolve. Each even turned out to be expert at waiting for a laugh, after a young ballet student, smitten with Billy, offered to show him her "hoo-hoo." None of the lads was in any rush to answer her, not with the audience so enjoying the moment. Each boy, too, made the most of the moment when he received the letter from the Royal Ballet School. The way each slowly moved his fingers over the envelope, postponing his learning what could well have been awful news, was terrific.

But even in the scenes where there was no particular conflict, the boys were top-notch. What a look of admiration each gave when he met his ballet teacher-to-be, Mrs. Wilkinson (Haydn Gwynne)—a look that said, "I don't know why I'm here—but may I stay a few minutes longer?" The boys characterized a lad who tried on his dancing exercises as if they were new clothes, and wasn't each surprised when he looked in the mirror and saw how well they fit? Trouble is, his father (Gregory Jbara) and brother Tony (Santino Fontana) hated that he was fiddling around with dance while they burned in their own private hell: *Billy Elliot* was set in 1984, and these men were part of the now-famous United Kingdom Mine Workers Strike.

And of course because this was a musical (and not a Doug Henning one) a kid cast as Billy would have to sing. With such yeoman demands placed on young men, somewhere along the line when composer Elton John and bookwriter-lyricist Lee Hall were creating the musical, one of them or a coworker must have said, "We might as well forget about this show right now. How can we possibly find a kid to do this eight times a week?" Well, they couldn't, and they never expected to. *Billy Elliot* offered its own mini-repertory company, in that three performers alternated as Billy, while two (David Bologna and Frank Dolce) shared the role of Michael, Billy's best friend, and the male who, pro-rated by age, must be the best-adjusted and most fearless transvestite in history.

Billy Elliot isn't a great musical, but it certainly is a good one. This is John's most truly theatrical score, and one can only imagine—let's say it again—how much better it might have been were John the type to be interested enough in musicals to attend rehearsals and previews.

There are effective moments in the book which Lee Hall based on his movie (though some may have come courtesy of director Stephen Daldry). How smart in the opening scene, where the miners were deciding whether or not to strike, that a bunch of uninvolved little kids ran around the room playing; that subtly reminds us that these coal porters were family men who desperately needed their income. We learned what was at stake through one of the most serious opening numbers in Broadway history.

Near the end of the show, we experienced Billy's greatest triumph yet—only to immediately learn that the miners had lost not only a year's pay, but also the strike. It was a moment almost as dramatically arresting as the one in *The King and I* where Anna and the King get the closest they've ever been (in "Shall We Dance?")—only to find, seconds later, that they're worlds apart again when the King is about to whip the renegade Tuptim.

While a lesser writer might have offered an utterly unselfish and inspiring dance instructor, Hall makes Mrs. Wilkinson like the teachers in *The Education of H*Y*M*A*N K*A*P*L*A*N*, who sang, "If you want to be an ever-lovin' teacher, you gotta be out of your ever-lovin' mind." Wilkinson may have had a cigarette dangling from her lower lip, but she was no Bob Fosse, and she knew it. There was a tender scene where Billy shared with her a letter his mother had written him when she knew she was dying. Billy knew every word by heart, and recited it as she reads. It gives the advice a parent always gives: "Be yourself." Yes, but the late Mrs. Elliot had no idea when she made that statement that Billy would pursue ballet. She might not have said the same thing had she survived, for she might not have understood the ballet world any more than her husband and older son did.

Interesting, though, that the miners annually staged a Christmas show where everyone sang and—yes—danced. (Guess they just rationalized that this was their "Once a Year Day.") Their song was called "Merry Christmas, Maggie Thatcher," and more than one Broadway visitor who saw *Billy Elliot* in London predicted that it might not be successful in New York, because it was too British-centric. When the 2000 hit *The Full Monty* morphed from movie to musical, the setting was changed from Sheffield, England to Buffalo, New York. *Billy Elliot* dared to stay in Northern England and not move to West Virginia. They didn't worry that American audiences would be hearing British accents as thick as a foggy day in London town.

The show also ran another, bigger risk: Would its story line seem too familiar? In *A Day in Hollywood*, a charming 1980 revue about Tinseltown, there was a song that offered a long, long list of film clichés; one was, "Gee, why can't I make you see I've got music inside of me, Pa?" That was *Billy Elliot*.

Fascinating, though, that the story wasn't about achieving fame and fortune, but "just" getting into a school. As any graduate of a conservatory can tell you, being accepted is just the start of struggle, which can be lifelong. The original *Billy Elliot* movie let us know that the kid made it; the stage show doesn't. Does this mean that we're in for *Billy Elliot: The Post–Ballet School Years?*

Billy Elliot. November 13, 2008–. Over 800 performances.

THE BIGGEST FLOP
9 to 5

It's the wrong time and the wrong place.

And another legendary pop songwriter bit the Broadway dust.

This time, it was country legend Dolly Parton who decided to write a score for a Broadway musical. She certainly knew the property she was adapting: *9 to 5*. In the 1980 film, Parton made her film debut as Mrs. Doralee Rhodes, whose lusty boss, Franklin Hart, wanted to seduce her at any cost.

The film was the second-highest grosser of its year, finishing only behind *The Empire Strikes Back*. Audiences responded not just to Parton, but also to Jane Fonda's Judy, a housewife whose husband left her for his secretary, and Lily Tomlin's Violet, whose intelligence and ability should have allowed her to break through the glass ceiling long ago.

But the musical version lasted little more than five months, and lost a reported $14 million. This despite four-time Emmy winner Allison Janney as Violet, and two *Wicked* alumnae—Stephanie J. Block, a former Elphaba, and Megan Hilty, a one-time G(a)linda—on the scene. The critics didn't rave, and the Tony nominating committee only gave four nods and no awards. Still, the producers hoped that women, who constitute the majority of theatergoers, would respond to the show at least as a pleasant night out.

The show was said to still take place in 1979, but no locale was specified. Nevertheless, the office seemed to be in New York. Aside from Doralee, everyone sounded Northeast Corridor urban—until the music started.

Parton's twangy sounds more often than not made for a strange dichotomy between Northern speaking voices and country singing voices. The lyrics, too, sounded as if they had a Southern sensibility, such as when an executive sang, "Well, shit, that don't hurt." One song brought on a group of singers clad in clerical robes, looking as if they were members of a Southern Baptist chorus.

This disconnect could have been easily remedied. Parton, bookwriter Patricia Resnick, and director Joe Mantello should have set the show in Nashville. The opening song ("9 to 5") showed people awakened by their alarm clocks, so one could have been a clock radio that blared, "The weather in Nashville is going to be cloudy today." If Southern accents had been added, the musical would have seemed more of a whole. As it was, at the end of the show the president of the company showed up looking exactly like Colonel Sanders—white suit and goatee—but even he didn't speak in a Southern accent.

Frankly, a show about oppressive and unenlightened male boss Mr. Hart (Marc Kudisch) and his mistreatment of his office "girls" might have seemed more apt if set down South. While the North has certainly seen its share of stinker bosses, the "good ol' boy" mentality seen in 9 to 5 seemed more right for an area of the country that had been slower to acknowledge one's civil rights.

A bigger problem may have been 9 to 5's now-ancient take on sexism. Hart told a colleague a joke—"How is a woman like Ex-Lax? They both irritate the crap out of you"—and the audience in the Marquis Theater moaned. That was eclipsed when Hart tried to blackmail Doralee into sleeping with him; the startled "Ohhhhh!" from the audience was not one that said, "I'm enjoying this show." The worst affront of all came when Hart said to Doralee, "You're nothing but a typewriter with tits." The "Ohhhhh!" after that one said, "I can't believe you think we're going to be entertained by this line."

Maybe 9 to 5 took veteran working women back to the way office life used to be—and they didn't want to go there. Perhaps younger workers, who hadn't experienced such discrimination firsthand, were appalled to see how men once treated women in an office environment. Envisioning an era when inequality was blatant and harassment was pervasive wasn't much fun for them. There are blacks who refuse to watch or read anything that has to do with slavery, and Jews who do not want to encounter Holocaust-themed properties. Granted, a sexually harassing boss is several rungs below those in sheer evil, but maybe women workers just didn't want to return to yesteryear, even in a shiny-bright Broadway musical.

Parton's score continued to be a liability. Audiences were supposed to laugh at Hart when he sang a seduction song to Doralee, but such lyrics as "I'd like to take those double-D's / And hold them oh-so-close to me" were more disgusting than funny. Parton should instead have given Doralee a song about how to avoid a sexually harassing boss every time she steps into his office. She would have come off as smarter, and avoided being a victim.

As it was, many women in the audience might have had a hard time getting behind Doralee. She sang of being a "Backwoods Barbie in a push-up bra" and wore inappropriate clothes to the office. While Parton's song and Doralee's character indicated a high comfort level with revealing clothing, some in the audience may have felt that Doralee wasn't helping herself with her choice of attire.

"Backwoods Barbie" was released more than a year before 9 *to* 5's debut, but it didn't do the show much good. In the old days, it would have been promoted as "from the upcoming new musical, 9 *to* 5." But Parton had written it as a pop song, and only later realized that she could recycle it as a song for her character. That's not the same thing.

Deep in the second act, Violet delivered a long, *spoken* harangue about the injustices she'd suffered at Hart's hands. In a musical, such a defining moment is always a song. Would Janney's singing voice have been inadequate to the demands of such a moment, even if it were "Rose's Turn Lite"? A more likely explanation was that Parton wasn't up to musicalizing the speech, for she was more comfortable writing pop songs than arias.

But Resnick's book was at fault, too. Many who have had terrible bosses may have occasionally wanted to kidnap and kill them, but few have gone beyond the fantasy stage. Violet, Judy, and Doralee did, but also demonstrated that two wrongs never make a right. Today's female worker probably would have preferred that 9 *to* 5's "heroines" find a legal, brains-not-brawn way to bring Hart to his deserved doom.

That Judy cried on her first day on the job may have rubbed today's female achievers the wrong way, too. Back in the sixties, militant feminists would go around pasting stickers on subway posters if they felt that "This ad insults women." Maybe theatergoers ultimately felt that 9 *to* 5 did, too.

9 *to* 5. April 30, 2009–September 6, 2009. 148 performances.

Finale

The last words go to—and come from—
Stephen Sondheim.

He's generally considered to be the greatest writer on Broadway during the fifty years we've covered. Five of his shows won Best Musical Tonys; five others were nominated as Best Musical. He has seven Tonys for writing scores, and four more nominations. He's also one of the few musical theater writers to win a Pulitzer Prize, for *Sunday in the Park with George*.

And yet Sondheim is only represented three times in this book of one hundred musicals–and always for having the biggest flop of the season: *Anyone Can Whistle* (1963–1964), *Merrily We Roll Along* (1981–1982), and *Wise Guys* (1999–2000).

Never once did Sondheim have the biggest hit of the season. While *A Funny Thing Happened on the Way to the Forum* was quite a success in 1961–1962, *How to Succeed in Business without Really Trying* was a bigger one. Although *Into the Woods* ran nearly two years, its main competition in 1987–1988, *The Phantom of the Opera*, has already run more than twelve times as long.

But attention must be paid to the greatest composer-lyricist that Broadway has ever known. And so we'll end the book by citing a few of his lyrics. All were written for specific characters in certain situations, and yet they can inadvertently be seen as commentaries on Broadway then and now.

Such as the lines in *Pacific Overtures'* last song: "See what's coming. See what's going. Next!" Lord knows that quite a bit has come and gone on Broadway. Most of the names cited in this book have died. Luckily some of their shows live on. But many musicals have indeed gone and are sadly forgotten. As Sondheim had Mrs. Lovett sing in *Sweeney Todd*, "Time's so fast. Now goes quickly—see? Now is past."

"Move On," Sondheim instructed in *Sunday in the Park with George*. Broadway has had to do that. While theater music had its distinctive, unique sound for much of the past fifty years, now it has been forced by critics and audiences to embrace the sound of pop and rock music. As Sondheim wrote in *Follies*, "Everybody has to go through stages like that."

But is it a stage? Perfect rhymes and correct stresses on syllables, once routinely found in most every show—and certainly in every Sondheim musical—are no longer valued; Tony Awards are now given to scores with dozens of sloppy lyrics. In *A Little Night Music*, Sondheim, though Madame Armfeldt, wondered, "Where is style? Where is skill? Where is forethought? Where's discretion of the heart? Where's passion in the art? Where's craft?" No one knew that when Sondheim wrote those lines in the early 1970s, there would now be far fewer of those qualities on Broadway today.

"Well, maybe next year," Sondheim also wrote in *A Little Night Music*. But don't bet on it. Longtime parents can certainly relate to lines from *Into the Woods*: "Children can only grow from something you love to something you lose." For many, the words "Broadway musical" can be substituted for "children."

And yet, as Sondheim asked in *Merrily We Roll Along*, "Why is it that old friends don't want old friends to change?" Many of us do want the Broadway musical to change—but in ways that improve it. The current state of affairs leaves us, as Sondheim wrote about a completely different subject in *Company*, "Sorry-grateful, regretful-happy."

Ah, well. As he wrote in *Merrily We Roll Along*, "We had a good thing going—going, gone."

Or is it? Although Broadway hasn't heard a totally new Sondheim score in the last fifteen years—since *Passion* closed in 1995—Sondheim has been represented on Broadway for at least part of each ensuing year with one of his previous shows. So audiences have had the chance to experience old-world Broadway quality.

In West Side Story, his first Broadway musical, Sondheim had his two lovers sing, "And make this endless day endless night." Here's hoping—and expecting—that no matter how much Broadway changes, Stephen Sondheim's music and lyrics will be displayed endlessly day and night.

Bibliography

BOOKS AND PLAY SCRIPTS

Albee, Edward. *Breakfast at Tiffany's*. Unpublished script, 1966.

Burrows, Abe. *Hellzapoppin'*. Unpublished script, 1976.

Coopersmith, Jerome. *Mata Hari*. Unpublished script, 1967.

Egri, Lajos. *The Art of Dramatic Writing*. New York: Simon and Schuster, 1946.

Goldman, William. *The Season*. New York: Harcourt Brace, 1969.

Guernsey, Otis. *The Best Plays of 1968–1969*. New York: Dodd Mead, 1970

Hanan, Stephen. *A Cat's Diary: How the Broadway Production of "Cats" Was Born*. Manchester, NH: Smith and Kraus, 2001.

Holmes, Rupert. *The Mystery of Edwin Drood*. New York: Nelson Doubleday, 1986.

Howard, Ken, and Edward Tivnan. *Act Natural: How to Speak to Any Audience*. New York: Random House, 2003.

Kimball, Robert, and Steve Nelson. *The Complete Lyrics of Frank Loesser*. New York: Knopf, 2003.

King, Larry L. *The "Whorehouse" Papers*. New York: Viking, 1982.

Kirkwood, James. *Diary of a Mad Playwright*. New York: E. P. Dutton, 1989.

Kissel, Howard. *The Abominable Showman*. New York: Applause, 1993.

Lehman, Ernest. *Sweet Smell of Success*. New York: Signet, 1957.

Lerner, Alan Jay. *Lolita, My Love*. Unpublished script, 1970.

Lerner, Alan Jay. *1600 Pennsylvania Avenue*. Unpublished script, 1970.

Mandelbaum, Ken. *"A Chorus Line" and the Musicals of Michael Bennett*. New York: St. Martin's, 1898.

Mandelbaum, Ken. *Not Since "Carrie."* New York: St. Martin's, 1991.

Merrill, Bob. *The Prince of Grand Street*. Unpublished script, 1978.

Miletich, Leo N. *Broadway's Prize-Winning Musicals*. London: Haworth, 1993.

Mordden, Ethan. *Coming Up Roses*. New York: Oxford University Press, 1998.

Mordden, Ethan. *The Happiest Corpse I've Ever Seen*. New York: Palgrave Macmillan, 2004.

Mordden, Ethan. *One More Kiss*. New York: Palgrave Macmillan, 2003.

Mordden, Ethan. *Open a New Window*. New York: Palgrave, 2001.

Norton, Elliott. *Broadway Down East*. Boston: Boston Public Library Books, 1977.

O'Donnell, Mark, and Thomas Meehan. *Cry-Baby*. Unpublished script, 2008.

Ostrow, Stuart. *Present at the Creation, Leaping in the Dark, and Going against the Grain*. New York: Applause, 2005.

Plummer, Christopher. *In Spite of Myself*. New York: Knopf, 2008.

Poole, Wakefield. *Dirty Poole*. Boston: Alyson, 2000.

Prince, Harold. *Contradictions*. New York: Dodd, Mead, 1974.

Rich, Frank. *Hot Seat*. New York: Random House, 1998.

Ropes, Bradford. *42nd Street*. New York: Grosset & Dunlap, 1932.

Rosenfeld, Lulla. *Jacob Adler: A Life on the Stage*. New York: Knopf, 1999.

Seff, Richard. *Supporting Player*. Bloomington, IN: Xlibris, 2007.

Staggs, Sam. *All about "All About Eve."* New York: St. Martin's, 2000.

Stevens, Leslie, and Duke, Vernon. *The Pink Jungle*. Unpublished script, 1959.

Suskin, Steven. *More Opening Nights on Broadway*. New York: Schirmer, 1997.

Suskin, Steven. *Opening Nights on Broadway*. New York: Schirmer, 1990.

Suskin, Steven. *Second Act Trouble*. New York: Applause, 2006.

Swayne, Steve. *How Sondheim Found His Sound*. Ann Arbor: University of Michigan, 2005.

Taylor, Theodore. *Jule: The Story of Composer Jule Styne*. New York: Random House, 1979.

Trapp, Maria Augusta. *The Story of the Trapp Family Singers*. New York: J. B. Lippincott, 1949.

Wasserman, Dale. *The Impossible Musical*. New York: Applause, 2003.

Yankee, Luke. *Just Outside the Spotlight*. New York: Backstage Books, 2006.

Zadan, Craig. *Sondheim & Co*. New York: Macmillan, 1974.

PERIODICALS AND WEBSITES

Internet Broadway Database. Ibdb.com.

London Theatre Record, Sept. 25–Oct 8, 1985 issue.

"The Sound of Money." *Mad* magazine. Spring 1970 issue.

Olson, John. "The Long and Winding Road to Road Show." *The Sondheim Review*, Winter 2008 issue.

Sondheim, Stephen. "*Wise Guys*: Work in Progress for 47 Years." *New York Times*, Sept. 12, 1999.

INTERVIEWS

Loni Ackerman

George Lee Andrews

Kelly Bishop

John Bowab

Wayne Bryan

Richard Chamberlain

Martin Charnin

Alexander H. Cohen

Brian Drutman

Joshua Ellis

Larry Fineberg

Richard Frankel

Rita Gardner

William Goldman

Ellen Greene

Michael Greif

Carol Hall

Marvin Hamlisch

Stephen Hanan

Rupert Holmes

Skip Koenig

Nathan Lane

Arthur Laurents

Linda Lavin

Galt MacDermot

William Martin

Natalie Mosco

Donna McKechnie

Randy Phillips

Justin Plowman

Gerome Ragni

Anthony Rapp

Stephen Schwartz

Richard Seff

Bert Silverberg

Sheila Smith

Stephen Sondheim

Charles Strouse

Pat Tolson

Bruce Vilanch